The Power of Peers in the Classroom

WHAT WORKS FOR SPECIAL-NEEDS LEARNERS

Karen R. Harris and Steve Graham, *Editors*

www.guilford.com/WWFSNL

This series addresses a significant need in the education of students who are at risk, those with disabilities, and all children and adolescents who struggle with learning or behavior. While researchers in special education, educational psychology, curriculum and instruction, and other fields have made great progress in understanding what works for struggling learners, the practical application of this research base remains quite limited. Books in the series present assessment, instructional, and classroom management methods that have strong empirical evidence. Written in a user-friendly format, each volume provides specific how-to instructions and examples of the use of proven procedures in schools. Coverage is sufficiently thorough and detailed to enable practitioners to implement the practices described; many titles include reproducible practical tools. Recent titles have Web pages where purchasers can download and print the reproducible materials.

RECENT VOLUMES

Teacher's Guide to ADHD
Robert Reid and Joseph Johnson

Vocabulary Instruction for Struggling Students
Patricia F. Vadasy and J. Ron Nelson

Preparing Effective Special Education Teachers
Nancy Mamlin

RTI for Reading at the Secondary Level: Recommended Literacy Practices
and Remaining Questions
Deborah K. Reed, Jade Wexler, and Sharon Vaughn

Inclusive Instruction: Evidence-Based Practices for Teaching Students with Disabilities
Mary T. Brownell, Sean J. Smith, Jean B. Crockett, and Cynthia C. Griffin

Universal Design for Learning in the Classroom: Practical Applications
Tracey E. Hall, Anne Meyer, and David H. Rose, Editors

Teacher's Guide to Effective Sentence Writing
Bruce Saddler

Strategy Instruction for Students with Learning Disabilities, Second Edition
Robert Reid, Torri Ortiz Lienemann, and Jessica L. Hagaman

Promoting Social Skills in the Inclusive Classroom
Kimber L. Wilkerson, Aaron B. T. Perzigian, and Jill K. Schurr

Teaching Word Recognition: Effective Strategies for Students
with Learning Difficulties, Second Edition
Rollanda E. O'Connor

Teaching Reading Comprehension to Students
with Learning Difficulties, Second Edition
Janette K. Klingner, Sharon Vaughn, and Alison Boardman

The Power of Peers in the Classroom:
Enhancing Learning and Social Skills
Edited by Karen R. Harris and Lynn Meltzer

The Power of Peers in the Classroom

Enhancing Learning and Social Skills

Edited by

Karen R. Harris
Lynn Meltzer

THE GUILFORD PRESS
New York   London

© 2015 The Guilford Press
A Division of Guilford Publications, Inc.
370 Seventh Avenue, Suite 1200, New York, NY 10001
www.guilford.com

Printed in the United States of America

This book is printed on acid-free paper.

Last digit is print number: 9 8 7 6 5 4 3 2 1

Library of Congress Cataloging-in-Publication Data

The power of peers in the classroom : enhancing learning and social skills /
edited by Karen R. Harris, Lynn Meltzer.
     pages cm. — (What works for special-needs learners)
  Includes bibliographical references and index.
  ISBN 978-1-4625-2106-7 (paperback) — ISBN 978-1-4625-2107-4 (cloth)
  1. Peer teaching. 2. Children with disabilities—Education. I. Harris, Karen R.
II. Meltzer, Lynn.
  LB1031.5.P695 2015
  371.39′4—dc23
                                                                   2015005009

About the Editors

Karen R. Harris, EdD, is the Mary Emily Warner Professor in the Mary Lou Fulton Teachers College at Arizona State University and a former general and special education teacher. Her research focuses on theoretically based interventions for the development of academic and self-regulation abilities among at-risk students and those with disabilities, as well as effective models of inservice teacher preparation for writing instruction for all students. She developed the Self-Regulated Strategy Development model of strategies instruction. The former editor of the *Journal of Educational Psychology*, Dr. Harris is coauthor or coeditor of several books and over 200 peer-reviewed publications. She is a recipient of the Distinguished Researcher Award for Special Education Research from the American Educational Research Association and the Career Research Award from the International Council for Exceptional Children. She has served as president of Division 15 (Educational Psychology) of the American Psychological Association and as president of the Division for Research of the Council for Exceptional Children.

Lynn Meltzer, PhD, is President and Director of Research at the Research Institute for Learning and Development (ResearchILD) and Director of Assessment at the Institute for Learning and Development (ILD) in Lexington, Massachusetts. She is also an Associate in Education at the Harvard Graduate School of Education, and for 28 years was an Adjunct Associate Professor in the Department of Child Development at Tufts University. Dr. Meltzer is a fellow and past president of the International Academy for Research in Learning Disabilities and is the chair of the renowned Learning Differences Conference, which she founded in 1984, at the Harvard Graduate School of Education. Her 35 years of neuropsychological evaluations and clinical consultations with children, adolescents, and adults have emphasized the theory-to-practice cycle of knowledge. Her recent work with her ResearchILD colleagues has centered on the development of SMARTS Online, an evidence-based executive function and peer mentoring/coaching curriculum for middle and high school students. Dr. Meltzer has published extensively on executive function, metacognition, and flexible thinking as well as the assessment and treatment of learning and attention difficulties.

Contributors

Terese Aceves, PhD, School of Education, Loyola Marymount University, Los Angeles, California

Alison Boardman, PhD, School of Education, University of Colorado Boulder, Boulder, Colorado

Edward H. Bovey II, MA, School of Education and Human Development, University of Colorado Denver, Denver, Colorado

Pamela Buckley, PhD, School of Education, University of Colorado Boulder, Boulder, Colorado

Anne Mong Cramer, PhD, Division of Education, Human Development, and Social Sciences, Penn State Altoona, Altoona, Pennsylvania

Anya S. Evmenova, PhD, Department of Special Education and disAbility Research, College of Education and Human Development, George Mason University, Fairfax, Virginia

Douglas Fuchs, PhD, Department of Special Education, Peabody College, Vanderbilt University, Nashville, Tennessee

Lynn S. Fuchs, PhD, Department of Special Education, Peabody College, Vanderbilt University, Nashville, Tennessee

Michael Greschler, MEd, Research Institute for Learning and Development, Lexington, Massachusetts

Devin M. Kearns, PhD, Department of Educational Psychology, University of Connecticut, Storrs, Connecticut

Janette K. Klingner, PhD (deceased), School of Education, University of Colorado Boulder, Boulder, Colorado

Katelyn Kurkul, MA, Research Institute for Learning and Development, Lexington, Massachusetts; Department of Education, Boston University, Boston, Massachusetts

Cristin Jensen Lasser, PhD, School of Education, University of Colorado Boulder, Boulder, Colorado

Jenna L. Lequia, MS, Department of Rehabilitation Psychology and Special Education, University of Wisconsin–Madison, Madison, Wisconsin

Linda H. Mason, PhD, School of Education, University of North Carolina at Chapel Hill, Chapel Hill, North Carolina

Margo A. Mastropieri, PhD, Department of Special Education and disAbility Research, College of Education and Human Development, George Mason University, Fairfax, Virginia

Kristen L. McMaster, PhD, Department of Educational Psychology, University of Minnesota–Twin Cities, Minneapolis, Minnesota

Lynn Meltzer, PhD, Research Institute for Learning and Development, Lexington, Massachusetts; Harvard Graduate School of Education, Cambridge, Massachusetts

Brooke Moore, PhD, School of Education, University of Colorado Boulder, Boulder, Colorado

Sarah R. Powell, PhD, Department of Special Education, University of Texas at Austin, Austin, Texas

Kelley S. Regan, PhD, Department of Special Education and disAbility Research, College of Education and Human Development, George Mason University, Fairfax, Virginia

Colleen Reutebuch, PhD, The Meadows Center for Preventing Educational Risk, University of Texas at Austin, Austin, Texas

Catherine Richards-Tutor, PhD, College of Education, California State University Long Beach, Long Beach, California

Laura Sáenz, PhD, Department of Special Education, University of Texas–Pan American, Edinburg, Texas

Karla Scornavacco, PhD, School of Education, University of Colorado Boulder, Boulder, Colorado

Thomas E. Scruggs, PhD, Department of Special Education and disAbility Research, College of Education and Human Development, George Mason University, Fairfax, Virginia

Wendy Stacey, MS, Research Institute for Learning and Development, Lexington, Massachusetts

Phillip S. Strain, PhD, School of Education and Human Development, University of Colorado Denver, Denver, Colorado

Kimber L. Wilkerson, PhD, Department of Rehabilitation Psychology and Special Education, University of Wisconsin–Madison, Madison, Wisconsin

Preface

Numerous studies have demonstrated the powerful influence of peer support and social relationships on student development and performance. Peer group socialization is a major avenue through which children develop their identities and self-concepts, which, in turn, shape their future interactions (Rodkin & Ryan, 2012; Rubin, Bukowski, & Laursen, 2009). Furthermore, meta-analyses have shown the positive effects of peer coaching and tutoring on students' motivation, self-concept, academic behavior, attitudes toward learning, and academic achievement. Research has also shown that older peer mentors influence mentees' perceptions, connect them to a social support network, and reconnect them with supportive adult authority figures. Because the social and academic lives of children and adolescents are intertwined in the school context, it is important to develop programs for addressing both in tandem.

As schools continue to face the challenges of optimizing growth for students, teachers, and classrooms, interventions that systematically incorporate peer supports offer a powerful tool for improvement (Harris, Graham, & Mason, 2006; Meltzer, 2014). For struggling learners and students with special needs, the power of peer-enhanced approaches is clear. Research indicates that incorporating peer support programs or peer-based interventions in the classroom is a win–win situation for students with special needs and their peers. Such supports are often associated with increased motivation, improved school performance, higher attendance, lowered retention rates, reduced special education placement, higher scores on state- and nationally-mandated assessments, and social and emotional gains.

Despite the existing research base, there are very few available resources that provide guidelines for applying these findings to classroom practice and that guide teachers, administrators, and school support personnel in implementing evidence-based programs. Therefore, there is a serious need for a book that incorporates what we know about peer supports and peer-based interventions into teacher preparation, classrooms, and schools. This book meets that need, providing teachers with evidence-based practices for enhancing learning, development, and social relationships for students with learning challenges and other special needs.

Chapter 1, by Meltzer and colleagues, discusses the rationale as well as specific suggestions for blending the teaching of executive function processes with a peer coaching program. Chapter 2, by Regan et al., focuses on peer interactions in the content areas as a means of differentiating instruction. Chapter 3, by Cramer and Mason, focuses on literacy, examining the role of peer support in learning to write. Literacy is discussed further in Chapter 4, in which Scornavacco et al. examine the role of peer discourse in collaborative strategic reading, and in Chapter 5, in which Kearns et al. examine peer-assisted learning strategies (PALS) for reading.

Chapter 6, by Powell and Fuchs, addresses PALS for mathematics. Chapter 7, by Wilkerson and Lequia, focuses on the benefits of small-group instruction for learners with varying strengths and challenges. In Chapter 8, Richards-Tutor, Aceves, and Reutebuch address how peer support for English learners can make a difference in the classroom. Finally, in Chapter 9, Strain and Bovey discuss how preschool peers can influence social outcomes for students with special needs.

We hope that this text will be a useful resource for educators, administrators, and other school personnel who work tirelessly to support special–needs learners, and that this will be as good a read for you as it has been for us.

REFERENCES

Harris, K. R., Graham, S., & Mason, L. (2006). Improving the writing, knowledge, and motivation of struggling young writers: Effects of self-regulated strategy development with and without peer support. *American Educational Research Journal, 43*(2), 295–340.

Meltzer, L. J. (2014). Teaching executive functioning processes: Promoting metacognition, strategy use, and effort. In J. Naglieri & S. Goldstein (Eds.), *Handbook of executive functioning* (pp. 445–474). New York: Springer.

Rodkin, P. C., & Ryan, A. M. (2012). Child and adolescent peer relations in educational context. In K. R. Harris, S. Graham, & T. Urdan (Eds.), *APA educational psychology handbook: Individual differences and cultural and contextual factors* (Vol. 2, pp. 363–389). Washington, DC: American Psychological Association.

Rubin, K. H., Bukowski, K. H., & Laursen, B. (Eds.). (2009). *Handbook of peer interactions, relationships, and groups.* New York: Guilford Press.

Contents

Purchasers of this book can download and print
select materials from *www.guilford.com/harris-forms*.

CHAPTER 1

Executive Function and Peer Mentoring

Fostering Metacognitive Awareness, Effort, and Academic Success

LYNN MELTZER, MICHAEL GRESCHLER, KATELYN KURKUL, and WENDY STACEY

As students advance through the grades, their academic performance depends increasingly on their ability to organize, prioritize, think flexibly, access working memory, and self-monitor, all of which are critically important executive function processes (Barkley, 2012; Brown, 2006, 2014; Denckla, 2007; Meltzer, 2007, 2014). These processes underlie accurate and efficient performance on academic tasks that involve the synthesis of multiple subskills such as reading comprehension, writing, studying, test taking, and completion of long-term projects (Brown, 2014; Elliot & Dweck, 2005; Goldstein & Naglieri, 2014; Meltzer & Basho, 2010). Maintaining the motivation, effort, and emotional self-regulation needed to access these executive function processes is often challenging, especially for students with learning and attention difficulties (Brown, 2006; Meltzer, 2010, 2014; Meltzer & Krishnan, 2007). When classroom teaching emphasizes strategies that address executive function processes and is supplemented with peer mentoring and peer coaching, students are often more effective at sustaining the effort needed to apply these strategies to their schoolwork (Meltzer, Reddy, Greschler, & Kurkul, 2013; Meltzer, Kurkul, Reddy, & Basho, 2014b).

In this chapter, we discuss the rationale as well as specific suggestions for teaching executive function processes explicitly and for integrating strategy instruction with a school-based peer mentoring program. In the first sections, we provide a context for this chapter by defining executive function processes and the important roles of peer mentoring and peer coaching. In the following sections, we discuss specific teaching strategies as well as ways in which peer mentoring and peer coaching can strengthen students' metacognitive awareness and executive function strategies in six core areas: goal setting, cognitive flexibility, organizing, prioritizing, accessing working memory, and self-monitoring. Finally, we summarize our *SMARTS* Executive Function and Mentoring program, a research-based cross-grade peer mentoring program that has been successfully implemented in four middle schools and high schools over the past 6 years (Meltzer, 2013b, 2014; Meltzer et al., 2013). Throughout the chapter, we emphasize practical strategies that teachers can implement in the context of the curriculum as well as ways in which cross-grade peer mentoring and classroomwide peer coaching systems can be used by teachers to supplement and strengthen strategy instruction.

EXECUTIVE FUNCTION AND ACADEMIC PERFORMANCE

> My mind is like a bottle of ginger ale. I need the fizzy bubbles to settle
> before I can do what I need to do.—Ben, 9 years old, fifth grader

Executive function is an all-encompassing construct or "umbrella term" for the complex cognitive processes that underlie flexible, goal-directed responses in novel or difficult situations (Anderson, 2002). Over the years, a broad range of definitions and models have been proposed to explain executive function (Barkley, 2010, 2012; Denckla, 2007; Goldstein & Naglieri, 2014). In our work, we emphasize the importance of key executive function processes that affect academic performance, namely, goal setting, cognitive flexibility/shifting, organizing, prioritizing, working memory, and self-monitoring (see Table 1.1) (Meltzer, 2007, 2010, 2014).

These executive function processes are critically important for performance on academic tasks that involve the coordination and integration of different subskills such as reading comprehension, writing, summarizing, note taking, studying, completing projects in a timely manner, and submitting work on time (Barkley,

TABLE 1.1. Executive Function Processes Defined

Executive function process	Definition
Goal setting	Identifying short-term and long-term goals; figuring out a purpose and endpoint
Cognitive flexibility/shifting	Switching easily between approaches; looking again, in a brand-new way
Organizing	Arranging information systematically; sorting and categorizing information
Prioritizing	Ordering based on relative importance; identifying what's most important
Accessing working memory	Manipulating information mentally; juggling ideas in one's mind
Self-monitoring	Identifying errors and self-correcting; finding and fixing one's own mistakes

2010; Dawson & Guare, 2010; Denckla, 2007; Deshler, Ellis, & Lenz, 1996; Meltzer, 2010, 2014; Meltzer & Basho, 2010). Students who struggle with these executive function processes often experience frustration and failure, and they feel as if their brains are "clogged" with information. The paradigm that we use to explain these difficulties is based on the analogy of a "clogged funnel," as is reflected in Figure 1.1 (Meltzer, 2010, 2014; Meltzer & Krishnan, 2007).

Instruction that emphasizes executive function strategies and helps students to "unclog the funnel" can prevent these students' difficulties from increasing in severity as the curriculum complexity and pace intensify. A comprehensive discussion of these executive function weaknesses, as well as techniques and worksheets for teaching specific executive function strategies, can be found in another book in this series, *Promoting Executive Function in the Classroom* (Meltzer, 2010).

STRENGTHENING EXECUTIVE FUNCTION STRATEGIES WITH PEER MENTORING AND PEER COACHING

> In ninth grade, my teachers told me I was lazy and unmotivated because my homework was often incomplete. When my mentor helped me to use strategies for organizing and checking my work, my grades improved and I began to feel that it would be worthwhile to work hard in school. My mentor changed my life and helped me to reach my senior year.—Max, 18 years old, 12th grader

Peer mentoring and peer coaching can maximize the effectiveness of teaching executive function strategies. Through activities that emphasize students' profiles of strengths and weaknesses, mentor–mentee dyads and peer coaching pairs enhance their self-understanding and their ability to apply executive function strategies to their schoolwork. Our *SMARTS* Executive Function and Peer Mentoring program is an evidence-based program that has been successfully implemented in grades 7–12 in five schools in Boston, Massachusetts, over the past 5

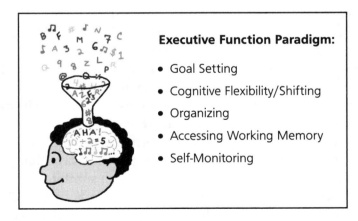

FIGURE 1.1. Executive function: The clogged funnel paradigm (revised). Copyright 2014 by Research ILD. Reprinted by permission.

years (Meltzer et al., 2011, 2013; Meltzer, 2014). In the last section of this chapter, we highlight the important features of our *SMARTS* program and summarize our research findings to date.

In this chapter, we address two slightly different models for using peer support to supplement and extend executive function strategy instruction: peer mentoring and peer coaching. When a *cross-grade peer mentoring* model is implemented, students from the upper grades are trained to become mentors and are then paired with mentees from the lower grades. A 2-year age difference is usually optimal (e.g., 11th graders paired with 9th graders or 8th graders paired with 6th graders). Mentors need to take leadership roles as they provide support and modeling to help their mentees apply the executive function strategies they have learned to their weekly homework. The logistics of creating a cross-grade peer mentoring program can be challenging; however, the creation of a schoolwide program promotes connectedness across the grades. When a *classroomwide peer coaching* model is implemented, pairing of students occurs within the same class or grade so that students are generally at similar developmental stages. There is no mentor or mentee; instead, pairs of students trade off the responsibility of being the "coach" and modeling new strategies for their partners. Peer coaching, which is logistically easier to implement, can therefore be used to supplement explicit strategy instruction within different content-area classes.

Within both models, peer mentors and peer coaches can encourage one another to reflect and think more deeply about their learning profiles and their use of executive function strategies (Meltzer et al., 2011; Meltzer, Basho, Reddy, & Kurkul, 2014a). In fact, participation in activities with peers who are at the same developmental level is a more powerful process for promoting self-awareness than introspection alone (Darling, 2005; Fuchs, Fuchs, Mathes, & Martinez, 2002). Furthermore, students often develop a stronger understanding of their own strengths and weaknesses as a result of the feelings of competence and autonomy prompted by their mentoring or coaching roles (Karcher, 2005).

Regardless of whether a peer mentoring or peer coaching model is used, special attention needs to be given to the processes used for pairing students. Mentor–mentee dyads need to be paired for a minimum of a year, whereas peer coaches can rotate more frequently within the same classes (Rhodes, 2005). It is important that teachers assign students to pairs in order to ensure that no students feel isolated and that the pairs are matched in ways that maximize learning. This process typically begins by informally assessing students' interests, self-understanding, metacognitive awareness, and the extent to which they apply executive function strategies to their schoolwork. Using this informal assessment information, peer mentoring or peer coaching dyads can be assigned in ways that maximize students' abilities to learn from each other. Students with similar profiles of strengths and weaknesses in strategy use and educational performance can help one another with academic tasks; however, in order to ensure that peer dyads develop a positive bond, students' shared interests (e.g., sports, music, video games) should also be taken into account.

Finally, a systematic approach to training peer mentors and peer coaches is critically important in order to strengthen instruction in executive function strategies. It is important to select mentors who are motivated and willing to take on a leadership role; therefore, an application and interview process is often helpful. An effective, evidence-based system for training peer mentors can be found in the National Mentoring Partnership *Elements of Effective Practice for Mentoring* (2005). This is also an excellent resource for best practices for mentor recruitment, screening, matching, monitoring, and support.

PROMOTING EXECUTIVE FUNCTION AND PEER MENTORING/COACHING ACROSS THE GRADES

> I stumbled and struggled and I had trouble in lots of areas, which made doing homework so slow. I am thankful to my sixth-grade teacher, who first taught me strategies for coping with my learning problem. I learned that if my approach was not working, I needed to take a step back, to think flexibly, and to approach my work in a different way by using strategies that could help me to get through.—Billy, 16 years old, 10th grader.

In this section, we discuss specific suggestions for creating strategic classrooms that promote students' metacognitive awareness and executive function strategy use. We focus on specific strategies for addressing metacognitive awareness as well as six important executive function processes, namely, goal setting, cognitive flexibility/shifting, organizing and prioritizing, accessing working memory, and self-monitoring. In each of these subsections, we discuss:

1. A general framework for understanding each executive function process.
2. Teaching strategies for addressing each executive function process in the context of the academic curriculum.
3. Systems for augmenting strategy instruction with peer mentoring and peer coaching.

The paradigm that guides these sections emphasizes the importance of metacognitive awareness as the foundation for teaching executive function strategies, which can then be strengthened through peer mentoring or peer coaching (see Figure 1.2). This paradigm is the cornerstone of our *SMARTS* Executive Function and Mentoring program, a cross-grade peer mentoring intervention that strengthens students' self-understanding and metacognitive awareness on an ongoing basis while teaching executive function strategies explicitly and systematically (see the final section of this chapter for more details).

It is beyond the scope of this chapter to detail the specific procedures used for teaching these executive function strategies in each academic area. Instead, we focus on a few examples of our *SMARTS* strategies for each of these executive function processes, and we discuss ways in which peer mentoring and peer coaching models can be effectively used to strengthen classroom instruction in these

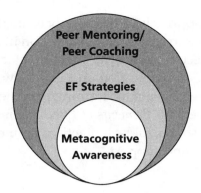

FIGURE 1.2. Promoting executive function: Augmenting strategy instruction with peer mentoring or peer coaching. Copyright 2013 by ResearchILD. Reprinted by permission.

areas. It should be noted that we have combined the executive function processes of organizing and prioritizing into one section, as these processes overlap extensively.

METACOGNITIVE AWARENESS

> After I began to understand why I was struggling in school, I began to understand how I learned best. When I did my homework, I worked hard to use the strategies that I learned from my teacher. The first time I did well on a test showed me that I wasn't dumb. I could do it!—Sam, 14 years old, ninth grader

Promoting metacognitive awareness and providing opportunities for students to think about their own thinking and learning create the foundation for teaching executive function strategies. Metacognitive awareness, a concept originally defined by Flavell (1979) and Brown, Bransford, Ferrara, and Campione (1983), refers to each student's understanding and beliefs about how he or she thinks and learns as well as the strategies that can be used to accomplish specific tasks. As students' metacognitive awareness increases, they begin to understand their strengths and weaknesses, which, in turn, influences their selection of specific executive function strategies (Meltzer, 2010; Meltzer, Katzir, Miller, Reddy, & Roditi, 2004a; Miller, Meltzer, Katzir-Cohen, & Houser, 2001). Metacognitive awareness also increases students' motivation to make the effort to master and use these strategies in their daily classwork and homework, which results in improved academic performance (Meltzer et al., 2004b; Meltzer, Basho, Reddy & Kurkul, 2014a; Meltzer, Reddy, Pollica, & Roditi, 2004c).

Teaching Techniques That Promote Metacognitive Awareness

Metacognitive awareness and effective strategy use are encouraged when teachers build a classroom culture that emphasizes strategy use and when they teach students what strategies are, why they should use strategies, and which strategies are effective for which tasks. To achieve this, teachers should begin by using formal and informal assessment methods that can help them to understand their students' self-perceptions and use of executive function strategies. One criterion-referenced assessment system that compares students', teachers', and parents' perceptions of students' self-understanding and strategy use is the Metacognitive Awareness System or MetaCOG (Meltzer et al., 2004a, 2004b, 2004c; Meltzer & Krishnan, 2007) (available at *www.researchild.org*). Teachers can use this brief assessment system as a baseline for understanding students' metacognitive awareness and strategy use and can tailor their instruction accordingly to promote and build metacognitive awareness. This MetaCOG survey system can also be readministered at the end of the school year to assess students' progress and to evaluate the effectiveness of strategy instruction. This metacognitive assessment system has been the foundation of our *SMARTS* Executive Function and Peer Mentoring intervention studies, which are summarized in the final section of this chapter (Meltzer, 2014; Meltzer et al., 2013).

Another practical and easily implemented technique for building metacognitive awareness is the consistent use of strategy reflection sheets that require students to reflect on and describe the processes and strategies they use for their classwork, homework, and test preparation. Strategy reflection sheets can incorporate a multiple-choice format, structured questions, or open-ended questions. As is evident from Figures 1.3a and 1.3b, this system also allows students to explain their strategy use to their peers, providing a structured approach for integrating executive function strategies with peer mentoring and peer coaching. By completing and sharing strategy reflection sheets, students begin to understand which strategies work well for them, as well as why, where, when, and how to apply specific strategies.

(a)

Strategy Reflection Sheet: Multiple-Choice Format

What strategies did you use for your writing assignment and preparing for your test?

____ Mapping and Webbing	____ Sentence Starters
____ Graphic Organizer	____ Personalized Editing Checklist
____ Linear Outline	____ Triple Note Tote
____ BOTEC	____ Other

(b)

Strategy Reflection Sheet: Open-Ended Format

What strategies did you use in order to prepare for this test or assignment?

I used a graphic organizer plus all my notes that I had and a textbook. Finally I used a little imagination.

FIGURE 1.3. Strategy reflection sheets for writing and test preparation: (a) multiple-choice and (b) open-ended question formats. Copyright 2004 by ResearchILD. Reprinted by permission.

TABLE 1.2. Strategy Reflections: Easy-to-Use Techniques for Building Metacognitive Awareness and Use of Executive Function Strategies

✓ *Strategy reflection sheets for homework*
   Students are graded for completing strategy reflection sheets for selected assignments to promote metacognitive awareness and strategic habits of mind.

✓ *Strategy shares*
   Brief daily or weekly discussion times for students to share their favorite personalized strategies from the week's homework.

✓ *Personalized strategy note cards and/or notebooks*
   Students record their favorite strategies on strategy note cards or in a strategy notebook to make practice easier at school and at home.

✓ *Strategy-of-the-week display board and strategy wall*
   Students' favorite strategies are showcased in different content areas on display boards. Students vote for a *Strategy of the Week* for display. By year-end, students' favorite personal strategies cover classroom walls.

Metacognitive awareness and effective strategy use are promoted when teachers make strategy use *count* in their classrooms (see Table 1.2). When grades for homework and tests include points for completing strategy reflection sheets, teachers promote strategic learning and strategic habits of mind in all students. Furthermore, daily or weekly strategy shares allow students to discuss their use of strategies with one another, a process that is strengthened through peer coaching.

Augmenting Strategy Instruction with Peer Mentoring and/or Peer Coaching

Metacognitive awareness and strategy instruction are strengthened when teachers group students into peer mentoring or peer coaching dyads. Self-understanding is also important for promoting supportive peer relationships, as groupings of peer mentors can be created based on students' interests, their self-reports about their strategy use on surveys such as the MetaCOG (see Table 1.3), and the "Know Yourself" strategy sheets (see Figure 1.4).

As is evident from Table 1.3, the MetaCOG Strategy Use Survey (STRATUS) and other MetaCOG questionnaires provide information about students' executive function strategies and effort that help teachers to match students in appropriate peer mentoring or peer coaching pairs. Information from these surveys can also be used to help students in mentoring and coaching pairs to understand the similarities and differences between their own strengths and weaknesses and the learning profiles of the students with whom they are paired. Additional information regarding students' self-understanding about their learning profiles can be obtained from the "Know Yourself" strategy sheets, which provide a structured system for encouraging students to think about their strengths and weaknesses to create visual displays of their learning profiles (see Figure 1.4).

TABLE 1.3. Selected Items from the MetaCOG Strategy Use Survey (MetaCOG STRATUS)

- I have trouble breaking down my homework into smaller, more manageable parts.
- I have trouble organizing my thoughts before I write.
- When I read or write, I struggle to figure out the main ideas.
- When I am learning something new, I connect it to something I already know.
- When I do my work, I ask if my answers make sense.
- If the method I am using to solve a problem is not working, I use another way of solving it.

Note. The STRATUS comprises 30 items. Copyright 2004, 2014 by ResearchILD. Reprinted by permission.

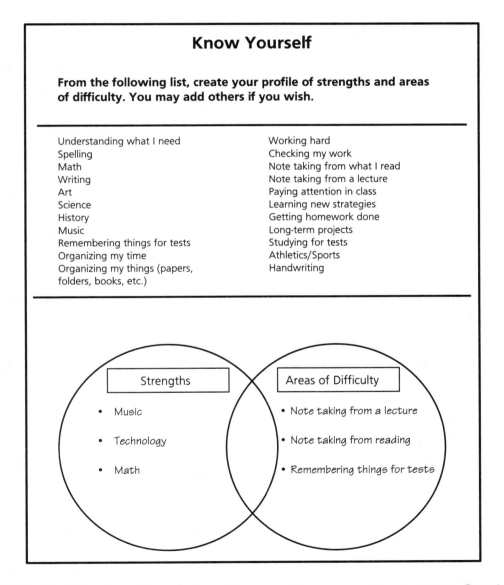

FIGURE 1.4. Know Yourself strategy sheet for promoting metacognitive awareness. Copyright 2014 by ResearchILD. Reprinted by permission.

Paired students can also help each other to increase their strategy use and self-understanding by discussing their learning profiles with one another and coaching one another as they reflect about the specific strategies that have been helpful to them in different areas.

In summary, promoting students' metacognitive awareness and self-understanding maximizes the effectiveness of teaching executive function strategies. Table 1.4 provides samples of practical and easily implemented classroom-based approaches that have been carried out systematically as part of the *SMARTS* intervention (Meltzer, 2014; Meltzer et al., 2013).

Once teachers have created a classroom culture that promotes metacognitive awareness, they can use this as a foundation for teaching executive function strategies in the context of the academic curriculum. In the sections below, we discuss specific teaching strategies for each of the core executive function processes as well as suggestions for augmenting strategy instruction with peer mentoring and peer coaching. These strategies have been implemented and evaluated over the past 5 years as part of the *SMARTS* intervention program for middle and high school students (Meltzer, 2014; Meltzer et al., 2013).

GOAL SETTING

> When students set goals without thinking through the steps, they are opening themselves up to all kinds of frustration and their self-esteem suffers. We need to teach students to think through their goals and to understand the steps they need to take to achieve them.—Sally J., middle school science teacher

Goal setting refers to the ability to set specific, realistic objectives that can be achieved within a defined period of time. Goal-setting strategies help students

TABLE 1.4. Fostering Metacognitive Awareness: Strengthening Students' Strategy Use through Peer Mentoring and Peer Coaching

Teacher	Peer mentor/peer coach
Teach executive function strategies explicitly and systematically.	Practice modeling the executive function strategies for each other.
Train peer mentors and peer coaches systematically (see last section in this chapter).	Interview each other using the *Know Yourself* worksheets.
Incorporate activities that help students to understand their strengths and areas of difficulty.	Ask each other how they think and learn and how they developed their strengths.
Assign strategy reflection sheets for homework and tests.	Interview each other to complete the strategy reflection sheets.
Make strategy use count by grading students based on their use of strategies.	Share effective strategies with each other. Display favorite strategies on strategy boards in the classroom.

to understand the task objectives, visualize the steps involved in accomplishing tasks, and organize the time and resources needed to complete tasks (Harris & Graham, 1999; Zimmerman, 2002). In addition, goal setting requires students to understand the big picture, to envision the end point of a task, and to recognize that goals need to be attainable (Krishnan, Feller, & Orkin, 2010).

Students often struggle to set realistic goals and to break their goals down into clear, meaningful steps. Clear goals are well defined, appropriately challenging, and make connections between day-to-day tasks and the desired long-term outcomes. Furthermore, when students set realistic and attainable goals, they need effective systems for tracking their progress and adapting their approaches when they encounter obstacles. Goal setting is also linked with students' awareness of their personal strengths and limitations as well as their ability to visualize the final outcome (Harris & Graham, 1999; Zimmerman, 2002). Helping students to create clear, appropriate, and well-developed goals can be challenging for teachers; therefore, a systematic approach is extremely important.

Teaching Goal-Setting Strategies

Teaching students to set effective goals requires strategies that help them to set and evaluate their goals systematically. The CANDO Goal-Setting Strategy is used in the *SMARTS* program to help students set realistic goals and to identify the steps they need to take to reach these goals (see Table 1.5). CANDO is an easy-to-remember mnemonic that helps students create realistic goals that help them succeed. For example, students take a vague goal such as "I want to be a better student" and transform this into a well-thought-out goal such as "I want to earn a 'B' in all of my academic classes by the end of the year." Strategies such as CANDO help students create goals that motivate them to succeed.

TABLE 1.5. The CANDO Goal-Setting Strategy

Mnemonics	Purpose	Example
Clear	Avoids the use of vague words	"I want to earn at least a B on my math tests."
Appropriate	States a goal that is attainable and realistic	"I will improve by at least one letter grade."
Numerical	Quantifies the goal so that progress is measurable	"I will study Spanish for 2 hours a week."
Doable	Breaks down the steps needed to achieve the goal	"In order to get a part in the play, I will have to sign up, audition, and practice."
Obstacles considered	Anticipates likely obstacles and incorporates potential solutions	"I feel like I'm stuck on my research paper; I need to schedule a meeting with the teacher and get help."

Note. Copyright 2009 by ResearchILD. Reprinted by permission.

Augmenting Strategy Instruction with Peer Mentoring and Peer Coaching

I told my mentee the only way to get good grades is to set goals. Even the littlest goal can make a big difference. She really appreciated that. Talking to her about goals made an impact on me too; I'm a role model, so I have to set a high standard for myself.—Trish, 17 years old, 11th-grade mentor

Even in the early elementary grades, strategies for setting appropriate goals can be modeled by peer mentors or peer coaches. Peer mentoring and peer coaching pairs can work together strategically to attain their goals and can help each other identify the steps needed to achieve their goals. Mentoring and coaching pairs can collaboratively estimate the amount of work involved in major projects and open-ended tasks and can select specific strategies for breaking down tasks into manageable parts, especially when there are multiple deadlines for different assignments.

The supportive nature of peer mentoring and coaching often helps to make goal-setting strategies more meaningful for students, as we have found in our *SMARTS* intervention studies (Meltzer et al., 2013, 2014b). Students evaluate each other's goals in an accepting and nonjudgmental way and can offer advice about ways of coping with obstacles that they may have encountered. For example, when using the CANDO goal-setting strategy (as shown in Figure 1.5), students can share ideas as they work together to set and evaluate each other's goals, and they can also focus on possible steps to achieve these goals.

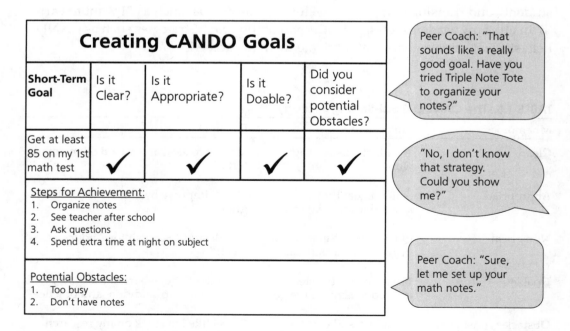

FIGURE 1.5. Mentor/coach CANDO goal-setting worksheet. Copyright 2007 by ResearchILD. Reprinted by permission.

As is evident from Figure 1.5, peer support also helps students organize and prioritize the steps they must take to achieve their goals and often motivates them to apply strategies to their daily schoolwork.

COGNITIVE FLEXIBILITY/SHIFTING

I learned a strategy for note taking that works great for me. It's really cool because it helps me figure out different ways that I can represent one thing when I write or study. It's all about shifting perspectives and seeing things from a different light. So, it's cool.—Jan, 13 years old, seventh grader

In the classroom setting, the ability to shift approaches and to synthesize information in novel ways is essential for effective reading, writing, math problem solving, note taking, studying, and test taking. When reading text, students need to shift between the concrete and abstract, between the literal and symbolic, and between major themes and relevant details (Block & Pressley, 2002; Cartwright, 2008a, 2008b, 2008c). Similarly, when writing, students must shift between their own perspective and that of the reader, and between the important concepts and supporting information. In the math domain, students need to shift from the words and sentences in math problems to the numbers, operations, algorithms, and equations in order to solve problems (Roditi & Steinberg, 2007). Finally, studying and test taking require students to shift among multiple topics, problem types, and formats as information is often presented differently in textbooks, homework, and tests. Teaching students to problem-solve and think flexibly is critically important to ensure that they can "unclog the funnel" and successfully master the increasingly complex curriculum as they advance through the grades.

Teaching Cognitive Flexibility and Flexible Thinking Strategies

Students need to be systematically taught how to interpret information in more than one way, to change their approaches when needed, and to choose a new strategy when one is not working. Three-column note-taking systems such as the *SMARTS* Triple Note Tote strategy (see Figure 1.6) can be taught across the grades and content areas. As we have shown in our *SMARTS* intervention studies, this strategy helps students to shift flexibly from the major themes to the details and back again for reading, writing, summarizing, note taking, and studying (Meltzer & Bagnato, 2010; Roditi & Steinberg, 2007; Meltzer, Pollica, & Barzillai, 2007).

As is evident from the figure, the first column of the Triple Note Tote is used for students to write down major themes, core concepts, or key questions; in the second column, they can record the relevant details, and in the third column, they list their strategy for remembering the information. The last column is critically important as this ensures that students develop personalized strategies for memorizing and retrieving the required information on quizzes and tests. The Triple Note Tote strategy is useful for summarizing, planning writing assignments, note taking, and studying as this helps students to organize and prioritize so that they can extract information from a variety of sources, including textbooks, homework assignments, and class notes. Shifting strategies also help students to switch flexibly between math operations. For example, complex multiplication and division require them to shift from one operation (e.g., addition) to a different operation (e.g., subtraction). Furthermore, students need to learn how to shift between problem formats for math homework and tests and to identify the key words, operations, and information needed to solve word problems flexibly.

FIGURE 1.6. The Triple Note Tote strategy: A system for shifting between major concepts and relevant details (Meltzer & Basho, 2010). Copyright 2007 by ResearchILD. Reprinted by permission.

Augmenting Strategy Instruction with Peer Mentoring and Peer Coaching

We tried the Triple Note Tote strategy together to help us switch from the main ideas to the details when we were reading our history books. The student I was coaching said she didn't like this strategy, but when I explained it to her in a different way, she really got it. She even explained it to the whole class!—Gene, 15 years old, ninth grader

Strategies for promoting cognitive flexibility can be strengthened with peer coaching and peer mentoring to create opportunities for students to solve problems from different perspectives across a variety of different content areas. When students are involved in peer discussions, they are exposed to multiple viewpoints and can learn how to approach problems from the perspective of their peers (Fuchs, Fuchs & Burish, 2000; Yuill, 2007). Students can also coach each other as they complete structured academic tasks that require them to use different strategies. These activities help all students to reflect and to think actively about which study strategies are most effective for different types of test formats and content areas. For example, when studying for a history test, peers can work together to create study guides using the Triple Note Tote strategy to help them shift between the main ideas and details. Similarly, when completing math homework or studying for math tests, peers can coach one another to shift between the different steps for solving word problems. For example, peers can use the KNOW shifting strategy to shift from organizing the information needed to solve the word problem to selecting the appropriate operation to calculating the answer (see Figure 1.7).

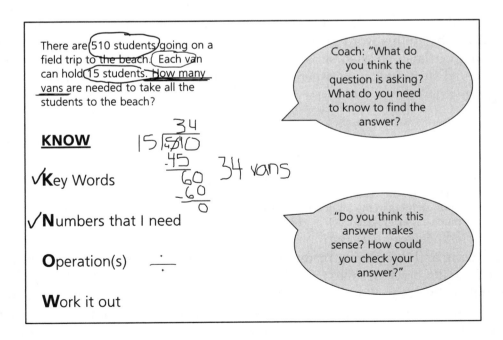

FIGURE 1.7. KNOW strategy math worksheet.

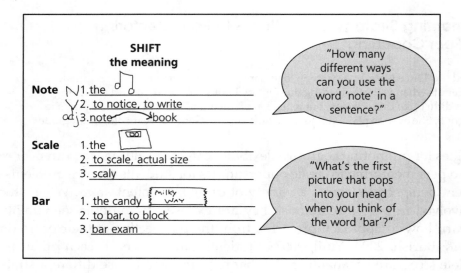

FIGURE 1.8. Shifty Words strategy worksheet.

When reading, writing, and studying, students also need to learn strategies for shifting between word meanings at the sentence and paragraph levels and for recognizing that words can change meaning in relation to context. One example of such a strategy that can be easily augmented through peer mentoring and peer coaching is shown in Figure 1.8.

As is evident from Figure 1.8, peer mentors and peer coaches can help one another to use the Shifty Words strategy when words or sentences do not make sense and to ask themselves questions such as "Does this word have more than one meaning?" "Can this word be used as both a noun and a verb?" "Can a different syllable in this word give it a different meaning?" Peer mentoring and peer coaching can also be used successfully in classrooms at different levels to help students to shift flexibly between literal and figurative interpretations of text in language arts, science, and history.

ORGANIZING AND PRIORITIZING

Everything was a mess! My backpack, my locker, my notes were so messy even I couldn't read them! I learned that using structure could really save me. I put dividers in my binder and started using multicolumn notes, and it was much easier to keep track of my work.—John, 21 years old, college student

Organizing and prioritizing materials, ideas, and information are important executive function processes that underlie most academic and life tasks. Strategies for systematically organizing and prioritizing time, materials, and ideas are essential for overall academic performance and particularly for reading comprehension, writing, note taking, studying, and test preparation. These executive function strategies assume greater importance in late elementary school when students are presented with an increasingly large volume of detailed information. When strategies for organizing and prioritizing are taught systematically in the context of school assignments, students are more likely to generalize these strategies and to succeed academically (Krishnan et al., 2010). Peer coaches can help students to organize and prioritize by ensuring that they use systematic approaches for organizing their materials, information, and ideas and applying these strategies to their schoolwork and homework, as summarized below.

Teaching Organizing and Prioritizing Strategies

When classroom teaching incorporates strategies for organizing and prioritizing ideas and information, students' performance improves in reading comprehension, written language, note taking, and studying (Meltzer et al., 2004a, 2004b, 2004c). For reading comprehension and written language, the structure imposed by a three-column note-taking system, such as the *SMARTS* Triple Note Tote strategy (see Figure 1.6 in the previous section), helps students to organize and prioritize information, find the main ideas, and separate the relevant from less relevant details. More specifically, in the area of written language, students benefit from explicit templates that match both the goals of the assignment and their learning profiles (Graham & Harris, 2003; Harris & Graham, 1996). These strategies help students to break down writing tasks into manageable parts, to organize their ideas, and to monitor their own performance (Graham, Harris, & Mason, 2005; Mason, Harris & Graham, 2011; Santangelo, Harris, & Graham, 2008). To structure the writing process further, a strategy such as BOTEC uses a mnemonic and visual image to help students focus on the important steps involved in writing, namely: **B**rainstorm, **O**rganize thoughts, generate a **T**opic sentence or Thesis statement, **E**laborate by providing **E**vidence, and draw a **C**onclusion (Meltzer et al., 2005) (see Figure 1.9).

Augmenting Strategy Instruction with Peer Mentoring and Peer Coaching

One day my mentee opened his bag, and it was just a huge pile of stuff. I said, "Okay, we can clean this." We came up with a new system, helped him put everything where it belonged, and we were done in 20 minutes. I think we were both surprised by that.—Chris, 17 years old, 11th-grade mentor

Peer support can increase students' motivation to use strategies for organizing and prioritizing on a long-term basis. Organizational strategies are also more engaging when peer mentors and peer coaches help one another to implement these strategies. Peer mentors and peer coaches can work together to organize their folders, binders, book bags, and other materials systematically and consistently. For example, using the *SMARTS* Four C's strategy (see Table 1.6) peer mentoring and peer coaching pairs can practice the four C's of organization in the context

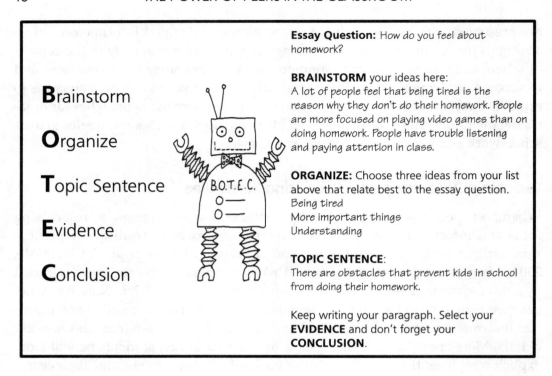

Essay Question: *How do you feel about homework?*

BRAINSTORM your ideas here:
A lot of people feel that being tired is the reason why they don't do their homework. People are more focused on playing video games than on doing homework. People have trouble listening and paying attention in class.

ORGANIZE: *Choose three ideas from your list above that relate best to the essay question.*
Being tired
More important things
Understanding

TOPIC SENTENCE:
There are obstacles that prevent kids in school from doing their homework.

Keep writing your paragraph. Select your **EVIDENCE** and don't forget your **CONCLUSION**.

FIGURE 1.9. The BOTEC strategy for generating written language. Copyright 2005 by ResearchILD. Reprinted by permission.

TABLE 1.6. The Four C's Strategy for Organizing Materials: Mentor/Coach Questions

The four C's strategy	Mentor/coach guiding questions
Clean: Clean out binders and separate them into items to keep for school, items to file at home, and items to recycle or throw away.	How should we *clean* out our backpacks? Should we make separate piles?
Customize: Use accessories such as binder tabs or colored pocket folders to create an individualized organization system. Develop a color-coding system for folders, books, etc. (e.g., blue for math, red for social studies).	How should we *customize* our organizational systems (e.g., color-coding based on subject, labeling, or pockets)?
Categorize: Create separate places for filing materials according to classes and assignment types (e.g., notes, quizzes).	How would you *categorize* your materials? Do you want to separate your materials based on your classes (e.g., math, history) or types of assignments?
Continue: Find time, weekly or monthly, to clear out binders and tweak organizational system.	How should we make sure we *continue* to keep up our organizational systems? Should we do it every Friday?

Note. Copyright 2013 by ResearchILD. Reprinted by permission.

of a backpack relay race (see Table 1.6) (Kurkul & Greschler, 2013). When this strategy is used in the *SMARTS* program, students are given messy backpacks that they are required to organize in relay teams as they search for specific items designated by the teacher. This relay team activity helps students to realize that effective organizational systems ultimately save them time. Peers help each other apply the lessons learned from the backpack relay race to systems for organizing and prioritizing their school materials when they prepare for tests or complete their homework.

ACCESSING WORKING MEMORY

> I used to think I was really bad at math. I could never remember anything!
> Then I learned to create crazy phrases and acronyms to help me remember
> and it's so much easier now!—Katie, 10 years old, fourth grader

Working memory refers to the ability to store information for short time periods while simultaneously manipulating the information mentally (e.g., holding the main themes in mind while sorting through the details or calculating math problems mentally). Baddeley (2006) and Swanson and Sáez (2003) have proposed that working memory often functions as the central executive function that directs all other cognitive processes, including students' abilities to inhibit impulses, shift attention, and direct effort to a specific task. Working memory therefore plays a critical role in efficient and accurate learning (Swanson, 2001; Swanson & Hoskyn, 2001; Swanson & Sáez, 2003).

Memorizing information in the classroom is heavily dependent on the extent to which students can focus and sustain attention in order to make connections, retain information, and retrieve relevant details (Tannock, 2008). In fact, attention and memory are so strongly linked that the two processes are often viewed as part of the same executive process (Swanson & Sáez, 2003). To remember, retain, and retrieve information, students benefit from strategies for sustaining their attention, attaching meaning to information, and chunking information to reduce the memory load (Kincaid & Trautman, 2010).

Teaching Working Memory Strategies

Working memory strategies are associated with teaching strategies for organizing and prioritizing information in meaningful ways to reduce the memory load. Mnemonics comprise one of the most effective methods for chunking information and retaining important details so that information can be mentally manipulated in working memory (Mastropieri & Scruggs, 1998; Scruggs & Mastropieri, 2000; Fontana, Scruggs, Mastropieri, 2007; Scruggs, Mastropieri, Berkeley, & Marshak, 2010). Teaching mnemonic strategies (e.g., key words, peg words, acronyms, acrostics) encourages students to connect new information to what they already know, make meaningful connections to seemingly disconnected details, and improve retention of information (Mastropieri & Scruggs, 1998; Mastropieri et al., 2001; Regan, Evmanova, Mastropieri, & Scruggs, Chapter 2, this volume; Scruggs & Mastropieri, 2000). For example, in the *SMARTS* program, we teach students to remember the states and their capitals by region, using crazy phrases that help them to organize, sequence, and chunk the information so that there are fewer details to memorize. Some students prefer to use visual strategies, such as personalized diagrams, cartoons, graphic organizers, and templates (Kincaid & Trautman, 2010). Chants, rhymes, and songs are also important to teach to students who rely on verbal or auditory strategies to memorize. As students learn and practice memory strategies, they benefit from modeling and support from teachers and peer mentors, who can encourage them to create their own memory strategies that match their individual learning profiles and to practice applying these strategies to their schoolwork (Kincaid & Trautman, 2010).

Augmenting Strategy Instruction with Peer Mentoring and Peer Coaching

Peer mentoring and peer coaching can help students to identify memory strategies that best fit their individual learning profiles. The positive support and encourage-

TABLE 1.7. Strategies for Enhancing Working Memory: Peer Mentoring/Coaching Strategies That Augment Classroom Teaching

Strategy	Content information	Mentor/coach guiding questions
Directions	Following multistep, auditory directions	"Let's see how many steps you can hold in your mind. Ready, I will read only two directions and then add on to see how many you can follow accurately."
Crazy phrases	To recall the six states in New England: Maine, New Hampshire, Massachusetts, Vermont, Rhode Island, and Connecticut.	"Can you make up a wacky phrase to remember names, places, or events in a specific order?" *My Neighbor Makes Valuable Coins.*
Acronyms	To remember the formula for cellular respiration: Glucose and Oxygen yield Water, ATP, and Carbon Dioxide	"Can you think of a real or nonsense word (or words) using the first letter of each of these key words?" GO-WAC
Cartoons	The definition of the word *capacious*.	"Can you create a meaningful memory strategy to help you remember the definition?"
Rhymes	The date of the Stamp Act.	"Can you use a rhyme or song to help you remember factual information?" *In 1765, the Stamp Act Was Alive.*

ment offered by peers encourages students to go beyond rote memory or simple rehearsal and helps them to learn how to use memory strategies effectively (see Regan, Evmenova, Mastropieri, & Scruggs, Chapter 2, this volume). Table 1.7 provides examples of memory strategies that peers can work on together for completing homework or studying for tests.

Some students prefer visual strategies such as cartooning, whereas others prefer auditory strategies such as rhymes. By sharing these strategies, peer mentoring and peer coaching dyads expose students to novel approaches that they might not otherwise consider. When students practice these strategies with the support of their peers, they improve their understanding that different strategies are helpful for different types of tasks.

SELF-MONITORING

> If a kid keeps getting D's on his test, but he doesn't stop to think
> about why he's getting a D, he can't do any better. You have to look
> at your tests and find patterns in your mistakes, then you can see the
> hard stuff coming and be prepared.—Jake, 17 years old, 11th grader

Self-monitoring refers to the ways in which learners manage their cognitive and metacognitive processes to track their own performance (Zimmerman, 2000; Zimmerman & Kitsantas, 1997; Zimmerman & Schunk, 2001; Santangelo et al., 2008). When students self-monitor, they review their progress toward their goals, evaluate the outcomes, and redirect their effort as needed. The ability to self-monitor is strongly associated with metacognitive awareness as well as cognitive flexibility. Therefore, students' use of self-monitoring strategies depends on their ability to recognize when, how, and why to use specific strategies so that they can evaluate the outcome of their strategy use, revise their strategies, and continually adjust their use of strategies based on the task demands (Meltzer & Bagnato, 2010).

Teaching Self-Monitoring Strategies

Students need systematic, structured, and scaffolded instruction in self-monitoring strategies so that they can become independent learners who do not rely on others to complete academic tasks (Graham & Harris, 2003; Graham et al., 2005; Reid & Lienemann, 2006). Self-monitoring strategies are important in all academic areas and are particularly important in the writing domain, where students need to shift mindsets from that of the "writer" to that of the "editor" so that they can identify their own errors. Students often realize that their writing is weak, but they often do not know how to revise the structure or organization to improve the content (Graham et al., 2005; Santangelo et al., 2008). For persuasive writing, students often benefit from explicit instruction to monitor their inclusion of the basic structural components of writing, such as topic sentences, supporting details, and paragraph endings (Graham & Harris, 2003). Self-regulated strategy development (SRSD) is a widely used evidence-based system that provides students with specific strategies for brainstorming, writing, and editing their work (Graham et al., 2005; Harris & Graham, 1996; Mong Cramer & Mason, Chapter 3, this volume).

In addition to rubrics, students benefit from a guided process for analyzing several of their writing samples to determine their most common mistakes so that they can develop personalized editing checklists (Meltzer & Bagnato, 2010; Graham et al., 2005; Santangelo et al., 2008). Personalized checklists and acronyms for editing particular types of assignments help students to self-check strategically so that they make fewer errors (Meltzer & Bagnato, 2010; Graham et al., 2005; Mason et al., 2011).

Similarly, personalized checking strategies are critically important for homework completion, studying, and taking tests in all content areas. Most students, especially students with learning and attention difficulties, need explicit instruction focused on how to check their work and how to identify their most common errors. Figure 1.10 illustrates a strategy for teaching students to check their tests that incorporates a "crazy phrase" for those students who more easily remember verbal information (Meltzer & Bagnato, 2010). Students can be taught to use this strategy as a model and then to develop personalized checking strategies for use in the different content areas.

Augmenting Strategy Instruction with Peer Mentoring and Peer Coaching

Peer support and peer coaching help students to invest the extra effort needed to create effective, individualized self-monitoring strategies. The Top 3 Hits strategy (see Figure 1.11) requires students to analyze their own work. For example, in the *SMARTS* program, students work in peer mentoring and coaching pairs to review previous tests and assignments with the goal of identifying common patterns of errors. For each subject, they select the three most common errors and

---

Checking Strategies for Tests

Name
✓ Did I write my name on the test?

Directions
✓ Did I follow the directions?

Strategies
✓ Did I use my strategies?

Corrections
✓ Did I check and make corrections?

Never **D**rink **S**our **C**offee!

FIGURE 1.10. Self-checking strategy for tests. Copyright 2013 by ResearchILD. Reprinted by permission.

John's Top 3 Hits for Math Tests

- Positive and Negative Signs

  Strategy: Did I highlight all of the signs to make sure that I added and subtracted positive and negative numbers correctly?

- Unit of Measure Labels

  Strategy: Did I underline the unit of measurement in the problem and include this in my answer ($, cm, in, m, etc.)?

- Operations

  Strategy: Did I check all my math operations to make sure that I used the correct operation (add vs. subtract; multiply vs. divide)?

FIGURE 1.11. Top 3 Hits strategy for checking tests: Student sample.

devise a strategy for remembering to check for these errors in their work. Students can develop systems for anticipating and correcting their own common errors on assignments, and they are more likely to use these editing strategies because of their collaborations within their mentoring or coaching dyads.

Students' motivation and emotional mindsets frequently affect their willingness to make the effort needed to check and correct multiple drafts of their work, processes that are critically important for long-term academic and life success (Dweck, 2008; Margalit, 2004). Peer mentoring and peer coaching can be particularly effective for motivating students to stop, reflect, and make the effort to use self-monitoring and other executive function strategies.

In conclusion, Table 1.8 provides a summary of selected strategies that have been discussed in this chapter for teaching executive function processes in the context of the academic content in order to help students "unclog the funnel" so that they can perform efficiently in the classroom. In the next section of this chapter, we describe the *SMARTS* Executive Function and Peer Mentoring program, an example of an evidence-based program that integrates the teaching of executive function strategies with peer mentoring (Meltzer, 2013b, 2014; Meltzer et al., 2013, 2014b).

THE *SMARTS* EXECUTIVE FUNCTION AND PEER MENTORING PROGRAM

SMARTS has taught me strategies for coping with my learning problem because if you're not getting anything done and you feel stuck, it's no use staying there. If something is not working, you need to take a step back, shift perspectives, and approach your work in a different way. I now know which strategies work for me and I feel more confident when I use these in my schoolwork.—Billy, 14 years old, eighth grader

Over the past 6 years, the *SMARTS* Executive Function and Mentoring program has been implemented and evaluated as a cross-grade mentoring intervention

TABLE 1.8. Summary of Selected Teaching Strategies for the Key Executive Function Processes

Executive function processes	Selected teaching strategies
Goal setting • Planning and allocating time. • Estimating time. • Adjusting time and effort.	Students complete goal-setting worksheets independently.
Cognitive flexibility/shifting flexibly • Shifting flexibly between major themes and details when reading, writing, studying. • Shifting between math operations and word problems. • Shifting between multiple meanings in words.	Teach strategies that foster flexible thinking (e.g., *Shifty Words* strategy, *Triple Note Tote*).
Organizing and prioritizing • Organizing work space, materials, and time. • Organizing and prioritizing concepts and ideas. • Figuring out which information is critical and which details are less relevant.	Teach students to use *Triple Note Tote* to organize and prioritize notes. Introduce *BOTEC* for organizing and prioritizing ideas for writing.
Accessing working memory • Chunking information to memorize and mentally manipulate details for multistep tasks (e.g., mental computation, note taking). • Accessing critically important details for solving complex math problems. • Remembering key concepts while taking notes.	Enhance working memory by teaching memory strategies (e.g., *crazy phrases, acronyms, cartoons,* and *rhymes*).
Self-monitoring • Using personalized error checklists for editing. • Checking final calculations with estimates of correct answers in math.	Help students to identify their common mistakes in writing and math and to develop personalized error checklists.

for middle and high school students in grades 7–12 in four low-income schools (Meltzer, 2014; Meltzer et al., 2013). *SMARTS* is an acronym for **S**trategies, **M**otivation, **A**wareness, **R**esilience, **T**alents, and **S**uccess, and each of these strands is a core component of this blended program (Meltzer, 2013a; Meltzer, Reddy, Brach, & Kurkul, 2012; Meltzer et al., 2011, 2013, 2014a). The *SMARTS* intervention program is anchored in a theoretical paradigm (see Figure 1.12) that integrates the teaching of selected executive function strategies with peer mentoring and peer coaching (Meltzer, 2013a, 2013b; Meltzer et al., 2011, 2012, 2013, 2014a). *SMARTS* is designed to promote the key processes that are the underpinnings for resilience and success, namely, metacognitive awareness, effort, academic self-concept, and executive function strategies (see Figure 1.12). Using a resilience framework, we connect these processes with the positive social effects of peer mentoring to foster academic success and resilience in all students with a specific focus on students with learning difficulties.

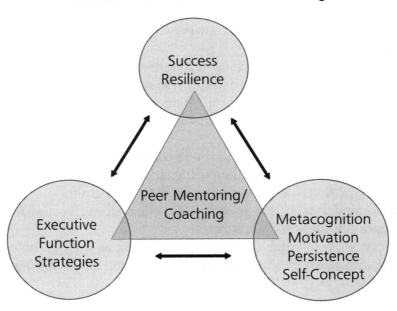

FIGURE 1.12. Theoretical paradigm underlying the *SMARTS* Executive Function and Mentoring program (Meltzer 2007, 2010). Copyright 2007 by ResearchILD. Reprinted by permission.

The objectives of *SMARTS* are twofold. The first goal is to ensure that teachers provide explicit teaching of executive function strategies that are linked with the curriculum so that students can apply these strategies to their classwork, homework, and tests (Gray, Meltzer, & Upton, 2008; Meltzer, 2010; Meltzer & Basho, 2010; Meltzer, 2014). The second goal is to strengthen students' motivation to use executive function strategies and to enhance their academic self-concept, effort, and resilience by building a supportive peer mentoring and peer coaching community in schools. The ultimate goal of *SMARTS* is to increase opportunities for academic and life success for all students, especially for students with learning and attention difficulties.

SMARTS Program Overview

The following principles guide the *SMARTS* peer-mentoring and peer-coaching intervention (Meltzer, 2013b, 2014; Meltzer et al., 2013, 2014a):

- Teachers are trained to create a culture of strategy use in their classrooms and to promote metacognitive awareness in their students by embedding executive function strategies in their curriculum and daily teaching practices.
- Teachers understand and acknowledge the interactions among effort, executive function strategies, academic self-concept, and classroom performance as well as the cycle that builds persistence, resilience, and long-term academic success.

- Teachers foster metacognitive awareness, flexible thinking, and strategic mindsets in their students.
- Teachers implement peer mentoring or peer coaching programs to provide a powerful forum for helping students to develop metacognitive awareness, to understand their learning profiles, and to apply executive function strategies to their schoolwork and homework by building these programs into the school day.
- Students view themselves as part of a community of learners who can help one another through peer mentoring and peer coaching. Emotional self-regulation is also strengthened as part of this program.
- Students understand that executive function strategies and focused effort are important for academic success.
- Students begin to value the *process* of learning as they become cognitively flexible and learn to shift flexibly during problem solving and other academic tasks.
- Students recognize that effort, persistence, and determination are critical for fostering academic and life success.

To implement the *SMARTS* curriculum across the grades and within individual classrooms, there is an emphasis on three major components: (1) executive function strategy instruction, (2) mentor training, and (3) application of executive function strategies to a group project selected by mentors and mentees. The curriculum comprises 30 strategies in the core executive function areas that can be taught over the course of the school year and integrated with content-area instruction across the grades with a focus on:

- Increasing students' metacognitive awareness.
- Improving students' understanding and use of executive function strategies in five broad areas: goal setting, shifting flexibly, organizing and prioritizing, accessing working memory, and self-monitoring.
- Increasing students' effort in school and their motivation to improve their academic performance.
- Promoting peer mentoring and peer coaching skills through training.

Mentor training is a critically important component of the *SMARTS* program. Peer mentors need explicit instruction in techniques for coaching their mentees and providing them with the empathy, praise, and attention that promote positive change (Larose & Tarabulsky, 2005). The *SMARTS* mentor training lessons focus on teaching mentors about their roles as supportive, empathic communicators and have been developed in accordance with the guidelines for best practices (National Mentoring Partnership, 2005). Mentors are trained to build strong mutual interpersonal connections with their mentees based on mutuality, trust, and empathy, which are the hallmarks of successful mentoring relationships (Rhodes, 2005). Through this mentor training, students learn effective mentoring strategies and gain the self-efficacy that is essential for successful mentoring (Darling, 2005). Mentor–mentee pairs work together to learn and practice executive function strategies, with mentors coaching their mentees and helping to build their self-confidence. Strong mentor–mentee relationships encourage mentors to examine and model the executive function strategies they use and to think more deeply about their goals and learning profiles. To reinforce learning and application of these strategies, the *SMARTS* curriculum culminates in a project that focuses on improving students' engagement, motivation, strategy use, and effort (see Figure 1.13).

SMARTS Intervention Studies: Summary of Findings

Findings from four *SMARTS* intervention studies with middle and high school students in four low-income inner-city schools in Boston, Massachusetts, have shown that positive mentoring relationships increase students' motivation, effort, and strategy use, resulting in improved self-concept and self-efficacy (Meltzer et al., 2011, 2012, 2013, 2014b). More specifically, students in stronger peer mentoring relationships displayed significantly higher levels of effort and strategy use in comparison with students in weak peer mentoring dyads (Meltzer et al., 2013, 2014b). These students also used strategies more frequently and consistently in their classwork, homework, projects, studying, and tests. Interestingly, students in stronger peer mentoring relationships also showed higher levels of metacognitive awareness as evidenced in their completed strategy reflection sheets as well as in their ability to identify and correctly apply executive function strategies. Furthermore, they showed significantly higher levels of resilience in comparison with students in weak peer mentoring relationships (e.g., *"I do not let problems stop me from reaching my goals"*). In other words, the social support offered by mentors who could connect with their mentees' social and emotional needs helped mentees to feel more confident and better equipped to deal with the many academic and other challenges in school (Meltzer et al., 2014b).

Our findings have also highlighted the importance of strengthening students' cognitive flexibility and teaching students strategies for thinking flexibly. Specifically, *SMARTS* students with higher cognitive flexibility scores were more goal oriented and more persistent and showed more effort in school (Meltzer et al., 2011).

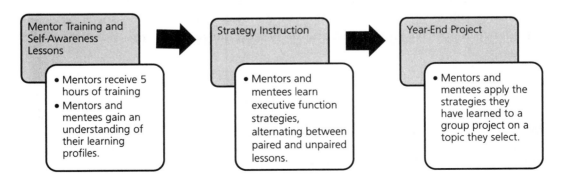

FIGURE 1.13. *SMARTS* cross-grade peer mentor training system.

These more flexible students also used more strategies in their schoolwork and were more organized. Classroom teachers rated these students as having stronger academic performance and as checking their work more frequently (Meltzer et al., 2011). Furthermore, the social connections provided by peer mentoring increased students' engagement in the learning process as well as their goal-orientation and motivation. Overall, students' cognitive flexibility, academic self-concept, and goal orientation all influenced their effort, persistence, and academic performance.

These findings emphasize the importance of increasing students' self-understanding, knowledge of executive function strategies, and academic self-concept. Together, these initiate a positive cycle in which students show increased effort and self-concept as well as more consistent use of executive function strategies, resulting in improved academic performance (Meltzer & Basho, 2010; Meltzer et al., 2007). Stronger academic performance helps students to feel more engaged and more invested in making the effort to use strategies in their classwork, homework, and long-term projects, the foundations of academic and life success (Meltzer, 2013b, 2014; Meltzer et al., 2011, 2013).

CONCLUSIONS

The growing presence of technology and the fast pace of our 21st-century classrooms has resulted in increased pressure on students to set goals, problem-solve flexibly, organize, prioritize, and self-monitor. As a result, schools are placing more emphasis on the importance of promoting metacognitive awareness in students and teaching executive function processes explicitly and systematically. Peer mentoring and peer coaching are powerful techniques that educators can use to extend and deepen the effects of teaching executive function strategies. One example of a research-based intervention is our *SMARTS* Executive Function and Mentoring program, which is designed to promote the key processes that are the foundation of resilience and success, namely, academic self-concept, use of executive function strategies, and effort. Our findings have shown that students in positive peer mentoring relationships use executive function strategies more consistently in their classwork, homework, projects, and tests, and that they feel more confident in school. When executive function strategy instruction is integrated with peer mentoring, schools provide students with a strong foundation for developing self-confidence, a positive work ethic, and resilience, the gateways to academic and life success.

ACKNOWLEDGMENTS

A special thanks to a number of colleagues and graduate interns for their excellent suggestions and invaluable help with the preparation of this chapter, in particular, Sage Bagnato, Kalyani Krishnan, Anna Lavelle, Ranjini Reddy, Julie Sayer, Nancy Trautman, Caitlin DeCortin, and Emily Holding.

Thanks too to the dedicated staff of the Research Institute for Learning and Development (ResearchILD) for their support and help, in particular, Bethany Roditi, Thelma Segal, Mimi Ballard, Jamie Cutler, and Abigail DeMille.

Finally, thanks to the following foundations for their support of this work over the past few years: Stacy Parker Fischer and the Oak Foundation, Peg Lovett and the Cisco Foundation, Shire, and Bain Children's Charities.

REFERENCES

Anderson, P. (2002). Assessment and development of executive functioning (EF) in childhood. *Child Neuropsychologia, 8*(2), 71–82.

Baddeley, A. (2006). Working memory, an overview. In S. Pickering (Ed.), *Working memory and education* (pp. 3–26). Burlington, MA: Academic Press.

Barkley, R. (2010). Evaluating executive functioning deficits in everyday life. *ADHD Report, 18*(6), 9–10.

Barkley, R. (2012). *Executive functions: What they are, how they work, and why they evolved.* New York: Guilford Press.

Block, C. C., & Pressley, M. (Eds.). (2002). *Comprehension instruction: Research-based best practices.* New York: Guilford Press.

Brown, A. L., Bransford, J. D., Ferrara, R. A., & Campione, J. C. (1983). Learning, remembering and understanding. In P. H. Mussen (Ed.), *Handbook of child psychology* (Vol. 3, pp. 77–166). New York: Wiley.

Brown, T. (2006). Executive functions and ADHD: Implications of two conflicting views, *International Journal of Disability, Development and Education, 53*(1), 35–46.

Brown, T. (2014). *Smart but stuck: Emotions in teens and adults with ADHD.* San Francisco: Jossey-Bass.

Cartwright, K. B. (Ed.). (2008a). *Literacy processes: Cognitive flexibility in learning and teaching.* New York: Guilford Press.

Cartwright, K. B. (2008b). Introduction to literacy processes: Cognitive flexibility in learning and teaching. In K. B. Cartwright (Ed.), *Literacy processes: Cognitive flexibility in learning and teaching* (pp. 3–18). New York: Guilford Press.

Cartwright, K. B. (2008c). Concluding reflections: What can we learn from considering implications of representational development and flexibility for literacy teaching and learning? In K. B. Cartwright (Ed.), *Literacy processes: Cognitive flexibility in learning and teaching* (pp. 359–371). New York: Guilford Press.

Darling, N. (2005). Mentoring adolescents. In D. DuBois & M. Karcher (Eds.), *Handbook of youth mentoring* (pp. 177–190). Thousand Oaks, CA: Sage.

Dawson, P., & Guare, R. (2010). *Executive skills in children and adolescents: A practical guide to assessment and intervention* (2nd ed.). New York: Guilford Press.

Denckla, M. B. (2007). Executive function: Binding together the definitions of attention deficit/hyperactivity disorder and learning disabilities. In L. Meltzer (Ed.), *Executive function in education: From theory to practice* (pp. 5–19). New York: Guilford Press.

Deshler, D., Ellis, E., & Lenz, K. (Eds.). (1996). *Teaching adolescents with learning disabilities: Strategies and methods* (2nd ed.). Denver: Love.

Dweck, C. S. (2008). *Mindset: The new psychology of success.* New York: Random House.

Elliot, A. J., & Dweck, C. S. (2005). Competence and motivation: Competence as the core of achievement motivation. In A. J. Elliot & C. S. Dweck (Eds.), *Handbook of competence and motivation* (pp. 3–15). New York: Guilford Press.

Flavell, J. H. (1979). Metacognition and cognitive monitoring: A new area of cognitive developmental inquiry. *American Psychologist, 34,* 906–911.

Fontana, J., Scruggs, T., & Mastropieri, M. (2007). Mnemonic strategy instruction in inclusive secondary social studies classes. *Remedial and Special Education, 28*(6), 345–355.

Fuchs, D., Fuchs, L. S., & Burish, P. (2000). Peer-assisted learning strategies: An evidence-based approach to promote reading achievement. *Learning Disabilities Research and Practice, 15*(2), 85–91.

Fuchs, D., Fuchs, L. S., Mathes, P. G., & Martinez, E. A. (2002). Preliminary evidence on the social standing of students with learning disabilities in PALS and no-PALS classrooms. *Learning Disabilities Research and Practice, 17*(4), 205–215.

Goldstein, S., & Naglieri, J. (Eds.). (2014). *Handbook of executive functioning.* New York: Springer.

Graham, S., & Harris, K. R. (2003). Students with learning disabilities and the process of writing: A meta-analysis of SRSD studies. In H. L. Swanson, K. R. Harris, & S. Graham (Eds.), *Handbook of learning disabilities* (pp. 383–402). New York: Guilford Press.

Graham, S., Harris, K. R., & Mason, L. (2005). Improving the writing performance, knowledge, and self-efficacy of struggling young writers: The effects of self-regulated strategy development. *Contemporary Educational Psychology, 30*(2), 207–241.

Gray, L., Meltzer, C., & Upton, M. (2008). *The SMARTS peer mentoring program: Fostering self-understanding and resilience across the grades.* Paper presented at the 23rd Annual Learning Differences Conference, Harvard Graduate School of Education, Cambridge, MA.

Harris, K. R., & Graham, S. (1996). *Making the writing process work: Strategies for composition and self-regulation.* Cambridge, MA: Brookline Books.

Harris, K. R., & Graham, S. (1999). *Making the writing process work: Strategies for composition and self-regulation* (2nd ed.). Cambridge, MA: Brookline Books.

Karcher, M. (2005). Cross-age peer mentoring. In D. DuBois & M. Karcher (Eds.), *Handbook of youth mentoring* (pp. 266–285). Thousand Oaks, CA: Sage.

Kincaid, K., & Trautman, N. (2010). Remembering: Teaching students how to retain and mentally manipulate information. In L. Meltzer (Ed.), *Promoting executive function in the classroom* (pp. 110–139). New York: Guilford Press.

Krishnan, K., Feller, M. J., & Orkin, M. (2010). Goal setting, planning, and prioritizing: The foundations of effective learning. In L. Meltzer (Ed.), *Promoting executive function in the classroom* (pp. 57–85). New York: Guilford Press.

Kurkul, K., & Greschler, M. (2013, October). *Motivating students to be organized.* Paper presented at the 4th Annual Executive Function Conference, Lexington, MA.

Larose, S., & Tarabulsky, G. (2005). Academically at-risk students. In D. DuBois & M. Karcher (Eds.), *Handbook of youth mentoring* (pp. 440–453). Thousand Oaks, CA: Sage.

Margalit, M. (2004). Second-generation research on resilience: Social-emotional aspects of children with learning disabilities. *Learning Disabilities Research and Practice, 19*(1), 45–48.

Mason, L., Harris, K., & Graham, S. (2011). Self-regulated strategy development for students with writing difficulties. *Theory into Practice, 50*(1), 20–27.

Mastropieri, M. A., & Scruggs, T. E. (1998). Enhancing school success with mnemonic strategies. *Intervention in School and Clinic, 33*, 201–208.

Mastropieri, M., Scruggs, T., Mohler, L., Beranek, M., Spencer, V., & Boon, R. T. (2001). Can middle school students with serious reading difficulties help each other learn anything? *Learning Disabilities Research and Practice, 16*(1), 18–27.

Meltzer, L. J. (Ed.). (2007). *Executive function in education: From theory to practice.* New York: Guilford Press.

Meltzer, L. J. (Ed.). (2010). *Promoting executive function in the classroom.* New York: Guilford Press.

Meltzer, L. J. (2013a, February). *The influence of peer mentoring relationships on effort, executive function, and resilience in students with learning difficulties.* Paper presented at the Pacific Coast Research Conference, San Diego, CA.

Meltzer, L. J. (2013b). Executive function and metacognition in students with learning disabilities: New approaches to assessment and intervention. *International Journal for Research in Learning Disabilities, 1*(2), 31–63.

Meltzer, L. J. (2014). Teaching executive functioning processes: Promoting metacognition, strategy use, and effort. In J. Naglieri & S. Goldstein (Eds.), *Handbook of executive functioning* (pp. 445–474). New York: Springer.

Meltzer, L. J., & Bagnato, J. S. (2010). Shifting and flexible problem solving: The anchors for academic success. In L. Meltzer (Ed.), *Promoting executive function in the classroom* (pp. 140–159). New York: Guilford Press.

Meltzer, L. J., & Basho, S. (2010). Creating a classroom wide executive function culture that fosters strategy use, motivation, and resilience. In L. Meltzer (Ed.), *Promoting executive function in the classroom* (pp. 28–54). New York: Guilford Press.

Meltzer, L. J., Basho, S., Reddy, R., & Kurkul, K. (2014a). *The SMARTS executive function and mentoring program: Fostering executive function, effort, and academic self-concept in students with learning difficulties.* Manuscript submitted for publication.

Meltzer, L. J., Katzir, T., Miller, L., Reddy, R., & Roditi, B. (2004a). Academic self-perceptions, effort, and strategy use in students with learning disabilities: Changes over time. *Learning Disabilities Research and Practice, 19*(2), 99–108.

Meltzer, L. J., & Krishnan, K. (2007). Executive function difficulties and learning disabilities: Understandings and misunderstandings. In L. Meltzer (Ed.), *Executive function in education: From theory to practice* (pp. 77–106). New York: Guilford Press.

Meltzer, L. J., Kurkul, K., Reddy, R., & Basho, S. (2014b, February). *Executive function strategies: The link between effort and academic self-concept.* Paper presented at the Pacific Coast Research Conference, San Diego, CA.

Meltzer, L. J., Pollica, L., & Barzillai, M. (2007). Executive function in the classroom: Embedding strategy instruction into daily teaching practices. In L. Meltzer (Ed.), *Executive function in education: From theory to practice* (pp. 165–194). New York: Guilford Press.

Meltzer, L. J., Reddy, R., Brach, E., & Kurkul, K. (2012, June). *Executive function, effort, and academic performance: Enhancing strategy instruction with peer mentoring.* Paper presented at the 35th Annual International Academy for Research in Learning Disabilities Conference, Padua, Italy.

Meltzer, L. J., Reddy, R., Brach, E., Kurkul, K., Stacey, W., & Ross, E. (2011, April). *The SMARTS mentoring program: Fostering self-concept, motivation, and executive function strategies in students with learning difficulties.* Paper presented at the Annual Conference of the American Educational Research Association, New Orleans, LA.

Meltzer, L. J., Reddy, R., Greschler, M., & Kurkul, K. (2013, June). *Executive function and effort: The effects of peer mentoring in students with learning differences.* Paper presented at the 37th Annual Conference of the International Academy for Research in Learning Disabilities, Boston, MA.

Meltzer, L. J., Reddy, R., Pollica, L., & Roditi, B. (2004c). Academic success in students with learning disabilities: The roles of self-understanding, strategy use, and effort. *Thalamus, 22*(1), 16–32.

Meltzer, L. J., Reddy, R., Sales, L., Roditi, B., Sayer, J., & Theokas, C. (2004b). Positive and negative self-perceptions: Is there a cyclical relationship between teachers' and students' perceptions of effort, strategy use, and academic performance? *Learning Disabilities Research and Practice, 19*(1), 33–44.

Meltzer, L. J., Roditi, B., Taber, S., Kniffin, L., Stein, J., Steinberg, J., et al. (2005). *Essay express.* Watertown, MA: ResearchILD and FableVision.

Miller, L. J., Meltzer, L., Katzir-Cohen, T., & Houser, R. (2001). Academic heterogeneity in students with learning disabilities. *Thalamus, 19*(1), 20–33.

National Mentoring Partnership. (2005). *Elements of effective practice for mentoring* (3rd ed.). Alexandria, VA: MENTOR.

Reid, R., & Lienemann, T. O. (2006). *Strategy instruction for students with learning disabilities*. New York: Guilford Press.

Rhodes, J. E. (2005). Concepts, frameworks, and foundations. In D. DuBois & M. Karcher (Eds.), *Handbook of youth mentoring* (pp. 30–43). Thousand Oaks, CA: Sage.

Roditi, B. N., & Steinberg, J. (2007). The strategic math classroom: Executive function processes and mathematics learning. In L. Meltzer (Ed.), *Executive function in education: From theory to practice* (pp. 237–261). New York: Guilford Press.

Santangelo, T., Harris, K. R., & Graham, S. (2008). Using self-regulated strategy development to support students who have "Trubol Giting Thangs Into Werds." *Remedial and Special Education, 29*(2), 78–89.

Scruggs, T. E., & Mastropieri, M. A. (2000). The effectiveness of mnemonic instruction for students with learning and behavior problems: An update and research synthesis. *Journal of Behavioral Education, 10,* 163–173.

Scruggs, T., Mastropieri, M., Berkeley, S., & Marshak, L. (2010). Mnemonic strategies: Evidence-based practice and practice-based evidence. *Intervention in School and Clinic, 46*(2), 79–86.

Swanson, H. L. (2001). Research on intervention for adolescents with learning disabilities: A meta-analysis of outcomes related to high-order processing. *Elementary School Journal, 101,* 331–348.

Swanson, H. L., & Hoskyn, M. (2001). Instructing adolescents with learning disabilities: A component and composite analysis. *Learning Disabilities Research and Practice, 16*(2), 109–119.

Swanson, H. L., & Sáez, L. (2003). Memory difficulties in children and adults with learning disabilities. In H. L. Swanson, K. R. Harris, & S. Graham (Eds.), *Handbook of learning disabilities* (pp. 182–198). New York: Guilford Press.

Tannock, R. (2008, March). *Inattention and working memory: Effects on academic performance.* Symposium conducted at the Harvard Graduate School of Education 23rd Annual Learning Differences Conference, Cambridge, MA.

Yuill, N. (2007). Visiting Joke City: How can talking about jokes foster metalinguistic awareness in poor comprehenders? In D. S. McNamara (Ed.), *Reading comprehension strategies: Theories, interventions, and technologies*. New York: Erlbaum.

Zimmerman, B. J. (2000). Attaining self-regulation: A social cognitive perspective. In M. Boekaerts, P. R. Pintrich, & M. Zeidner (Eds.), *Handbook of self-regulation* (pp. 13–39). San Diego, CA: Academic Press.

Zimmerman, B. J. (2002). Becoming a self-regulated learner: An overview. *Theory into Practice, 41*(2), 64–70.

Zimmerman, B. J., & Kitsantas, A. (1997). Developmental phases in self-regulation: Shifting from process to outcome goals. *Journal of Educational Psychology, 89,* 29–36.

Zimmerman, B. J., & Schunk, D. H. (Eds.). (2001). *Self-regulated learning and academic achievement: Theoretical perspectives*. Mahwah, NJ: Erlbaum.

CHAPTER 2

Peer Interactions in the Content Areas

Using Differentiated Instruction Strategies

KELLEY S. REGAN, ANYA S. EVMENOVA, MARGO A. MASTROPIERI,
and THOMAS E. SCRUGGS

> Learning is more effective when it is an active
> rather than a passive process.
> —EURIPIDES

Teachers should use differentiated approaches to instruction to support the learning of students with disabilities. In inclusive classrooms, differentiation can be accomplished by using peers to help all students access the curriculum. Strategies for doing so are particularly important for teachers to use in science and history classrooms, where students are exposed to abstract concepts, unfamiliar vocabulary, and an abundant amount of information. This chapter provides an overview of the challenges that students with and without disabilities face in content areas such as science and history. Thereafter, we identify research-based strategies demonstrated with positive outcomes for students with and without disabilities in secondary classrooms. The primary focus of this chapter is to summarize several differentiated instruction strategies considered beneficial for students in inclusive science and history classrooms. Recent research using peer tutoring, peer mediation, and peer-assisted learning activities with various levels of differentiated instruction will be described within a framework that encompasses critically effective elements of teaching. Inservice and preservice teachers will be exposed to explicit strategies for using peers in inclusive classrooms to support the learning of students with disabilities in science and history classrooms. Additional ways technology can be implemented within a peer-tutoring format in science and history content-area classrooms will also be addressed. Finally, we discuss step-by-step peer-mediated strategies for engaging students in the learning process with differentiated curriculum enhancements using mnemonic strategies, content cards, tiered game folders, and specific technology-based interventions.

INCLUSIVE CLASSROOM INSTRUCTION

Over the past decade, increasing numbers of students with learning disabilities (LD) have been spending more than 80% of their school day in inclusive classrooms (Cortiella, 2011). Today's inclusive classrooms include students who are culturally and linguistically diverse, students with emotional and behavioral disabilities, students with mild autism, and/or at-risk students. Learning in the content areas can be especially challenging as many students between grades 4 and 12 struggle to read on grade level (Biancarosa & Snow, 2006) and are challenged with critical thinking and memory deficits (Vaughn & Bos, 2009). Compounding these challenges, inclusive classroom instruction typically requires teachers to provide whole-class lectures that include complex vocabulary, abstract concepts, and complex reading activities. Furthermore, the pace of instruction is rapid, given end-of-year statewide high-stakes testing. Unfortunately, this fast pace frequently results in fewer opportunities for students to learn and apply new content in classes. Students with disabilities and those at risk for failure typically perform better when provided with multiple relevant and interesting practice activities (e.g., Mastropieri & Scruggs, 2014).

CONTENT AREAS: SCIENCE AND HISTORY

The content areas of focus in this chapter, science and history, are especially challenging beyond third grade when students are required to memorize a vast amount of declarative information and new vocabulary, regularly read text independently, and respond to questions. Students in social studies classes, for example, may need to memorize names of historical figures and sequence critical turning points in human history (e.g., the industrial revolution). History curricula also require students to interpret primary and secondary source documents and to make connections between the past and present, and analyze and interpret maps with physical features. Across science curricula (e.g., physical science, life science, biology, physics, chemistry), as students develop skills of systematic inquiry, they are exposed to complex concepts and vocabulary. In fact, compared to other content areas, the amount of new vocabulary introduced in science classes may be the most challenging for students with and without disabilities (Groves, 1995). A review of secondary content textbooks reveals that current texts are filled with factual information in history (Berkeley, King-Sears, Hott, & Bradley-Black, 2014) and in science (Mastropieri & Scruggs, 1994). Thus, textbooks for social studies and science instruction often fail to meet the varied needs of students in inclusive classrooms as they lack adequate structure, and also include a tremendous amount of new vocabulary with insufficient definitions (Mastropieri, Scruggs, & Graetz, 2003a).

WHY DIFFERENTIATE INSTRUCTION?

The vocabulary and concepts of science and social studies curricula are especially challenging for students with disabilities when teachers use abstract presentations and text-based approaches (Scruggs, Mastropieri, & Okolo, 2008). The 2003 National Longitudinal Transition Study (NLTS-2) reported that one-third of teachers are using the general education curriculum without any modifications and few students with LD receive substantial modifications to the curriculum, if any (Wagner, Newman, Cameto, Levine, & Garza, 2006). Furthermore, previous research has indicated that inclusive classroom instruction may involve only teacher-led, whole-class instruction with lecture and discussion formats (Scruggs, Mastropieri, & McDuffie, 2007) that primarily involve interactions mediated through the teacher (Okolo, Ferretti, & MacArthur, 2007). If modifications are not employed, one assumption is that class textbooks are being used with little differentiation or curriculum enhancements to support student learning. This practice is not sufficient for facilitating students' reading comprehension, information processing, understanding of challenging concepts, and recall of factual information. It is important that teacher practitioners use research-based strategies *and* provide quality instruction for students with and without disabilities in the content areas.

WHAT RESEARCH-BASED STRATEGIES SHOULD BE USED IN THE CONTENT AREAS?

Fortunately, recent studies of content-area instruction have provided teachers with a wealth of research-based strategies to support students with and without disabilities in secondary classrooms (Okilwa & Shelby, 2010; Scruggs, Mastropieri, Berkeley, & Graetz, 2010; Wexler, Reed, Pyle, Mitchell, & Barton, 2013). Scruggs et al.'s (2010) meta-analysis included 68 investigations, from 1984 to 2006, of effective interventions in content-area instruction (i.e., science, social studies, and English) for students with disabilities at the middle school and high school level. Over 2,514 students (80% of students with LD) were participants in these studies. This meta-analysis revealed eight categories of the best evidence-based practices at the secondary level for teachers to use in their content-area classrooms. The effective interventions supported students with memorizing essential information, learning new facts and vocabulary, and staying engaged while learning complex concepts in the content areas. The interventions were evaluated using a descriptive statistic known as an effect size. An effect size allows practitioners to understand the strength of a particular intervention or the likelihood that students with LD will respond favorably when the intervention is employed in the classroom versus when it is not employed. Effect sizes describe how well a practice "works" on a numeric scale. As a rule of thumb, interventions or strategies with an effect size less than 0.40 are said to have a minimal effect on student learning, a moderate effect size ranges from 0.40 to 0.70, and a high positive effect on student learning would be described with a value greater than 0.80. To what extent do the content-area interventions for students with disabilities at the middle school and high school levels "work"? The interventions in Scruggs et al.'s (2010) meta-analysis were variable but fell in the moderate (e.g., 0.40 to 0.70) to high (e.g., >0.80) range, revealing a collection of effective practices for use in content-area instruction at secondary levels. The instructional practices and the corresponding effect size were as follows:

- Peer-mediated learning = 0.48
- Hands-on learning = 0.58
- Computer-assisted learning = 0.62
- Spatial learning strategies, using tables and charts = 0.83
- Study aids (e.g., highlighting, framed outlines, guided notes) = 0.94
- Learning strategy instruction (e.g., study skills, note-taking skills) = 1.09
- Mnemonic instruction (e.g., key words, peg words, and letter strategies to facilitate memory) = 1.39
- Systematic, explicit instruction in specific contexts = 1.68 (Scruggs, 2012)

These interventions help students with learning disabilities to "attend more carefully or think more systematically about the content to be learned" (Scruggs, 2012).

DESIGNING DIFFERENTIATED INSTRUCTION WITH PEERS

In the inclusive classroom, differentiation of instruction should be a primary practice since teachers can plan for instruction that accounts for the individual needs of students. The goal of differentiated instruction is to maximize learning for all students (Tomlinson, 2003). Teachers design differentiated instruction to improve relevant practice activities and to facilitate memory and comprehension. For example, from the given list of practices above, study aids, mnemonic instruction, and strategy instruction can be provided during peer-mediated learning and facilitated using hands-on materials in small groups or pairs versus whole-class instruction. In fact, approaches to differentiation that have used peer tutoring and peer-assisted learning games have resulted in positive effects on student performance in social studies (e.g., Gersten, Baker, Smith-Johnson, Dimino, & Peterson, 2006; Mastropieri, Scruggs, Spencer, & Fontana, 2003b; Scruggs, Mastropieri, & Marshak, 2012; Spencer, Scruggs, Mastropieri, 2003) and science (e.g., Bowman-Perrott, Greenwood, & Tapia, 2007; Mastropieri et al., 2006; Scruggs, Mastropieri, Bakken, & Brigham, 1993; Simpkins, Mastropieri, & Scruggs, 2009). The materials that students use in small groups can also be differentiated for particular learners, so that students can be supported or challenged as necessary. For example, a game-based approach to science instruction supports students with disabilities so that they can perform comparably or above their peers in inclusive classrooms (Mastropieri et al., 1998).

DIFFERENTIATED CURRICULUM ENHANCEMENTS

The interventions identified for use in content-area instruction at secondary levels can be differentiated and also implemented within a peer-tutoring format in inclusive social studies and science classrooms. Mastropieri and Scruggs (2012, 2014) investigated this notion in their design of differentiated curriculum enhancements (DCEs) in inclusive high school chemistry classes (Mastropieri, Scruggs, & Graetz, 2005) and middle school history classes (Mastropieri, Scruggs, & Marshak, 2008). The DCE investigations included classwide peer mediation using embedded mnemonic strategies (Marshak, Mastropieri, & Scruggs, 2011), manipulatives including games (Mastropieri et al., 2006; Simpkins et al., 2009), graphing and charting skills (Mastropieri et al., 2006), and peer tutoring using content sheets (McDuffie, Mastropieri, & Scruggs, 2009). Generally, when peers in inclusive classes use these DCEs and learn in small groups or in dyads, a student with a disability is paired with a higher-achieving student. The teacher provides modeling and guides both students to follow the specific rules and procedures for the tutor and tutee during the paired games. Research findings reveal that when secondary students with and without disabilities use differentiated approaches and work with peers, their learning in the content areas is significantly higher compared with students who are taught using more traditional approaches (Okilwa & Shelby, 2010; Stenhoff & Lignugaris/Kraft, 2007; Wexler et al., 2013).

In the remainder of this chapter, we provide examples of how peer-mediated strategies can give teachers an opportunity to differentiate instruction and support student learning in inclusive content-area classrooms. The examples are framed by PASS, an acronym representing key variables that teachers should embody when delivering quality instruction.

QUALITY INSTRUCTION: PASS

As with every research-based practice, peer tutoring and peer mediation in the content areas can only succeed when critical elements of quality instruction are emphasized in the classroom. Elements of effective instruction that support the learning of students with disabilities require instructors to provide rules and procedures, identify errors and provide feedback, use elaborative strategies, and monitor, evaluate, and document progress. In inclusive settings where differentiated instruction is provided for all students, teachers can follow the PASS approach (Mastropieri & Scruggs, 2002, 2014; Scruggs & Mastropieri, 1995). PASS represents key elements for teacher practitioners to use as a guide for planning, delivering, and evaluating effective inclusive instruction (Mastropieri & Scruggs, 2014). To summarize, PASS is an acronym for:

1. **P**rioritize instruction.
2. **A**dapt instruction, materials, or the environment.
3. **S**ystematically teach with the "SCREAM" variables (i.e., s̲tructure, c̲larity, r̲edundancy, e̲nthusiasm, a̲ppropriate rate, and m̲aximized engagement).
4. **S**ystematically evaluate the outcomes of instruction.

Prioritize Instruction

Prioritizing instruction is especially important given the ever-expansive content that teachers need to cover and the short amount of time during the school day allotted for content coverage. Thoughtful planning is necessary to prioritize teaching objectives and to maximize the coverage of these objectives. For example, fifth graders evaluated by a high-stakes science test at the end of the school year need to know particular content in targeted units of study. The content in these units should be a priority. Therefore, teachers would prioritize the following concepts and vocabulary for the Earth and Space unit: *meteorologist, clouds, hurricanes, barometers*, and *continental shelf*. For students with disabilities, priorities may be determined on an individual basis that will likely involve the objectives included on individualized educational plans (IEPs). The pace of instruction can also be individualized, providing ample practice for some students and engaging others with a heightened knowledge of concepts. When prioritizing and planning instruction, teachers need to give careful consideration to the materials for teaching the scope and sequence of the curriculum (i.e., adopted textbooks, supplemental materials). Accessible instructional materials emphasize salient information and include text enhancements such as text-to-speech, spatial organizers, graphs, and tables to support student comprehension.

Adapt Instruction, Materials, or the Environment

Adaptations to the instruction, materials, and/or the environment are made to differentiate the learning needs of students in inclusive settings. An adaptation is typically based on students' physical, sensory, language, literacy, and emotional/behavioral characteristics. Using hands-on activities during instruction is an adaptation, as is using software for reading text, directly teaching literacy skills, embedding technological adaptations for computer use, and using peer mediation and cooperative learning methods of instruction. When considering adaptations to instruction, teachers should recognize the different types of learning they are attempting to facilitate for the learner(s). For example, some information is factual (e.g., names of people or events, vocabulary definitions), while other information is more conceptual so that students need to understand the key concepts or "big ideas." In addition, students may perform at different levels of learning. Learning levels range from first acquiring new knowledge and building fluency to skillfully generalizing previous knowledge to new situations. For example, a history teacher may create tiered levels of folder games for students to "play" with peers in order to review vocabulary and challenging concepts. The folders and game materials can be strategically color coded so that students at level 1 difficulty can identify terms that correspond with the provided definitions, whereas level 2 can require students to produce original definitions of the terms or concepts. That is, for any level of learning, teachers can differentiate expectations by asking students to *identify* or *produce* relevant responses. Identification is a response such as pointing or selecting an answer from a list of choices. Production is typically more challenging since the responses involve writing, saying, spelling, or demonstrating a behavior.

Systematically Teach with the SCREAM Variables to Maximize Engagement and Learning

Once teachers are familiar with *what* to teach and consider any adaptations needed for differentiation, a teacher should be sure to teach systematically. Teaching systematically will ensure maximized student engagement and student learning. Systematic teaching involves the SCREAM variables: structure, clarity, redundancy, enthusiasm, appropriate rate, and maximized engagement through questioning and feedback (Mastropieri & Scruggs, 2002, 2014). These variables are represented below:

1. **S**tructured lessons are organized and purposeful when students understand their roles, they know what is expected in the classroom, and they are more apt to maintain attention. For strategies encompassing peer-tutoring formats, the explicitness of roles and procedures is especially important since the instruction is student centered.

2. **C**larity is practiced by teachers when the presentation explicitly addresses the lesson objective, the vocabulary used is familiar to students, visuals are used to support communication, and concrete, explicit examples are provided. Consider a peer-tutoring lesson in which students, for example, have a cue card with supportive statements to provide to a peer when he or she answers incorrectly to a prompt.

3. **R**edundancy supports student learning because it provides another opportunity for students to practice the primary learning objective in new ways. Teachers who provide effective instruction provide students multiple opportunities to practice newly acquired skills.

4. **E**nthusiasm is a critical teaching behavior that can motivate students to attend in a learning environment that is fun and highly engaging.

5. Teachers should use an **A**ppropriate rate when teaching. A brisk presentation rate with frequent questioning of students is ideal.

6. **M**aximized academic engagement and student time on task are critical for student learning. Academic engagement is enhanced when teachers use effective questioning techniques, streamline transition activities, provide positive feedback, and target relevant class discussions. When teaching a strategy to students in an

inclusive classroom, for example, it is important for teachers to observe students practicing the strategy and provide feedback to students, as well as verbalize what they do well during a peer-tutoring arrangement and be mindful of their roles and the procedures for peer mediation.

Systematically Evaluate the Outcomes of Instruction

Teachers need to systematically evaluate how students are progressing toward a learning objective. Systematic evaluation allows teachers to frequently monitor and adjust instruction based on student performance. Student outcomes can be determined by frequent formative evaluations, curriculum-based measurements, pre–posttests, and/or practice activities that students can complete during guided and independent practice opportunities. Another component of systematic evaluation involves the inclusion of students in this process. Students can self-evaluate, document, and monitor their performance, independent of the teacher. For example, after students complete a strategy involving a review of history content, the teacher can ask them to record the number of items they responded to correctly on a dated self-evaluation record sheet.

The PASS variables provide a framework that encompasses critically effective elements of teaching. The variables are relevant to all aspects of effective instruction including modeling, guided practice, and independent practice. Explicit modeling by teachers is essential (Regan & Berkeley, 2012), and relevant opportunities to practice specific skills and strategies can also be provided within the classroom through the use of structured peer mediation with differentiated materials.

HOW CAN TEACHERS USE THE PASS FRAMEWORK?

Peer mediation in the content areas is only successful when critical elements of quality instruction are emphasized in the classroom. Quality instruction must include relevant additional supplemental practice for students. The instructional framework, PASS, can be used during the guided practice component of instructional lessons. When planning instruction, teachers can effectively differentiate these practice opportunities with peer-mediated strategies, supplemental tutoring, and DCE activities. In order to explicitly demonstrate how teachers can use the PASS framework while employing research-based peer-mediated strategies for students with and without disabilities in the content areas, we will present detailed explanations and explicit examples from specific studies. Within the four themes of PASS, we will detail two examples of a classwide peer-tutoring strategy used with middle school students in social studies and in science classes. Three more examples will demonstrate how DCE materials in science enhanced the learning of elementary and secondary students with and without disabilities. We will conclude with additional suggestions for teachers as to how technology can be used to support peer-mediated strategies for all students, including those with learning disabilities, in inclusive content-based classrooms.

Prioritize Instruction

Teachers follow their state's curriculum guide to determine what to teach students in a particular grade level and content area. The state standards provide the key concepts and ideas that each student should know in order to pass a high-stakes test in that content area. With that end in mind, teachers may use long-term instructional planning to ensure that the essential knowledge included in the scope and sequence of the curriculum is addressed in a timely manner. The essential knowledge is targeted content that teachers will need to ensure that students have ample opportunities to practice. One way to ensure that teachers have time to reinforce this content is to supplement their instruction with peer-mediated strategies. The time needed to cover the vast content is rarely sufficient to even meet the needs of many typical learners, and peer-mediated strategy instruction is one time-efficient way to differentiate instruction for varied learners in an inclusive setting. For example, one particular challenge for students with and without disabilities is the vast vocabulary and concepts that are a part of the essential knowledge included in units of science and history. Peers are an underutilized resource for supporting students' understanding of unfamiliar concepts in science and history.

History

For example, seventh graders in a history class may need to acquire the knowledge and skills identified in a state's curricula titled *United States History: 1865 to the Present*. These history standards may include the following units: Industrialism, the Progressive Movement, and Imperialism (Spanish-American War). In these units of study, students learn about the emergence of modern America and how life changed after the Civil War, including the impact of industrial growth on the United States. In order to support student understanding of the vocabulary and concepts in the units, teachers must first prioritize the targeted vocabulary of each unit, anticipating those terms that will be particularly challenging for students with and without disabilities. After identifying the essential concepts, the history teacher can supplement instruction by providing an opportunity for pairs of students to review the concepts and vocabulary.

Science

Similarly, in an eighth-grade life science class, a teacher may need to cover the following five units: (1) cell division through meiosis and mitosis, (2) analyzing personal traits and characteristics, (3) Mendel's work, (4) the probability of traits and basic concepts of genetics, and (5) DNA. In addition to developing the skills of scientific investigation, reasoning, logic, and understanding the nature of science, students may be required to investigate and understand the following key concepts: DNA, the function of genes and chromosomes, genotypes, phenotypes, dominant and recessive traits, individuals who contributed to our understanding of genetics, and how organisms change over time (e.g., mutation, adaptation, extinction, evolution, genetic variation). The complexity of this information requires teachers to prioritize the critical concepts for students. One way to do this is for teachers to ask district or school personnel to identify the most critical need area based on the previous year's high-stakes test results. Further, teachers could consider the critical concepts most relevant for that specific grade level as well as subsequent grades. For example, many scientific concepts and principles are relevant across disciplines, including the skills of thinking critically and strategically to solve real-world problems. Therefore, supporting students' understanding of these concepts and utilizing strategies that can serve as a review of these concepts would be a wise priority for instruction.

When teachers are familiar with the curriculum as well as their students' individualized needs, they can more effectively select the salient concepts and important vocabulary that their students may struggle with but still need to learn. These issues can be identified from class performance in years past, results from high-stakes testing, and essential knowledge identified in state curriculum guidelines. Once the content of instruction has been prioritized, opportunities can be provided for practice using peer-mediated strategies.

Adapt Instruction and Materials

Teachers who know the curriculum and their students' needs are better prepared to adapt instruction and materials as necessary. Inclusive instruction requires teachers to modify and adapt materials for the diverse learning needs of students. Considering the characteristics of students with disabilities, quality instruction includes materials that are engaging, visually appealing, tactile, clear, motivating, and memorable. DCEs including mnemonics, content sheets, and leveled game materials are easily adapted to facilitate learning for all students in the classroom. When used in a classwide peer-tutoring format, the benefits are significant for students with disabilities. In a peer-tutoring format, the teacher pairs a student with a disability with a typically achieving student. Specific instructional examples of how DCEs and peer interactions can be used in science and history classrooms across varied grade levels are detailed in the following sections (Marshak, Mastropieri, & Scruggs, 2011; Mastropieri, Scruggs, & Graetz, 2005; Mastropieri et al., 2006; McDuffie et al., 2009; Simpkins et al., 2009). Teachers can easily adapt these DCEs in order to match their own curricular content.

Mnemonics and Peer Interactions

The first type of DCE includes mnemonics. A mnemonic strategy, or a tool to support recall of information, is particularly helpful in the content areas when there is vast vocabulary to recall. After prioritizing the key concepts and/or vocabulary terms that students need to know, teachers should develop materials that reinforce students' recall of challenging concepts. One type of mnemonic is the key word method. This method involves identifying a "key word" that is familiar to the learner, *sounds* like the new word, and is easily visualized (Mastropieri & Scruggs, 1989; Scruggs & Mastropieri, 2000). A picture is created to imprint the association of the familiar with the unfamiliar interacting together. In an inclusive classroom, teachers place the selected images on two-sided notecards. One side of the card displays the image (generated from clip art) that represents a mnemonic associated with the targeted content to be learned.

Before students can begin to work in dyads, teachers need to model the use of these cards; explain student roles, rules, and procedures; and provide opportunities for students to practice. This process may take a few days, especially if students have never participated in peer-tutoring interactions. Two examples are described to illustrate how mnemonics can be used with peers to differentiate instruction in inclusive science and history classrooms.

SCIENCE

Our first example illustrates how a mnemonic strategy used in a classwide peer-tutoring format has been used to assist high school students in mastering important chemistry content (Mastropieri et al., 2005). High school student pairs were provided with two-sided content cards. On one side of the card was a mnemonic, and the other side contained scripted questions and comments to be rehearsed, depending on the tutees' responses. Materials were designed to include questions requiring substantial expansion and elaboration of relevant information as well as recall. All students in inclusive classrooms participated as both tutors and tutees. For the tutor, the content card included all of the prompts to ask the tutee as well as the potential responses of the tutees. The content cards began with a question, such as *What is a mole?* If the tutee responded correctly, the tutor skipped the strategic information and asked the questions about additional elaborations and expansions on the content, and then asked for additional examples of the content in order to promote comprehension of the concept (e.g., *What are examples of moles?*). If, however, the tutee was unable to state the correct response, the tutor showed an interactive illustration depicting a mnemonic strategy (see Figure 2.1). The interactive

Your weight in grams is . . .

FIGURE 2.1. Key word mnemonic: *mole.* The atomic weight in grams of a compound or an element.

illustration was accompanied by an explanation provided by the tutor, who said: "Think of the word *mole*. Then think of this picture of a mole on a scale looking at his weight in grams to help you remember that *mole* is the weight in grams of an atomic element." The tutor then asked the tutee what a mole was and what was happening in the illustration that represented the definition of a mole. Another example of a content card is provided in Figure 2.2.

HISTORY

Similarly, for a U.S. history unit such as the Progressive Movement, a classwide peer-tutoring format with embedded mnemonics is very helpful (Marshak et al., 2011). In this unit, students were unfamiliar with the word *unions*. The key word for unions was *onions*. Figure 2.3, for example, presents a picture that has onions interacting in a way associated with the meaning of the term *unions*. For the industrialism unit, an unfamiliar term for students was *John D. Rockefeller* (see Figure 2.4). Therefore, the key word was *rock*. A picture of a rock with oil pouring over it was intended to trigger students to recall that John D. Rockefeller is a businessman who controlled the oil business.

Content Sheets

Content sheets are another example of DCEs (McDuffie et al., 2009). The concept is similar to that of the key word mnemonic strategy, but images are not included on the content sheets. Rather, the targeted concepts and vocabulary are embedded on 8½" × 11" card stock and include prompts as well as the script to be rehearsed by the tutor with his or her tutee. For example, a content sheet in a seventh-grade life science class would read, "List the four nitrogenous bases." The corresponding answer on the content sheet would be, "Guanine, cytosine, adenine, and thymine." Other prompts may include "What are proteins used for?" "Who made the first model of a DNA molecule?" "Why is the order of nitrogen bases important?" and "What is the outside or 'handrails' of the DNA model made of?" Before students could complete tutoring sessions with the content sheets, the teacher would need to teach them the rules and procedures for the tutoring session. As students take turns acting as tutors and tutees, procedures should include systems for switching tutor and tutee roles after a specific number of questions as well as suggestions for providing feedback to tutees who provide correct or partially correct answers. Teachers can list the specific dialogue cues directly on the content sheets. Providing structure and using supportive materials encourage positive peer-tutoring sessions (Fulk & King, 2001; Kroeger, Burton, & Preston, 2009).

Differentiated Game Materials and Peer Interactions

A third DCE strategy to support student learning of science concepts and vocabulary comprises the use of dyads or groups of three peers working together using

What is the Periodic Table?

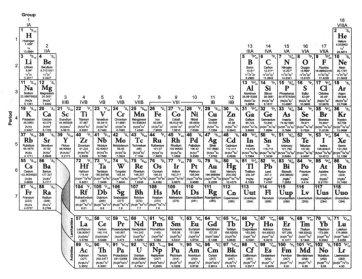

Answer: A tabular arrangement of all known elements, organized by properties.

If your partner is correct, go to →
If your partner doesn't know the answer, review the strategy.

Strategy: Think of the word *table* (chart) for the periodic table, and think of the table of all the elements.

Then ask →
What is the strategy to remember the periodic table?

Then ask again →
What is the periodic table?

Then ask →
What else is important about the periodic table?

[Answers may include: Properties are arranged by periods (rows) and groups (columns).]

Then ask →
What are other characteristics of the periodic table?

[Answers may include: **Increase across periods:** Mass, electron affinity, ionization energy; **Decrease across periods:** Size; **Increase across groups** (top to bottom): Reactivity, atomic radius; **Decrease across groups** (top to bottom): Electron affinity, electron negativity, ionization.]

Then ask →
What are the components of the periodic table?

[Answers may include: alkali metals, alkaline earth metals, transition elements, metalloids, noble gases, lanthanides, actinides.]

FIGURE 2.2. Content tutoring materials for a tutee in a high school chemistry class.

Ask:	What are unions?
Listen for:	Group of people who fight for better working conditions.
If correct:	Go on to the next card.
If wrong:	Say: The key word for union is *onion*.
Say:	To help you remember that unions are a group of people who fight for better working conditions, remember this picture of a group of onions demanding better working conditions.
Ask	What are unions?
Listen for:	Group of people who fight for better working conditions.
If correct:	Go on to the next card.
If wrong:	Start again on this card.

FIGURE 2.3. Mnemonic for the term *union* and script on back of note card.

differentiated game materials. The DCEs used in Mastropieri et al.'s (2006) and Simpkins et al.'s (2009) investigation included "tiered activities" presented in a game folder format that were developed on varying levels of difficulty. The materials that were developed to reinforce prioritized concepts were leveled by student ability (i.e., low, middle, or high). Students could complete all levels of games at their own pace, mastering each level before moving on to the next level. Teachers identified the levels by using different-colored folders (Level 1 = yellow; Level 2 = blue; Level 3 = red).

For middle school students in a science class studying the Scientific Investigation unit, games included matching exercises (e.g., Concentration, Jeopardy), measuring activities, paired questioning, and graphing activities (see Table 2.1) (Mastropieri et al., 2006). Each game was maintained inside a file folder. On the left side of the file folder were the directions for the game and answer key(s) as

Rockefeller (ROCK)   Businessman who controlled
                                                      the oil business.

Ask:	Who was John Rockefeller?
Listen for:	Businessman who controlled the oil business.
If correct:	Go on to the next card.
If wrong:	Say: The key word for Rockefeller is *rock*.
Say:	To help you remember that Rockefeller was a businessman who controlled the oil business, remember this picture of a rock with oil on top of it.
Ask:	Who is John Rockefeller?
Listen for:	Businessman who controlled the oil business.
If correct:	Go on to the next card.
If wrong:	Start again on this card.

FIGURE 2.4. Key word mnemonic for key information, John D. Rockefeller, and script on back of note card.

needed. In some of the games, answer keys and/or a list of useful hints were provided, as needed. In the right pocket were the materials needed, such as a game board, laminated dry-erase sheets, a ruler, scoring/recording sheets, or question/answer cards. If game pieces were needed, small pocket sleeves were attached to the folder. Any playing cards were maintained in the folder with a rubber band. Since game materials could be shared across the classroom and used multiple times, the directions, game boards, game materials, and so forth were laminated for durability (see Figure 2.5).

The tiered games were differentiated. For example, Level 1 games provided many prompts to students, Level 2 games provided fewer prompts, and Level 3 contained no prompts. To demonstrate, we will describe the quantitative/quali-

TABLE 2.1. "Tiered" Science Folder Games

Name of game	Key concepts	Objective of game
Experimental Design	Independent variable; dependent variable; hypothesis; constants; repeated trials	*Level 1*: Match independent and dependent variables *Levels 2 and 3*: Identify hypothesis, independent, and/or dependent variables within given scenario
Mission Possible	Chart; data set; line graph; bar graph; circle graph	Generate simple line, bar, and circle graphs of increasing difficulty from Level 1 to Levels 2 to 3
Hangman	Science vocabulary	Solve mystery word before all body parts are drawn (Level 1 includes "hints")
Concentration	Science vocabulary	Match vocabulary word to definition
Liquid Measurement	Liquid measurement in milliliters	Identify container (out of three choices) with target measurement
Jeopardy	Science vocabulary	Earn points by giving questions to provided answers
Quantitative/ Qualitative	Quantitative data Qualitative data	*Level 1*: students can "guess" qualitative and quantitative attributes *Level 2*: students discern between qualitative and quantitative attributes given prompts *Level 3*: students discern between qualitative and quantitative attributes without prompts
Measurement	Measurement of height and width using SI	*Levels 1, 2, and 3:* measure height and width of objects and record on record sheet

FIGURE 2.5. Three of the eight folder games and teacher manual for increasing science learning.

tative game. To reinforce the concepts of quantitative and qualitative data, Level 1, the lowest activity level, required students to read a statement on a series of cards (e.g., "The student had long, curly, black hair"; "The snake was 15 centimeters long") and identify whether this was a quantitative or qualitative statement. A game board accompanied the Level 1 game. The game board was marked with a start position for students to position their selected game piece. The game pieces moved along a path of 31 randomized red and blue spaces until the finish line. The directions to play the Level 1 game included:

1. Each player should choose a playing piece.
2. Everyone starts on the start box.
3. Players should play in alphabetical order.
4. Draw a card and read the statement aloud.
5. Determine if the statement is quantitative or qualitative.
6. State the answer aloud and verify that it is correct by checking the back of the card.
7. If you are correct, move your player piece to the right box.
   a. If the statement is qualitative, move it to the next blue box.
   b. If the statement is quantitative, move it to the next red box.
8. Whichever player makes it to the finish box first wins!
9. At the end of the game, record your overall rating and time on your master record sheet.

Level 2 required students to generate three quantitative and qualitative observations from given illustrations. They were to complete an answer sheet that prompted them to record their quantitative and qualitative observations. Prompts for quantitative observations included "How much or how many" and prompts for qualitative observations included the word *Describe*. Level 3 for the quantitative/qualitative game required students to identify observations given more illustrations, *without* any prompts. Low-ability students and all students with disabilities were required to begin with Level 1 materials. To be certain all students mastered each level before moving on to the next, they monitored their own progress using recording sheets. The record sheet was completed after every game session. Students recorded their answer/score on the sheet provided across from the corresponding game and colored folder. They played the game with their partner(s) until they mastered the game. They also recorded how long they played the game.

Similarly, the differentiated curriculum enhancements that included leveled folder games were effective for fifth-grade students in a science class who were studying units on Earth and space as well as light and sound (Simpkins et al., 2009). The five games "played" in pairs at the elementary level included Jeopardy, Motor Cross Raceway, Hangman, Concentration, and Tic-Tac-Toe. The games and the relevant game directions, game pieces (e.g., small toy cars, numbered cubes), and game materials were maintained in individual folders (see Figures 2.6 and 2.7 for Jeopardy materials).

FIGURE 2.6. Jeopardy game-based science activity mounted inside a file folder.

There were two levels of difficulty for each student in the pair. Level 1 required students to identify the correct answer (identification), whereas Level 2 required students to produce relevant responses (production). A comparison of these two levels or types of prompts is provided in Table 2.2. It is assumed that higher-level students spend less time on Level 1 games (identification items) and students with disabilities spend more time on Level 1 games. Level 1 games include items with prompts, correct responses, and an answer sheet for self-correction. The Level 2 materials were production items and included a statement or a question that did not provide a prompt. An answer sheet for self-correction was included in the file folder. When using the games, the students completed a sheet to identify the game they completed, the length of time spent on that game, and how they per-

---

1. Shuffle the cards and place them into the slots on the Jeopardy board with the answers showing.
2. Player A chooses a card for 10, 20, 30, or 40 points.
3. Player B reads the statement on the card.
4. Player A gives the answer in the form of a question.
5. Player B removes the card and looks at the answer hidden at the bottom of the card.

- If correct: Player A enters points on the score sheet.
- If incorrect: set card aside for the next round—no points given.
- Once all the cards have been read, switch players and start at the beginning.
- Player with the highest total wins.
- At the end of the game, record your overall score and time on your master record sheet.

FIGURE 2.7. Jeopardy directions on laminated cardstock inside science game folders.

TABLE 2.2. Examples of Jeopardy's Identification and Production Items for Earth and Space Unit Assessment

Level 1: Identification	Level 2: Production

A scientist that studies meteorology is known as . . .
    a. What is a meteorologist?
    b. What is a gastronomist?
	A scientist that studies meteorology is known as . . .

This cloud is puffy and looks like a cotton ball.
    a. What is a stratus cloud?
    b. What is a cumulus cloud?
	This cloud is puffy and looks like a cotton ball.

Electrical charges that build up in clouds.
    a. What is lightning?
    b. What is a shock?
	Electrical charges that build up in clouds are . . .

ceived their progress toward completing the game(s). Again, components of self-monitoring and self-evaluation were embedded throughout the peer-mediated session.

Key Points

In inclusive classrooms, peer-mediated strategies provide opportunities for teachers to differentiate instruction and to support students with disabilities. DCEs can include embedded mnemonics, content sheets, and leveled file folder games. Later in this chapter, we will describe how teachers can consider ways to use another DCE, *technology*, in a peer-mediated format as well.

Teachers can differentiate curriculum enhancements in several ways. First, the amount of time students need to spend with the materials before mastering the content can be adapted. For example, pairs of students can use the materials for reviewing concepts during the first 10 or last 10 minutes of every class. Second, the materials can be modified based on the number of prompts provided to students to facilitate their responses. Third, the materials can be adapted according to student ability (i.e., low, middle, or high). That is, a student with a lower ability level may be asked to identify the correct answer while a student of higher ability may be asked to produce an example of a concept. Students' ability levels may be determined in a variety of ways. These may include (1) interpreting screening data from assessments completed at intervals during the school year, (2) interpreting progress monitoring data on particular targeted skills for individual learners, such as reading fluency or vocabulary, and/or (3) looking at unit test scores in that content area.

Teachers should allocate time toward creating some of the materials shown in the figures and tables. If laminated and stored adequately, the materials can be reused each year, and the strategies taught have lasting effects on students' learning.

Systematically Teach

Systematic teaching of peer-mediated strategies using differentiated curriculum enhancements involves six key processes: Structure, Clarity, Redundancy, Enthusiasm, Appropriate rate, and Maximize academic engagement (SCREAM).

Structure

First, the structure and clarity of peer roles are a significant component of peer-mediated strategies. Peer roles must be clearly defined, and the lesson should be structured so that students know what to expect in the classroom. For example, in Marshak et al.'s (2011) study, one student in the dyad was referred to as the "general" (tutor) and the other student was the "admiral" (tutee). To create optimal dyads, teachers can be strategic. One way to pair the dyads is to use the achievement distribution in the class. For example, in Marshak et al.'s (2011) study, students were ranked from the highest performing (#1) to the lowest performing (#30), then the list was split to match students. For example, #1 was paired with #15, #2 with #14, #16 with #30, #17 with #29, and so on. Teachers may find it necessary to modify the matching of pairs based on individual personality characteristics.

Clarity

Second, the DCEs provide visuals to support communication between the students in each pair. These visuals can include the actual words and/or directions for students to follow during the peer-mediated interactions. Questions and explicit feedback can be written on the content cards to be read by peers verbatim, and the game folders can include the game directions for students to refer to when working in their dyads. Game directions for Motor Cross Raceway, Science Hangman, Tic-Tac-Toe, and Sorry are provided in Table 2.3 (Simpkins, 2007).

For the DCEs with embedded mnemonics (Marshak et al., 2011), a picture was placed on the front of the card and instructions were written on the back of the card to support student interactions. Figure 2.3, for example, shows the side of the card with the image to help students recall the meaning of the word *union*. Below the image is an example of a dialogue that could ensue between the general and the admiral. The generals, in this example, are playing the role of the "tutor." The general *knows* what to say because his script is on the back of the card. If the admiral does not respond accurately, the partner rereads the strategy on the back of the card again. During the dyad practice, students progress through all of the cards and then switch roles. At the end of the activity, students monitor their progress. For example, students record on their tracking sheet the number of cards they have completed correctly. They also record the date and length of time used to review the cards. The teacher then collects the student folders and envelope containing the mnemonic cards.

TABLE 2.3. Directions for Folder Games as Used in Simpkins's (2007) Study of Science Units

Motor Cross Raceway

This activity can be played with up to three players. Choose your game piece and begin at Start. Roll die and move the number of spaces indicated on the die. If you land on a space with words (flat tire, crash, mud pit, move two spaces, need motor oil, accelerate one space, battery dead, spin, finish ahead), you receive an extra roll of the die. Choose a Motor Cross Raceway card and answer the question (check the answer key for correct answers). If you answer the question/statement correctly, you can stay on that space. If you answer incorrectly, you have to move back one space. The player who reaches the finish first will win the game. Alternate directions: if the player answers the question/statement incorrectly, he or she has to move back to Start or loses a turn. The players should record their overall rating and time on the student record sheet.

Science Hangman

This activity can be played in pairs or groups of more students. Partners will have an opportunity to play each role. One student will read the question on the card to his or her partner. Then the student will draw the number of spaces needed to solve the mystery word. The hint can be given if needed, when playing Level 1. The partner will say a letter. If the letter belongs in the mystery word, it will be written in its appropriate space. If the letter does not belong in the mystery word, it will be written in the missed letters box, and a specific body part (i.e., head, body, arms, and legs) will be drawn for each incorrect response. The partner will continue giving letters until the mystery word is solved or all body parts are drawn. The partners record his or her overall rating and time on the record sheet, and then switch roles.

Tic-Tac-Toe

Decide which player will be "X" and which will be "O." Decide which player will go first. Player 1 should choose a question card. If she answers the question correctly, she can place the marker on that space; if she answers incorrectly, her opponent can have a chance at answering the question. If the opponent answers correctly, he can place his marker on the space, then take his turn to choose a question card; the partner who has three in a row across or diagonally wins the game. The players should record their overall rating and time on their record sheet.

Sorry

This activity is a modification of the popular board game and can be played with up to four players. Players should place the SORRY cards face down on the appropriate square. Students should choose game pieces (red, blue, yellow, or green). The game begins after all game pieces are placed on the start circle of the appropriate color. Player 1 rolls the die to determine how many spaces he will move. Once the player has moved, he should choose a card, read the statement/question aloud, and provide an answer. If the player provides the correct answer, he stays in his space. If the player provides an incorrect answer, he has to move back one space. Play continues until all game pieces have been moved around the board and have arrived in the home space. The player who arrives home first is the winner. The players should record their overall rating and time on the student record sheet.

Maximize Engagement

Third, in order to maximize student engagement when employing peer-mediated strategies, the teacher should teach the students the rules and procedures involved in the tutoring sessions. Since students take turns acting as tutor and tutee, the teacher needs to model how to switch tutor and tutee roles after so many questions/cards and how to provide feedback to tutees who provide the correct answer and/or a partially correct answer. A sample dialogue in Table 2.4 between tutor and tutee illustrates the tutoring procedure.

In contrast, when student pairs use the DCEs involving the game folders, as demonstrated in Mastropieri et al.'s (2006) and Simpkins's (2009) science investigations, teachers can present directions to students on how to play the games as they begin a single game. Thus, directions can be provided for games students actually use, rather than reviewing all games at once. Furthermore, for secondary learners, the procedures for the content cards can simulate how they were used in Mastropieri et al.'s (2005) high school chemistry class. Rules and procedures are provided for the peer-tutoring format (see Table 2.5); however, students are able to skip using the provided strategic materials. When this is the case, students can be asked higher-level questions that require them to expand and elaborate on content. This feature of the strategy may be more appealing in inclusive classes in which some teachers, but not all, require strategies and high-level content and concepts to be taught. Moreover, students' time on task and attention is best maintained when instruction can match ability level.

Redundancy

For redundancy, ample practice of tutoring rules and procedures should be provided in the classroom. In previous investigations, students were taught to use the differentiated materials with the game folder format in four 90-minute science

---

TABLE 2.4. Tutor and Tutee Dialogue with Content Sheets in Science Class

Tutor: What are proteins used for?

Tutee: To break down sugar. (*incorrect*)

Tutor: Proteins are used to build cells, tissues, and organs, and to perform all life processes. What are proteins used for?

Tutee: Proteins build organs and help you live. (*partially correct*)

Tutor: That is partially correct; can you think of anything else?

Tutee: Build cells. (*partially correct*)

Tutor: Proteins are used to build cells, tissues, and organs, and to perform all life processes. What are proteins used for?

Tutee: Proteins are used to build cells, tissues, and organs, and to perform all life processes. (*correct*)

Tutor: Good job!

TABLE 2.5. Tutoring Rules and Procedures for Peer Tutoring in High School Chemistry

Rules	Procedures
Talk only to your partner about the peer-tutoring program.	First student asks questions on one to five cards while second student listens and answers questions.
Talk in a quiet voice.	
	Switch roles and turn to the beginning section; second student asks first student the questions.
Cooperate with your partner.	
Do your best.	

classes, and subsequent practice opportunities were provided in 45-minute sessions for a 12-week period (Mastropieri et al., 2006). Elementary grade participants in Simpkins et al.'s (2009) study used 45- to 60-minute science periods to complete one to two of the games. Approximately 20 minutes of the class session was allocated for students to work with a peer and complete the games. For all examples, teachers monitored student pairs when walking around the room, providing clarity, support, and feedback as needed.

Key Points

Systematic teaching of peer-mediated strategies allows teachers to effectively differentiate instruction for students in inclusive classrooms. In order for student pairs to participate effectively with the materials in a peer-tutoring format, teachers should provide structure, clarity of roles and procedures, and opportunities for practice, and maximize engagement. Finally, teachers need to also consider the two remaining variables of SCREAM inherent in effective instruction: enthusiasm and appropriate rate. Expressing enthusiasm for learning and for using hands-on materials can be contagious, so lead by example. Ensure that the classroom is a safe environment with positive energy conducive to learning. Also, teachers who effectively differentiate instruction are aware of when to slow down and/or present information at a quick pace. An appropriate rate of instruction will support students with disabilities to achieve comparably if not above their peers.

<u>S</u>ystematically Evaluate Outcomes

When using any instructional strategy, teachers should systematically evaluate student performance in order to inform future practice. Specifically, teachers would want to know if, and to what degree, peer-mediated strategies with differentiated curriculum enhancements support students as they progress toward a learning objective. In classrooms, teachers usually assess student performance using pre–posttests. Further, teachers want to know if students are motivated and receptive to peer interactions in inclusive science and history classrooms. In order to assess student perceptions, teachers can observe and ask students to provide feedback. Likewise, teacher perceptions of peer-mediated strategies to differentiate instruction should be determined, as well. To illustrate, we now will describe how history and science classrooms used pre–posttest data to monitor student performance and how teachers and students perceived the peer-mediated instruction and DCE materials.

Student Performance

Students who have used DCEs with embedded mnemonics, content sheets, or game materials during classwide peer tutoring were evaluated using pre–posttests. For example, in Marshak et al's (2011) study, students were asked to complete a 60-item posttest as a measure of knowledge across three history units (e.g., Industrialism, the Progressive Movement, and Imperialism). In order to monitor student performance in history class, the teachers first identified 60 test items for all three units to be of importance for students meeting state testing standards. Of the 60 items, 30 were selected as the basis for the content included on the cards with the embedded mnemonics. These were considered to be the "targeted items" in the investigation. Each of the three units had a 20-item, multiple-choice test that included targeted and nontargeted items. The pre–posttests consisted of 60 total multiple-choice questions (20 items per unit) with half of the questions included as the targeted items (see Table 2.6 for sample items). After 12 weeks of instruction, a similar, but reordered test served as the posttest.

Findings for all three units revealed significant differences favoring students who used peer-mediated strategies with DCEs. Across all three units, the effect sizes for those students who participated with DCEs involving embedded mnemonics were in the moderate to high range for both general education and special education students (e.g., 0.64 to 0.81). Students with and without disabilities who used the mnemonic strategies to learn relevant vocabulary and concepts performed better on the posttest. In fact, the performance of students with disabilities was as high as those without disabilities.

Positive outcomes were also reported in Mastropieri et al.'s (2006) investigation involving eighth graders in science. The pre–posttest of the Scientific Investigation unit consisted of 34 multiple-choice items. Results indicated that the students who participated in peer mediation with the DCEs involving leveled game folders significantly outperformed students who did not participate. Interestingly, students with disabilities who used the folder games in pairs demonstrated a higher effect size (e.g., 1.15) than students without disabilities. Stronger performance was also identified for students who used embedded mnemonic strategies to learn higher-level concepts in a high school chemistry class (Mastropieri et al., 2005). Findings revealed that the high school students with and without disabilities who used peer-mediated strategies with DCEs showed stronger performance than students who received traditional instruction in chemistry.

TABLE 2.6. Sample Items from a Social Studies Unit Pre–Posttest

What was the final straw that caused the United States to declare war on Spain?

   a. The invasion of Cuba
   b. The invasion of Puerto Rico
   c. The explosion of the USS *Maine*
   d. The murder of a U.S. government official in Cuba

How did yellow journalism help cause the Spanish-American War?

   a. They reported what was happening in Hawaii.
   b. Newspaper owners published made-up stories to make Americans hate Spain.
   c. They made up stories about Cuba to get people to vote against a war.
   d. They reported on events in Puerto Rico.

Workers wanted to change all of the following EXCEPT . . .

   a. long hours
   b. unsafe working conditions
   c. distance from their tenement to the factory
   d. low wages

Which industrialist is most commonly associated with the oil industry?

   a. Andrew Carnegie
   b. Cornelius Vanderbilt
   c. John D. Rockefeller
   d. J. P. Morgan

What are unions?

   a. Groups of people who wanted longer working hours and less pay
   b. Places where workers were paid
   c. Groups of people that would work for free
   d. Groups of people who fought for better working conditions

Where did the steel industry grow into a huge business?

   a. Pittsburgh
   b. Chicago
   c. New York City
   d. Boston

Identification and Production Items

In order to systematically evaluate the outcomes of instruction, teachers should consider including both identification and production items on pre- and posttests. The demands of production items are typically more challenging than identification items that provide answer choices. For example, to determine the effects of classwide peer tutoring with content sheets on student learning in science, the units' pre- and posttests included 10 production items and 25 identification items (McDuffie et al., 2009) (see Table 2.7 for sample items). For each of the unit tests in this example, students using DCEs with embedded content sheets outperformed students in the traditional instructional setting. Further analyses revealed relatively higher performance on the identification items versus the production items on the posttests.

Similarly, Simpkins et al.'s (2009) study employing DCEs with game folders evaluated student learning of science units (i.e., Earth and Space; Light and Sound) using 14 production and identification items. Positive effects favored those who participated in peer mediation involving game materials, with effect sizes surprisingly higher for the production test items (0.436) than the identification test items (0.237). Both higher- and lower-performing students were able to benefit because of the DCE materials.

TABLE 2.7. Production and Identification: Sample Test Items of a Science Pre–Posttest

Sample production items	Sample identification items
What is genetics?	What is a phenotype? a. The genetic makeup of an organism b. A form of a trait that masks another form of the same trait c. The physical appearance of an organism d. A form of a trait that appears to be hidden by another form of the same trait
What is the purpose of a Punnet square?	What is an allele? a. The genetic makeup of an organism b. The different forms of a gene c. A form of a trait that has naturally evolved d. Cellular structure that carries genetic information

Student Perceptions

Survey data and student interviews from past studies have shown positive student perceptions about the use of DCE materials. For example, students who used DCEs with game materials expressed approval for the games on a 3-point self-evaluation scale (i.e., using smiley faces) (Mastropieri et al., 2006). Students who used the DCEs with embedded mnemonics actively participated, and their learning of content was reflected on posttest outcomes (Marshak et al., 2011). Similarly, students in Simpkins et al.'s (2009) study reported that the peer-tutoring procedures for the game folder activities were interesting, enjoyable, easy to use, and facilitated science learning. High school students also enjoyed using the elaborative and mnemonic strategies to learn chemistry content in a classwide peer-tutoring format (Mastropieri et al., 2005). In addition, observations of the chemistry classes indicated that higher-achieving students did not need to rely on the strategies embedded within the materials as frequently as the lower-achieving students. In fact, students with disabilities could have benefited from even more time with the tutoring materials if time could be allocated within the inclusive classroom. Overall, teachers appreciated the materials despite the pressure to proceed through the content at a rapid pace, given the end-of-year high-stakes testing.

Teacher Perceptions

In past studies, teachers who used the content sheets to learn science concepts were positive about classwide peer tutoring (McDuffie et al., 2009). Teachers reported that they enjoyed using peer tutoring and that they believed it was beneficial for students with and without disabilities. However, they did not indicate a preference for peer tutoring, and they reported that because peer tutoring was more noisy and unstructured, it was more challenging to keep students on task. Four teachers in Mastropieri et al.'s (2006) study reported using the games "a lot" or "fairly often" while two teachers reported using the DCEs less often than they had planned, given the challenges of finding time to implement the materials in their classes and covering the content for the end-of-year state high-stakes testing.

Key Points

In order to evaluate student performance following peer-mediated interactions with DCEs, inclusive classrooms teachers may use pre–posttests, quizzes, and/or observations. In the examples provided, both higher- and lower-performing students were able to benefit because of the DCE materials. That is, peer-mediated strategies offer opportunities for teachers to provide effective differentiated instruction to support students with disabilities in inclusive classrooms.

To monitor ongoing progress, teachers may also consider requiring students to record on their tracking sheet the number of cards they have completed correctly after each session. Students could also indicate the date and length of time spent reviewing the cards. For the tiered game folders, students could record and rate their performance on a 3-point self-evaluation scale. Self-evaluation components such as these support students' ability to learn independently and reinforce their self-regulatory skills.

Finally, studies have revealed positive perceptions of the peer-mediated strategies and the DCE materials, with students expressing a preference for these strategies when compared with traditional instruction. It must be noted that teachers should frequently check in with students after classwide peer-tutoring sessions to ensure that this type of instruction is favorable for all students in inclusive science and history classrooms.

ADDITIONAL PEER-MEDIATED STRATEGIES: USING TECHNOLOGY-BASED DCEs

Historically, technology-based interventions have been used to differentiate classroom instruction and to address students' individual needs. As these interventions are an important factor in 21st-century classrooms, we provide a brief discussion of the role that technology can play in peer-mediated learning in the content areas. One instructional intervention, computer-assisted instruction (CAI), has been found to be a moderately effective strategy for introducing content-based instruction to students with learning disabilities (Scruggs et al., 2010, 2012). CAI software provides individual practice, immediate feedback, and a summary of each student's performance. This software can support students in a specialized skill area such as word-level reading (e.g., Lexia Strategies for Older Students [SOS]).

In addition to CAI, many exciting technologies have been developed to support differentiated instruction for students with different abilities and needs. For example, virtual learning environments via technology as well as video-based curricula have recently been explored in both history and science classrooms. In addition, assistive technology can provide academic and/or behavioral supports that may be necessary to ensure active participation of students during peer-mediated instruction. When teachers use technology to supplement their instruction, they should use the PASS processes in order to ensure a seamless integration, as is discussed briefly below.

Prioritize Instruction

In recent years, multiple technology-based interventions have been developed to address state standards and to improve student performance on high-stakes tests across various content areas. Thus, web-based virtual environments have been utilized to support middle school students with and without disabilities as they learn history (e.g., Okolo, Englert, Bouck, Heutsche, & Wang, 2011) and science (e.g., Marino, Coyne, & Dunne, 2010). The Virtual History Museum, for example, was developed to introduce skills that eighth-grade students need to know in order to conduct historic investigations in diverse classrooms. Teachers can use this virtual experience to teach a variety of topics such as the causes of World War II or the early transportation revolution (*http://vhm.msu.edu/site/default.php*; Okolo et al., 2011). In turn, another virtual learning environment, called Alien Rescue, has been successfully used to introduce both state and national science standards in areas such as (1) scientific inquiry, (2) properties of matter, (3) motions and forces, (4) transfer of energy, (5) structure and function in living systems, (6) structure of the earth system, (7) science and technology, and many others (*http://alienrescue.edb.utexas.edu*; Marino et al., 2010). Whether the technology tool is complex, allowing teachers or students to specify or adjust the topic, or a simple video documentary that introduces the civil rights movement (Gersten et al., 2006), teachers should remember that, like any other strategy, technology needs to be prioritized and effectively integrated with instruction. Teachers can also use technology with all students to review the concepts and vocabulary pervasive in science and history curricula.

Adapt Instruction and Materials

Technology has been widely used to modify and adapt materials for students with diverse learning needs. Many technology-based interventions are designed to provide additional supports for struggling learners. For example, the Virtual History Museum allows teachers to differentiate all activity templates for students, by providing built-in supports such as feedback, scaffolds, additional explanations and directions, simplified versions of the activity, and/or text-to-speech features (Okolo et al., 2011). Peer-mediated exploration and cooperative discussions of the Alien Rescue virtual environment in heterogeneous groups allows all students to become familiar and comfortable with this complex technology-enhanced curriculum before they proceed through the Virtual Space Station independently (Marino et al., 2010).

Assistive Technology

While many general education teachers consider peer-mediated and cooperative learning strategies as a prominent instructional technique to meet the diverse needs of students with disabilities, especially in the content areas (Harper & Maheady, 2007; Maheady, Harper, & Mallettee, 2001), additional supports may be necessary to ensure active participation in activities by students with diverse needs (O'Brien & Wood, 2011). Students who struggle with reading, writing, spelling, handwriting, memory, and motor skills may rely on assistive technology adaptations to be successful in their peer-tutoring roles. Teachers can employ assistive technology in order to increase, maintain, or improve the academic capabilities of their students with and without disabilities. For example, students who struggle with vocabulary may benefit from text-to-speech supports available from either high-tech computer-based software or from tech solutions such as reading pens (e.g., Quicktionary pen) that allow them to scan any word in order to hear it being defined and read aloud. With this tool, students with disabilities can take on the role of tutor and lead the peer-mediated interactions in heterogeneous groups. In addition, simple low technology such as a Mini-Me, a short-message voice recorder with built-in playback options, may enhance classwide peer mediation to ensure appropriate instructional feedback that students can then provide to each other. Thus, low-performing students who are not entirely familiar with the content can still provide accurate feedback with the Mini-Me recorder attached to each peer-tutoring content sheet (Skylar, 2007; Wood, Mackiewicz, Van Norman, & Cooke, 2007). Furthermore, as an alternative to using a Mini-Me recorder, sound stickers can be used with the Livescribe Smartpen. As described with the Mini-Me, the teacher can prerecord accurate feedback onto the sound stickers, allowing students to play back audio notes from the interactive peer-tutoring cards used by the tutor/tutee.

Systematically Teach

Technology-based interventions, which follow principles of instructional design, embody the SCREAM variables by providing structure, clarity, redundancy, enthusiasm, appropriate rate, and maximized academic engagement. Students are typically highly engaged and motivated to use technology. In the Virtual History Museum, for example, students access historic information presented in virtual exhibits and complete activities assigned to them by the curator or a teacher/researcher in the virtual museum. Teachers can differentiate these activities for low-performing and high-performing students in an inclusive classroom. In fact, because technology-based interventions are student-centered, students can navigate at their own pace, and the technology has often been programmed to respond appropriately to student performance. In addition, technology provides ample opportunities for practicing key concepts and curriculum content. Using the Virtual History Museum as an example, students can explore artifacts including documents, images, videos, and music, as well as an accompanying text to review essential content (Okolo et al., 2011). Further, the Alien Rescue virtual environment includes 3-D videos, databases, advanced graphics, and animations introducing the STEM (i.e., Science, Technology, Engineering, and Mathematics) astronomy curriculum. One of the virtual activities requires students to watch a video with an embedded structured problem and then has the students proceed through five stages of scientific inquiry: exploration, preliminary research, advanced research, hypothesis testing, and justifying solutions. Multiple rooms in the virtual environment present different instruments and information in science, engineering, and mathematics that are necessary to learn the astronomy content (Marino et al., 2010). Teachers could certainly structure this virtual experience, or parts of the experience, using a peer-tutoring format. For example, a structured peer interaction that uses content cards could follow each of the five stages of scientific inquiry.

Peer Interactions

Whereas CAI is typically completed individually, teachers can implement technology-based interventions using peers in inclusive classrooms. For example, Gersten and his colleagues (2006) have employed a video-based curriculum in order to level the playing field for struggling readers in a history class and to facilitate meaningful peer interactions about the history content. Two groups of middle school students with and without learning difficulties watched a video documentary about the civil rights movement segmented into four 10-minute clips. Video instruction was also supplemented by textbook and article readings. Besides additional interactive activities such as (1) compare–contrast text structure activities to foster understanding, (2) narrative text structures to generate discussion questions and organize materials, and (c) inserted questions and teacher clarifications during the viewing of the videos, students in one of the groups also participated in heterogeneous peer dyad activities, where they used the Think-Pair-Share technique. During Think-Pair-Share, learners thought of an answer to a question, discussed this in pairs, and then shared their answers and a rationale with the entire class. In Gersten et al.'s (2006) study, students were specifically asked to discuss how they would feel if they were in a similar situation to the one presented in the video or text. In addition, partners alternated turns, each reading aloud one paragraph of text from the history textbook and/or an article and helping the other with unknown or difficult vocabulary. Thus, students with learning disabilities received immediate feedback from their partners to mediate any confusion as a result of their reading difficulties.

Systematically Evaluate Outcomes

Data collection and automatic reporting are built into many technology-based interventions. Teachers can require students to demonstrate their knowledge of a topic by assigning a variety of activities in the virtual environment such as writing essays, diary entries, newspaper articles, or position papers, as well as completing graphic organizers and quizzes (Okolo et al., 2011). If not built in, teachers can incorporate evaluation measures such as student content interviews and/or written essays to assess students' understanding of topics (Gersten et al., 2006). Observations can also be used to systematically evaluate the outcomes of the instruction. From observations, it may become apparent that specific students with and without disabilities are not engaging in peer-mediated discussions appropriately. Technology can then be used to teach the desired behaviors.

Using Technology to Teach Peer-Mediated Skills

To illustrate, O'Brien and Wood (2011) have used video modeling to explicitly teach high school students with learning disabilities how to effectively and efficiently engage in peer-mediated discussions in a social studies class. It is important for teachers to improve group interactions as well as the discussion skills that students need in order to participate in cooperative learning activities, which are widely used in many general education classrooms. O'Brien and Wood (2011) required three students with learning disabilities in an inclusive social studies classroom to engage in a simplified cooperative peer-mediated instructional strategy called Numbered Heads Together (NHT). During this strategy, students reviewed lesson materials as a group. Then, they were numbered and assigned randomly into smaller groups in order to discuss answers to content-relevant questions. Therefore, *all* students were given a chance to participate in a critical discussion about content. The teacher asked students to take turns reading an issue of *Current Events* aloud and then pose a discussion question. Students then moved into their assigned NHT discussion groups, discussed the article and the posed question, and shared their answers with the whole class after a 5-minute group discussion. During the video modeling sessions, students watched video clips featuring college students that demonstrated examples and nonexamples of contrived behaviors that could occur during their discussions with partners. Students also had a chance to discuss their observations of what worked and what didn't go well in the video examples/nonexamples. Some exemplary behaviors included restating the question, demonstrating active listening behaviors, maintaining eye contact, taking turns sharing their perspectives, actively working with the text, and reaching consensus about their answers. Nonexamples included being off task, making negative comments, ignoring or dominating the discussion, mocking other partners, and not paying attention to the materials or task, as well as engaging in off-task conversations. The use of videos to model desired behaviors during cooperative learning opportunities encouraged positive student behaviors and higher levels of content group discussion (O'Brien & Wood, 2011). Therefore, the students had task-oriented verbal interactions and their questions were associated with the content. These gains were maintained even after the video modeling was no longer used with the students.

SUMMARY OF DCE STUDIES

DCEs are appealing to teachers in inclusive classrooms for many reasons. In this section, we summarize the advantages of using DCEs in the context of the PASS variables.

- Foremost, students with and without disabilities require additional relevant supplemental practice. When teachers prioritize instruction, the essential content can be embedded in the mnemonics, content cards, or technology-based interventions and rehearsed in a classwide peer-tutoring format during science or history class. Teachers have the flexibility of allotting time in the daily schedule for students to interact in pairs to practice, review, and use the DCE materials.

- Materials used during practice sessions can be tiered or leveled to address student diversity in the classroom. Adaptation of instructional materials is essential for quality instruction. Teachers know their students best and should consider the ability levels of their students and the types of supports students may need in order to meet the learning objectives (e.g., prompts, embedded mnemonics, and scripts).

- Peer-mediated sessions can be differentiated by the amount of time that individuals are required to spend on each content card (Marshak, 2011; McDuffie et al., 2009). For example, if students are recording their performance after each tutoring session, teachers should predetermine the criterion for advancing to the next level. In addition, as demonstrated in Mastropieri et al.'s (2005) study, more advanced students in a chemistry class are able to focus on high-level content and concepts by skipping those embedded strategies that are unnecessary for their learning. Finally, modifying instruction to match student performance is inherently built into many technology-based interventions. The Virtual History Museum, for example, includes a variety of materials that could be flexibly explored at each student's individual pace (Okolo et al., 2011).

- Another reason teachers find DCEs appealing is that all students can reverse roles and function as tutors and tutees. This facilitation of inclusion efforts is most successful if teachers systematically teach. Specifically, teachers should structure the peer-mediated strategy, provide explicit modeling, show enthusiasm, create and use supportive materials, and give students ample opportunities to practice. Teachers should also consider using technology to provide explicit modeling of effective interactions (O'Brien & Wood, 2011). When students are clear as to their tutor or tutee role and how to use the materials, student engagement will be maximized.

Finally, teachers should systematically monitor student performance by developing pre–posttests and/or self-evaluations. Ways for students to monitor performance need to be embedded in the student procedures. That is, during the peer-mediated activities, students can test one another and also rate their own performance on a 3-point scale. In turn, students can build self-regulatory skills such as self-monitoring and self-evaluation.

FUTURE DEVELOPMENT OF ADDITIONAL STRATEGIES

A final strategy to highlight for practicing teachers and researchers is the use of content enhancements such as graphic organizers, including computer-based graphic organizers to support student learning in social studies and science. Content enhancement tools aid students' comprehension of text by spatially representing information through a variety of formats such as cause and effect, compare and contrast, and outlines. Several recent research reviews suggest that both paper-based and computer-based graphic organizers are effective strategies, especially in science, social studies, and written expression (Ciullo & Reutebuch, 2013; Dexter, Park, & Hughes, 2011; Gajria, Jitendra, Sood, & Sacks, 2007; Scruggs et al., 2010, 2012). However, all of the studies conducted to date have focused either on an individual student completing a graphic organizer or an instructor providing the content to be included on an instructor-generated graphic organizer (Ciullo & Reutebuch, 2013). Future research is needed to determine how a computer-based graphic organizer in a peer-mediated environment could potentially benefit students with and without disabilities in an inclusive science or social studies classroom. Furthermore, a computer-based graphic organizer could easily be differentiated with and without prompts in order to address the varied ability levels in the classroom, as demonstrated in earlier studies employing DCEs.

CONCLUSION

Peer-mediated strategies provide opportunities for teachers to differentiate instruction and to support students with learning disabilities in inclusive classrooms, especially in such content areas as science and social studies. In addition, both teachers and students have expressed positive attitudes toward using differentiated materials and peer-mediated instruction. Helpful strategies that have been discussed in this chapter include mnemonic strategies, DCEs, manipulatives including folder games, peer tutoring, and peer mediation using varied materials. For the success of all students, effective inclusive classrooms require a variety of differentiated instructional interventions like these to support student learning. In addition to these strategies, we briefly discussed some of the exciting advances of virtual learning and video modeling, and ways in which technology can be used to differentiate instruction and to help facilitate peer-mediated interactions. When preservice and inservice teachers are mindful of the critically effective elements of teaching and incorporate peer-mediated strategies in the classroom, they can effectively differentiate instruction. The use of differentiated instructional strategies that facilitate peer interaction is an approach that holds much promise for students with disabilities in inclusive classrooms.

REFERENCES

Berkeley, S., King-Sears, M. E., Hott, B. L., & Bradley-Black, K. (2014). Are history text-books more "considerate" after 20 years? *Journal of Special Education, 47*, 217–230.

Biancarosa, C., & Snow, C. E. (2006). *Reading next: A vision for action and research in middle and high school literacy: A report to Carnegie Corporation of New York.* Washington, DC: Alliance for Excellent Education.

Bowman-Perrott, L. J., Greenwood, C. R., & Tapia, Y. (2007). The efficacy of CWPT used in secondary alternative school classrooms with small teacher/pupil ratios and students with emotional and behavioral disorders. *Education and Treatment of Children, 30*(3), 65–87.

Cortiella, C. (2011). *The state of learning disabilities.* New York: National Center for LD.

Ciullo, S., & Reutebuch, C. (2013). Computer-based graphic organizers for students with LD: A systematic review of literature. *Learning Disabilities Research and Practice, 28*, 196–210.

Dexter, D. D., Park, Y. J., & Hughes, C. A. (2011). A meta-analytic review of graphic organizers and science instruction for adolescents with learning disabilities: Implications for the intermediate and secondary science classroom. *Learning Disabilities Research and Practice, 26*, 204–213.

Fulk, B. M., & King, K. (2001). Classwide peer tutoring at work. *TEACHING Exceptional Children, 34*(2), 49–53.

Gajria, M., Jitendra, A. K., Sood, S., & Sacks, G. (2007). Improving comprehension of expository text in students with LD: A research synthesis. *Journal of Learning Disabilities, 40*, 210–225.

Gersten, R., Baker, S. K., Smith-Johnson, J., Dimino, J., & Peterson, A. (2006). Eyes on the prize: Teaching complex historical content to middle school students with LD. *Exceptional Children, 72*, 264–280.

Groves, F. H. (1995). Science vocabulary load of selected secondary science textbooks. *School Science and Mathematics, 95*, 231–235.

Harper, G. F., & Maheady, L. (2007). Peer-mediated teaching and students with learning disabilities. *Intervention in School and Clinic, 43*, 101–107.

Kroeger, S. D., Burton, C., & Preston, C. (2009). Integrating evidence-based practices in middle science reading. *TEACHING Exceptional Children, 41*(3), 6–15.

Maheady, L., Harper, G. F., & Mallettee, B. (2001). Peer-mediated instruction and interventions and students with mild disabilities. *Remedial and Special Education, 22*, 4–14.

Marino, M. T., Coyne, M. D., & Dunn, M. W. (2010). The effects of technology-based altered readability levels on struggling readers' science comprehension. *Journal of Mathematics and Science Teaching, 29*, 31–49.

Marshak, L., Mastropieri, M. A., & Scruggs, T. E. (2011). Curriculum enhancements in inclusive secondary social studies classrooms. *Exceptionality: A Special Education Journal, 19*(2), 61–74.

Mastropieri, M. A., & Scruggs, T. E. (1989). Constructing more meaningful relationships: Mnemonic instruction for special populations. *Educational Psychology Review, 1*, 83–111.

Mastropieri, M. A., & Scruggs, T. E. (1994). Text-based vs. activities-oriented science curriculum: Implications for students with disabilities. *Remedial and Special Education, 15*, 72–85.

Mastropieri, M. A., & Scruggs, T. E. (2002). *Effective instruction for special education* (3rd ed.). Columbus, OH: Merrill.

Mastropieri, M. A., & Scruggs, T. E. (2012). How can teacher attitudes, co-teaching and differentiated instruction facilitate inclusion? In C. Boyle & K. Topping (Eds.), *What works in inclusion?* (pp. 153–163). Berkshire, UK: Open University Press.

Mastropieri, M. A., & Scruggs, T. E. (2014). The inclusive classroom: Strategies for effective differentiated instruction (5th ed.). Upper Saddle River, NJ: Prentice Hall.

Mastropieri, M. A., Scruggs, T. E., & Graetz, J. E. (2003a). Reading comprehension instruction for secondary students: Challenges for struggling students and teachers. *Learning Disability Quarterly, 26,* 103–116.

Mastropieri, M. A., Scruggs, T. E., & Graetz, J. (2005). Cognition and learning in inclusive high school chemistry classes. In T. E. Scruggs & M. A. Mastropieri (Eds.), *Cognition and learning in diverse settings: Advances in learning and behavioral disabilities* (Vol. 18, pp. 107–118). Oxford, UK: Elsevier.

Mastropieri, M. A., Scruggs, T. E., Mantzicopoulos, P. Y., Sturgeon, A., Goodwin, L., & Chung, S. (1998). "A place where living things affect and depend on each other": Qualitative and quantitative outcomes associated with inclusive science teaching. *Science Education, 82,* 163–179.

Mastropieri, M. A., Scruggs, T. E., Marshak, L. (2008). Training teachers, parents, and peers to implement effective teaching strategies for content area learning. In T. E. Scruggs & M. A. Mastropieri (Eds.), *Personal preparation: Advances in learning and behavioral disabilities* (vol. 21, pp. 311–329). Bingley, UK: Emerald.

Mastropieri, M. A., Scruggs, T. E., Norland, J., Berkeley, S., McDuffie, K., Tornquist, E. H., et al. (2006). Differentiated curriculum enhancement in inclusive middle school science: Effects on classroom and high-stakes tests. *Journal of Special Education, 40,* 130–137.

Mastropieri, M. A., Scruggs, T. E., Spencer, V., & Fontana, J. (2003b). Promoting success in high school world history: Peer tutoring versus guided notes. *Learning Disabilities Research and Practice, 18,* 52–65.

McDuffie, K. A., Mastropieri, M. A., & Scruggs, T. E. (2009). Promoting success in content area classes: Is value added through co-teaching? *Exceptional Children, 75,* 493–510.

O'Brien, C., & Wood, C. L. (2011). Video modeling of cooperative discussion group behaviors with students with learning disabilities in a secondary content-area classroom. *Journal of Special Education Technology, 26*(4), 25–40.

Okilwa, N. S. A., & Shelby, L. (2010). The effects of peer tutoring on academic performance of students with disabilities in grades 6 through 12: A synthesis of the literature. *Remedial and Special Education, 31,* 450–463.

Okolo, C. M., Englert, C. S., Bouck, E. C., Heutsche, A., & Wang, H. (2011). The Virtual History Museum: Learning U.S. history in diverse eighth-grade classrooms. *Remedial and Special Education, 32,* 417–428.

Okolo, C. M., Ferretti, R. P., & MacArthur, C. A. (2007). Talking about history: Discussions in a middle school inclusive classroom. *Journal of Learning Disabilities, 40,* 154–165.

Regan, K., & Berkeley, S. (2012). Effective reading and writing instruction: A focus on modeling. *Intervention in School and Clinic, 47,* 276–282.

Scruggs, T. E. (2012). Differential facilitation of learning outcomes: What does it tell us about learning disabilities and instructional programming? *International Journal for Research in Learning Disabilities, 1*(1), 4–20.

Scruggs, T. E., & Mastropieri, M. A. (1995). What makes special education special?: An analysis of the PASS variables in inclusion settings. *Journal of Special Education, 29,* 224–233.

Scruggs, T. E., & Mastropieri, M. A. (2000). The effectiveness of mnemonic instruction for students with learning and behavior problems: An update and research synthesis. *Journal of Behavioral Education, 10,* 163–173.

Scruggs, T. E., Mastropieri, M. A., Bakken, J. P., & Brigham, F. J. (1993). Reading vs. doing: The relative effects of textbook-based and inquiry-oriented approaches to science learning in special education classrooms. *Journal of Special Education, 27*, 1–15.

Scruggs, T. E., Mastropieri, M. A., Berkeley, S., & Graetz, J. (2010). Do special education interventions improve learning of secondary content? A meta-analysis. *Remedial and Special Education, 36*, 437–449.

Scruggs, T. E., Mastropieri, M. A., & Marshak, L. (2012). Peer mediated instruction in inclusive secondary social studies learning: Direct and indirect learning effects. *Learning Disabilities Research and Practice, 27*, 12–20.

Scruggs, T. E., Mastropieri, M. A., & McDuffie, K. A. (2007). Co-teaching in inclusive classrooms: A meta-synthesis of qualitative research. *Exceptional Children, 73*, 392–416.

Scruggs, T. E., Mastropieri, M. A., & Okolo, C. M. (2008). Science and social studies for students with disabilities. *Focus on Exceptional Children 41*(2), 1–24.

Simpkins, P. M. (2007). *The effect of differentiated curriculum enhancements on the achievement of at-risk and normally achieving students in 5th grade science* (Doctoral dissertation). Retrieved from ProQuest Dissertations and Theses database (UMI No. 3255809).

Simpkins, P. M., Mastropieri, M. A., & Scruggs, T. E. (2009). Differentiated curriculum enhancements in inclusive 5th grade science classes. *Remedial and Special Education, 30*, 200–308.

Skylar, A. A. (2007). Using assistive technology to include low-performing students in peer tutoring: A little help from Mini-Me. *Journal of Special Education Technology, 22*(1), 53–57.

Spencer, V., Scruggs, T. E., & Mastropieri, M. A. (2003). Content area learning in middle school social studies classrooms and students with emotional or behavioral disorders: A comparison of strategies. *Behavioral Disorders, 28*, 77–93.

Stenhoff, D. M., & Lignugaris/Kraft, B. (2007). A review of the effects of peer tutoring on students with mild disabilities in secondary settings. *Exceptional Children, 74*, 8–30.

Tomlinson, C. A. (2003). Deciding to teach them all. *Educational Leadership, 61*(2), 6–11.

Vaughn, S., & Bos, C. S. (2009). *Strategies for teaching students with learning and behavior problems* (7th ed.). Boston: Allyn and Bacon.

Wagner, M., Newman, L., Cameto, R., Levine, P., & Garza, N. (2006). An overview of findings from wave 2 of the National Longitudinal Transition Study-2 (NLTS2) (NCSER 2006-3004). Menlo Park, CA: SRI International.

Wexler, J., Reed, D. K., Pyle, N., Mitchell, M., & Barton, E. E. (2013). A synthesis of peer-mediated academic interventions for secondary struggling learners. *Journal of Learning Disabilities.* Available online.

Wood, C. L., Mackiewicz, S. M., Van Norman, R. K., & Cooke, N. L. (2007). Tutoring with technology. *Intervention in School and Clinic, 43*, 108–115.

CHAPTER 3

"Thank You for Helping Me Write a Better Paper"

Peer Support in Learning to Write

ANNE MONG CRAMER and LINDA H. MASON

Peer assistance for improving written expression has many well-documented advantages. When well implemented, peer assistance can benefit all students, especially those who struggle for mastery throughout the writing processes of planning, composing, revision, and editing. In addition, peers can support each other in fostering generalization and maintenance of learned writing strategies. In this chapter, we highlight the benefits of self-regulated strategy development (SRSD) instruction for peer-supported learning in writing. Procedures for teaching research-based strategies, tips for teaching low-achieving students how to give and receive effective feedback, and reproducible graphic organizers are included.

Writing has always been a foundational skill, a skill critical for success in academic and employment settings (National Commission on Writing, 2004). As recently as the turn of the 20th century, most communication outside of personal contact was through formal letters written in calligraphic cursive. As typewriters became prevalent, business writing became a joint venture between a typist and a business executive, the typist transcribing handwritten or orally dictated messages into formal letters and documents. This bears little resemblance to writing in today's workforce, where one is expected to generate content through word processing. In fact, electronic communication has replaced all but the most formal professional communiqués. Technological advancements, furthermore, have propelled writing into social media, the preferred means of communication for those born between 1983 and 2000, "Generation Y" (Miller, 2013). Beyond face-to-face communication, Generation Y communicates primarily through writing, preferring texting and instant messaging to phone calls.

From single-word tweets about the weather (e.g., "#Sunshine!") to creating professional reports and manuscripts, writing is an essential component of our personal and professional lives. Work, social, and educational needs justify the investment of academic learning time to develop fluent writing skills. Despite the emphasis on writing for informal social communication, formal writing remains a keystone of academic standards and assessment (Graham & Harris, 2013). In fact, recent U.S. Common Core State Standard initiatives (National Governors Association Center for Best Practices and Council of Chief State School Officers, 2013) demand that students across all academic areas (1) write arguments, informative/explanatory text, and narrative text; (2) write with clarity and cohesion to meet task, purpose, and audience; (3) plan and revise, edit, or rewrite; (4) use technology for production, publication, and collaboration; (5) write short and longer responses to demonstrate comprehension of subject matter; (6) use and integrate multiple sources while avoiding plagiarism; (7) use evidence from text to support writing; and (8) write in short and extended time frames.

Results of the 2011 National Assessment of Educational Progress (NAEP) indicated that 8th- and 12th-grade students in the United States performed at or below "basic" in the four evaluation benchmarks (i.e., below basic, basic, proficient, and advanced) for writing performance. Assessments over the past decade have indicated that nationally, U.S. students are not meeting the minimum expectations for writing in the academic curriculum. While these findings are alarming, they are not surprising given that 75% of students reported that they wrote for 30 minutes or less per day during English Language Arts, and even less in other content areas (U.S. Department of Education, 2011). Potentially compounding the problem, NAEP for 8th- and 12th-grade students utilized computer-based writing assessments for the first time in 2011, bringing another dimension of instruction, word-processing skills, to the assessment and accountability initiatives for students' writing performance.

In this chapter, we first describe the difficulties many students experience when writing. We also explore methods for teaching writing more effectively, specifically, how peer-mediated writing assists students within a wide ability range. We examine how writers and peer editors at all skill levels can collaborate and strengthen outcomes across the writing process. We then provide specific strategies that support peer-mediated writing and provide sample classroom materials that reinforce learning.

THE NEED FOR PEER-ASSISTED LEARNING IN WRITING

To support academic and professional writing, as noted previously, writing should be incorporated into all areas of the curriculum Common Core State Standards (National Governors Association Center for Best Practices and Council of Chief State School Officers, 2013). In this context, peer-assisted learning makes sense for struggling writers. First, in addition to instructional time and writing practice, becoming a proficient writer is dependent on appropriate feedback that fosters growth (Harris & Graham, 2009). Given that every student's work is unique, resulting in teacher conferences with only one student at a time, providing timely and quality feedback is difficult. Peer-mediated planning, composing, and editing increase the opportunities for student authors to discuss their writing and decrease the wait time for feedback. In fact, feedback received during peer conferencing has been established as effective in improving the completeness and quality of students' writing (Mong Cramer & Mason, 2014; MacArthur, Schwartz, & Graham, 1991a; MacArthur, Schwartz, & Graham, 1991a, 1991b; Wong, Butler, Ficzere, & Kuperis, 1997). Furthermore, Wong and colleagues (1997) found that students with learning disabilities (LD) rated student conferencing and teacher conferencing as equally effective. This is not to suggest that peer conferencing should replace teacher evaluation, feedback, and support; however, it does suggest that peers can serve as effective mediators for the writing process.

Peers as mediators can also address weaknesses in students' evaluation of their own writing, particularly for struggling writers, who often have difficulty in this area (Bartlett, 1982). These students often focus on superficial spelling and grammar changes with little attention to substantive meaning-altering changes (MacArthur & Graham, 1987). This skill deficit may be the result of disconnects between what the writer intended and what was actually written (MacArthur (2013). A struggling writer's failure to detect missing information or ambiguities may provide evidence for this disconnect. Without the benefit of another person to point out missing information, struggling writers may be unable to differentiate between what they wrote and what they were thinking while writing. Peer mediators can help to bridge the gap between the writer's intention and the end product.

Peer feedback can also support higher-level evaluation of clarity, organization, and cogency (MacArthur, Schwartz & Graham, 1991a; Stoddard & MacArthur, 1993). Grounded in Vygotsky's sociocultural learning theory, there is evidence that peers can provide meaningful support. Researchers note, however, that support is meaningful only when teachers provide students with explicit instruction on how to offer specific, constructive feedback in a socially appropriate manner (Dahl & Farnan, 1998; Fitzgerald & Stamm, 1990; Patthey-Chavez & Ferris, 1997). Without this instruction, students are more likely to give potentially hurtful negative feedback or random praise that preserves social relationships (Beach & Friedrich, 2006; Dipardo & Freedman, 1988). Needless to say, this type of feedback is ineffective for helping writers develop new skills. When effective feedback procedures have been learned, peer editors can support writing across the processes of planning, composing, revising, and editing.

CHARACTERISTICS OF THE WRITING PROCESSES AND THE ROLE OF PEERS

Peer-assisted learning in writing is generally conceived as an editor providing feedback and suggesting changes to an author's written draft. MacArthur (2013, p. 216), however, notes that "revision includes mental evaluation and revision of sentences before writing them, changes in text during writing, changes in plans, as well as evaluation and revision of complete drafts." Based on this thinking, all peer mediation in writing is part of the revision process, whether this occurs before, during, or after writing a draft. With this framework in mind, we examine how peer-assisted learning supports the critical stages of writing, namely planning a draft paper, composing the draft paper, and revising and editing the draft paper.

Writers vary in their knowledge and implementation of planning strategies. Experienced writers are more likely to practice advance planning by recording ideas and evaluating information prior to writing (Graham & Harris, 2007). Experienced writers organize their thoughts around a particular topic, identify the critical components of style associated with the writing genre, and develop content around these components. Experienced writers also consider the purpose of the paper and the needs of the audience, adjusting voice and content accordingly. On the other hand, inexperienced and struggling writers tend to write in a rapid-fire style known as "knowledge telling" (MacArthur & Graham, 1987). According to MacArthur and Graham, writing produced using this method is typically disjointed, lacks organization and cogency, and often deviates from the topic. Peer mediators can play an important role in revision by helping writers identify missing or ambiguous information and by brainstorming additional content during the planning process (Mong Cramer & Mason, 2014). When revision at the content level occurs during planning, writers are essentially front-loading their work to include refined information in their first draft, reducing the amount of revision needed at the end of the writing process.

During the composing process, peers can collaborate as coauthors, supporting one another in idea generation, word choice, cogency, and clarity. When two writers work together, the more experienced writer should share knowledge with, support, and encourage the less experienced writer. Stoddard and MacArthur (1993) reported that skills acquired during peer-assisted composing often generalize to future first drafts; the editor's feedback internalizes and becomes part of the writer's metacognitive process.

The terms *editing* and *revising* are often considered synonymous descriptors for the same function; however, revision functions differently than editing. Editing generally involves checking for spelling, grammar, punctuation, and other mechanical issues. Revising focuses on substantive content changes that affect meaning. Experienced writers recognize the benefits of deep revisions for adjusting meaning and clarifying thoughts. Struggling and inexperienced writers more often focus on surface-level changes that have little effect on meaning (MacArthur, 2013). In fact, fewer than 20% of revisions made by students with disabilities result in substantive differences (Graham, 1997; MacArthur & Graham, 1987). Revision is a three-phased learned process. For struggling writers, the three revision phases must be explicitly taught, modeled, and carefully scaffolded through guided practice.

Revision Phases

Three overarching revision phases are necessary for effective revision: *evaluation*, *detection*, and *repair* (Fitzgerald, 1987; Flower, Hayes, Carey, Schriver, & Stratman,

1986). *Evaluation* begins with identifying (1) the purpose for writing, such as to inform, to persuade, or to tell a story, (2) required primary traits (e.g., reasons and explanations for writing an opinion), and (3) intended audience. In peer-mediated learning, the peer editor should first form a general impression of the writing and then evaluate the writer's use of standard writing conventions (MacArthur, Graham, & Harris, 2004). Spelling and grammar are not technically a major factor in content evaluation unless serious mechanical issues interfere with the writer's meaning. Evaluation can be problematic for many student peer editors, especially for those students with learning and cognitive disabilities. These students (1) have problems identifying errors and inconsistencies in writing (Graham, 1997); (2) lack the strategic problem-solving skills needed for effective evaluation, resulting in proofreading rather than clarity (MacArthur et al., 2004); (3) do not understand that evaluation should occur during planning, composing, and revision/editing; and (4) have serious mechanical errors in their own writing and do not see similar errors that distract from noticing substantive content-related problems (Graham, 1990; Thomas, Englert, & Gregg, 1987).

Detection, although similar to evaluation, requires subtle differences in prerequisite skills such as knowledge of text and sentence structures and content-specific writing norms (Flower et al., 1986). Effective detection and diagnosis depends on the peer editor's experience and skill, as well as the complexity of the writer's content. For students with disabilities, who often have poor reading comprehension, limited writing skills, and limited understanding of what makes writing effective (Lane, 2004), the skills needed for higher-level detection and diagnosis are problematic. Without development of the prerequisite skills related to writing, students with disabilities are unlikely to be successful in their detection of writing problems (Stoddard & MacArthur, 1993).

Repair is the physical action taken to fix the problems (Flower et al., 1986). Writers must first decide whether to revise by reworking the existing text or to revise by fixing the problem through deletion and rewriting. Both options require a variety of strategies, including the ability to apply basic language and writing skills (MacArthur et al., 2004), skills that may be underdeveloped in students with disabilities (Morris Kindzierski, 2009). Changes of any kind will likely be difficult for students with weak language, writing, and mechanical skills.

Strategy instruction for revising, fortunately, has been effective in addressing the needs of struggling writers, including the needs of students with disabilities (Graham & Perin, 2007b; Troia, 2006). The family of peer-assisted strategies for revision, taught within the self-regulated strategy development SRSD instructional model, has been validated as especially effective for students' strategy acquisition and mastery of specific writing skills across genres. Although the term *self-regulated* may seem out of place in a book about the power of peers, the path to self-regulation is not an isolated journey, but one carefully guided by the support of others. In the next section, we introduce SRSD instruction and strategies that incorporate the power of peers to increase writing proficiency and build a community of skilled writers.

SELF-REGULATED STRATEGY DEVELOPMENT

SRSD, developed by Harris (Harris & Graham, 1985), has the largest evidence base in writing intervention studies across grade levels (Harris, Graham, Brindle, & Sandmel, 2009). The model supports student motivation, self-efficacy for writing, recognition of the positive effects of effort when applying the strategy, and emphasizes the importance of peer support and interaction (Harris & Graham, 2009). During SRSD instruction, peer-assisted planning and revision strategies are taught within six instructional stages: develop background knowledge, discuss it, model it, memorize it, support it, and provide independent practice (Mason, Harris, & Graham, 2011). An overview of the six instructional stages is presented in Table 3.1. Four procedures for teaching students to self-regulate their learning—goal setting, self-monitoring, self-instruction, and self-reinforcement—are embedded throughout the six stages. SRSD instruction is recursive; instructional stages are revisited as needed to support student mastery in applying the strategies to their writing, to reinforce maintenance, and/or to scaffold students' skills for generalization. For example, once a revision strategy is learned and students begin to apply the strategy to more complex writing tasks over time, the teacher provides guided support to ensure the student applies the strategy accurately to the new task. When transferring a peer-assisted revising strategy learned from one genre (e.g., persuasive writing) to another (e.g., informative writing), modeling and guided practice may need to be revisited.

Next, we review recommendations for teaching students to self-regulate learning; thereafter, we describe the integrated SRSD instructional model for strategy acquisition.

Self-Regulation

Proficient writers establish goals for task accomplishment, self-monitor progress, use positive self-instruction, and self-reinforce when they have met their goals (Harris, Graham, MacArthur, Reid, & Mason, 2011). Unfortunately, many students with disabilities lack these critical self-regulation skills for beginning and completing written expression tasks. During SRSD instruction, teachers explicitly teach and support procedures for building students' self-regulation. In initial SRSD instructional stages, for example, students are encouraged to set goals for doing their best to work collaboratively with their teacher and peer partners to learn new strategies. Later, the students set goals to apply the strategies to their writing. Self-monitoring reinforces students' goal setting; students examine their writing and chart or graph their strategy use to show improvement over time. When goals are not met, students are encouraged to collaborate with their peer partners to redirect efforts to improve writing. As students begin to learn and apply strategies, they add goals that include higher-level writing skills such as improving word choice and sentence type.

Students also learn to support writing by using self-instruction (i.e., self-speech) throughout the writing process. The teacher models self-instruction and

TABLE 3.1. Self-Regulated Strategy Development Stages of Instruction

1. *Develop and activate knowledge needed for writing and self-regulation*
   - Read and discuss anchor papers within the genre (persuasive essays, reports, etc.) to:
     - Develop declarative, procedural, and conditional knowledge.
     - Discuss guidelines for meaningful, appropriate, and constructive feedback.
   - While moving through instructional stages, continue to develop strategy components until students can identify critical genre components.
   - Discuss and examine writing and self-regulation strategies; begin development of peer-mediated roles; introduce goal setting and self-monitoring.

2. *Discuss it—Discourse is critical!*
   - Discuss present levels and previous experiences with writing, revising, and self-regulation; explore attitudes, beliefs, and perceptions about writing and revising, including how internal feedback and the feedback they have received from others influence their self-efficacy as writers.
   - Highlight the value of mastering powerful strategies and the power of utilizing peer feedback in becoming a stronger writer; evaluate and discuss examples and nonexamples of constructive feedback.
   - Explore peer-assisted learning sheets, graphic organizers, and other materials; discuss examples and nonexamples of when and where to use materials.
   - Graph baseline components of prior compositions to inform accurate goal setting; emphasize that baselines are starting points to help writers monitor personal growth; omit baseline graphing if focusing on low, pre-instruction performance would damage self-efficacy.
   - Continue discussion of writing, revising, and self-regulation strategies: purpose, benefits, and examples and nonexamples of useful generalization.
   - Develop students' commitment to learning the strategy and establish the teacher's role as a partner in learning; emphasize the influence of effort and appropriate use of the strategy in becoming a stronger writer and editor.

3. *Model it—Model writing and conferencing*
   - Model planning, writing, revision conferences, and making revisions.
   - Analyze and critique the modeling; discuss where adjustments might increase effectiveness.
   - Support development of self-regulation strategies across the writing and revising process and other academic assignments.
   - Continue generalization support.

4. *Memorize it*
   - Develop and encourage writers to memorize the strategy components (mnemonics, self-regulation steps, and strategy applications) from the early stages of strategy acquisition, and continue working toward memorization throughout the lessons.
   - Confirm that students have memorized the mnemonics and their meaning prior to independent practice.

5. *Support it*
   - Use strategy charts, graphic organizers, and self-instruction sheets to work collaboratively with students to foster mastery of planning, writing, and revising strategies.
   - Assist students in developing preliminary goals relative to genre elements and task characteristics that are both achievable and challenging; criterion levels increase gradually to meet mastery-level performance.
   - Fade supports such as prompts, guidance, and use of support materials on an individual basis to support independence and promote generalization to other settings.

(continued)

TABLE 3.1. *(continued)*

- Self-regulation components (goal setting, self-instructions, self-monitoring, and self-reinforcement) that are incorporated into each lesson can be further enhanced by encouraging students to begin managing the writing environment, using imagery, and critically analyzing and using feedback from past and present editors.
- Plan for maintenance and continue support of generalization.

6. *Independent performance*
- Students demonstrate mastery of planning, writing, revising, and self-regulation strategies independently; teachers monitor and provide scaffolded support.
- Encourage cooperative pairs to work with new partners to support generalization.
- Continue to discuss plans for maintenance and generalization.

Note. Stages 1 and 2 are often combined; pacing for lessons and stages is individualized to student need; some stages may require more than one lesson; instruction is recursive in nature with stages being revisited as necessary to support mastery.

assists students in developing personal and peer group self-instructions (see Table 3.2 for types of personal and group self-instructions). Self-reinforcement supports writing performance across all phases, from positive self-instruction and visual representation of progress through self-monitoring.

Stages of Strategy Acquisition

As noted previously, the stages of strategy acquisition are flexible and designed to meet the writer's needs during demanding writing tasks. In describing the stages, we focus on teaching a planning strategy for writing an opinion (e.g., POW [**P**ick my idea, **O**rganize my notes, **W**rite and say more] + TREE [**T**opic sentence,

TABLE 3.2. Personal and Peer Self-Instruction Examples

Self-instruction	Personal self-instruction	Peer group self-instruction
Problem definition	"What do I need to do?"	"I need to ask my peer to check my paper."
Focus on attention and planning	"How do I get started?"	"We need to focus on the strategy steps."
Strategy use	"I'm not sure about this step."	"I need to ask my peer or my teacher."
Self-evaluation and error correcting	"How am I doing? Did I remember everything?"	"I forgot to check my peer's paper for a good ending sentence. I need to go back and do that."
Coping and self-control	"This may take a long time, but if I follow the steps it will be easier."	"My partner can help me to follow the steps if I get stuck."
Self-reinforcement	"My paper is much better."	"I think I really helped my peer. He seems to like my suggestions."

Reasons, **E**xplanations, **E**nding **S**entence]) as well as teaching specific strategies for peer revision (e.g., Peer Revising Strategy).

Develop Preskills and Background Knowledge

Teachers begin SRSD instruction by developing students' skills and knowledge for working with a peer during the writing process and learning a strategy. Rules for providing constructive feedback are presented during this stage. Students and the teacher, for example, describe examples of working with peers to accomplish and improve other tasks such as skills in other academic subject areas, sports, and playing games. The teacher also develops the students' knowledge, as needed, for using strategies in genre-specific writing.

Discuss It

During *"discuss it,"* the teacher introduces the strategy mnemonic and each strategy step, and explains the specific benefits of the strategy for improving writing. As the teacher describes the strategy, students review strategy mnemonic charts, peer-assisted learning sheets, graphic organizers, and so forth. When teaching a planning strategy, the teacher and students evaluate an anchor paper for strategy-specific components. Students examine their previously written papers in comparison with the new strategy. Students graph their performance to provide a baseline for self-monitoring. When discussing a peer-assisted revision strategy, students and the teacher evaluate examples and nonexamples of constructive feedback specific to each strategy step. Students and the teacher evaluate papers previously written without peer feedback and graph criteria elements to establish the baseline for self-monitoring. For both planning and revision strategies, peers and the teacher work collaboratively to establish criterion goals. In this early stage, students also set goals to learn the strategy mnemonic and strategy steps.

Model It

Cognitive modeling, modeling while thinking out loud, is the heart of good strategy instruction (Association for Supervision and Curriculum Development [ASCD], 2002). During modeling, the teacher uses the strategies, self-regulation procedures, and instructional materials to complete the writing task. Positive self-instructions are developed and modeled; negative self-instructions are identified and corrected. For peer-revision strategies, the teacher can model with another teacher, support staff, or a student. Student pairs that have mastered the strategy can also model. Modeling must be planned and practiced in advance, regardless of who models! Modeling should demonstrate to the students the benefit of using the strategy by providing a relatively seamless example of how the strategy and peer assistance benefit writing. After modeling, students develop personal self-instructions to use during peer feedback and writing.

Memorize It

Memorization begins when students are first introduced to the strategy in the *"discuss it"* stage. For many students, memorizing the strategy mnemonic and strategy steps requires little support. For students struggling with memorization, group or peer-repeated practice is recommended. "Rapid fire" cue cards, whiteboards or chalkboards, and oral practice for memorization can be used prior to or after a lesson. Memorization is important for building fluency in strategy use, increasing correct strategy application, and reducing the dependency on teacher-developed instructional materials. Students with significant memory difficulties may continue to use support materials such as cue cards, mnemonic sheets, and graphic organizers.

Support It

During *"support it,"* the teacher works collaboratively with students by scaffolding assistance, a process that shifts responsibility from the teacher to the students and student pairs. In addition, the teacher monitors students' use of strategies and self-regulation procedures by providing explicit, specific feedback. For example, the teacher supports students' self-monitoring by asking peer pairs to count the number of strategy elements planned or written, and to graph results. If an element has been incorrectly identified, the teacher revisits the *"discuss it"* stage explicitly and explains the element again. Given the important role of self-instruction in student motivation to write, the teacher should address negative self-instructions immediately. It may also be necessary to model effective use of self-instruction again. Collaborative practice and guided practice are repeated until students demonstrate strategy mastery and are able to work with their peer partners independently.

Independent Practice

During independent practice, students work independently with their peer partner while the teacher monitors performance to ensure the maintenance of learning over time. As noted in *"support it,"* the teacher should revisit any stage of strategy instruction as needed. In addition, the teacher should foster generalization of peer support and the strategies learned in other subjects, classrooms, and writing tasks. Finally, students' growth and progress are celebrated.

SRSD Revision Research

As noted previously, SRSD instruction effectively facilitates peer-assisted learning across the writing process. The effects of SRSD for reciprocal peer revision for personal narratives, for example, have been examined with fourth- through eighth-grade students in self-contained classrooms (MacArthur et al., 1991a; MacArthur,

Graham, Schwartz, & Shafer, 1995) and resource rooms (Stoddard & MacArthur, 1993). Morris Kindzierski (2009) compared the effects of SRSD for peer revision to individual revision of descriptive essays written and revised by students with emotional and behavioral disorders (EBD). Mong Cramer and Mason (2014) examined the effects of SRSD for peer revision during planning while working with middle school students with EBD. All of these researchers reported increased holistic quality and gains for specific component qualities (i.e., primary traits, organization, and clarity) following SRSD instruction and peer-revision conferencing. In addition, across research studies, students provided positive feedback about revising with peers. Morris Kindzierski (2009) reported decreases in antisocial verbal exchanges between students following SRSD instruction. Mong Cramer and Mason (2014) also observed an important finding, an increase in time spent revising when students were evaluating a peer's work in comparison with the time spent reviewing their own work. In summary, SRSD peer-revision instruction fosters quality feedback and increases student time and effort invested in revising, resulting in improved organization, clarity, and completeness of written products.

In the next section, we describe these research-evaluated approaches in the context of (1) hand- or computer-written essays, (2) revision, and (3) generalization and maintenance. Research findings and implications are also noted. Especially when working with students with disabilities, it is critically important to work from a strong evidence base. The majority of research in writing focuses on instruction for planning and/or revising strategies (e.g., Graham & Perin, 2007a). When planning for peer-mediated writing interventions, again, the research focuses primarily on planning and revising with peer support. Detailed descriptions of all the noted SRSD instructional components, complete lesson plans, and reproducible materials for the strategies are available in two texts: *Powerful Writing Strategies for All Students* (Harris, Graham, Mason, & Friedlander, 2008) and *Powerful Strategies for Improving Reading and Writing in Content Areas* (Mason, Reid, & Hagaman, 2012). The video *Teaching Students with Learning Disabilities: Using Learning Strategies* (ASCD, 2002) features SRSD instruction implemented in elementary and middle school classrooms. Online interactive tutorials on SRSD are available at *http://iris. peabody.vanderbilt.edu/pow/chalcycle.html.*

Peer-Assisted Strategies to Support Planning

Skilled writers develop ideas and concepts from memory, understand their audience, evaluate ideas and concepts, and then translate ideas and concepts into written text (Flower & Hayes, 1980). Unfortunately, many students with disabilities struggle with generating ideas and putting ideas into an organized plan for writing (Scardamalia & Bereiter, 1987; Graham, 1990). Through peer-assisted techniques for brainstorming and planning, writers can address these difficulties early in the writing process.

Narratives

Real or imagined experiences and events are described in narrative writing. The Common Core State Standards (National Governors Association Center for Best Practices and Council of Chief State School Officers, 2013) note that students should be able to write well-written and well-structured narratives that include (1) problems, situations, or observations; (2) rich and vivid descriptions; (3) a variety of techniques for sequencing events; and (4) a reflective conclusion. Although narrative text structures are generally familiar because of students' background knowledge through reading and hearing stories, writing complex narratives across academic domains can be difficult for many students. Sophisticated narrative writing is important across the curriculum, for example, in social studies for writing biographies and in science for writing about occurrences during a natural event (e.g., hurricane, earthquake). An effective story grammar strategy is SRSD for the C-SPACE mnemonic (**C**haracters—Who are the characters in the story?; **S**etting—Where and when did the story take place?; **P**urpose—What does the main character try to do?; **A**ction —What does the main character do to achieve the goal?; **C**onclusion—What is the result of the action?; **E**motions —What are the reactions and feelings of the main character?) (MacArthur, et al., 1991b). C-SPACE assists students in using familiar story grammar elements as a guide for identifying and incorporating effective narrative elements into writing. Instruction includes teaching student pairs to brainstorm and plan, and to evaluate and provide feedback for the story grammar components (see Mason et al., 2011, for peer-assistance biographies).

As in all instructional strategies described in this chapter, lessons for C-SPACE include the six stages of SRSD instruction and the four self-regulation procedures. Instructional materials include a C-SPACE mnemonic chart, self-monitoring sheet, graphic organizer, and peer feedback guides (see Figures 3.1 and 3.2 for sample organizer and guide). Initial instruction focuses on a single narrative type. When students have learned C-SPACE, teachers can begin generalizing the strategy to other tasks. Introduction to the C-SPACE strategy mnemonic and steps begins with the teacher and students discussing the benefits of the strategy and peer assistance for improving narrative writing. Guidelines for effective peer feedback are described; examples and nonexamples are noted. Peer pairs identify C-SPACE strategy steps elements in a sample narrative, then evaluate their performance on a previously written narrative. Next, a teacher-pair team, or a student-pair team models how to use the C-SPACE strategy with all instructional materials. Modeling includes using the peer feedback guides for brainstorming ideas and for receiving feedback for the narrative planned on the graphic organizer. Peer practice in implementing all steps of C-SPACE is scaffolded; the teacher gradually fades support as students work toward independence. Students continue to provide and receive feedback while writing narratives without teacher assistance and without the C-SPACE instructional materials.

Planning a Narrative		
Characters Who is in this story?	**Setting** Time and place	**Purpose** What the characters try to do
Action What the characters do	**Conclusion** Results	**Emotions** Reactions and feelings

FIGURE 3.1. Personal narrative graphic organizer. Based on Mason, Reid, and Hagaman (2012).

Author's Feedback
☐ Brainstorm
☐ Create plan (use graphic organizer)
☐ Use your notes to tell your story to a partner
☐ Listen to feedback
☐ Make notes
☐ Using feedback, write your narrative

Peer's Feedback	
☐ Listen	
☐ Tell what you liked about the narrative	
☐ Discuss ideas using C-SPACE	
☐ C—Characters	☐ A—Action
☐ S—Setting	☐ C—Conclusion
☐ P—Problem	☐ E—Emotion

FIGURE 3.2. C-SPACE author and partner feedback guide. Based on Mason, Reid, and Hagaman (2012).

Informative Writing

Informative writing is commonly used to enhance content-area knowledge or demonstrate understanding of learned information (MacArthur & Philippakos, 2010). Students are expected to write papers that "examine and convey complex ideas, concepts, and information clearly and accurately through the effective selection, organization, and analysis of content" (CCSS; National Governors Association Center for Best Practices and Council of Chief State School Officers, 2013). Teaching students to implement peer-assisted strategies throughout the writing process alleviates difficulties they may encounter, allowing them to focus on synthesis and exploration of content. Using SRSD for the PLAN & WRITE strategy (PLAN: **P**ay attention to the prompt, **L**ist main ideas, **A**dd supporting ideas, **N**umber your ideas; WRITE: **W**ork from your plan to develop your thesis statement, **R**emember your goals, Include transition words, Try to use different kinds of sentences, and Exciting, interesting, $100,000 words)[1] develops and strengthens students' skills for information essay writing (De La Paz, 1999). The PLAN & WRITE informative strategy (Harris et al., 2008) has been used for summative writing assessments and can be adapted for complex writing tasks where students are asked to synthesize learning across multiple readings and classroom activities (i.e., reports). SRSD for PLAN & WRITE focuses students' attention on identifying and organizing main ideas and supporting details during planning. During the WRITE phase, students focus on elements such as transitions, sentence structure, and word choice to enhance cogency and interest.

Instructional procedures for PLAN & WRITE follow the SRSD stages for strategy acquisition and self-regulation (see Harris et al., 2008, for lessons and instructional materials). Mini-lessons with different student objectives, such as improving sentence writing and word choice, are infused throughout the lessons. Instructional materials include a PLAN & WRITE mnemonic chart, brainstorming sheet, planning sheet, revision checklist (see Figure 3.3), model essays, worksheets outlining goals for proficient writing, lists for characteristics of good essays, and different kinds of sentences. Guidelines for teaching students to work in pairs are provided (see Table 3.3).

In the beginning lessons, the teacher sets the purpose for learning the strategy, discusses strategy steps, models writing an essay, and begins to facilitate student memorization of the strategy. In the following lessons, students learn to (1) identify a thesis sentence, transition words, types of sentences, and essay parts using a model essay; (2) identify essay parts and synonyms in a different essay; (3) review pronoun and verb agreement; and (4) revise an essay. During these lessons, student pairs or small groups use the revision checklist to evaluate and revise model essays. Students then establish goals and compose an essay collaboratively. Teachers provide guided practice to support student pairs or small groups in setting goals and composing essays. Teachers also monitor students' use of the revision checklist until they are able to demonstrate effective revision performance. In final lessons, students write essays independently and revise essays in pairs.

The effects of PLAN & WRITE for expository essays were examined in a single subject study with 22 middle school students with and without LD in general education classrooms (De La Paz, 1999). Researchers examined written plans for completeness and accuracy using a 6-point scale (0 = no planning to 5 = accurate map or outline). Only 7% of the participants did any advanced planning during baseline. Planning was generally of two types: a listing of words or a complete first draft. Following instruction, all students created formal plans, with 55% earning the top score of 6 points, indicating a complete plan with appropriate follow-

---

[1]PLAN & WRITE was developed and evaluated by De La Paz and Graham (2002) to support students' competency test writing.

Revision Checklist

Directions: Read each item. Place a checkmark in the box next to each statement that describes the paper as it is written now, and an "x" in the box next to each statement where changes may be needed.

Ideas and Development

☐ Addresses the topic by answering all parts of the writing prompt.

☐ Good development, including many elaborated and extended details.

☐ Details/examples are presented in a way that helps the reader understand.

☐ Ideas are clearly written and well illustrated.

☐ The paper is interesting to read.

Organization and Coherence

☐ Topic is clear.

☐ Writer stays on topic.

☐ Paper is organized and flows smoothly from one idea to the next.

☐ Paper's introduction, body paragraphs, and conclusion are clear.

☐ Transitions are used to link sentences or paragraphs.

Vocabulary

☐ Words selected are appropriate, specific, and varied.

☐ Synonyms are used appropriately.

Sentence Structure, Grammar, and Usage

☐ Different kinds of sentences are used.

☐ The paper is easy to read and has few (or no) grammar or word usage errors.

FIGURE 3.3. PLAN & WRITE revision checklist. Based on Harris, Graham, Mason, and Friedlander (2008).

TABLE 3.3. Guidelines for Teaching Students to Work in Pairs

Model	Appropriate feedback with the sample papers
Explain	The relationship between goal setting and receiving and using feedback: writer selects goals; reader gives feedback; writer uses feedback for revision, and writer sets new goals.
Emphasize	Revision is a process that can be done while and after composing. Revising is about making improvement in ideas!
Establish procedures and rules	• Establish pairs, write names on revision checklist (writer/reader) • Pairs share goals and exchange papers • Students read their partner's essay: o No marks on the original essay o Use quiet voices to talk about the paper o Make a minimum of two positive comments o Make a minimum of two suggestions o Include specific ideas and questions o Exchange revision checklists o Ask questions o Work independently to make changes o Ask the teacher for help if needed o Set new goals
Provide practice	Give students time to independently practice planning and revising papers.

Note. Based on Harris, Graham, Mason, & Friedlander (2008).

through relative to essay development. An additional 20% of students provided a complete outline but had some level of redundancy or missing elements.

De La Paz (1999) also compared writing of seventh- and eighth-grade students with LD to low-, average-, and high-achieving writers (12 to 14 years). Results indicated mean scores more than doubled between baseline and post-instruction across the three measures (essay quality, length, and number of essay elements written) and across all four groups of learners. Length of essays improved across all groups with the number of words written ranging from mean (M) = 70.6 [standard deviation (SD): 20.0] to M = 108.8 (40.7) at baseline, to post-instruction range of M = 176.6 (31.9) to M = 220.9 (18). The number of essay elements ranged from M = 8.3 (2.2) to M = 13.0 (3.0) elements at baseline to M = 23.0 (4.5) to M = 28.7 (1.7) at post-instruction. Finally, quality measures on an 8-point scale from 0 (lowest score) to 7 (highest score) doubled, with baseline ranging from M = 1.9 (0.4) to M = 2.7 (0.8), and post-instruction ranging M = 4.7 (0.8) to M = 5.8 (0.4). An important finding from this research was the universal benefit of the PLAN & WRITE strategy for all students in the classroom.

Persuasive Writing

The Common Core State Standards (National Governors Association Center for Best Practices and Council of Chief State School Officers, 2013) note that for persuasive writing, students should be able to (1) introduce and acknowledge claims, (2) identify opposing claims, (3) organize reasons and evidence logically, and (4) write a concluding statement that supports the argument presented. One recently evaluated approach combined well-validated SRSD for the POW (**P**ick my idea, **Orga**nize my notes, **W**rite and say more) + TREE (**T**opic sentence, **R**easons—three or more, **E**xplanations—one for each reason, and **E**nding—wrap it up right) strategy (Harris et al., 2008) with a new revision strategy, LEAF (**L**isten as the author reads, **E**xplain what you like best, **A**sk evaluation questions, **F**inalize your comments) (Mong Cramer, & Mason, 2014). LEAF's structured format guides peers through the process of providing meaningful feedback during planning, before students write a first draft. Peers evaluate each other's persuasive plans for inconsistencies or missing information. Peers also support each other by brainstorming additional ideas to address missing critical components or incomplete information.

Following the procedures for effective SRSD instruction, students receive POW + TREE for persuasive writing instruction first. The first LEAF lesson focuses on establishing prior experience by giving and receiving feedback and activating prior knowledge about how the feedback students have received in the past made them feel. The teacher leads discussion of the social dynamics of peer feedback and introduces the terms *specific, constructive*, and *appropriate* as guidelines for meaningful feedback. The teacher and students evaluate and analyze teacher-prepared examples and nonexamples of effective feedback. The teacher uses the LEAF Mnemonic Chart (Figure 3.4) to explain the reciprocal nature of POW + TREE and LEAF, and illustrates how each strategy supports students so that they can become better editors.

After discussing the strategy, the teacher explicitly models a peer-revision conference using the LEAF Peer Revision Guide (see Figures 3.5a and 3.5b). This graphic organizer supports evaluation and discussion between editor and author, prompting evaluation and critique of critical components of a persuasive response. The teacher and students discuss feedback from a variety of perspectives including identifying (1) the nonvocalized private thoughts the editor should not share and (2) the types of useful, corrective feedback. It is important for peers to understand that praise without suggestions for improvement (e.g., "This is really good!") does not help the author improve writing. Equally important, feedback that is critical, sarcastic, embarrassing, or demeaning discourages the author and may limit new idea exploration. A good editor presents a balance of praise and critique, and offers both with a high level of specificity. For example, rather than saying, "This reason is good, but I don't like the second reason," on the topic of whether students should have homework on weekends, editors could say, "Your reason, 'because that's when families do things together,' is a really good reason because most teachers like to do things with their families on weekends, too. The reason, 'because we're sick of school by the end of the week,' might not be very persuasive to a teacher. It sounds like you don't like what they teach and it might make them feel bad. Instead, you could say that you need rest at the end of the week. I think teachers get tired, too, and they might understand that reason better."

POW + TREE
with
LEAF Revision

POW + TREE

P Pick my idea

O Organize my notes

W Write and say more

TOPIC Sentence
Tell what you believe.

REASONS—3 or More
Why do I believe this?
Will my readers believe this?
Do I have a counter reason?
Does it change my belief?

EXPLAIN Reasons
Say more about each reason.

ENDING
Wrap it up right!

LEAF

Listen
- Take turns listening to each other read your planners.

Explain what you liked best.
- Which reasons are strongest?
- What makes them good reasons?

Ask yourself evaluation questions based on your partner's planner and record your thoughts below.
- Parts?
  Is the author's planner complete?
- Is it logical?
  Who is the author trying to persuade? What could the author add to make it more persuasive?
- Details?
  Where could the author add more details?
  Do you have any suggestions?
- Clarity?
  Is there any part that is hard to understand?
  Could something be clearer?

Finalize your comments.
- Discuss questions and suggestions with the author.
- Return planner to the author.

FIGURE 3.4. LEAF mnemonic chart.

LEAF Peer Revision Guide

Author _____   Essay Topic _____

Editor _____   Date _____

Good feedback is specific—constructive—appropriate

_____ **Listen**   Take turns listening to each other reading your planners.

_____ **Explain** what you liked best.

_____ **Ask yourself** evaluation questions about your partner's plan. Record your thoughts.

_____ **Finalize** your comments. Discuss questions and suggestions with the author.

Return the planner and your revision guide to the author.

Which reasons are strongest, and what makes them good reasons?

_____

_____

_____

_____

_____

_____

_____

_____

Parts? Is the author's planner complete? TOPIC _____

R1 _____   E1 _____

R2 _____   E2 _____

R3 _____   E3 _____

Counter _____

Refute _____

Ending _____   Extra? _____

FIGURE 3.5a. LEAF Peer Revision Guide (Side A).

Who is the author trying to persuade? _____

What could the author do to make it more persuasive? _____

_____

_____

_____

Is it logical? Yes No If no, why is it not logical? _____

_____

_____

_____

Details? Where could the author add more details? _____

_____

_____

_____

_____

Do you have any suggestions? _____

_____

_____

_____

_____

Clarity. Is there anything that is hard to understand? Could something be clearer?

_____

_____

_____

_____

_____

_____

_____

_____

_____

_____

_____

Discuss your questions and suggestions with the author.

FIGURE 3.5b. LEAF Peer Revision Guide (Side B).

After observing the teacher modeling a LEAF peer conference, students write supportive revision self-statements to guide their interactions while working as editors. The teacher and students discuss the vocabulary listed on the revision guide (*strongest, persuade, convinced, logical, support, clarity, specific, constructive*, and *appropriate*), and then practice editorial skills.

Next, students and the teacher collaboratively complete a mock revision conference using a LEAF Revision Guide based on a sample plan. After collaborative practice, students practice with their partner using one of their own plans. Editors are encouraged to look for opportunities to make their partner's plans even better while teachers monitor conferences closely for appropriate interaction. Each conference begins with the author reading and describing the plan aloud and the editor responding with a positive statement explaining what they liked best and noting the reason they felt was strongest. Editors then work independently to evaluate and diagnose their partner's work. Upon completion of evaluation, authors and editors meet together for a summative conference where the editor shares suggestions for revisions. Authors consider the feedback and make changes they believe would improve their final draft. To preserve individual choice, the editor's comments are noted to be suggestions, not mandates. The author has final control of content.

Preliminary research on LEAF suggests that students with EBD can provide and use effective feedback when working with peers (Mong Cramer & Mason, in press). Four pairs of students in sixth through eighth grade participated in a single subject study that examined the effects of SRSD for POW + TREE with LEAF for persuasive writing. Data were collected across phases related to the completed draft (holistic quality on an 8-point scale, length, and number of critical elements); the quality and type of feedback; and the implementation of feedback. Holistic quality was the most informative measure of the final product in terms of evaluating effectiveness. Scores increased between baseline and post-instruction for all eight participants. Baseline quality scores ranged from $M = 2.4$ (0.89) to $M = 4.4$ (0.89). Following instruction in POW + TREE, quality scores ranged from $M = 3.3$ (4.16) to $M = 8.0$ (0), with three of the eight students at the ceiling of 8. Following instruction in LEAF, quality scores ranged from $M = 6.0$ (1.73) to $M = 8.0$ (0), with an additional student reaching the ceiling. The three highest-performing students who had reached the ceiling of 8 after POW + TREE instruction remained at ceiling. For students who had not yet reached mastery, however, the addition of LEAF stabilized their writing quality. Results suggested positive benefits on the quality of writing for struggling writers.

In addition to the effect of SRSD for POW + TREE and LEAF on student performance, the recommendations given by student editors and the use of those recommendations by the authors in the completed drafts were examined (Mong Cramer & Mason, 2014). Feedback was evaluated using a 3-point scale (no benefit, moderate benefit, substantial benefit) and implemented recommendations were counted. Of the 91 recommendations made, 13 were rated as no benefit, 38 were rated as moderate benefit, and 40 were rated as substantial benefit. Examination of the use of feedback found that most participants used the recommendations they received, whether it was beneficial or not. Nine of the 13 "no benefit" recommendations were used, perhaps indicating that additional research is needed for critiquing the quality of feedback. Of the "moderate benefit" recommendations, 36 of the 38 were implemented, and 38 of the 40 recommendations rated as "substantial benefit" were incorporated into completed drafts. While further study of SRSD for POW + TREE and LEAF is needed to test the efficacy of the approach, and further development of critical analysis of feedback is warranted, these preliminary results are promising.

Peer-Assisted Strategies to Support Revising

Common Core State Standards (National Governors Association Center for Best Practices and Council of Chief State School Officers, 2013) initiatives state that students develop and strengthen writing for a specific purpose and audience by revising, editing, rewriting, or trying a new approach. Two peer-assisted revising strategies, Peer Revising Strategy (MacArthur, et al., 1991a; MacArthur et al., 1995; Stoddard & MacArthur, 1993)[2] and Compare, Diagnose, and Operate (CDO; Scardamalia & Bereiter, 1983), have been taught and evaluated within the SRSD instructional framework. (See Harris et al., 2008, for Peer Revising Strategy and CDO lessons and instructional materials.)

Peer Revising Strategy

The Peer Revising Strategy is a two-part peer-assisted strategy for revising and proofreading. Instructional materials include the Peer Revising Strategy Checklist and Ask Your Partner sheet (see Figure 3.6), the proofreading checklist, and paper for writing notes. In initial lessons, the teacher describes the benefits of revising and proofreading and models ways of using strategies. For the first peer-revision phase, students read aloud and discuss their peer partners' papers. The partner (reader) identifies strengths and provides constructive feedback about specific aspects such as places where more detail would be helpful or where the text is unclear. The peer partner (author) then writes notes for clarification and elaboration. For the second phase of the strategy, proofreading, student partners focus on discussing changes for mechanical errors. The peer partners take turns serving as reader and author. The teacher carefully monitors the partners' feedback quality and time spent discussing revisions so that each author has an equivalent opportunity to write a better paper. Authors write final essays based on their partners' recommendations.

MacArthur et al. (1991a) examined the pre- and post-instruction narrative writing responses of 29 students with LD between fourth and sixth grade in a self-

---

[2]The Peer Revising Strategies were developed by MacArthur and colleagues and evaluated with computer-written essays.

Ask Your Partner

PARTS?

Does it have a good beginning, middle, or ending?

ORDER?

Does the paper follow a logical sequence?

DETAILS?

Where can more details be added?

CLARITY?

Is there any part that is hard to understand?

The Peer Revising Strategy Checklist

Part 1. Revising	Notes	Part 2. Proofreading
Listen and READ ____		CHECK your paper ____ and correct errors
TELL what the paper ____ is about		EXCHANGE papers and check for errors in:
Tell what you like best ____		SENTENCES ____
READ and make notes ____		CAPITALS ____
Is everything CLEAR? ____		PUNCTUATION ____
Can any DETAILS ____ be added?		SPELLING ____
DISCUSS your ____ suggestions with the author		DISCUSS corrections

FIGURE 3.6. Peer Revising Strategy and Checklist. Based on Harris, Graham, Mason, and Friedlander (2008).

contained suburban classroom. Assessed holistically based on an 8-point scale, writing was examined through a wide-angle lens of multiple factors such as content, organization, and style, without special emphasis on any one aspect. MacArthur and colleagues reported that when peer revision was applied to the C-SPACE narrative strategy (see Harris et al., 2008), holistic scores nearly doubled from $M = 2.77$ (1.77) at baseline to 4.27 (1.25) following instruction.

To evaluate the effect of meaningful feedback, macro- and micro-level changes made by the students were also examined (MacArthur et al., 1991a). At the macro level, the quality of changes made between drafts was reported on a 4-point rational number scale (−2 to +2), the sign of the number indicating a positive or negative influence on quality. At pretest, the changes made between drafts had a negligible effect on quality. Following instruction the changes between drafts significantly improved the holistic quality of the written response $t(12) = 2.21$, $p = .024$. At the micro level, changes were counted and their impact assessed. Substantive changes altered content, while surface-level changes addressed mechanical corrections. Students in the peer revision condition made significantly more changes at posttest (pretest $M = 0.39$, posttest $M = 2.39$). Comparing individual and peer-revision groups, students working in peer-revision groups made significantly more substantive changes (peer revision $M = 2.39$, individual $M = 1.23$). There was no significant difference between pre- and posttest nonsurface revisions when students were working individually.

MacArthur et al. (1991a) also categorized changes in two ways: (1) changes that do or do not alter meaning and (2) changes that improve or do not improve quality. The majority of both substantive changes (pretest 75%; posttest 81%) and surface-level changes (pretest 63%; posttest 74%) improved the quality of the essays. Similar percentages were reported for the changes that affected meaning. These findings indicate that writers with LD who receive instruction in peer-assisted revision may make higher-quality changes that improve the overall quality of their narrative essays. Results of the MacArthur et al. (1991a, 1991b) and Mong Cramer and Mason (2014) studies indicate that to maximize the effectiveness of peer revision, teachers should provide peer-assisted revision instruction in how to identify problems and how to provide meaningful feedback. This instruction assists student editors in giving more meaningful, substantive feedback and supports writers in using the feedback received from their editors.

The CDO Strategy

The CDO strategy (Compare, Diagnose, Operate) assists students in managing revision component processes at the sentence level. *Compare* involves identifying the needed revision by first reading the sentence. In *diagnose*, writers identify potential problems, and in *operate*, revision is specified and executed (Graham & Harris, 2005). This framework guides the revision process to coordinate individual elements in the student's writing. Students can use the CDO strategy to independently revise their own writing or work with peers. Procedures for teaching CDO peer-assisted revision are similar to those for other SRSD peer-assisted approaches. The teacher builds background knowledge for working with peers; explicitly describes the purpose and benefit of the strategy; models while thinking aloud through the strategy steps with all instructional materials; and supports student-peer implementation for independent use of the strategy. Given the number of CDO steps, writers may require extra practice to reach memorization. Until the strategy is memorized, student pairs select and use the diagnose cards (e.g., is the sentence believable, understandable, useful, and interesting) and operate cards (e.g., rewrite, change wording, add or delete) to guide the revision process. Instructional materials include the CDO mnemonic chart, CDO Revising Strategy directions (see Figure 3.7), CDO memorization flash cards, CDO sentence diagnose cards (see Figure 3.8), and CDO operate cards (see Figure 3.9).

The effectiveness of CDO was examined in a study involving 90 students in the fourth, sixth, and eighth grades (Scardamalia & Bereiter, 1983). Students practiced the CDO strategy in one of two conditions: (1) at the sentence level, pausing after writing each sentence to evaluate, or (2) following completion of a full

---

CDO Revising Strategy

Step 1. Compare: Read the sentence.

Step 2. Diagnose: Select the best evaluation cards.
   This doesn't sound right.
   This is not what I meant to say.
   The essay is not in the right order.
   People may not understand what I wrote.
   I am getting away from my main point.
   This is a weak or incomplete idea.
   The problem is _____.

Step 3. Operate: Select a tactic card.
   Add: Add examples, information, details, etc.
   Leave this part out: Delete a part (word, phrase, sentence, etc.).
   Rewrite: Say it (word, phrase, sentence, etc.) in a different way.
   Change the wording: Rearrange information (word, phrase, sentence, etc.).

Step 4. Operate: Make your revision.

FIGURE 3.7. CDO Revising Strategy directions. Based on Harris, Graham, Mason, and Friedlander (2008).

Does this sound right?	Will my reader believe or understand this?
Is this what I meant to say?	Is this sentence useful?
Will my reader be interested in this?	This sentence is good!

FIGURE 3.8. CDO sentence diagnose cards. Based on Harris, Graham, Mason, and Friedlander (2008).

ADD	DELETE
REWRITE	CHANGE

FIGURE 3.9. CDO operate cards. Based on Harris, Graham, Mason, and Friedlander (2008).

draft. Both groups produced final responses of similar persuasive quality and made changes that were beneficial to the topic, with positive changes outnumbering neutral changes. However, the positive changes had little effect on the holistic quality of the final piece. The nature of the changes was generally related to small portions of text, and participants tended to avoid more complex issues of cogency with the theme.

In addition to scoring students' writing improvement, evaluation statements for each sentence were compared to the evaluation statement selected by the author. Results indicated that statements were either a direct match or a valid alternative statement; fewer than 10% of fourth graders, 5% of sixth graders, and no eighth graders made choices judged as completely inappropriate. In addition, researchers evaluated the remedial tactics selected by students and found little variation by age or condition with several notable exceptions. While fourth graders chose to leave the sentence "as is" more frequently than sixth and eighth graders, there was no significant difference in the frequency of the choice to leave the sentence "as is" across all three grades. There was, however, some variation between treatment groups surrounding the remediation tactic, calling for further explanation or the addition of an example. In the postdraft condition, 6–8% of the total tactical choices involved adding further information to remediate a problem. In the sentence-by-sentence evaluation group, 18–20% of the total tactical choices involved adding more information.

The ultimate application of any revision strategy is the ability to execute the correction effectively. In evaluating students' execution, Scardamalia and Bereiter (1983) noted that students demonstrated relative competence in evaluating, diagnosing, and planning for revision. However, the extent to which the solution is worse than the original for some students may indicate a language deficit. The results of this early study suggest evidence of executive function limitations and cognitive overload related to the complexity of content generation and the demands of written expression (see Chapter 1 for a discussion of executive function strategies). In later research, these complex cognitive functions were noted to be supported (e.g., De La Paz, 1999; MacArthur et al., 1995; Mong Cramer & Mason, 2014) when teachers used explicit instruction for teaching peer revision.

Supporting Generalization and Maintenance

Students with disabilities generally do not transfer strategies across classrooms, writing tasks, and genres without teacher-guided support (Graham & Harris, 2005). In addition, students with disabilities often do not maintain learned strategies. When transferring a peer-assisted strategy, it is important that teachers consider revisiting SRSD stages of instruction and self-regulation procedures. For example, if the Peer Revising Strategy is taught for opinion papers written with the POW + TREE strategy, modeling and providing guided practice may be needed to teach students to transfer the revising strategy to a narrative writing strategy. Goals and procedures for self-monitoring and self-instructions may also need modifications to meet the new task. Additionally, teacher-supported booster sessions are recommended to support student maintenance in using the strategies over time. As previously noted, the teacher should revisit any of the SRSD instructional stages as needed!

Peers can be supportive about reminding each other to use learned strategies over time and across settings. Based on findings in two studies (Graham, Harris & Mason, 2005), researchers recommend that partners be established for helping with transfer and generalization of the strategies beginning in the second phase of instruction, *"discuss it,"* during which teachers help students to consider other settings and academic tasks where the strategy might be useful. Goals can be established for (1) transferring to other tasks such as writing homework or journaling, and (2) helping "each other by pointing out situations when they might transfer" (Harris et al., 2008, p. 162). In the beginning of each lesson, the teacher can ask the student pairs to describe when they transferred and how they helped their partner. Efforts made to transfer and help each other are recorded (see Figure 3.10 for transfer sheet for the POW + TREE strategy) and positive reinforcement for effort is provided.

CONCLUSIONS AND FUTURE DIRECTIONS

Continued work focused on the development of effective peer-mediated writing strategies will benefit both teachers and students. As budgets for education shrink and class sizes increase, the need to increase opportunities for students to provide each other with feedback, and ultimately incorporate feedback into their self-regulated work, becomes increasingly important. Peer-mediated learning can reduce teacher demands so that teachers can focus expertise and give attention where it is most needed. Peers working in cooperative groups can assist with scaffolded instruction by supporting one another with strategy acquisition, memorization, and application (Reid, Lienemann, & Hagaman, 2013). In writing, peers can support one another with idea generation and planning (De La Paz, 1999; Mong Cramer & Mason, 2014) and revising (MacArthur, et al., 1991a, 1991b; MacArthur et al., 1995; Stoddard & MacArthur, 1993; Scardamalia & Bereiter, 1983.)

Technology for written language is changing rapidly and profoundly influencing our modes of communication. In the future, it is possible that writing and social conversation will become as outdated as the handwritten letter; however, the processes underlying the act of writing—generating ideas, planning and organizing ideas into a rational stream of thought, and revising and editing—will continue. Given the complexity of these writing processes, peer-assisted learning strategies will be even more important for supporting student learning.

POW + TREE

I Transferred My Strategy to . . .	I Helped My Partner to . . .

FIGURE 3.10. POW + TREE peer partner and transfer sheet. Based on Harris, Graham, Mason, and Friedlander (2008).

REFERENCES

Association for Supervision and Curriculum Development. (2002). *Teaching students with learning disabilities: Using learning strategies.* Retrieved from *http://shop.ascd.org/Default. aspx?TabID=55&ProductId=1553.*

Bartlett, E. J. (1982). *Learning to revise: Some component processes.* New York: Academic Press.

Beach, R., & Friedrich, T. (2006). Response to writing. In C. A. MacArthur, S. Graham, & J. Fitzgerald (Eds.), *Handbook of writing research* (pp. 222–234). New York: Guilford Press.

Dahl, K., & Farnan, N. (1998). *Children's writing: Perspectives from research.* Newark, DE: International Reading Association.

De La Paz, S. (1999). Self-regulated strategy instruction in regular education settings: Improving outcomes for students with and without learning disabilities. *Learning Disabilities Research and Practice, 14,* 92–106.

De La Paz, S., & Graham, S. (2002). Explicitly teaching strategies, skills, and knowledge: Writing instruction in middle school classrooms. *Journal of Educational Psychology, 94,* 687–698.

Dipardo, A., & Freedman, S. (1988). Peer response groups in writing classroom: Theoretic foundations and new directions. *Review of Educational Research, 58,* 119–149.

Fitzgerald, J. (1987). Research on revision in writing. *Review of Educational Research, 57,* 481–506.

Fitzgerald, J., & Stamm, C. (1990). Effects of group conferences on first graders' revision in writing. *Written Communication, 7,* 96–135.

Flower, L. S., & Hayes, J. R. (1980). Identifying the organization of writing processes. In L. W. Gregg & E. R. Steinberg (Eds.), *Cognitive processes in writing* (pp. 31–50). Hillsdale, NJ: Erlbaum.

Flower, L., Hayes, J., Carey, L., Schriver, K., & Stratman, J. (1986). Detection, diagnosis, and the strategies of revision. *College Composition and Communication, 37,* 16–55.

Graham, S. (1990). The role of production factors in learning disabled students' compositions. *Journal of Educational Psychology, 82,* 781–791.

Graham, S. (1997). Executive control in the revising of students with learning and writing difficulties. *Journal of Educational Psychology, 89,* 223–234.

Graham, S., & Harris, K. R. (2005). *Writing better: Effective strategies for teaching students with learning difficulties.* Baltimore, MD: Brookes.

Graham, S., & Harris, K. (2007). Best practices in teaching planning. In S. Graham, C. MacArthur, & J. Fitzgerald (Eds.), *Best practices in writing instruction* (pp. 119–140). New York: Guilford Press.

Graham, S., & Harris, K. R. (2013). Common Core State Standards, writing, and students with LD: Recommendations. *Learning Disabilities Research and Practice, 28,* 28–37.

Graham, S., Harris, K. R., & Mason, L. H. (2005). Improving the writing performance, knowledge, and self-efficacy of struggling young writers: The effects of self-regulated strategy development. *Contemporary Educational Psychology, 30,* 207–241.

Graham, S., & Perin, D. (2007a). A meta-analysis of writing instruction for adolescent students. *Journal of Educational Psychology, 99,* 445–476.

Graham, S., & Perin, D. (2007b). *Writing next: Effective strategies to improve writing of adolescents in middle and high schools—A report to Carnegie Corporation of New York.* Washington, DC: Alliance for Excellent Education.

Harris, K. R., & Graham, S. (1985). Improving learning disabled students' composition skills: Self-control strategy training. *Learning Disability Quarterly, 8,* 27–36.

Harris, K. R., & Graham, S. (2009). Self-regulated strategy development in writing: Premises, evolution, and the future. *British Journal of Educational Psychology* (Monograph series), *6,* 113–135.

Harris, K. R., Graham, S., Brindle, M., & Sandmel, K. (2009). Metacognition and children's writing. In D. Hacker, J. Dunlosky, & A. Graesser (Eds.), *Handbook of metacognition in education* (pp. 131–153). Mahwah, NJ: Erlbaum.

Harris, K. R., Graham, S., MacArthur, C., Reid, R., & Mason, L. H. (2011). Self-regulated learning processes and children's writing. In B. Zimmerman & D. Schunk (Eds.), *Handbook of self-regulation of learning and performance* (pp. 187–201). Danvers, MA: Routledge.

Harris, K. R., Graham, S., & Mason, L. H. (2006). Self-regulated strategy development for 2nd-grade students who struggle with writing. *American Educational Research Journal, 43*, 295–340.

Harris, K. R., Graham, S., Mason, L., & Friedlander, B. (2008). *Powerful writing strategies for all students.* Baltimore, MD: Brookes.

Lane, K. L. (2004). Academic instruction and tutoring interventions for students with emotional and behavioral disorders: 1990 to the present. In R. B. Rutherford, Jr., M. M. Quinn, & S. R. Mathur (Eds.), *Handbook of research in emotional and behavioral disorders* (pp. 462–486). New York: Guilford Press.

MacArthur, C. A. (2013). Best practices in teaching evaluation and revision. In S. Graham, C. MacArthur, & J. Fitzgerald (Eds.), *Best practices in writing instruction* (2nd ed., pp. 215–238). New York: Guilford Press.

MacArthur, C. A., & Graham, S. (1987). LD students composing under three methods of text production: Handwriting, word processing, and dictation. *Journal of Special Education, 21*, 22–42.

MacArthur, C. A., Graham, S., & Harris, K. R. (2004). Insights from instructional research on revision with struggling writers. In L. Allal, L. Chanquoy, & P. Largy (Eds.), *Revision: Cognitive and instructional processes* (pp. 125–137). Boston: Kluwer Academic.

MacArthur, C., Graham, S., Schwartz, S., & Shafer, W. (1995). Evaluation of a writing instruction model that integrated a process approach, strategy instruction, and word processing. *Learning Disability Quarterly, 18*, 278–291.

MacArthur, C., & Philippakos, Z. (2011). Instruction in a strategy for compare-contrast writing. *Exceptional Children, 76*, 438–456.

MacArthur, C., Schwartz, S., & Graham, S. (1991a). Effects of a reciprocal peer revision strategy in special education classrooms. *Learning Disabilities Research and Practice, 6*, 201–210.

MacArthur, C. A., Schwartz, S. S., & Graham, S. (1991b). A model for writing instruction: Integrating word-processing and strategy instruction into a process approach to writing. *Learning Disabilities Research and Practice, 6*, 230–236.

Mason, L. H., Harris, K. R., & Graham, S. (2011). Self-Regulated strategy development for students with writing difficulties. *Theory into Practice, 50*, 20–27.

Mason, L. H., Kubina, R. M., Valasa, L. L., & Cramer, A. M. (2010). Evaluating effective writing instruction for adolescent students in an emotional and behavioral support setting. *Behavioral Disorders, 35*, 140–156.

Mason, L. H., Reid, R., & Hagaman, J. (2012). *Building comprehension in adolescents: Powerful strategies for improving reading and writing in content areas.* Baltimore, MD: Brookes.

Miller, M. (2013). Communication style in the multi-generational workplace. Retrieved November 30, 2013, from *www.business2community.com/communications/communication-style-multi-generational-workplace-0693986#!oKTKy*.

Mong Cramer, A., & Mason, L. H. (2014). The effects of strategy instruction for writing and revising persuasive quick writes for middle school students with emotional behavioral disorders. *Behavioral Disorders, 40*, 37–51.

Morris Kindzierski, C. M. (2009). "I like it the way it is!": Peer-revision writing strategies for students with emotional behavioral disorders. *Preventing School Failure, 54*, 51–59.

National Commission on Writing (2004). Writing: A ticket to work . . . or a ticket out: A survey of business leaders. Retrieved February 6, 2015, from *www.collegeboard.com/prod_downloads/writingcom/writing-ticket-to-work.pdf*.

National Governors Association Center for Best Practices & Council of Chief State School Offi-cers. (2013). *Common Core State Standards.* Washington, DC: Author.

Patthey-Chavez, G. G., & Ferris, D. (1997). Writing conferences and the weaving of multi-voiced texts in college composition. *Research in the Teaching of English, 31,* 51–90.

Reid, R., Lienemann, T. O., & Hagaman, J. L. (2013). *Strategy instruction for students with learning disabilities* (2nd ed.). New York: Guilford Press.

Scardamalia, M., & Bereiter, C. (1983). The development of evaluative, diagnostic, and remedial capabilities in children's composing. In M. Martlew (Ed.), *The psychology of written language: A developmental approach* (pp. 67–95). London: Wiley.

Scardamalia, M., & Bereiter, C. (1987). Knowledge telling and knowledge transforming in writ-ten composition. In S. Rosenberg (Ed.), *Advances in applied psycholinguistics* (Vol. 2, pp. 142–175). New York: Cambridge University Press.

Stoddard, B., & MacArthur, C. A. (1993). A peer editor strategy: Guiding learning-disabled stu-dents in response and revision. *Research in the Teaching of English, 27,* 76–103.

Thomas, C. C., Englert, C. S., & Gregg, S. (1987). An analysis of errors and strategies in the expository writing of learning disabled students. *Remedial and Special Education, 8,* 21–30.

Troia, G. (2006). Writing instruction for students with learning disabilities. In C. MacArthur, S. Graham, & J. Fitzgerald (Eds.), *Handbook of writing research* (pp. 324–336). New York: Guilford Press.

U.S. Department of Education, Institute of Education Sciences, National Center for Education Statistics. (2011). *2011 Writing Framework for the National Assessment of Educational Progress.* Washington, DC: U.S. Government Printing Office.

Wong, B. Y. L., Butler, D. L., Ficzere, S. A., & Kuperis, S. (1997). Teaching adolescents with learn-ing disabilities and low achievers to plan, write, and revise compare-and-contrast essays. *Learning Disabilities Research and Practice, 12,* 2–15.

CHAPTER 4

Using Collaborative Strategic Reading to Promote Student Discourse

Karla Scornavacco, Brooke Moore, Alison Boardman,
Cristin Jensen Lasser, Pamela Buckley, and Janette K. Klingner

"Would you rather read silently and write a summary by yourself," asked Ms. Drake, a seventh-grade teacher in a high-poverty urban middle school, "or would you rather do it with a group of people, and get to talk about it?" Ms. Drake posed this question during an end-of-year interview about her use of the multicomponent reading instructional model called collaborative strategic reading (CSR). The question was a rhetorical one, meant to make a point about reasons she would continue using CSR in her classroom. As many educators like Ms. Drake know, it takes more than just assigning students to groups and handing them a reading to ensure they learn important content, practice key reading skills, and ponder essential questions of a unit. In this chapter, we provide a description of CSR and examples to help teachers increase opportunities for students to discuss what they are reading in class within small groups to promote comprehension.

CSR is an instructional model that supports students in developing metacognitive awareness and learning strategies for enhanced reading comprehension (Klingner, Vaughn, Boardman, & Swanson, 2012; Klingner, Vaughn, & Schumm, 1998). Students learn to use multiple reading strategies embedded within a routine in heterogeneous, collaborative groups that include opportunities for peer discussion of text—before, during, and after reading (see Appendix 4.1). The general structure of this routine includes:

- Brainstorming (i.e., connecting with prior knowledge), and setting a purpose for reading (**Preview**).
- Monitoring understanding and taking steps to figure out unknown words or confusing concepts (**Click and Clunk**).
- Determining the main idea of designated sections of texts (**Get the Gist**).
- Generating questions and reviewing key ideas and information after reading (**Wrap-Up**).

As a multicomponent model, CSR attends to the needs of a wide variety of learners and includes explicit supports for English language learners (ELLs), students with learning disabilities (LD), and struggling readers. Moreover, CSR can strengthen students' ability to learn with, and from, each other when reading complex texts.

This chapter begins with an overview of the importance of attending to peer discourse in classrooms to promote reading comprehension. Next, the chapter offers a description of CSR, including an explanation of the ways in which the collaborative structure of CSR guides the social construction of knowledge (Vygotsky, 1978) and provides opportunities for academic language development and content learning (August & Shanahan, 2006; Genesee, Lindholm-Leary, Saunders, & Christian, 2005). We also describe studies evaluating CSR's positive outcomes for students with learning disabilities and struggling readers, average and high-achieving students, and ELLs in multiple settings and across grade levels. To support teachers in facilitating peer learning in CSR classrooms, we then turn our attention to the classroom materials and techniques used by CSR teachers to promote high-quality discussions and group collaboration among peers. Throughout the chapter, we provide examples of student discourse in real classrooms so that we can continue to learn from the conversations of students.

PROMOTING READING COMPREHENSION WITH PEER DISCOURSE

Speech develops in humans around the need to communicate our experiences to others (Rogoff, 2003; Vygotsky, 1978). As we communicate and engage in discourse, concepts and ideas dynamically emerge and are shared with others in order to engage in social activities (Engeström & Sannino, 2010; Lave & Wenger, 1991). Talking about texts in school enables students to build on each other's ideas and make sense of what they are reading. Take, for instance, an exchange within a group of four students in a sixth-grade science classroom studying the transmission of diseases. Students were reading an article about germs and illnesses. At the end of a section of the text, student-led groups stopped to write on their own and then talked about the main idea, or "gist," as it is called in CSR, of what they had just read:

BRIAN: OK, I put that there are four types of germs and they are bacteria, viruses, fungi, and protozoa.

CARLA: I put germs are so tiny that they cannot be seen and sneak into your body.

ANGEL: I put that germs are living organisms that invade your body.

DIEGO: There are four types of germs that could affect your body. (Classroom observation, April 30, 2013)

After sharing each gist, students then offered one another feedback. For example, Brian said to Diego, "You could . . . add . . . more detail. So that's like, one, just putting one thing." Then Angel followed up by saying, "Like, you could put like how they invade your body." Within a few minutes all four students had written, discussed, and then revised their gist statements to reflect a more thorough understanding of the entire section of the text. The concept of communicable disease was developed and shared among the group of students. Knowledge and thinking become distributed among students as they come together to talk through and accomplish the task of comprehending a text (Cole & Engeström, 1993; Lave & Wenger, 1991).

Learning in individuals involves a zone of proximal development, which Vygotsky (1978) described as "the distance between the actual developmental level as determined by independent problem solving and the level of potential development as determined through problem solving under adult guidance or *in collaboration with capable peers*" (p. 86, emphasis added). CSR is a structured reading comprehension model that facilitates student interactions, thereby creating opportunities for students to offer each other explanations and feedback. As described in the next sections, the routines and scaffolds of CSR provide an optimal level of support designed to facilitate student interactions in a low-pressure environment of full participation and strategy use. For diverse and exceptional learners, interactive dialogue among peers coupled with explicit feedback and support from their teacher can enhance reading comprehension (Fuchs, Fuchs, Mathes, & Lipsey, 2000; Gersten, Fuchs, Williams, & Baker, 2001; Swanson, Hoskyn, & Lee, 1999; Vaughn, Gersten, & Chard, 2000).

THE IMPORTANCE OF STRATEGY INSTRUCTION

As with comprehension strategy instruction in general, a fundamental principle of CSR is that struggling readers can learn to apply reading behaviors used by good readers and subsequently improve their ability to comprehend text (Kamil et al., 2008; Klingner et al., 2012; Paris, Wasik, & Turner, 1991; Pressley & Afflerbach, 1995). To develop conceptual knowledge and foster cognitive processes, students need strategies that they can draw from automatically to help them along in their learning (Brown, Bransford, Ferrara, & Campione, 1983). More experienced readers, for instance, automatically employ strategies when their comprehension fails; they metacognitively notice that their comprehension is faltering and apply a strategy to repair it (Pressley, Borkowski, & Schneider, 2010). However, struggling readers may not be aware that their comprehension is breaking down, and they may need more explicit instruction in reading comprehension strategy use (Berkeley, Mastropieri, & Scruggs, 2011; Edmonds et al., 2009).

Researchers have explored the use of comprehension strategies to guide students in capturing the key concepts in text: (1) plan for reading (e.g., prediction, brainstorming; Anderson & Pearson, 1984); (2) monitor their understanding while they read (e.g., summarization; Baker & Brown, 1984; Malone & Mastropieri, 1992); and (3) ensure that they comprehend what they read after reading (e.g., question generation, clarification; Collins, Brown, & Newman, 1989; Simmonds, 1992). For strong readers, making these strategies visible through instruction and practice is important to transition them into "potentially conscious" and "potentially controllable" use of these strategies (Pressley et al., 2010). Students who struggle with complex text require more support (Gajria, Jitendra, Sood, & Sacks, 2007; Gersten et al., 2001).

CSR combines these research-based reading comprehension strategies, essential for all students, by having students brainstorm before reading, monitor for understanding and determine main ideas while reading, and generate questions and review key ideas following reading (Klingner et al., 1998, 2012). Furthermore, there is a key element of student collaboration within each of these strategies as students talk with each other (and with the teacher) about the text at different points of the reading process, guided by student roles and suggested sentence starters (e.g., "Each of us wrote something about _____").

Collaborative strategies can facilitate discourse that is productive. Cohen (1994) explained that "productivity" in talk helps students develop higher levels of thinking, creates interactions that foster equity among peers, and builds prosocial skills (e.g., cooperation, reciprocity). Researchers suggest that educators develop and practice a repertoire of classroom discourse features to ensure that all students have the right and space to speak and all know how to actively listen to others (Cazden, 2001; Michaels, O'Connor, & Resnick, 2008). Certain conditions and routines are known to support students in collaborative discourse: grouping students heterogeneously, assigning roles, setting clear objectives, teaching social skills, providing them with talking prompts, and monitoring student interactions with each other (Klingner et al., 2012; Stevens & Slavin, 1995).

Benefits of Peer Discourse When Using Reading Comprehension Strategies

In a traditional teacher-centered classroom, few students get the chance to contribute to large-group discussions, leaving many students as passive recipients of the learning. When peer discourse is encouraged, more students have the opportunity to actively create knowledge for themselves and for others. "In the ideal discussion-based classroom community, students have the right to speak and the obligation to explicate their reasoning, providing warranted evidence for their claims so that others can understand and critique their arguments" (Michaels et al., 2008, p. 284). Students benefit from engaging in high-level dialogue with others in a variety of ways, each of which is related to the other.

Interpersonal Skill Development

When students engage in discourse with other students in cooperative learning groups, one outcome is the development of prosocial, interpersonal skills (Cohen, 1994). In order to complete an assigned group task or solve a problem cooperatively, students must rely on positive interdependence, holding each other accountable to complete the work (Johnson & Johnson, 1999; Slavin, 1996). Productive group work often depends on students developing social cohesion by caring about each other's contributions to the team and developing a desire for all students in the group to be successful (Slavin, Hurley, & Chamberlain, 2003).

Educators, however, must foster the development of positive interpersonal skills through tasks that require collaboration and the contribution of all students to learn something new. As Slavin (2011) notes, "When the group task is to *do* something, rather than to *learn* something, the participation of less able students may be seen as interference rather than help" (p. 8). Poole (2008), for instance, conducted a detailed interactional analysis of two heterogeneous reading groups and found that the least proficient readers in each group not only read less, but were interrupted more often than the other students. CSR attempts to counter these situations by promoting participation among *all* students in each small group. Students, for instance, have time to write down their ideas before sharing, and each group member follows prompts on role cards to encourage discussion among all students.

Motivation

Motivation is influenced by both social processes (e.g., group dynamics) and by individual processes (e.g., priorities for learning, different learning styles; Järvelä, Violet, & Järvenoja, 2010). Teachers can foster motivation during peer work by assigning group rewards based on individual learning and each student's contribution (Oxford, 1997; Slavin, 1996). Guiding students to be reflective of their contributions to the team goal supports the development of cooperative skills and fosters the motivation to learn (Gillies & Boyle, 2010; Hogan, Natasi, & Pressley. 2000).

Metacognition

When students engage in peer discourse, they restructure each other's thinking through "cognitive elaboration" (Slavin, 2011). As Cazden (2001) noted, "students will be more apt to actively struggle with new ideas—rephrasing them, arguing with them, conceptually trying them out, and verbally trying them on—when they are spoken by (less authoritative) peers than by the (more authoritative) teacher" (p. 111). Elaborating on others' ideas is a metacognitive strategy, as students are developing awareness of their own (and others') misunderstandings while simultaneously working to "fix" them up (Gillies, 2003; Stevens & Slavin, 1995). Peer work also supports self-regulated learning (Azevdeo, 2009). As Zimmerman (2008) wrote, self-regulated learners seek help from peers and "are metacognitively, motivationally and behaviorally active participants in their own learning process" (p. 167).

Equity

Finally, engaging in peer discourse while working collaboratively with others has the potential to establish equity in the classroom as it fosters deliberate democracy (Michaels et al., 2008). In their research on equity in classrooms, Cohen and Lotan (1995) drew on the idea of "expectation states theory" suggesting that social stratification exists in classrooms where the dominance of high-status students is reinforced (e.g., being called on more often, expected to know the answer) and lower-status student participation is minimized. When teachers assign students to heterogeneous groups and hold them accountable for monitoring the contribution of ideas and solutions, more students have the opportunity to share the task of learning (Kotsopoulos, 2010). This is one of the key goals of CSR.

Participation Structures for Diverse and Exceptional Learners

Placing students into heterogeneous groups also creates the opportunity for students to capitalize on a variety of interests and knowledge as expertise is distributed across the group (Cole & Engeström, 1993; Klingner & Vaughn, 1996). If students are well supported so that all group members' ideas are welcomed, their differences can be minimized, and each can contribute his or her own understanding and perspective to the group so that all can learn (Gutiérrez & Stone, 1997). As described in the following sections, the structure and resources in CSR provide students with LD access to texts so they can participate, but also have support in knowing what to do when grappling with complex texts and how to take necessary steps to strengthen comprehension. The structure and resources of CSR allow for students with LD to engage in high-level discourse with peers without disabilities. O'Connor and Jenkins (2013) noted the benefits of peer discourse in cooperative groupings if "students with LD (learning disabilities) have time and opportunity to use the language of content and instruction, and to argue through a point of view" (p. 521).

Grouping ELLs with both native English-speaking peers and other students who speak their mother tongue promotes the use of cross-linguistic conversations to make meaning of content presented in English. Additionally, Tharp (1982) suggested that ELLs benefit when teachers allot instructional time for small-group discussion. During this time, the dominant participation structure entails informal, overlapping, and voluntary speech, mutual participation among teachers and students, and co-narration (Tharp, 1982). Because ELLs participate in discussions among peers and their feedback may be received in a less threatening and consequently more receptive manner, peer discourse in small heterogeneously grouped settings also helps build oral language proficiency for ELL students.

Not only do these types of conversations mitigate the affective filter for ELL students' later participation in whole-class conversational settings, they also serve the purpose of enhancing students' metalinguistic awareness (Hayes, Rueda, & Chilton, 2009). Providing ELL students access to educational experiences through native language supports can have an empowering effect, as demonstrated in the following interaction (Klingner et al., 2012) about an excerpt from the reading passage: "The fishermen of Minamata began protesting against Chisso Corporation in 1959. They demanded compensation, and that Chisso quit dumping toxic waste."

DANIEL: What does *compensate* mean?

ALEX: I am not sure, but I know what *recompensa* means in Spanish. It means you pay back someone when you hurt them.

DANIEL: Oh, so you think they wanted money from the company?

ALEX: Yeah, that makes sense. I guess it's pretty cool to be bilingual.

Ultimately, when teachers value students' native language and combine its usage with effective professional practices, like CSR, students are successful and engaged.

COLLABORATIVE STRATEGIC READING

Origins of CSR

CSR draws on Palincsar and Brown's reciprocal teaching (1984), which focused on improving students' reading comprehension skills through the guided practice of specific reading strategies. In small groups, the students participating in reciprocal teaching engage in a text collaboratively using four assigned roles: Summarizer, Questioner, Clarifier, and Predictor (Oczkus, 2010). After reading a section of assigned text, each student completes a task, depending upon his or her role. The teacher gradually releases responsibility for dialogue about the text to the students. As in reciprocal teaching, students in CSR are introduced to, and consistently practice and use, reading comprehension strategies throughout a lesson. However, unlike reciprocal teaching, students in CSR classes engage in *all* aspects of the lesson.

Guided by their peers, who assume one of the four roles of CSR, students move through different stages of collaboration: working independently (e.g., brainstorming what they already know about a topic, writing their own main idea gist statement, writing and answering their own questions), sharing and discussing their individually developed ideas across the group (e.g., asking and answering each other's questions), and then working toward building consensus about the theme or main purpose of a text. These levels of collaboration within a CSR lesson are briefly listed in Figure 4.1. Students move between these levels of collaboration with the support of each other and the structured routine of CSR along with the guidance of their teacher as a facilitator of reading engagement and knowledge building.

Students collaborate before, during, and after the reading activities of CSR using content-related texts (e.g., textbook section, article related to the curriculum, chapter of a novel) that are divided into sections. The length of the text may vary depending on such factors as grade level, text complexity, and proficiency at using reading strategies. The final sections of this chapter illustrate ways in which students engage in the CSR strategies together and how their teachers can facilitate productive discourse about the reading.

Research on CSR

Over a period of more than 15 years, CSR has been studied using both qualitative and quantitative research designs. CSR results have demonstrated positive outcomes for all students, with benefits for struggling readers, students with disabilities, and ELLs.

To investigate the impact of CSR on student reading comprehension outcomes, three experimental design studies have been conducted in which classes of students were either randomly assigned to CSR ("treatment") or to a comparison ("business-as-usual") condition. This process of randomization is the most reliable method of creating homogeneous research groups without introducing potential biases or judgments in determining which students receive treatment. Vaughn et al. (2011) conducted an experimental design study in diverse middle school language arts and reading classes, and findings showed that CSR classes out-

---

Level 4: Connection/Consensus Building
Student group goes beyond literal comprehension of text; talk of the group connects to purpose of the lesson and/or other topics of study; students make real-world connections.

Level 3: Discussion
Student activity includes negotiations, feedback, and/or revisions based on the ideas of others in the group.

Level 2: Sharing
Student activity includes sharing ideas, but not evaluating or elaborating on those ideas.

Level 1: Independent Work

FIGURE 4.1. Levels of collaboration within a CSR lesson.

performed comparison students. Boardman, Klingner, Buckley, Annamma, and Jensen (in press) also used an experimental design to examine the impact of CSR when implemented in science and social studies classes in diverse urban middle schools, noting that the CSR students outperformed similar students in comparison classes. In a third experimental study conducted with upper elementary classrooms, Klingner, Boardman, Buckley, and Reutebuch (2014) found that students with LD who received CSR instruction in inclusive classrooms made significantly greater gains than students with LD in the comparison inclusive classrooms.

The earlier qualitative and quasi-experimental studies examined the ways in which CSR influenced the reading outcomes and content learning of diverse and exceptional learners. Klingner et al. (1998) studied CSR in diverse, inclusive fourth-grade classrooms. Results demonstrated that students in CSR classrooms made greater gains on a standardized reading comprehension measure compared with students in a comparison typical classroom condition. Yet, students in both conditions demonstrated equal proficiency in their knowledge of social studies content. In a subsequent study (Klingner & Vaughn, 2000), CSR was implemented with fifth-grade ELLs. Data included audio-recorded group discussions with analysis focusing on the input of ELLs and bilingual students. Results showed that target students demonstrated high levels of academic engagement, and students helped each other understand word meanings and make sense of their science textbook. Klingner, Vaughn, Arguelles, Hughes, and Leftwich (2004) focused on linguistically and culturally diverse inclusive fourth-grade social studies classrooms, comparing CSR classes to non-CSR classes. Students in CSR classrooms improved more on a standardized reading comprehension measure than comparison students. Relative to other subgroups of students in this study, low-achieving students made the highest gains. Taken together, these studies suggest that the collaborative reading process of CSR is helping to close the achievement gap for struggling readers.

CSR Strategies in the Classroom

This next section highlights the processes of CSR using examples from classrooms. Each of the examples derives from our partnership with an urban school district supporting an initiative to integrate CSR into all middle school science, social studies, and language arts classes. The purpose of this section is to illustrate how CSR works in the classroom. In the following sections, we offer more details about the materials and resources that the students in these examples use as cues and supports, and then describe ways in which teachers can introduce and continually refine the approaches they use to support students to engage in CSR.

Preview

A student's opportunity to learn with and from his or her peers starts with the Preview portion of the CSR lesson cycle. In a CSR preview, the students tap into their background knowledge and share something they already know about the topic of the reading. The teacher leads this portion of the lesson to support students' connections with relevant content and the purpose for reading.

In a seventh-grade science lesson about the Gulf of Mexico oil spill, for instance, Ms. White asked students to brainstorm some reasons her students might want to separate substances and how they might do that. Students wrote down their brainstorms, and then starting with the Leader, they shared what they had written:

> Juan: "Some of the reasons you'd want to separate substances is to get the bad things out of the good things like water. And you might separate them by extracting them out."
>
> Jill: "Some of the reasons why you would want to separate two substances is because it's not really good, like for example, H_2O and oil don't really fit because it can affect a whole environment."
>
> Alejandra: "Some of the reasons you might separate substances is because like when two things are bad next to each other you can get really sick from it."
>
> David: "I would like to separate substances for chemical reasons that our sea water could be defective and I would take out the oil. I would filter the water with the oil." (Classroom observation, February 2011)

The quality of the discourse during the sharing portion of the preview is typically at a more foundational, basic level. As demonstrated by the previous dialogue in Ms. White's class, students were not yet discussing, providing feedback, or evaluating each other's responses. In terms of a schema of levels of collaboration (see Figure 4.1), the students started at Level 1, working quietly and independently to generate their brainstorms, and then moved into Level 2, sharing. This process is intentional as it allows students to grow more comfortable with each other as each student has something to share (in this example above, students started discussing the topic of separating substances). During the Preview stage of CSR, students also start to build a group understanding of the text as they hear multiple ideas for activating their schema about what to think about when reading the text as a group.

The key Preview steps for a teacher to follow in a CSR lesson include:

1. Introduce the topic.
2. Prompt students to write and share responses to a brainstorm question that activates prior knowledge and is focused on the purpose of the reading.
3. If needed, preteach one to three key words or concepts that are used in the text and are important for comprehension and content learning. Teachers preteach these words with a picture or other visual, or with a quick word study (e.g., looking at prefixes, roots, suffixes). Teachers might also point out difficult words or proper nouns as appropriate.
4. State the purpose for reading.

Click and Clunk

The quality of the students' discourse deepens as students turn to one another for support in figuring out the meaning of words or concepts that impede their understanding. After reading a section of text aloud, students identify "clunks" (unknown words or phrases) and use "fix-up strategies" (see Appendix 4.3) to figure out the meaning of the clunk. In the example below, students discuss ideas about the meaning of the word *vast* identified in a textbook chapter about the rise and fall of the Islamic civilization.

> LUCY: Okay, what do you guys think *vast* means?
>
> BRIAN: Hmmm, that's a tricky one.
>
> (*All look at reading.*)
>
> BRIAN: Let's use our flipcharts.
>
> (*Three students open up their flipbooks.*)[1]
>
> LUCY: (*reading sentence from textbook*) "Over the next 500 years Islamic civilizations spread throughout this vast area." (*looking up at group*) Seems like kind of a spread out or big area.
>
> BRIAN: I think it's throughout this small area (*using hand gestures*) because it's talking how it was small and then it's growing.
>
> LUCY: No, I think it's vast because up here in this one (*pointing to a sentence earlier in the text; two other girls follow along, looking at that section in text as well*). It says, "Spain and North Africa and much of Central Asia." That's *a lot* of area. It's like huge.
>
> BRIAN: So, would it be a lot?
>
> LUCY: Like vast or big. (Classroom observation, May 8, 2013)

Lucy started this process by asking her peers: "Who had a clunk?" (See Clunk Expert Role Card in Appendix 4.3.) Since *vast* was a word that most of the students did not know, Lucy continued by asking for ideas about its meaning. In the exchange, Lucy was the group member who offered a final definition. Notice, however, that she may not have done so without the aid of Brian. Lucy turned to the text for support and prompted her group to reread a section of text that not only supported her understanding of the word *vast* but also reinforced key information about the spread of the Islamic civilization (the topic of the lesson). Together, the students moved into a level of collaborative discussion (Level 3), negotiating the meaning of an important word in the text.

---

[1] "Flipbooks" are a collection of CSR resources that students have on their desks for support. A flipbook includes lists of word parts (i.e., prefixes, root words, suffixes) and cognates, as well as a list of question stems.

The Click and Clunk process, in its entirety, refers to a metacognitive process in which students recognize when they have a breakdown in understanding and need to take corrective action. Students refer to "clicks" as times when they understand what they are reading (like hearing the "clicks" of the grooves in a skateboard riding along on the sidewalk), and "clunks" as times when they have a breakdown in understanding (like the "clunk" of a skateboard accident, prompting the rider to refine her technique and try again). Students use one or more of four fix-up strategies to figure out the meaning of these clunks. The back of the Clunk Expert Role Card (Appendix 4.3) outlines the four fix-up strategies. The first two strategies prompt students to use context clues in the same sentence (Fix-Up Strategy 1) and in surrounding sentences (Fix-Up Strategy 2). The next two strategies direct students to examine the word, looking for word parts (Fix-Up Strategy 3) or cognates in another language (Fix-Up Strategy 4).

As with all of CSR, students use each other for support when figuring out the meaning of unknown words or phrases. Teachers may need to model examples of clunks in their own reading as a way to reiterate that readers may not understand every word but can use strategies (and each other) to repair comprehension. Should someone know the word, the Clunk Expert guides the group to put the definition back into the sentence to make sure it makes sense. Thus, all students are actively checking the definition even if just one person knew (all or some of) the meaning of the word or phrase.

Get the Gist

Students continue to learn from and with each other during the Gist process of CSR. When students "get the gist" they are synthesizing important information from an entire section of text. This requires higher-order thinking skills as students must differentiate between what is important, compared to what is merely interesting, and find a common connection among all the details of the passage. Each student must also put the information into his or her own words.

At the start of Get the Gist, students talk through what might be the most important "who" or "what" of a section. For instance, in the example below, four students in a social studies class for ELLs were figuring out the most important "who" or "what" of a section of the textbook about preventing disease in ancient China.

IAN: Who or what, what is it? I think it's about giving the

KENDRA: Transporting, not giving.

IAN: But how do they do that? By using vaccines, right?

JIN: No, they can expose. Like it's if I cough on you, or touch you, then that's exposing.

IAN: But the most important "who" or "what," what is it?

JIN: Mmm.

ADRIANA: Smallpox, I think.

JIN: Why, but why did they highlight *vaccine* in here (*pointing to textbook*). Why did they highlight it in blue?

IAN: Because it's an [unintelligible].

KENDRA: Because it's for clunks, if someone doesn't understand vaccination.

ADRIANA: It's vocabulary. But OK, what do you think is the "who" or "what"?

IAN: I think it's the ancient Chinese exposed—

KENDRA: It's only two words. We're not doing the 10-word gist.

IAN: I know, but how can the gist be—It's like the ancient Chinese exposed the smallpox by vaccines.

ALL: Yeah, yeah.

IAN: And we know what a vaccine is (*reads definition in textbook*).

ADRIANA: It protects.

IAN: Yeah, yeah right.

KENDRA: We have to figure out the most important "who" or "what."

IAN: Ah, what is it?

ADRIANA: Preventing disease from smallpox?

KENDRA: Yeah.

IAN: Two words.

ADRIANA: Preventing smallpox.

KENDRA: Preventing disease.

IAN: Yeah. (Classroom observation, March 2011)

In discussing the key ideas about this section of text, students were rereading, clarifying, asking each other questions, using academic language such as *exposing*, as well as elaborating on and explaining the key concept of vaccines in ancient China. The students then wrote their own gists and discussed the quality of those gists (see back of Gist Expert Role Card, Appendix 4.4).

Wrap-Up: Questioning and Review

The final stages of a CSR lesson cycle prompt student groups to attend to what was learned in the entire reading and to formulate teacher-like questions about key content and ideas of the reading. There are two parts to the wrap-up: question generation and review.

QUESTION GENERATION

Facilitated by the Question Expert, students write leveled questions about what was read and share them with members of their group. Examples of the three levels of questions (Right There, Think and Search, and Author and You) are listed in the Question Expert Role Card (see Appendix 4.5). Students can also refer to a list of sentence stems corresponding to each question type (Klinger et al., 2012). For instance, sample Right There question stems include:

- Who was it that _____?
- What is _____?
- What was the turning point in _____?
- When did _____ happen?

Think and Search question stems that require synthesis or combining information include:

- Who was _____ and what did he (or she) do?
- What were some of the reasons for _____?
- How was the problem of _____ solved?
- How are _____ and _____ different?

Author and You question stems that prompt students to make connections or inferences include:

- Why is _____ a good or a bad thing?
- How would you feel if _____?
- What do you think would have happened if _____?
- What else could we do to solve the problem of _____?

As the students use Question Answer Relationships (QAR), such as those proposed by Raphael (1986) in collaborative settings, they must consider information in the text as well as their background knowledge and each other's ideas. The following is an exchange between four students reviewing an article on sleep habits of young teens. Students use textual evidence as well as each other for support in coming to a group understanding of the effects of not sleeping:

ANGEL: Who would like to read one of their questions? Sabina?

SABINA: What are the effects of not sleeping?

ANGEL: OK, who would like to answer it? Damien?

DAMIEN: Your behaviors can change in many ways. You can be irritated and any other emotion . . .

ANGEL: OK . . .

PILAR: I have the same question.

ANGEL: OK, Pilar.

PILAR: I have the same question.

ANGEL: Yeah, but someone can . . .

PILAR: What are the effects of not getting enough sleeping?

ANGEL: The effects of not getting enough sleeping is you get cranky, irritated, and also distracted.

PILAR: There is more here (*pointing to the text*).

ANGEL: And also you have bad behavior . . .

SABINA: What about the other page?

(*Students turn to back of the card.*)

SABINA: There's more.

PILAR: And it can affect your immune system.

ANGEL: Yeah. (Classroom observation, May 9, 2013)

These students expanded on each other's thinking by using prompts from the cue cards and, most important, each other and the text. The students shared the responsibility for coming to a group understanding of key points in the text.

Throughout this process, the Question Expert supports his or her peers in generating questions that connect to the purpose of the lesson. There are better, and not as good, questions in CSR. The more proficient questions grapple with important parts of the text and not random details. Teachers, too, can guide question generation to promote content understanding. For example, a teacher may require students to create questions that connect to the learning objective or to include a key vocabulary word into one of their questions as a way to reinforce the learning of that term and prompt students to use academic language with each other.

REVIEW

Review is the final step in the CSR process, and is facilitated first by the Leader of the group and then by the teacher. Prompted by the Leader, students individually compose a summary review statement about the key information and ideas of the text, and then share and discuss within groups what each person has written. The helping behaviors of the students continue, as they push each other to use textual evidence and elaborate on their reasons for including what they wrote in their statements. Finally, the teacher brings the class together for a whole-class wrap-up as a way to reinforce key ideas of the reading and its connection to the larger purpose of the unit's goals (see Figure 4.2 for a list of sample follow-up activities for content and wrap-ups).

Clunk
- Create individualized vocabulary quizzes using the students' own clunks.
- Add clunks to word walls, with their definitions.

Gist
- Write gists on board and evaluate (explicitly say why they prefer one to another).
- Pass out problematic gists and have students rewrite.

Questions
- Take questions and play jeopardy (or some other game) the next day.
- Tell students you will use their questions on a quiz and do so.

General (all strategies and/or content)
- Have students debrief about the functioning of their group by identifying one thing they did well and one thing they need to work on next time. Share with the class.
- Use Numbered Heads Together to review key responses: Teacher poses a question and all groups "put their heads together" to figure out the answer. The teacher randomly selects a table number and role card, and the student at that table with that role answers the question to the whole class.

FIGURE 4.2. Sample follow-up activities for a CSR lesson.

CSR Resources

As literacy coaches and researchers, we are often asked how to support the development of classrooms that look like the ones in the videos we use to demonstrate best practices. (For sample videos and CSR resources, see *www.csrcolorado.org*.) Teachers asking these questions are not referring to the lighting or the camera angle of the video clips, but the fact that students are talking to one another, looking back at the text, and elaborating or questioning what each student is offering as an important idea or connection to the unit's goals. The CSR excerpts shared in this chapter were conducted in heterogeneous classrooms in urban school districts with students who reflect the socioeconomic diversity of the schools. There is seldom any hidden magic in these classrooms; the teachers and students have all been *practicing* the CSR strategies with each other while using well-designed materials as helpful supports. Foundational to this practice is instruction that:

- Promotes peer collaboration in student-led groups so that students are purveyors of information and ideas, rather than the teacher being the giver of all information.
- Includes deliberate supports that students can use to guide their discussions and attention to the reading.

To answer the "how" questions—how to set up a CSR classroom for success, how to facilitate academic language development, how to ensure students support one another—we turn to the CSR classroom materials and resources as guides for what occurs in a CSR lesson.

Cooperative Learning Group Roles

CSR introduces students to the use of important cooperative learning group roles. Drawing on the work of Palincsar and Brown (1984), CSR roles are designed to give each student a specific task that contributes to the learning occurring in the group. A unique aspect of CSR roles is that students engage in every aspect of CSR, guided by the strategy expert who facilitates the group's discussion and learning. The four group roles are:

1. *Leader*: Guides the group to participate and help one another through all the steps of CSR. The leader keeps track of time, keeps the group working together, and guides the final student-led review of the text.
2. *Clunk Expert*: Guides the group in using fix-up strategies to figure out the meaning of unknown words or concepts.
3. *Gist Expert*: Guides the group through a collective understanding of the main ideas of a section of text by helping the group determine the most important "who" or "what" and the key ideas about the "who" or "what," then writing their own gists and discussing them for quality.
4. *Question Expert*: Guides the group in generating and sharing leveled questions that address important information from the reading.

Over time, students learn to lead their group through each part of the CSR lesson cycle by using the different roles (Klingner et al., 2012). In subsequent sections,

✏️	Write your questions and the answers in your learning log.
💬	Who would like to share his or her best question?
💬	Who would like to answer that question?
📖	Where in the text did you find the information to answer that question?

FIGURE 4.3. Excerpt from Question Expert Role Card. From Klingner, Vaughn, Boardman, and Swanson (2012). Reprinted with permission from John Wiley & Sons, Inc.

we will elaborate on ways teachers can support students in learning to use these roles well.

Role cards (Appendices 4.2–4.5) are important support mechanisms that scaffold students' learning of both reading comprehension and cooperative learning strategies (Berkeley et al., 2011; Stevens & Slavin, 1995). First, each role card guides the group through the steps of a strategy. Icons are also used to indicate the extent of collaboration (e.g., the talk bubble refers to discussion time, and the pencil refers to individual thinking and writing time). In an excerpt from the Question Expert Card shown in Figure 4.3, for instance, notice how students are prompted to follow a process involving both individual work and exchanging of ideas based on the text.

Students who find it difficult to enter an academic discussion are supported through the routine provided on the card, and by learning common structures of academic discourse (Cazden, 2001; Michaels et al., 2008). The sentence stems on the back of the Leader and Gist Expert cards, for instance, help students collaborate with one another by offering discussion frames that lead students to question, clarify, elaborate, and give feedback (see Figure 4.4).

CSR Learning Log

The CSR learning log is a place for students to capture and refine their thinking about the important ideas from the reading (see Appendix 4.6, adapted from Klingner et al., 2012). At each stage of the lesson cycle, students write individual responses and then share and discuss their ideas with their group members. Students are encouraged to go back and improve their work as they clarify their thinking about the text.

To encourage participation:
- (name), what do you think of _____?
- (name), why do you think that?
- (name), I like what you said about _____ because _____.
- Who can add on to what (name) just said?

To monitor participation:
- Did everyone hear that?
- I'm noticing that _____.

To discuss gists:
- What is similar and different about our gists?
- Our gists all include _____.
- Each of us wrote something about _____.

FIGURE 4.4. Sample sentence stems on the back of the CSR role cards. From Klingner, Vaughn, Boardman, and Swanson (2012). Reprinted with permission from John Wiley & Sons, Inc.

The CSR learning log is a type of graphic organizer and a record of student thinking that supports the link between the development of reading and writing (Hebert, Gillespie, & Graham, 2012). There are multiple advantages of using the CSR learning log: built-in wait time, a reminder of the CSR routine, and a record of student learning that teachers can review, share, or use for offering feedback and figuring out instructional next steps. Students are more prepared for what to do next and can go back to their work to review or improve it. Students can also use the learning logs to study for quizzes or as prompts for discussions.

CSR Rubrics

CSR offers numerous rubrics that support students' understanding with explicit criteria of what CSR should "look like and sound like" when students contribute to their group's understanding of the text. Given a goal of enhancing peer discourse, the rubrics serve as a reminder and guide to ways students might talk about a text together. The rubrics also offer an accountability mechanism of each student's individual work during the lesson cycle (Gillies, 2003; Gillies & Boyle, 2010).

CSR teachers select which rubric(s) to use based on the focus of the lesson and the students' familiarity with the expectations of the class. In addition to a Learning Log Rubric that attends to the students' final written work (Appendix 4.7), there are also rubrics focused on supporting quality peer interactions, including a group process rubric and rubric for each CSR role (e.g., a Leader Role Rubric as shown in Figure 4.5). These rubrics direct students to self-assess their guidance of their group based on strategies used (e.g., all students in my group wrote their own gist before discussing) and also on their collaborative efforts by helping students think about what worked well and setting possible goals for improvement.

CSR resources offer students specific and explicit support that purposefully promotes quality student interactions in collaborative group work. Once students are engaged in high-quality discussions around texts, the resources will not be utilized with as much regularity. Yet, introducing these resources, and reinforcing the use of them in CSR lessons, facilitates the growth and automaticity of both reading comprehension and collaborative strategies and skills.

Introducing CSR to Your Students

When introducing CSR to students, teachers often start with CSR introductory lesson plans and an expert role-alike group lesson for students. By introducing the CSR before, during, and after reading strategies separately, teachers provide students opportunities to learn the basics of each strategy and practice applying each expert role. Teachers also introduce and reinforce the suggested CSR rules as a way to articulate expectations about the need for respect and collaboration in the classroom.

Group Names: _____ Date: _____

Leader—Group Work Debrief

	YES (2)	SOMETIMES (1)	NOT REALLY (0)	
The **Leader** kept the group moving through all the parts of CSR.				
The **Leader** kept track of time.				
The **Leader** guided the group to write and share their review statements.				
We all **shared, discussed,** and **listened** to one another. We asked each other questions and helped one another.				Total
TOTAL SCORE				

One thing we did really well . . .

One thing we could do better next time . . .

FIGURE 4.5. Leader Role Rubric. From Klingner, Vaughn, Boardman, and Swanson (2012). Reprinted with permission from John Wiley & Sons, Inc.

Introductory CSR Lessons

Teachers usually lead students through five introductory CSR strategy lessons that align with before, during, and after reading strategies. Each lesson takes approximately 30–50 minutes to implement and is structured in the following way: "I Do" (teacher models), "We Do" (teacher and students practice), "You Do" (students work either independently or collaboratively to apply strategies). The first lesson introduces students to Preview. The second is about Click and Clunk; the third is about Gist; and the fourth and fifth are about Questioning and Review.

The "I Do" portion of the Gist lesson, for example, starts with the teacher stating the importance of monitoring understanding while reading and stopping to self-check for understanding. The teacher also tells students they will be writing down their gists at the end of a section of text and explains that this process can help them check to make sure they are figuring out what is most important in a passage of text. The teacher concludes this portion of the lesson by modeling how to Get the Gist using a piece of content-related text.

For the "We Do" portion of the Gist lesson, the teacher helps the whole class write a gist by following the three steps modeled previously. Together, the teacher and students name the most important "who" or "what" from a piece of text. They discuss the most important information about the "who" or "what," and they co-construct a gist in about 10 words or less. This same process is repeated for the "You Do" activity. Students work with a partner to identify the most important "who" or "what" and then discuss the most important information about that "who" or "what" based on what was read. Then on their own, students practice writing a gist in about 10 words or less and read it aloud to their partner. The gist mini-lesson concludes with a review of the Gist Expert Role Card and gist rubric. Gist Experts are instructed to make sure that all students in the group write their own gists, to lead the group in sharing and discussing the quality of their gists, and to support their group in improving their gists.

Role-Alike Group Lesson

After teachers and students have completed the five introductory CSR strategy lessons, the teacher guides students through an activity in cooperative learning. The purpose of the lesson is for students to become experts in their assigned CSR roles and to share the functions and responsibilities of their role with others in the group. Like the strategy introductory lessons, the cooperative learning lesson is structured in the "I Do" (teacher models), "We Do" (teacher and students practice), "You Do" (students work either independently or collaboratively to apply strategies) format.

During the "I Do" portion of the lesson, the teacher begins with a discussion about why collaboration and dialogue are important. The teacher explains that students work together to comprehend challenging, content-related texts by learning and using specific CSR roles. Accountability within the context of CSR is described as holding each other to a higher standard of learning by discussing ideas using evidence from the text, demonstrating a willingness to challenge other's ideas respectfully, and listening while others are speaking.

At the onset of each lesson, the teacher assigns students to designated CSR expert roles. In the role-alike activity, students are grouped with others who have the same role (Leaders together, Clunk Experts together, Gist Experts together, Question Experts together). Students quickly and quietly move into their role-alike groups while the teacher distributes the role cards based on student's assigned role. Next, for the "We Do/You Do" portion of the lesson, the teacher facilitates a jigsaw activity intended for students to learn more about the roles. For the activity, students are given the following instructions: become the expert in your role by working with others who have this role too; read your role card; and as a group, discuss and answer questions about your role (i.e., What are the responsibilities of someone in this role? Why is this role important? How do you think this role works together with the other roles?).

After students engage in a 5- to 10-minute discussion within their role-alike groups, students return to their assigned CSR group to share what they have learned. Starting with the Leader role, each student is given 1 minute to share his or her role in the group. The students then rotate through all the expert roles (Clunk Expert, Gist Expert, and Question Expert). While students work in small groups, they practice listening to each other by taking notes on what their peers will be doing as experts in their group. Afterward, the teacher brings the whole class together to highlight examples of students using inclusive dialogue and textual references (e.g., elaborating, clarifying).

The role-alike lesson concludes after the teacher distributes the Group Process Rubric and has students discuss how students will use the rubric to rate their work as a team. During this time, students use the rubric to set specific goals for their first full CSR lesson (e.g., "We will work on making sure that we all participate equally in our conversations").

---

1. Talk only to the members of your group.
2. Talk only about your work.
3. Use 6-inch voices (loud enough so that only those sitting at your table can hear you).
4. When you have a question, ask the Leader to raise his or her hand to get help from the teacher.

FIGURE 4.6. CSR rules.

CSR Rules

Suggested CSR rules are provided for all teachers in the cooperative learning (role-alike) lesson plan (see Figure 4.6). These rules were established based on research implementing CSR in culturally and linguistically diverse classrooms (Klingner et al., 2012). The rules are fourfold and the final rule, in particular, reinforces the need to first ask one another a question before turning to the teacher for help. Without this rule, a student may call a teacher over and ask a question that another student in his or her group already knew how to answer.

Transitioning to Student-Facilitated Groups

When first learning CSR, students benefit from teachers who scaffold the process by introducing each strategy one at a time and then demonstrating the CSR cycle in a way that *transitions* from more teacher-controlled to teacher-facilitated and student-directed learning. Teachers support this transition process by taking the following steps:

1. *Modeling CSR with a section of the reading*: The teacher talks through the process as if she were the Leader, the Clunk Expert, and the Gist Expert.
2. *Acting as the Leader* and selecting a group of three students to go through the process with him or her. The rest of the class follows along, and the entire class debriefs the process and then proceeds with the next section as partners or in a group of four.
3. *Controlling the timing.* The teacher may offer explicit directions that include pacing, such as, "read the first section and identify your clunks. You have five minutes, go." Or, "You have 2 minutes to write your gist. There should be no talking. Go."

Promoting High-Quality Discussions in CSR

Throughout the year, teachers support students in becoming more active, helpful contributors to their group's understanding of a reading. Teachers often discover the need to fine-tune or reteach a strategy to a group of students who are struggling with a particular component while the rest of the class works in their CSR groups. Teachers may also discover a need to pull the whole class together to reiterate and reinforce expectations for group work. This section describes some of the ways we have seen teachers guide students to recognize and develop their own specific, actionable steps for working together to better understand content-rich texts in the classroom.

Stating Expectations

At the outset of a CSR lesson, teachers can remind students of a key expectation of group work. "CSR leaders," said one social studies teacher, "I expect that you will keep your groups focused today and ensure that everyone in the group plays their role well, including using both sides of the role cards to ensure that your group has a deep and meaningful discussion about the ideas in the text" (Coach field notes, May 23, 2013).

The teacher can then focus his or her feedback on the ways in which Leaders are prompting group members to use both sides of the role cards, for example, "Josie is pointing to the guiding questions at the back of the gist card as a reminder to her Gist Expert to talk about the quality of each other's gists." This teacher may also want to get the class's attention midway through the lesson to give a "temperature check" on the ways in which groups are talking with one another about key content of the reading. The teacher can display the back of the Leader card on the document camera (or PowerPoint; see Appendix 4.2) and point out which sentence starters he or she heard Leaders use for encouraging equitable participation.

Stating what a teacher expects to see may be as simple as students having role cards visible next to their learning logs and readings. Or, the stated expectation may be a little more elaborate as students progress with CSR. For instance, a teacher might state, "Question Experts, I expect to hear discussions about the *quality* of each other's questions and responses. At least one person in your group will say something that is strong about the response, and another person will offer a suggestion of an additional place in the text to find more information." Making this statement once at the beginning of the class is just a start. Teachers must also remind students, spotlight groups that are heeding the expectations, and, when necessary, offer students options for what they can say or do in situations when the peer interactions are not yet as strong as they might be as the year progresses.

Showing Models of Students at Work

Students also learn from seeing other students in action. In our district partnership project we offer six different 2- to 4-minute video clips of students using the strategies effectively together with minimal support from their teachers. (For sample videos and CSR resources, see *www.csrcolorado.org*.) Many teachers have used these clips in their classes. Teachers, for instance, use the corresponding note taker (see Appendix 4.8 for the Teacher's Guide to the Gist Clip), which helps students focus on how collaboration works within a component of CSR. The note taker includes eight categories for describing what students are doing and not doing and what materials are being used. Many teachers support students in narrowing the focus of viewing the clip by asking them to take notes on one or two categories at a time. After watching the video clip, students share and discuss their observations of their assigned categories. Teachers often show the video clip a second time so students can see and hear more of what their peers noticed about the ways the students were discussing the reading.

Many CSR teachers also make videos of their own students during a CSR lesson and play a short clip (1–2 minutes) from the recording back for the class. When watching the video with students, teachers elaborate on what they expect to see more of (and less of) when using CSR in the classroom. This process also allows students opportunities to ask questions about expectations and to get more ideas for how to listen, question, elaborate on concepts, and provide feedback for one another. For example, Ms. VanArk, a ninth-grade language arts teacher in a low-income urban high school, explained to CSR researchers in an end-of-year interview: "During semester one I filmed one of the groups that was doing a nice job [of reading a text together using academic language] and used that as an indicator of proficiency to show to the other classes." Ms. VanArk proceeded to say that she "could click on the film and [her students] could see and hear the students in that group using the cue cards." The clip was under 1 minute long, and in the video Ms. VanArk told her students, "Here is an example of a group using academic language that moved them into the green area of the rubric, the proficient area." Ms. VanArk further elaborated in her interview: "From that moment forward it became really clear what was expected in groups" (Interview, May 7, 2013). With the ubiquity of cell phones and iPads with cameras, teachers have more options for capturing examples of expectations on film, as did Ms. VanArk, so other students can learn from their peers.

Offering Feedback

When students are engaged in using CSR to read and discuss challenging texts, teachers can offer supportive feedback. Feedback varies, depending on students' needs. Throughout a typical CSR lesson, a teacher will offer supportive feedback for a variety of reasons: prompting or reminding students to use CSR procedures or materials, ensuring students are understanding the content of the text, and monitoring group processing (e.g., all students are contributing, experts are guiding their groups, students are using accountable talk to agree or disagree). Before a teacher offers feedback, a quick assessment of the status of the group is necessary. For example, when students worked in cooperative groups in Ms. Smith's class, she quietly approached each group to listen in as students talked. Students knew to continue working when Ms. Smith approached, allowing the teacher time to glance at each student's learning logs. If the students' logs reflected clear definitions of clunks, and a rich understanding of the section reflected in gist statements, Ms. Smith listened to the group's dialogue, checking for misunderstandings of content and ensuring that each group member was participating in the conversation. Ms. Smith's constructive feedback was offered when needed.

Supportive feedback falls along a continuum ranging from explicit prompting of strategy use to use of guiding questions that target students' higher-order thinking about the content (Hargreaves, 2013). While a teacher must ensure that students are "getting" the content, he or she must also foster students' use of CSR strategies and collaboration. After a teacher has determined the status of the group, the teacher's first move is to question the expert (as Ms. Smith demonstrated in the clip above). For example, in Emma Jackson's seventh-grade science class, Ms. Jackson approached a group and asked, "Clunk Expert, how did your group determine the meaning of 'tertiary'?" Once the expert responded, Ms. Jackson probed a bit further: "And Leader, did you all agree with that definition?" Finally, Ms. Jackson reminded them of a key strategy, "When you put that definition back into the text, did it make sense?" (Classroom observation, April 2012). In this quick 3-minute dialogue, Ms. Jackson offered feedback related to roles and process (e.g., reminders and questions to the Clunk Expert and Leader), fostered collaboration (e.g., how did the group work together toward consensus?), and reminded them of specific strategies (e.g., returning to the text).

Finally, teachers can provide supportive feedback to groups by giving students rubrics specific to each student's own role, or to the students' work as a group together. In Ms. Delgado's fifth-period social studies class, each table of students had a laminated copy of the group process rubric located in the center of their table. As Ms. Delgado moved around the room, monitoring each group's work and conversations, she quietly noted where a group was in terms of participation, support they were giving each other, and how well they were problem solving as a team. Groups that worked well together were rewarded at the end of the class. Groups that were not functioning at a proficient level had the opportunity to discuss their progress and set goals for the next day. Ms. Delgado gave her students explicit feedback related to how they did as a group: "Today, I noticed that Michael was not participating in conversations. Leader, did you consider using the back of your role card to help your group? If you notice someone is not participating, make sure that you ask that group member specific questions, or make sure that everyone in your group pauses to give that person time to think and share" (Classroom observation, April 2012). For diverse and exceptional learners, who tend to have lower levels of engagement in general education classrooms, attention to group processing like Ms. Delgado's may increase students' awareness of their participation and lead to more productive interactions and increased work quality.

Engaging Students in Self-Reflection

Engaging students in the explicit examination of their own actions and learning (Russell, 2005; Valli, 1997) can also hold the potential for fostering collaborative engagement. Even with the help of CSR rubrics to guide student self-reflection, students may not know how to be reflective of their own work, or may simply fill out the rubric with what they think the teacher wants to hear (Kotsopoulos, 2010). The use of video as a self-reflection tool, on the other hand, gives students the opportunity to see themselves as they interact with others in their cooperative groups. Through the use of video, students can become aware of their off-task activity and how this hinders their group process. They also notice moments when they are contributing positively toward the collective learning.

Ms. Kade, for instance, recorded each of her sixth-grade social studies cooperative learning groups for 10 minutes when her students were using CSR, and then had them watch themselves while scoring their group process with the rubric. In conversations with each group after they watched their recording, Ms. Kade was pleased with what students noticed. "One of my lowest readers never realized how much he actually helped his peers until watching the video clip. He kept pointing out to his group members, 'Look! I helped you just then with your gist!' And off-task group behavior has changed dramatically! They know what CSR looks like, and they do it in their own groups now" (Classroom observation, March 2012).

CONCLUSION

The review of literature on reading strategy instruction attained widespread and political recognition with the publication of the National Reading Panel's report (National Reading Panel, 2000). CSR includes five of the strategies that the panel identified as having a solid research base (as determined with experimental and quasi-experimental designed studies) for improving students' reading comprehension: comprehension monitoring; cooperative learning; question answering; question generation; and summarization. When teachers are new to CSR, they may notice that it consists of reading comprehension strategies they may have already been using in their classrooms. These teachers, however, do not necessarily use all of these strategies in tandem with such a strong focus on a content goal and deliberate attention to group discourse skills.

It can take time and practice for students to develop effective reading comprehension strategies that they can apply when reading other texts. For this reason, CSR teachers are explicit about a targeted skill or strategy and explain to the students that this is a vehicle for making sense of the content. Equally important, CSR teachers offer students deliberate support in learning how to use these strategies together as peers in the classroom. To facilitate their discussions, the students use multiple resources to come to group consensus on the essential key ideas and information in a reading. These resources include—but are not limited to—the use of role cards, discussions with one another, and teachers' stated expectations and guidance. The collaborative and discursive strategies developed by CSR are lifelong skills that can be transferred to other group work situations, and they can be used when students are tackling important, yet sometimes difficult, text across content areas.

ACKNOWLEDGMENTS

The classroom examples in this chapter derive from a 5-year research project and partnership with a large urban school district that introduced and scaled up CSR districtwide in its middle school classrooms. The district was awarded an Investing in Innovation (i3) validation grant from the U.S. Department of Education in 2010 with the goal of bringing CSR to science, social studies, and language arts classrooms in all district middle schools. By supporting CSR in its schools, the district is committed to making an essential feature of CSR a reality in the classroom: Providing the opportunity for students to talk with each other in a structured, supportive way about reading so that they learn important content *and* strengthen reading comprehension skills.

We wish to thank the members of our district partnership, especially the teachers, as well as Bridgett Bird, Deborah Blake, Laura Henderson, Emily Holmes, Vera Ananda, and Vivian Masket, whose insights on instructional support and development of resource materials have helped improve CSR. Many examples in this chapter were developed from their hard work.

The contents of this chapter were developed under Grant No. U396B100143 (Investing in Innovation) from the Department of Education. However, they do not necessarily represent the policy of the U.S. Department of Education, and endorsement by the federal government should not be assumed. For more information about CSR Colorado, including CSR resources and tips, see *www.csrcolorado.org*.

REFERENCES

Anderson, R. C., & Pearson, P. D. (1984). A schema theoretic view of basic processes in reading. In P. D. Pearson (Ed.), *Handbook of reading research* (pp. 255–291). New York: Longman.

August, D., & Shanahan, T. (2006). *Developing literacy in second-language learners: Report of the National Literacy Panel on Language-Minority Children and Youth*. Mahwah, NJ: Erlbaum.

Azevdeo, R. (2009). Theoretical, conceptual, methodological, and instructional issues in research on metacognition and self-regulated learning: A discussion. *Metacognition Learning, 4*, 87–95.

Baker, L., & Brown, A. L. (1984). Metacognitive skills of reading. In P. D. Pearson (Ed.), *Handbook of reading research* (pp. 353–394). New York: Longman.

Berkeley, S., Mastropieri, M. A., & Scruggs, T. E. (2011). Reading comprehension strategy instruction and attribution retraining for secondary students with learning and other mild disabilities. *Journal of Learning Disabilities, 44*(1), 18–32.

Boardman, A., Klingner, J. K., Buckley, P., Annamma, S., & Jensen. C. (in press). Collaborative Strategic Reading in content classes: Results from year 1 of a randomized control trial. Manuscript submitted to *Reading and Writing: An Interdisciplinary Journal*.

Brown, A. L., Bransford, J. D., Ferrara, R. A., & Campione, J. C. (1983). Learning, remembering, and understanding. In P. Mussen (Ed.), *Handbook of child psychology* (Vol. 3, pp. 77–166). New York: Wiley.

Cazden, C. B. (2001). *Classroom discourse: The language of teaching and learning* (2nd ed.). Portsmouth, NH: Heinemann.

Cohen, E. G. (1994). Restructuring the classroom: Conditions for productive small groups. *Review of Educational Research, 64*(1), 1–35.

Cohen, E. G., & Lotan, R. A. (1995). Producing equal-status interaction in the heterogeneous classroom. *American Educational Research Journal, 32*(1), 99–120.

Cole, M., & Engeström, Y. (1993). A cultural-historical approach to distributed cognition. In G. Salomon (Ed.), *Distributed cognitions: Psychological and educational considerations*. Cambridge, UK: Cambridge University Press.

Collins, A., Brown, J. S., & Newman, S. (1989). Cognitive apprenticeship: Teaching the craft of reading, writing and mathematics. In L. B. Resnick (Ed.), *Knowing, learning, and instruction: Essays in honor of Robert Glaser* (pp. 453–494). Hillsdale, NJ: Erlbaum.

Edmonds, M. S., Vaughn, S., Wexler, J., Reutebuch, C. K., Cable, A., Tackett, K. K., et al. (2009). A synthesis of reading interventions and effects on reading comprehension outcomes for older struggling readers. *Review of Educational Research, 79*, 262–300.

Engeström, Y., & Sannino, A. (2010). Studies of expansive learning: Foundations, findings and future challenges. *Educational Research Review, 5*(1), 1–24.

Fuchs, D., Fuchs, L. S., Mathes, P. G., & Lipsey, M. W. (2000). Reading differences between low-achieving students with and without learning disabilities: A meta-analysis. In R. Gersten, E. P. Schiller, & S. Vaughn (Eds.), *Contemporary special education research* (pp. 81–104). Mahwah, NJ: Erlbaum.

Gajria, M., Jitendra, A. K., Sood, S., & Sacks, G. (2007). Improving comprehension of expository text in students with LD: A research synthesis. *Journal of Learning Disabilities, 40*, 210–225.

Genesee, F., Lindholm-Leary, K., Saunders, W., & Christian, D. (2005). English language learners in U.S. schools: An overview of research findings. *Journal of Education for Students Placed at Risk, 10*(4), 363–385.

Gersten, R. M., Fuchs, L. S., Williams, J. P., & Baker, S. (2001). Teaching reading comprehension strategies to students with learning disabilities: A review of research. *Review of Educational Research, 71*, 279–320.

Gillies, R. M. (2003). The behaviors, interactions, and perceptions of junior high school students during small-group learning. *Journal of Educational Psychology, 95*(1), 137–147.

Gillies, R. M., & Boyle, M. (2010). Teachers' reflections on cooperative learning: Issues of implementation. *Teaching and Teacher Education, 26*, 933–940.

Gutiérrez, K. D., & Stone, L. D. (1997). A cultural-historical view of learning and learning disabilities: Participating in a community of learners. *Learning Disabilities Research and Practice, 12*(2), 123–131.

Hargreaves, E. (2013). Inquiring into children's experiences of teacher feedback: Reconceptualizing assessment for learning. *Oxford Review of Education, 39*(2), 229–246.

Hayes, K., Rueda, R., & Chilton, S. (2009). Scaffolding language, literacy, and academic content in English and Spanish: The linguistic highway from Mesoamerica to Southern California. *English Teaching: Practice and Critique, 8*(2), 137–166.

Hebert, M., Gillespie, A., & Graham, S. (2012). Comparing effects of different writing activities on reading comprehension: A meta-analysis. *Reading and Writing, 26*, 111–138.

Hogan, K., Natasi, B. K., & Pressley, M. (2000). Discourse patterns and collaborative scientific reasoning in peer and teacher-guided discussions. *Cognition and Instruction, 17*(4), 379–432.

Järvelä, S., Violet, S., & Järvenoja, H. (2010). Research on motivation in collaborative learning: Moving beyond the cognitive-situative divide and combining individual and social processes. *Educational Psychologist, 45*(1), 15–27.

Johnson, D. W., & Johnson, R. T. (1999). Making cooperative learning work. *Theory into Practice, 38*(2), 67–73.

Kamil, M. L., Borman, G. D., Dole, J., Kral, C. C., Salinger, T., & Torgesen, J. (2008). *Improving adolescent literacy: Effective classroom and intervention practices: A practice guide* (NCEE#2008–4027). Washington, DC: National Center for Education Evaluation and Regional Assistance, Institute of Education Sciences, U.S. Department of Education. Retrieved from *http://ies.ed.gov/ncee/wwc.*

Klingner, J. K., Boardman, A., Buckley, P., & Reutebuch, C. K. (2014, April). *Collaborative strategic reading for students with LD in upper elementary classrooms.* Poster presented at the Council for Exceptional Children Convention and Expo, Philadelphia, PA.

Klingner, J. K., & Vaughn, S. (1996). Reciprocal teaching of reading comprehension strategies for students with learning disabilities who use English as a second language. *Elementary School Journal, 96*(3), 275–293.

Klingner, J. K., & Vaughn, S. (2000). The helping behaviors of fifth graders while using collaborative strategic reading during ESL content classes. *Tesol Quarterly, 34*(1), 69–98.

Klingner, J. K., Vaughn, S., Arguelles, M. E., Hughes, M. T., & Leftwich, S. A. (2004). Collaborative strategic reading "real-world" lessons from classroom teachers. *Remedial and Special Education, 25*(5), 291–302.

Klingner, J. K., Vaughn, S., Boardman, A. G., & Swanson, E. (2012). *Now we get it!: Boosting comprehension with collaborative strategic reading.* San Francisco: Jossey-Bass.

Klingner, J. K., Vaughn, S., & Schumm, J. S. (1998). Collaborative strategic reading during social studies in heterogeneous fourth-grade classrooms. *Elementary School Journal, 99*, 3–22.

Kotsopoulos, D. (2010). When collaborative is not collaborative: Supporting student learning through self-surveillance. *International Journal of Educational Research, 49*, 129–140.

Lave, J., & Wenger, E. (1991). *Situated learning: Legitimate peripheral participation*. Cambridge, UK: University of Cambridge Press.

Malone, L. D., & Mastropieri, M. A. (1992). Reading comprehension instruction: Summarization and self-monitoring training for students with learning disabilities. *Exceptional Children, 58,* 270–279.

Michaels, S., O'Connor, C., & Resnick, L. B. (2008). Deliberative discourse idealized and realized: Accountable talk in the classroom and in civic life. *Studies in Philosophy and Education, 27*(4), 283–297.

National Reading Panel. (2000). *Report of the national reading panel: Teaching children to read*. Washington, DC: National Institute of Child Health and Human Development.

O'Connor, R. E., & Jenkins, J. R. (2013). Cooperative learning for students with learning disabilities: Advice and caution derived from evidence. In H. L. Swanson, K. R. Harris, & S. Graham (Eds.), *Handbook of learning disabilities* (2nd ed., pp. 507–525). New York: Guilford Press.

Oczkus, L. D. (2010). *Reciprocal teaching at work: Powerful strategies and lessons for improving reading comprehension*. Newark, DE: International Reading Association.

Oxford, R. L. (1997). Cooperative learning, collaborative learning, and interaction: Three communicative strands in the language classroom. *Modern Language Journal, 81*(4), 443–456.

Palincsar, A. S., & Brown, A. L. (1984). Reciprocal teaching of comprehension-fostering and comprehension-monitoring activities. *Cognition and Instruction, 1*(2), 117–175.

Paris, S. G., Wasik, B., & Turner, J. C. (1991). The development of strategic readers. In R. Barr, M. L. Kamil, P. B. Mosenthal, & P. D. Pearson (Eds.), *Handbook of reading research* (Vol. 2, pp. 609–640). Hillsdale, NJ: Erlbaum.

Poole, D. (2008). Interactional differentiation in the mixed-ability group: A situated view of two struggling readers. *Reading Research Quarterly, 43*(3), 228–250.

Pressley, M., & Afflerbach, P. (1995). *Verbal protocols of reading: The nature of constructively responsive reading*. Mahwah, NJ: Erlbaum.

Pressley, M., Borkowski, J. G., & Schneider, W. (2010). Cognitive strategies: Good strategy users coordinate metacognition and knowledge. *Annals of Child Development, 4,* 89–129.

Raphael, T. E. (1986). Teaching question answer relationships, revisited. *Reading Teacher, 39*(6), 516–522.

Rogoff, B. (2003). *The cultural nature of human development*. New York: Oxford University Press.

Russell, T. (2005). Can reflective practice be taught? *Reflective Practice, 6*(2), 199–204.

Schön, D. (1983). *A reflective practitioner: How professionals think in action*. New York: Basic Books.

Simmonds, E. P. M. (1992). The effects of teacher training and implementation of two methods for improving the comprehension skills of students with learning disabilities. *Learning Disabilities Research and Practice, 7,* 194–198.

Slavin, R. E. (1996). Research on cooperative learning and achievement: What we know, what we need to know. *Contemporary Educational Psychology, 21,* 43–69.

Slavin, R. E. (2011). Instruction based on cooperative learning. *Handbook of research on learning and Instruction,* 344–360.

Slavin, R. E., Hurley, E. A., & Chamberlain, A. (2003). Cooperative learning and achievement: Theory and research. In W. M. Reynolds, G. E. Miller, & I. B. Weiner (Eds.), *Handbook of psychology: Educational psychology* (Vol. 7, pp. 177–198). Hoboken, NJ: Wiley.

Stevens, R. J., & Slavin, R. E. (1995). Effects of a cooperative learning approach in reading and writing on academically handicapped and nonhandicapped students. *Elementary School Journal, 95*(3), 241–262.

Swanson, H. L., Hoskyn, M., & Lee, C. (1999). *Interventions for students with learning disabilities: A meta-analysis of treatment outcomes*. New York: Guilford Press.

Tharp, R. G. (1982). The effective instruction of comprehension: Results and description of the Kamehameha Early Education Program. *Reading Research Quarterly, 17,* 503–527.

Valli, L. (1997). Listening to other voices: A description of teacher reflection in the United States. *Peabody Journal of Education, 72*(1), 67–88.

Vaughn, S., Gersten, R., & Chard, D. J. (2000). The underlying message in LD intervention research: Findings from research syntheses. *Exceptional Children, 67,* 99–114.

Vaughn, S., Klingner, J. K., Swanson, E., Boardman, A. G., Roberts, G., Mohammed, S. S., et al. (2011). Efficacy of collaborative strategic reading with middle school students. *American Education Research Journal, 48*(4), 938–964.

Vygotsky, L. S. (1978). *Mind in society: The development of higher psychological processes.* Cambridge, MA: Harvard University Press.

Zimmerman, B. J. (2008). Investigating self-regulation and motivation: Historical background, methodological developments, and future prospects. *American Educational Research Journal, 45*(1), 166–183.

APPENDIX 4.1. CSR diagram.

COLLABORATIVE STRATEGIC READING

Before Reading

PREVIEW

1. Engage
Identify the topic.

2. Brainstorm
Connect with what you already know.

3. Set the purpose
Consider the purpose for reading.

During Reading

CLICK & CLUNK

1. Look for clunks
Find words or ideas you don't understand.

2. Use fix-up strategies
· Re-read the sentence with the clunk.
· Re-read sentences before and after clunk.
· Look for prefixes, suffixes and root words.
· Look for cognates.

GET THE GIST

1. Figure out the main idea
· Determine the most important who or what.
· Find the most important information about the who or what.
· Write a brief gist statement.

After Reading

WRAP UP

1. Question
Write three types of questions that can be answered by reading the passage and thinking about what you already know.

· Right There
· Think and Search
· Author and You

2. Review
Identify the most important information.

CSR Colorado
Read. Lead. Succeed.

Reprinted with permission from the Meadows Center for Preventing Educational Risk (2009).

APPENDIX 4.2. Leader Role Card.

CSR CUE CARD

CSR Leader

DURING READING

Read

Who would like to read this section?

Click and Clunk

Write your clunks in your learning log.

Clunk Expert, please help us.

Get the Gist

It's time to get the gist. Gist Expert, please help us.

[Repeat all of the steps in this section for each section of the text.]

AFTER READING

Questions

It's time to ask questions. Question Expert, please help us.

Review

Now it's time to write the Review in our learning logs. Write one or two sentences containing the most important information about the text.

Who would like to share? Remember to say why your ideas are the most important.

Use the text to explain your thinking.

CSR CUE CARD
Job Description

The leader's job is to guide the group through all the steps of CSR. The leader keeps track of time, keeps the group working together and leads the review.

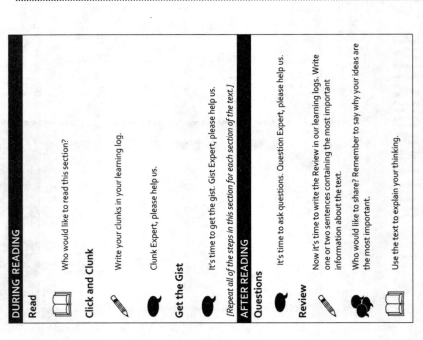

The **Leader** guides the group to participate and help one another:

To encourage participation:

- _____(name)_____, what do you think of _____?

- _____(name)_____, why do you think that?

- _____(name)_____, I like what you said about _____ because _____.

- Who can add on to what _____(name)_____ just said?

To monitor participation:

- Did everyone hear that?

- I'm noticing that _____.

To reflect on today's work:

- Something that went well today was _____.

- Next time we need to work on _____.

- Is there anything else that would help us do better next time?

CSR Colorado
Read. Lead. Succeed.

From Klingner, Vaughn, Boardman, and Swanson (2012). Reprinted with permission from John Wiley & Sons, Inc.

APPENDIX 4.3. Clunk Expert Role Card.

CSR CUE CARD

Clunk Expert

DURING READING

Click and Clunk

Who has a clunk? Does anyone know the meaning of the clunk?

If YES, someone knows the meaning of the clunk:

Please explain what the clunk means and why you think so.

Let's reread the sentence and make sure that definition makes sense.

Write the definition in your learning log.

If NO, no one knows the meaning of the clunk:

Use Fix-Up Strategies to define the clunk.

Let's reread the sentence and make sure that definition makes sense.

Write the definition in your learning log.

[Repeat all of the steps in this section for each clunk.]

CSR CUE CARD

Job Description

The Clunk Expert makes sure that students write their clunks in their learning logs. The Clunk Expert also helps students use Fix-Up Strategies to figure out the meaning of unknown words or ideas.

Fix-Up Strategies

DURING READING

1. Reread the sentence with the clunk and look for key ideas to help you figure out the word. Think about what makes sense.

2. Reread the sentences before and after the sentence with the clunk, looking for clues that help us figure out the clunk.

3. Break the word apart and look for word parts (prefixes, suffixes, root words) or smaller words you know.

4. Look for a cognate that makes sense.

135

From Klingner, Vaughn, Boardman, and Swanson (2012). Reprinted with permission from John Wiley & Sons, Inc.

APPENDIX 4.4. Gist Expert Role Card.

CSR CUE CARD

Gist Expert

DURING READING

Get the Gist

What is the most important "who" or "what" in this section? Does everyone agree? Why or why not? What is the most important information about the who or what?

Use the text to explain your thinking.

Everyone, think of your own gist and write it in your learning log.

Let's share our gists.

Let's discuss our gists using the questions on the back of this card.

Use the text to explain your thinking.

CSR CUE CARD

Job Description

The Gist Expert makes sure that all the students in the group write their own gists. The Gist Expert also leads the group in sharing their gists and discussing the quality of the gists. High-quality gists contain the most important "who" or "what") and the most important information about the topic. Gists should be about 10 words.

DURING READING

Discussion of Gists

1. What is similar and different about our gists?

2. Our gists all include _____.

3. Each of us wrote something about _____.

4. I think _____'s gist is the best gist because _____.

5. Let's check the quality of our gists.
   - Do all our gists include only the most important information?
   - Do all gists leave out unnecessary details?
   - Are all gists about 10 words?
   - Are all gists complete sentences?

   If not, what can we do to help each other improve the quality of our gists?
   - What if you changed _____?
   - Could you add something about _____?

From Klingner, Vaughn, Boardman, and Swanson (2012). Reprinted with permission from John Wiley & Sons, Inc.

CSR Colorado
Read. Lead. Succeed.

APPENDIX 4.5. Question Expert Role Card.

Question Expert

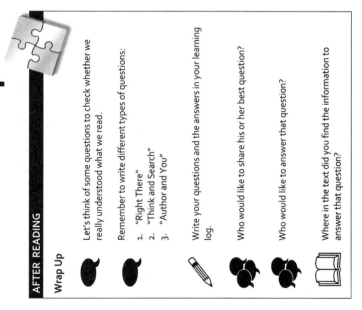

The Question Expert guides the group in coming up with questions that address important information from the reading. The Question Expert makes sure that students ask different levels of questions. The Question Expert checks to see that all students write questions and answers.

HOW TO WRITE A "RIGHT THERE" QUESTION

Write a question that will help you and your group to remember an important fact from the text.

Example: *"What is an earthquake?"* The answer is found "right there" in one sentence of the text. *"An earthquake is a vibration that travels through the Earth's crust."*

HOW TO WRITE A "THINK AND SEARCH" QUESTION

Write a question that will help you and your group to synthesize and remember important information from different sections of the text.

Example: *"How are different groups of people affected by land use in the Amazon rainforest?"* The answer is found by searching in several different parts of the text.

HOW TO WRITE AN "AUTHOR AND YOU" QUESTION

Write a question that will help you and your group to make connections to the text. Your question should help you connect the text to something you have already learned and/or to the big idea you are studying.

Examples: *"How is the energy transfer we read about today similar to or different from the energy transfer we learned about in last week's experiment?"* or *"Why are power and authority important to consider as we study westward expansion?"*

AFTER READING

Wrap Up

 Let's think of some questions to check whether we really understood what we read.

 Remember to write different types of questions:

1. "Right There"
2. "Think and Search"
3. "Author and You"

 Write your questions and the answers in your learning log.

Who would like to share his or her best question?

Who would like to answer that question?

Where in the text did you find the information to answer that question?

CSR Colorado
Read. Lead. Succeed.

From Klingner, Vaughn, Boardman, and Swanson (2012). Reprinted with permission from John Wiley & Sons, Inc.

CSR Learning Log

Name _____ Date _____ Period _____

Today's Topic _____

Before Reading: Preview

Brainstorm: Connections to prior knowledge

Key Vocabulary

_____ = _____

_____ = _____

Purpose:

During Reading: Section 1

Clunks

_____ = _____

_____ = _____

_____ = _____

Gist

During Reading: Section 2

Clunks

_____ = _____

_____ = _____

_____ = _____

Gist

During Reading: Section 3

🔑 **Clunks**

_____ = _____

_____ = _____

_____ = _____

💡 **Gist**

After Reading: Wrap-Up

Questions: (write questions and answers)

Q:

A:

Q:

A:

Q:

A:

Review: (Connect to the purpose / CLO)

APPENDIX 4.7. Learning Log Rubric. *(page 1 of 2)*

Learning Log Rubric

Name _____

Lesson Date _____ Passage _____

	Proficient 3	Becoming Proficient 2	Not Proficient 1	Score
Before				
Brainstorm	• Brainstorm is directly related to the topic	• Brainstorm is *somewhat* related to the topic	• Brainstorm is not at all related to the topic • Text appears to be copied	
During				
ID Clunks	• Student selects appropriate clunks: common rather than proper nouns • Self-monitoring: no apparent clunk avoidance	• Limited evidence of self-monitoring: clunks are only chosen based on previously selected words (by teacher or book—underlined, boldfaced) • Clunks are words student already know	• No clunks listed when they are expected	
Use Fix-Up Strategies	• Use of any of four fix-up strategies to find the meaning of the clunk • Brief definition is given	• Does not use fix-up strategies correctly • Asks the teacher instead of using fix-up strategy	• Lists clunk with no definition • Uses a dictionary before attempting a fix-up strategy	
Get the Gist	• Names who/what and most important information about who/what • Gist captures overall idea of section • Gist is paraphrased and is approximately 10 words • Gist is a complete sentence	• Names who/what but focuses on details rather than the main idea • Gist is overly general • Gist is partially synthesized • Part of gist may be copied from the text	• Incorrectly names who/what • Focuses on details rather than the main idea • Gist may be copied exactly from the text • Gist is an incomplete sentence	

(continued)

From Klingner, Vaughn, Boardman, and Swanson (2012). Reprinted with permission from John Wiley & Sons, Inc.

From *The Power of Peers in the Classroom: Enhancing Learning and Social Skills*, edited by Karen R. Harris and Lynn Meltzer. Copyright 2015 by The Guilford Press. Permission to photocopy this material is granted to purchasers of this book for personal use only (see copyright page for details). Purchasers can download additional copies of this material from *www.guilford.com/harris-forms*.

140

	Proficient 3	Becoming Proficient 2	Not Proficient 1	Score
After				
Ask and Answer Questions	• More than one question type is used • Important ideas from text are captured in the questions • Questions are written in question format • Answers to questions can be found by looking in the text • Answers are written in learning log	• More than one question type is used • Important ideas are inconsistently captured in the questions • Lacks most important ideas • Answers to questions can be found by looking in the text • Answers are written in learning log	• Only one question type is given when more are expected • Important ideas are not captured in the questions • Questions are written as statements • Questions are not related to the text • Questions do not support comprehension of the text • Answers are not provided	
Review	• Statement reflects important information • Brief but complete sentence(s) • Review is paraphrased	• Reflects important information but is detail-focused	• Lacks important information • Detail-focused • Possibly copied from the text	

Comments:

TOTAL:

141

APPENDIX 4.8. Teacher's Guide for the CSR Gist Collaboration Video Clip.

This note taker is designed to help students focus on how collaboration works within the Gist strategy. There are eight categories in the table, so you may want to assign students to focus on two or so categories at a time so they capture more detailed notes. After watching the video clip, students can share and discuss their observations about their assigned categories. You may also want to show the video clip a second time.

Possible observations are listed below.

What materials do the students have on their desks?	• Expert Role Cards • Learning Logs • Reading • Something to write with
What do the students appear to be doing?	• Focusing on Gists • Reading and writing—"most important idea about the topic" • Taking turns sharing gists and listening—"mine was ..."—"OK, read yours ..."
What are the students NOT doing?	• Goofing off • Talking to other groups • Ignoring their group • Talking about topics not related to the reading
What is the overall volume in the room?	• Pretty quiet • Talking so their group members can hear • Groups around the room are not loud or distracting to others
Can you tell any of the roles?	• Gist Expert = girl. • "OK, so before you write your gist think about the most important idea about the topic . . . and then write it down." • She also says, "Go ahead and read. We'll share our gists." • She listens to the boy's gist and helps him improve it ("that doesn't make sense . . . you could have written . . .")
At what times are students working independently?	• Each student writes his/her own gist on his/her Learning Log
Who is sharing gists with the group? Are they all the same?	• Each student shares • Gists are NOT the same
Who is helping to improve someone's gist, and how is he/she helping?	• Listening to one another • Responding to one another • Girl/Gist Expert: "that doesn't make sense . . . you could have written . . ." • Boy (Student 2)—does not let them move on to the next section. Says, "No, but the bad part . . ." • Gist Expert explains what she wrote (that fits into the "bad part") • Reread parts of the text

Peer-Assisted Learning Strategies to Improve Students' Word Recognition and Reading Comprehension

DEVIN M. KEARNS, DOUGLAS FUCHS, LYNN S. FUCHS,
KRISTEN L. MCMASTER, and LAURA SÁENZ

As every classroom teacher can attest, providing differentiated instruction for all students is often very challenging (Fuchs, Fuchs, Mathes, & Simmons, 1997). Students have a wide range of needs—some students are below grade level and others above, some students may not speak English as their first language, and likely some students have disabilities (cf. Fuchs & Fuchs, 2003). It can be very difficult for teachers to meet all of these needs at the same time. It is even harder because most teachers have limited time to plan. As a result, many teachers feel compelled to target instruction for the students "at the middle," thus limiting the growth of both low- and high-achieving students (Baker & Zigmond, 1990).

Peer-Assisted Learning Strategies (PALS) for Reading is a set of programs that help teachers differentiate reading instruction without creating individualized materials. The PALS programs are research-based, peer-mediated, and improve student achievement by providing students with intensive, sustained practice of important reading skills. There are four levels of PALS: Kindergarten, First Grade, Grades 2–6, and High School. In Kindergarten PALS (K-PALS) and First Grade PALS, children build word recognition skills. In Grades 2–6 PALS and High School PALS, students develop reading comprehension and fluency. In all levels of PALS, children work in pairs to complete reading activities, following clear, simple procedures prescribed by the program. PALS also includes a reinforcement system to keep students on task and provide positive feedback for completing academic tasks.

The purpose of this chapter is to provide readers with a detailed introduction to the PALS Reading programs. This chapter will not provide enough detail to start PALS—for that, the appropriate manual is needed—but it will explain the activities involved, how children learn them and do them, and what role the teacher plays. We hope this explanation is clear enough to help teachers and instructional leaders decide whether PALS fits the needs of their students.

In the following sections, we begin by describing the general design of the PALS programs. Then, we describe the research that has shown PALS improves reading skills. Next, we describe each of the levels of the programs, K-PALS, First Grade PALS, Grades 2–6 PALS, and High School PALS in detail. We explain how the activities work and provide examples to make clear how the procedures work. Finally, we describe practices to plan for PALS, start implementation, and sustain use of the program.

OVERVIEW OF PALS READING

Design of the PALS Programs

PALS focuses on reading skills that are important for each grade level (e.g., National Institute of Child Health and Human Development, 2000; Scarborough, 2001; Snow, Burns, & Griffin, 1998; see Table 5.1). In PALS, most or all of the activities are conducted in pairs. PALS is *same-age* peer tutoring, that is, the students are in the same grade. The pairs are created so that one student is higher in reading skill than the other. In most cases, high-performing readers are paired with average-performing readers, and average-performing readers are paired with low-performing readers. This system typically assures that students vary in reading skill but also assures the skill difference is not extreme. With a moderate difference in reading skill, both students often benefit from PALS.

TABLE 5.1. PALS Programs, Lessons, and Skills

Program	Lessons	Skills covered
Kindergarten PALS	72	Phonological awareness, grapheme–phoneme correspondence, decoding (phonics), sight word reading, reading fluency
First Grade PALS	70	Grapheme–phoneme correspondence, decoding (phonics), sight word reading, reading fluency
PALS for Grades 2–6	12 training lessons	Reading fluency, reading comprehension (summarizing, retelling, predicting)
High School PALS	6 training lessons	Reading fluency, reading comprehension (summarizing, retelling, predicting)

For all PALS activities, all students do two jobs, serving both as the *Coach* and the *Reader*. As the Coach, the student watches the Reader and provides help when needed. As the Reader, the student reads, responds to prompts from the Coach, and accepts the Coach's help. The Coach follows explicit, scripted instructions to prompt the Reader and provide help when the Reader is stuck or makes a mistake. The precise job descriptions, procedures, and prompts are designed to keep both students engaged in academic learning throughout the PALS lesson. One example of the way the procedures promote engagement is K-PALS teachers tell students that when the Coach and Reader complete a K-PALS activity, they immediately return to the beginning of the activity and practice it again.

PALS also includes a motivation system to keep the pair focused on academic tasks. In all versions except High School PALS, pairs earn points for completing PALS activities. For example, pairs earn 5 points in First Grade PALS every time they finish reading a list of sight words. Pairs earn rewards for earning points. In K-PALS, each pair receives praise from the teacher and applause from the class when they earn 100 points. In First Grade PALS and Grades 2–6 PALS, the class is divided into two teams, and pairs' points go toward a team total. The team that accumulates the most points in a week is the Winning Team and gets to stand and take a bow, while the teacher and the other team applauds for them. In High School PALS, students earn PALS Dollars instead of points. The dollars are accumulated over time and are used to "buy" prizes from the PALS Store.

Research on PALS Reading

Over the past 20 years, Doug Fuchs, Lynn S. Fuchs, and their colleagues at Vanderbilt University conducted a series of studies in which they designed different versions of PALS in collaboration with teachers (e.g., Fuchs, Fuchs, & Burish, 2000). The PALS programs were tested using rigorous methods of evaluation that allow us to say that PALS is a research-based program. Due to the research results, the U.S. Department of Education's What Works Clearinghouse (*http://ies.ed.gov/ncee/wwc*) lists Kindergarten PALS and First Grade PALS as effective interventions for improving beginning readers' alphabetics skills. Their review of evidence on Grades 2–6 PALS determined it is effective for improving students' reading comprehension skills and the reading achievement of English language learners (ELLs) and students with learning disabilities (LD). We describe the results of some representative studies below.

Kindergarten PALS' Effectiveness

Two main studies were conducted to evaluate the effectiveness of Kindergarten PALS (K-PALS) Reading. Fuchs et al. (2001b) found that K-PALS students had greater improvement than students in control condition (i.e., without PALS) in phonological awareness, grapheme–phoneme correspondence (GPC; i.e., letter–sounds like c = /k/), word reading, decoding, and fluency. On average, effect sizes were greater than 0.50 in standard deviation units, representing about an additional half grade-level of improvement.[1] Put differently, this means that at least 70% of students in K-PALS did better than the students in the control classrooms (Lipsey et al., 2012). Stein et al. (2008) conducted a large-scale, multisite study of K-PALS and found that students who participated in K-PALS were better at GPC fluency than students who did not participate in K-PALS. Based on these findings, Hollands et al. (2013) indicated that K-PALS was one of the most cost-effective programs available for beginning readers, compared with other programs with positive evidence from the What Works Clearinghouse. Fuchs et al. (2002b) and Rafdal, McMaster, McConnell, D. Fuchs, and L. S. Fuchs (2011) also found that K-PALS led to positive effects for students with disabilities.

First Grade PALS Effectiveness

Fuchs et al. (2001a) found that students who participated in First Grade PALS performed better than students in a no-PALS comparison condition on measures of phonological awareness, decoding, word recognition, and spelling after 22 weeks of implementation, with effect sizes of about 0.50. Fuchs et al. (2001b) also found students in First Grade PALS did better than students in the comparison condition on measures of reading comprehension and fluency, with effects between 0.20 and 0.30 standard deviations, about the difference between a student at the 50th percentile and one at the 60th percentile.

Grades 2–6 PALS Effectiveness

PALS Reading for Grades 2–6 was tested by Fuchs and colleagues (1997). They found that students of teachers who implemented PALS had larger gains in fluency and reading comprehension than students in comparison classrooms where PALS was not implemented. These effects, observed both for average-achieving (ES = 0.56) and low-achieving (ES = 0.55) students, were larger than the expected growth of students between third and sixth grade. On average, students in these grades are expected to have a between-grade growth equal to an effect size between 0.32 and 0.40 (Lipsey et al., 2012). Students identified with LD also made significant—albeit smaller—gains (ES = 0.22). Sáenz, Fuchs, and Fuchs (2005) showed ELLs in third through sixth grade—including high-, average-, and low-achieving students and students with LD—all improved their reading skills through PALS. Students with LD in PALS classrooms also experienced more social acceptance than did students with LD in comparison classrooms (Dion, Fuchs, & Fuchs, 2005; Fuchs, Fuchs, Mathes, & Martinez, 2002a).

---

[1]Cohen (1988) suggested using 0.2 to describe a "small" but meaningful effect, 0.5 to describe a "medium" effect, and 0.8 to describe a "large" effect.

High School PALS Effectiveness

The High School version of PALS was shown to improve the reading comprehension skills of high schoolers in self-contained special education or remedial-reading classrooms, with an effect size of 0.34 (Fuchs, Fuchs, & Kazdan, 1999). These data indicated that more than 60% of the students in the PALS condition had scores above students in the comparison group. In high schools, standardized reading gains year to year are less than 0.20 on average (Lipsey et al., 2012), so this effect of 0.34 represents more than a year's growth, compared to what is generally expected in high school.

PALS PROGRAMS

K-PALS Reading

K-PALS Activities

There are three parts to each K-PALS lesson, summarized in Table 5.2. First, there is a teacher-directed *Sound Play* activity that provides phonological awareness practice. Second, there is a *Decoding Lesson* that the class practices as a whole group and that the students then complete in pairs. The Decoding Lesson includes activities to practice reading GPC (*What Sound?*), sight word recognition (*Sight Words*), decoding words (*Sound Boxes*), and reading sentences with fluency (*Reading Sentences*). The last activity is *Partner Reading*, which students complete in pairs using teacher-selected texts. This activity is introduced about halfway through the program.

When the students do the Decoding Lesson in their pairs, the students are paired by reading skill level, as previously indicated (See "Design of the PALS Programs" pp. 144–145, for details on creating pairs.) The student who reads first (given the title of *Reader* because this is the first job this student has) is lower in reading skill than the student who reads second. The student who reads second is given the title of the *Coach*, because this student coaches first. During the Decoding Lesson and Partner Reading, both students do the jobs of Coach and Reader. After the Reader completes one section of the Decoding Lesson, the partners switch jobs. Then, the Reader coaches and the Coach reads.

SOUND PLAY ACTIVITIES

The teacher-led Sound Play for phonological awareness takes between 3 and 5 minutes. The Sound Play activities include no letters and focus on improving beginning readers' awareness of the spoken syllables, rimes (vowels and trailing consonants; e.g., the sound of -*at* in *cat*), and phonemes (individual sounds; e.g., the sounds of *c, a,* and *t* in *cat*) within words. The activities change every three to six lessons. Each addresses a different phonological awareness skill, as described in Table 5.3. The Sound Play lessons often contain sounds students will practice during the Decoding Lesson.

TABLE 5.2. Kindergarten PALS (K-PALS) Activities and Academic Purposes

Activity	Summary	Purpose	Lesson introduced
Sound Play	Teachers lead students in activities that practice sound identification, rhyming, and sound blending.	Phonological awareness development	Intro 1[a]
Decoding Lesson	Students work in Coach/Reader pairs to complete the four activities below.		
What Sound?	The Coach points at alphabet letters and asks the Reader "What sound?" The Reader gives the sound.	Grapheme–phoneme correspondence knowledge	1
Sight Words	The Coach points at high-frequency sight words and says "What word?" The Reader reads the word.	Sight word reading skill	5
Sound Boxes	The Coach tells the Reader to "Say the word slowly" and then to "Sing it and read it." The Reader first says the sounds slowly, then sings them, then reads the word.	Decoding practice	3
Reading Sentences	The Coach tells the Reader, "Read the sentence," and the Reader reads it.	Sentence fluency	29
Partner Reading	The First Reader reads a page and then the Second Reader rereads the same page.	Passage fluency and comprehension	39

[a]Intro 1 refers to a set of four 5-minute lessons conducted the week before formal K-PALS instruction begins. These short lessons include instruction about the purpose of K-PALS, information that the students will work in pairs, and practice with very simple phonological awareness activities.

Teachers begin implementing Sound Play during an Introduction Week. In that week, the students learn the purpose of K-PALS, learn they will work with a partner to complete K-PALS activities, and practice the first Sound Play activities. In Introduction Lessons 1 and 2, the Sound Play activities involve syllable clapping, a simple activity with which most students are successful. The lessons help the students understand what will happen during Sound Play. In Introduction Lessons 3 and 4, students learn the First Sound A activity, described in Table 5.3.

Figure 5.1 illustrates the First Sound A activity. The teacher repeats each Sound Play activity at least twice. The teacher also adds additional practice if the students do not understand the activity or perform poorly on the items.

STUDENT DECODING LESSONS

After Sound Play, the students complete four activities using a Student Decoding Lesson sheet. The Student Decoding Lesson sheet for Lesson 29 is shown in Figure 5.2. The teacher practices all of the activities with the whole class before the stu-

TABLE 5.3. K-PALS Sound Play Activities

Activity	Sample	Purpose and Procedure	First Lesson	Total Lessons
First Sound A	Intro Lesson 3	*Purpose*: To identify words' initial phonemes. *Procedure*: Teacher says two words with target phoneme, and students choose between two pictures.	Intro 3	10
First Sound B	Lesson 5	*Purpose*: To identify words' initial phonemes. *Procedure*: Teacher says one word with target phoneme, and students choose between three pictures.	5	12
Rhyming	Lesson 9	*Purpose*: To identify words that rhyme. *Procedure*: Teacher says two words with target rime, and students choose between two pictures.	9	8
Guess My Word A	Lesson 13	*Purpose*: To blend phonemes to form spoken words. *Procedure*: Teacher says the four words that rhyme. Then, she says one of the word's phonemes while pointing at large top boxes. Students repeat the sounds and say the word they make.	13	16

(continued)

TABLE 5.3. *(continued)*

Activity	Sample	Purpose and Procedure	First Lesson	Total Lessons
Guess My Word B		*Purpose*: To blend phonemes to form spoken words. *Procedure*: Same as Guess My Word A, except words all begin with the same phoneme.	17	8
Guess My Word Mix	Same as above, with pictures that contain a variety of phonemes	*Purpose*: To blend phonemes to form spoken words. *Procedure*: Same as Guess My Word A, except words contain a variety of phonemes.	48	8
Last Sound		*Purpose*: To identify words' final phonemes. *Procedure*: Teacher says two words with target phoneme, and students choose between two pictures.	37	12

Note. Adapted from *Peer-Assisted Learning Strategies Kindergarten Reading Teacher Manual* by D. Fuchs, et al.(n.d.) Adapted with permission.

Intro Lesson 3

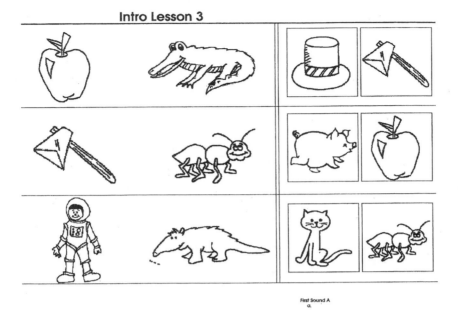

First Sound A
a.

FIGURE 5.1. First Sound A (Sound Play activity). For the first item on the page, the teacher says, *"Apple,* /a/ (IPA: /æ/). *Alligator,* /a/. What starts with /a/, *hat* or *axe*?" The students respond, *"Axe,* /a/." If the students make an error, the teacher corrects the class by saying the correct answer and repeating the item. From D. Fuchs et al. (n.d.). Reprinted with permission from the authors.

dents complete the activities in pairs. During the whole-class practice, the teacher shows the students the entire Student Decoding Lesson sheet with an overhead projector, with a document camera, or on a Smart Board. If none of these technologies are available, the teacher can write the lesson on chart paper or use the K-PALS Large Print Manual (see Table 5.4 for a list of all materials needed for all versions of PALS). The teacher acts as the Coach and the students are all Readers. The teacher shows the students how to prompt the Reader and how to provide corrective feedback when the Reader makes a mistake. The teacher also asks students to take turns as the Coach. During the first few lessons, the teacher selects coaches who can model correct prompting and corrections. Later, the teacher selects students who may need to review coaching procedures. The class practices the activities as many times as the teacher feels is needed.

The What Sound? activity is the first activity in the Student Decoding Lesson, designed to improve recall of GPCs. In K-PALS, GPCs are taught for the 26 alphabet letters (*q* is taught as *qu* = /kw/) and the consonant digraphs *sh, ch, th,* and *ck.* During the activity, the Coach points at each grapheme (letter pattern). Here is a sample script for the What Sound activity for Lesson 29, shown in Figure 5.2 (top section):

COACH: (*Points at* g.) What sound?
READER: /g/.

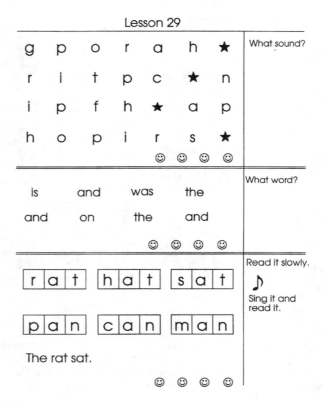

FIGURE 5.2. The Student Decoding Lesson sheet for K-PALS Lesson 29, the first lesson in which the students complete all four activities (What Sound?, Sight Words, Sound Boxes, and Sentences). The teacher practices the entire sheet with the whole class before they do it in pairs. For each of the three sections, both students must complete the activities before they move on to the next section. When each student finishes reading a section, the Coach places a slash through the happy face, and the students then switch jobs. From D. Fuchs et al. (n.d.). Reprinted with permission from the authors.

The students are taught to pronounce the sounds without a trailing "uh" (IPA: /ə/), or schwa, sound.[2] Many adults have difficulty removing the schwa from their pronunciations as well, so we wish to remind readers that the addition of schwa to consonant sounds distorts them. If asked to blend "kuh" (IPA: /kə/), "ah" (IPA: /æ/), and "tuh" (IPA: /tə/), a student is likely to think *cuh-att-tuh* (IPA: /kə 'æ tə/) is correct rather than *cat* (Elbro, de Jong, Houter, & Nielsen, 2012). Thus, teachers must be careful with their own pronunciations. We are often asked whether we should be similarly persnickety about students' pronunciations. Generally, we do not advise correcting students if they add schwa, as this is likely to be more confusing than helpful. Moreover, with good teacher modeling, students are less likely to distort the sounds. Teachers might occasionally have students practice

---

[2]In this chapter, we use a simple system for representing sounds, placing graphemes (letters or letter combinations that represent a single sound) between slashes. For readers familiar with the International Phonetic Alphabet (IPA), we also include the formal IPA symbols in parentheses afterward.

TABLE 5.4. Information about PALS Reading Materials

Item	Kinder-garten	First grade	Grades 2–6	High school	Number needed	Source
Teacher materials						
Teacher manual	Y	Y	Y	Y	1 per classroom	Order from PALS website
Timer for the teacher	Y	Y	Y	Y	1 per classroom	Purchase separately
Large-print manual	Y	N	N	N	1 per classroom; optional	Order from PALS website (optional)
DVD	Y	N	Y	Y	1 per classroom; optional	Order from PALS website (optional)
Transparencies/scans for Smart Board/document camera/large-print versions	Y	Y	Y	Y	1 set per classroom	Make from teacher manual
Pair materials						
Folders	Y	Y	Y	Y	1 per pair	Purchase separately
Point sheets	Y	Y	Y	N	1 per pair per week	Copy from teacher manual
Lesson sheets	Y	Y	N	N	1 per pair per lesson	Copy from teacher manual
Question Card and Correction Card	N	N	Y	Y	1 each per pair	Copy from teacher manual
Trade books, chapter books, or other texts	N	Y	Y	Y	1 per pair per week/month	Purchase separately; use existing
Decodable books	Y	Y	N	N	1 per pair per day	Purchase separately; use existing
Individual student materials						
PALS Activity Packet	N	N	Y	Y	1 per student	Copy from teacher manual
Earnings sheet	N	N	N	Y	1 per student per week	Copy from teacher manual
Check register, checks, PALS catalog	N	N	N	Y	1 per student	Copy from teacher manual
PALS note-taking sheets	N	N	N	Y	1 per student	Copy from teacher manual
Rewards						
PALS catalog items	N	N	N	Y	multiple	Purchase separately
PALS bookmarks	Y	Y	N	N	multiple	Copy from teacher manual

Note. The PALS website is accessible at *kc.vanderbilt.edu/pals.*

saying the sounds without adding schwa, but correcting every occurrence will likely reduce students' enthusiasm about doing K-PALS without perfecting their pronunciations.

If the Reader makes a mistake, the Coach immediately provides corrective feedback, as shown in Figure 5.3. This serves as an illustration of the correction procedures, all of which include (1) immediate correction of the error by the Coach, with emphasis on the correct response rather than the error, (2) repetition of the correct response by the Reader, and (3) repeating the entire line. Repeating the line serves both to increase the degree of practice and as a deterrent against careless errors because there is a cost associated with making a mistake.

Stars are placed at intervals in the What Sound? section of the K-PALS Student Decoding Lesson sheet, as shown in the top section of Figure 5.2, to prompt the Coach to provide positive social reinforcement to the Reader by saying "Good work," or providing some similar praise. When the Reader completes the activity, the Coach uses a pencil to mark a slash through the happy face. Coaches are taught not to fill in the happy faces, so as not to waste time. After the Coach marks the happy face, the students switch jobs and the Coach becomes the Reader. When both students finish What Sound?, they go on to Sight Words without prompting from the teacher.

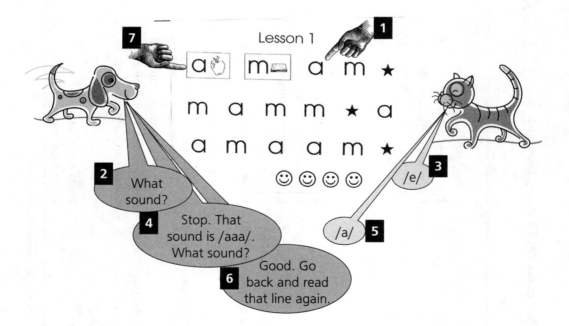

FIGURE 5.3. The correction procedure for What Sound?, where the numbers in black squares represent the sequence. In this case, the dog is the Coach and the cat is the Reader. The Coach points at a letter [1] and says, "What sound?" [2]. The Reader responds and makes an error, saying, "/e/" (IPA: /ɛ/) [3]. The Coach says, "Stop, that sound is /aaa/ (IPA: /æææ/). What sound?" [4]. The Reader repeats it [5]. The Coach tells the Reader, "Good. Go back and read that line again" [6]. The Coach then returns to the beginning of the line [7] and asks, "What sound?" for the first item again. The lesson in this figure is from D. Fuchs et al. (n.d.). Reprinted with permission from the authors.

The Sight Words activity improves students' knowledge of 21 high-frequency sight words taken from the Dolch list (Dolch, 1936). The procedure is as follows:

COACH: (*Points at* and.) What word?
READER: *And.*

If the Reader makes an error, the Coach corrects the Reader in the following way:

COACH: (*Points at* was.) What word?
READER: *What.*
COACH: Stop. That word is *was.* What word?
READER: *Was.*
COACH: Good. Start the line again.

Each student does Sight Words once before the pair moves on to Sound Boxes.

The Sound Boxes activity improves students' decoding—or phonics—skills. Students use a synthetic phonics procedure—that is, matching graphemes to phonemes and blending those sounds together to pronounce a word. For Sound Boxes, the letters representing individual sounds appear in boxes (sometimes called Elkonin boxes after the Russian psychologist who recommended their use; Clay, 1985) to draw students' attention to the connection between words' letters and sounds. Notably, both letters in a digraph occupy one box to show they say one sound. For example, the word *chop* is presented as [*ch*] [*o*] [*p*] to emphasize that the letters *ch* represent /ch/ (IPA: /tʃ/). The procedure is as follows:

COACH: Read it slowly.
READER: (*Slowly moves finger between boxes in* rat.) /rrraaat/ (IPA: /rrræææt/).
COACH: Sing it and read it.
READER: (*Moves finger under word.*) /rraat/ (IPA: /rrææt/) (*in a sing-songy voice, to promote blending of the phonemes. Moves finger under word again.*) *Rat.*

Errors during Sound Boxes are corrected using the same general form as for the other activities, as follows, for the word *hat* pronounced /hit/ (IPA: /hɪt/):

COACH: Read it slowly.
READER: /hiiit/ (IPA: /hɪɪɪt/).
COACH: Stop, that word is /haaat/ (IPA: /hæææt/), /haat/ (IPA: /hææt/) (*in a sing-songy voice.*) *Hat.* What word?
READER: /haaat/ (IPA: /hæææt/), /haat/ (IPA: /hææt/) (*in a sing-songy voice.*) *Hat.*
COACH: Good. Start the line again. (*Reader points at first word on line.*)

In Lesson 29, the Sentences activity is added. The Coach merely says, "Read the sentence," and the Reader does so. Errors are corrected as with errors during Sight Words or Sound Boxes.

When students finish the Decoding Lesson each day, they count their happy faces. They mark one point on the point sheet for each face (see Figure 5.4). When the pair fills their point sheet, the teacher recognizes the students for completing it by asking the class to applaud for the pair, by posting their completed point sheets on a K-PALS bulletin board, or with some other method that provides social reinforcement.

PARTNER READING

In Lesson 39, or about the 10th week of K-PALS, pairs begin Partner Reading. In this activity, the Coach reads a sentence and the Reader repeats it, which is the opposite of the Student Decoding Lesson order, in which the Reader reads first. The Coach—who is a better reader—can provide a fluent model for the Reader, which allows the Reader to benefit more from the repeated reading. Repeated reading is thought to improve reading fluency—and potentially reading comprehension—in elementary school students (e.g., O'Connor, White, & Swanson, 2007; Sindelar,

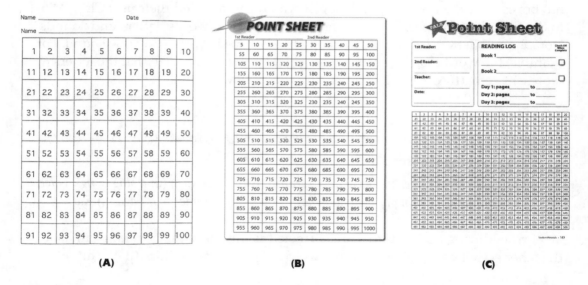

FIGURE 5.4. PALS point sheets: (A) the K-PALS sheet; (B) the First Grade sheet; (C) the Grades 2–6 sheet. In K-PALS, pairs get 1 point for each happy face on the Student Decoding Lesson sheet and 1 point for each time they finish reading a book. In First Grade, pairs get 5 points for each happy face on the Student Decoding Lesson sheet and 5 points for each time they finish reading a book. In Grades 2–6 PALS, students receive 1 point per sentence read during Partner Reading, up to 10 points for their Retell, and 3 points for each completed cycle of Paragraph Shrinking or Partner Reading activities. Figure 5.4A from D. Fuchs et al. (n.d.). Reprinted with permission from the authors. Figure 5.4B from D. Fuchs et al. (2011). Reprinted with permission from the authors. Figure 5.4C from D. Fuchs et al. (2008). Reprinted with permission from the authors.

Monda, & O'Shea, 1990). The teacher selects books at the "instructional level" (Burns, 2007) of the lower-performing reader, meaning this student can read the book with 93% to 97% accuracy (that is, about 1 mistake every 20 or 25 words). The higher-performing reader should be able to read the book at the independent level, between 98% and 100% accuracy (that is, no more than 2 mistakes per 100 words). One alternative way of assuring students can read the book is for the teacher to model reading a book for the whole class, and all of the pairs read the same book.

During Partner Reading, the correction for missed words is the same as that in Sight Words for sight words and Sound Boxes for decodable words. If neither student knows how to say a word, the Coach raises his or her hand to get the teacher's attention, and the Reader continues reading. When possible, the teacher tells the pair the word they have missed. The pair repeats it and resumes reading. When the pair finishes reading a book, they mark a point on the point sheet. Pairs read one book at least six times before asking the teacher for a new book.

First Grade PALS Reading

Overview of First Grade PALS Reading

First Grade PALS Reading, like K-PALS, emphasizes basic skills in reading. Students participate in activities focused on learning GPCs, practicing sight words, decoding, and fluency. Unlike K-PALS, First Grade PALS activities are almost all done in pairs. The teacher begins the lesson by conducting a whole-class activity called *Hearing Sounds and Sounding Out*. Then, the student pairs complete the *Student Decoding Lesson*, which is similar to K-PALS' Decoding Lesson. After about 10 weeks of First Grade PALS implementation, teachers introduce *Partner Reading*, as in K-PALS. The times for each activity are prescribed, and the teacher tells the students when to move to the next one (see Table 5.5).

In each pair, the students are called the *First Reader* and the *Second Reader*, based on whether they read first. The students are paired high-average and average-low (there are more details on pairing in a subsequent section), and the First Reader is the lower-performing reader. Both students act as Coach and Reader, as in K-PALS.

First Grade PALS Activities

The teacher first introduces new sounds and conducts the Hearing Sounds and Sounding Out whole-class activity. Then, the students complete most of the remaining activities using the Student Decoding Lesson sheet. Each activity is described below.

TEACHER-DIRECTED HEARING SOUNDS AND SOUNDING OUT

The teacher leads the class in this activity that combines phonological awareness and decoding. Figure 5.5 illustrates how the activity is conducted. During

TABLE 5.5. First-Grade PALS Reading Activities and Academic Purposes

Activity	Summary	Purpose	Time	First lesson
Hearing Sounds and Sounding Out	The teacher leads the class in identifying the sounds in a spoken word. Then, the class sounds the word out together and reads it quickly. The same words are used for the Hearing Sounds and Sounding Out activities.	Phonemic awareness and decoding practice	~3 min	3
Saying Sounds	The Coach points at alphabet letters and asks the Reader, "What sound?" The Reader gives the sound.	Grapheme–phoneme correspondence knowledge	3 min	1
Sounding Out	The Coach tells the Reader to "sound it out" and then to "read it fast." The Reader first says the sounds slowly and then reads the word.	Decoding practice	4 min	4
Sight Words	The Coach tells the Reader to "read the words." The Reader reads the entire word list.	Sight word reading skill	3 min	5
Stories	The Coach tells the Reader, "Read the sentence," and the Reader reads it.	Passage reading fluency	5 min	6
Speed Game	Each student reads the words in the Sight Words or Stories activity as quickly as she can three times. Her goal is to read more words the second or third time.	Word identification fluency or passage reading fluency	~5 min	7
Partner Reading	The First Reader reads a page and then the Second Reader rereads the same page.	Passage fluency and comprehension	~10 min	30

the Hearing Sounds part of the Hearing Sounds and Sounding Out activity, the teacher does not point at the lesson page, although it is visible. To conduct this part of the lesson, the teacher holds the teacher manual in the left hand and uses the right hand to guide the students through segmenting the word orally. To do this, the teacher holds up the right hand, palm toward the body. Then, the teacher puts up one finger for each sound in the word, beginning with the thumb. It is important that the students see the first finger on the left side, so that the direction of the fingers follows the direction of print. Figure 5.6 illustrates how to do this. During the Sounding Out part of the Hearing Sounds and Sounding Out activity, the teacher then points to the word and prompts the students to "sound it out" and "read it fast," pointing to each letter as the students blend the sounds in the word.

FIGURE 5.5. Procedure for conducting teacher-directed Hearing Sounds and Sounding Out. The teacher holds up the Hearing Sounds and Sounding Out lesson page, printed in the teacher manual in large print. She then tells the class to say the sounds in a word [1]. She does not point at the lesson page because this is the "Hearing Sounds" part of the activity to practice phonemic awareness. As the students say the sounds [2], she holds up one finger for each sound they say. Then, the teacher tells the students to sound out the word [3] and slides her finger under each letter as the students say the sounds [4]. The students pronounce the sounds continuously (/cheeeksss/ [IPA: /tʃɛɛɛksss/]) rather than one by one (/ch/, /e/, /k/, /s/). Finally, the teacher tells the students to say the word [5], and the students say it normally [6]. From D. Fuchs et al. (2011). Reprinted with permission from the authors.

If the students make mistakes, the teacher says, for example, "Stop, that word is /kaaat/ (IPA: /kæææt/), *cat*. Sound it out." Students then sound it out. The teacher instructs the students to read it fast and has the class start the line again. The Sounding Out procedure and correction are the same as the one the Coach uses in the Student Decoding Lesson. Once the teacher has completed Hearing Sounds and Sounding Out, the teacher introduces any new sight words the students will encounter during the Student Decoding Lesson. A box around the sight word shows it is a new sight word, as illustrated in Figure 5.7 (for *what*). Then, the students complete the Saying Sounds, Sounding Out, and Sight Words activities for 3 minutes, 4 minutes, and 3 minutes, respectively. Figure 5.7 shows each of these (see boxes 1, 2, and 3).

STUDENT DECODING LESSON

The Saying Sounds activity is identical to the What Sound? activity in K-PALS. The Sounding Out activity is identical to the Sounding Out part of the teacher-directed Hearing Sounds and Sounding Out activity. It is important that the students not do the Hearing Sounds part of the activity (i.e., putting up the fingers and pronouncing the phonemes). For the Sight Words activity, the Coach simply says, "Read the

Instructions	Hand shape	Teacher language	Student language

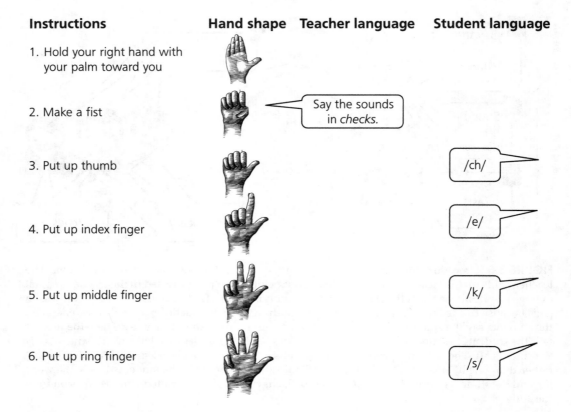

1. Hold your right hand with your palm toward you

2. Make a fist — Say the sounds in *checks*.

3. Put up thumb — /ch/

4. Put up index finger — /e/

5. Put up middle finger — /k/

6. Put up ring finger — /s/

FIGURE 5.6. Hand shapes for conducting Hearing Sounds activity in First Grade PALS. This diagram shows the hand shapes from the teacher's point of view. The students see the fingers coming up from left to right, following the direction of print.

words," and the Reader reads them without stopping for further prompts from the Coach (as was done in K-PALS). Notably, the First Grade PALS sight words are often grouped in phrases, and teachers often encourage students to say the phrases together. There are corrections for each of these activities that are the same as the corrections described for What Sound?, Sight Words, and Sounding Out previously. The Reader always repeats the line whenever there is a mistake.

When the First Reader completes an activity once, the Coach marks a happy face and 5 points on the point sheet. The First Grade point sheet contains 400 points rather than 100 as in K-PALS, and the points go toward a team total (described further below). Then, the students switch jobs and the Second Reader completes the activity. If the time allotted for the activity has not elapsed when both readers have completed the activity once, the First Reader becomes the Reader again and does the activity again. Pairs can continue earning points and work on the same activity until the teacher's timer goes off.

After Sight Words, the teacher teaches the students any new *Rocket Words* needed to read the story. Rocket Words are words the students could not decode using only the GPCs learned in First Grade PALS, which have not been taught as sight words, and which are needed to read the story. The teacher briefly teaches

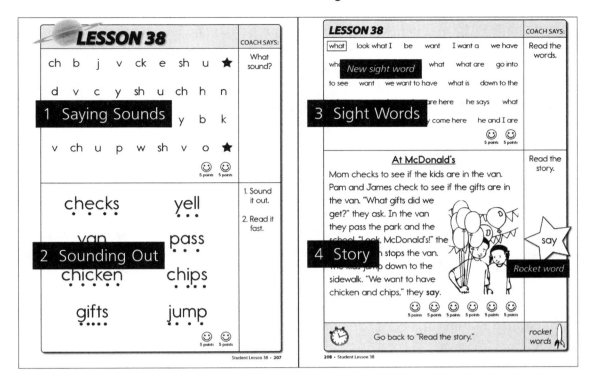

FIGURE 5.7. First Grade PALS Reading student lesson sheet for Lesson 38. From D. Fuchs et al. (2011). Reprinted with permission from the authors.

these as she would teach sight words. Then, the teacher reads the story aloud to the class as they follow along. Finally, the students return to their pairs and read the story in pairs for 5 minutes.

SPEED GAME

The Speed Game is an individual student activity to increase reading speed, although the students continue sitting with their partner. During this activity, the First Reader returns to the Sight Words section of the Student Decoding Lesson, and the teacher gives the First Reader 30 seconds to read as far as possible in the section. As the First Reader reads, the Second Reader coaches and corrects mistakes by just saying the correct word. The First Reader simply repeats the word and continues reading. This correction procedure limits the time taken from the Reader during this speeded activity.

When the teacher's timer goes off, the First Reader circles the last word he read and puts his initial on the page. Then, the First Reader reads again for 30 seconds, circles the last word, and writes his/her initials by the circle. This is done a third time. If the First Reader got further the second or third time, he marks an X through one of the rockets on his Speed Game chart. When he fills up the chart, he gets a bookmark and a new chart. A bookmark template is provided in the

First Grade PALS manual. A sample Speed Game chart and bookmark template are shown in Figure 5.8.

When the First Reader has finished, the Second Reader tries to beat his own time on the second or third reading as well. The students do not compete directly against each other, so each student has his own Speed Game Chart. Once the students reach Lesson 29, the Speed Game switches from reading the sight words to reading the story to emphasize passage fluency.

PARTNER READING

In Week 10 of First Grade PALS, around Lesson 30, the teacher introduces the pairs to Partner Reading. For this activity, the teacher explains that the Second Reader reads a page first and the First Reader reads it second. This is because—as in K-PALS—the stronger reader can model for the weaker reader. As in K-PALS, the text should be at the instructional level of the lower reader and the independent level of the higher reader. The students get a happy face and 5 points each time they finish reading the book. They read for a total of 10 minutes each PALS session.

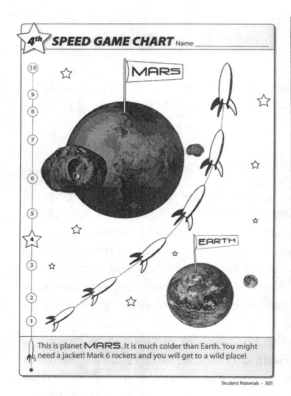
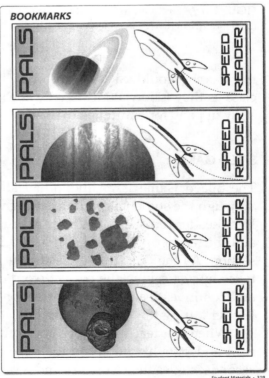

FIGURE 5.8. A sample First Grade PALS Speed Game Chart and bookmark template. From D. Fuchs et al. (2011). Reprinted with permission from the authors.

POINTS AND TEAMS

In First Grade PALS, the pairs are placed into two teams. The teacher determines the teams ahead of time, taking care to balance the teams so that each team has an equal number of stronger and weaker pairs. At the end of each week, the teacher tallies the points of all the pairs on each team and declares the Winning Team and the Second Place Team. The Winning Team stands up, takes a bow, and receives applause from the Second Place Team. The Second Place Team receives applause but does not get to take a bow. The use of the points toward the team total links the points to peer praise and makes the points more meaningful. Alternative rewards may be used, but we encourage teachers to use rewards that provide social reinforcement and cost very little or nothing (e.g., free time).

Grades 2–6 PALS Reading

Grades 2–6 PALS Reading changes the emphasis from the word recognition skills that comprised much of K-PALS and First Grade PALS lessons. Grades 2–6 PALS focuses on fluency and reading comprehension, in line with the emphasis on these skills in these grades as well as the expectations of the Common Core State Standards (despite being developed before them). Grades 2–6 PALS comprises four activities, *Partner Reading*, *Retell*, *Paragraph Shrinking*, and *Prediction Relay*. The length of each activity is prescribed, and the teacher tells the students when to move to the next activity. Table 5.6 provides a brief description of the activities and times. Pairs use the point sheet (Figure 5.4c) to record points for completing tasks during each activity.

Students are given the titles of First Reader and Second Reader in Grades 2–6 PALS, as in First Grade PALS. In contrast with First Grade PALS, however, the First Reader in Grades 2–6 PALS is the higher-performing reader, and the Second Reader is the lower-performing reader. Table 5. 7 provides a guide to the titles of the students in the pair, as they differ by level and mean different things. In Grades 2–6 PALS, the higher-performing reader is the First Reader because the texts are not controlled in terms of the words used, and it is important that the stronger reader models accurate, fluent reading for the lower-performing reader. Nonetheless, both students act as Coach and Reader, the higher-performing reader reading first and the lower-performing reader coaching first. Each pair reads a text at the instructional level of the lower-performing reader, following the same guidelines described above (i.e., 93–97% accuracy for the lower-performing reader; 98–100% accuracy for the higher-performing reader).

Grades 2–6 PALS has 12 training lessons, completed in the first 3 or 4 weeks of PALS implementation. After training is completed, the four activities are completely peer directed and take a minimum of 35 minutes to complete. We recommend teachers allot 40 or 45 minutes to provide feedback and instructional support to the class. In our research studies, teachers have generally implemented PALS three times a week.

TABLE 5.6. Grades 2–6 PALS and High School PALS Activities and Academic Purposes

Activity	Summary	Purpose	Time	Lessons taught
Partner Reading	The First Reader reads the text. When time is up, the Second Reader rereads the same text.	Passage fluency	10 min[a]	2–3
Retell	The Second Reader retells what was read during Partner Reading.[b]	Retelling	2 min[c]	4–5
Paragraph Shrinking	The First Reader reads a paragraph. The Second Reader, as Coach, asks the Paragraph Shrinking Questions, and the First Reader answers them. When time is up, the Second Reader does the same activities.	Summarizing	10 min[a]	6–8
Prediction Relay	The First Reader makes a prediction, reads half a page, and says whether the prediction came true. The Coach monitors the reading and asks the Prediction Relay questions. When time is up, the Second Reader does the same activities.	Predicting/ inference	10 min[a]	10–11

[a]The First Reader reads for 5 minutes. When the timer goes off, the Second Reader reads for 5 minutes.
[b]Sometimes teachers have students alternate Retell, the First Reader saying the first thing that happened and the Second Reader the second thing, and so on.
[c]In second grade, Retell lasts 1 minute.

TABLE 5.7. Titles of Students in Each Pair by PALS Program Level

Level	Title if reading first	Title if reading second	Higher reader	Job order switching
Kindergarten	Reader	Coach	Coach	Yes, for Partner Reading
First Grade	First Reader	Second Reader	Second Reader	Yes, for Partner Reading
Grades 2–6	First Reader	Second Reader	First Reader	No
High School	First Reader	Second Reader	First Reader	No

Note. In Kindergarten and First Grade PALS, the lower-performing reader reads first during the Decoding Lesson and second during Partner Reading.

Grades 2–6 PALS Activities

Teachers introduce students to the four activities through the 12 training lessons. These lessons are scripted, and the Grades 2–6 PALS manual also includes "Guiding Points" for teachers to use in lieu of scripts. We recommend using the scripts because we have observed that students understand the lessons better and the teachers finish the lessons faster when they use the scripts. Figure 5.9 shows a sample training lesson.

PARTNER READING

The First Reader reads for 5 minutes. The Second Reader coaches. When the teacher's timer goes off after 5 minutes, the students switch jobs and the Second Reader rereads the text the First Reader just read, starting at the same spot the First Reader

★ **INTRODUCTION TO PARAGRAPH SHRINKING**

Guiding Points

Introduce Paragraph Shrinking. Explain the following key point:

Each Reader will read for 5 minutes. After each paragraph, the reader will shrink the information into a main idea statement.

How long does the First Reader read during Paragraph Shrinking?

How long does the Second Reader read during Paragraph Shrinking?

By shrinking a paragraph down to 10 words or less, what are we creating?

How often does the reader stop to make a main idea statement?

Tell students that making main idea statements will help them to build comprehension skills.

A main idea statement is made up of 2 parts:

- **The most important who or what in the paragraph**

- **The most important thing about the who or what**

Use T-2.2 (Question Card).

Great! Now let's get excited about our next PALS activity. It's called Paragraph Shrinking. In Paragraph Shrinking, you'll shrink the information in each paragraph into a main idea statement. The main idea statement tells the most important idea in the paragraph. What does the main idea statement tell us?

STUDENTS: *The most important idea in the paragraph.*

As in Partner Reading, each Reader will read for 5 minutes. How long will each Reader read during Paragraph Shrinking?

STUDENTS: *Five minutes.*

That's right. At the end of each paragraph read, the Reader will stop to create a main idea statement. The Reader will go through 3 steps to create a main idea statement that is 10 words or less. When we shrink a paragraph down to 10 words or less, what are we creating?

STUDENTS: *A main idea statement.*

How often does the reader stop to make a main idea statement?

STUDENTS: *After every paragraph.*

That's right! Paragraph Shrinking will help you make good main idea statements. Being able to make good main idea statements will strengthen your reading comprehension. A main idea statement is made up of 2 parts:

- The most important who or what in the paragraph

- The most important thing about the who or what

⬥(T) Use Transparency 2.3 (Question Card - page 2).

Everyone, look at your Question Card. Point to the section where it says "Paragraph Shrinking."

Pause for students to point.

These are the 3 things the Coach will ask the Reader to do after each paragraph to help them make a good main idea statement. Let's read them together:

62 · Day 6: Introduction to Paragraph Shrinking

FIGURE 5.9. A sample from Training Lesson 6. The gray bar on the left contains the Guiding Points and the right side shows the script. From D. Fuchs et al. (2011). Reprinted with permission from the authors.

began. Teachers sometimes give each pair a sticky note to mark their starting spot, as pairs sometimes forget where they started.

In Partner Reading, the Coach has two jobs. The Coach's primary job is to follow along as the Reader reads and check the Reader's mistakes. Table 5.8 shows the four types of errors the Reader might make and the Coach's response to each one. In all cases, the Reader rereads the sentence that contained an error. The Coach's second job is to mark a point on the point sheet for each sentence the Reader reads.

Coaches sometimes have difficulty simultaneously paying attention to the Reader and marking a point for each sentence. A simple way to address this problem is to have the Coach count the points on his or her fingers and mark the point sheet once the Reader gets 5 points. Another possible solution is to assign a number of points per page (usually 5 or 10) and have the Coach mark the point sheet when they finish the page.

RETELL

After Partner Reading, each pair retells what they just read for 2 minutes. The First Reader coaches and asks the Second Reader, "What happened first?" and the Second Reader says the first event in the section read. The First Reader continues

TABLE 5.8. Reader Errors and Coach Responses

Error type (language used with students)	How Reader reads "This was invitation enough."	Coach actions and prompts	Reader responses to Coach prompts
Addition (Adding a word or word ending)	*This was not enough invitation.*	→ Points to location of addition. **You added a word. Read the sentence again**.?	→ *This was invitation enough.*
Hesitation (Waiting longer than 4 seconds)	*This was [pause] . . .*	→ Counts to 4 on fingers. Points at "invitation." **Check it.** **That word is invitation. What word?** **Good. Read the sentence again.**	→ *I need some help.* → *Invitation.* → *This was invitation enough.*
Mispronunciation (Saying the wrong word or word ending)	*This was inviting enough.*	→ Points at "invitation." **Check it.** **That word is invitation. What word?** **Good. Read the sentence again.**	→ *I need some help.* → *Invitation.* → *This was invitation enough.*
Omission (Leaving out a word or word ending)	*This was enough.*	→ Points at "invitation." **Check it.** **Good. Read the sentence again.**	→ *Oh! Invitation.* → *This was invitation enough.*

Note. Reader language is written in *italics*. Coach actions are shown in plain text, and Coach language is written in **bold**.

asking what happened, and the Second Reader continues to retell. The students are permitted to look at the text as they retell. If the Second Reader skips an event, retells incorrectly, or gets stuck, the First Reader simply tells the Second Reader the answer. When Retell ends, each pair can award itself up to 10 points, self-monitored and based on whether they retold all of the events in the text they read. Teachers provide guidance to help pairs make good decisions about the number of points they deserve.

PARAGRAPH SHRINKING

After Retell, the First Reader reads new text for 5 minutes, and the pair shrinks as many paragraphs as they can. Generally, pairs shrink two or three paragraphs. When the timer goes off, the Second Reader reads new text for 5 minutes, and the pair shrinks more paragraphs. To do Paragraph Shrinking, the Coach stops the pair after they read a paragraph (or several short paragraphs, when there is dialogue), and prompts the Reader to perform the three Paragraph Shrinking steps. Figure 5.10 illustrates the steps in Paragraph Shrinking.

PREDICTION RELAY

The final Grades 2–6 PALS activity requires the Reader to make a prediction, read half a page, and check the prediction by telling whether the prediction was accurate. The Coach prompts the Reader to make a prediction by asking "What do you predict will happen next?" for fiction and "What do you predict you will learn next?" for nonfiction. After reading half a page, the Coach asks the Reader "Did your prediction come true?" and the Reader responds simply "Yes," "No," or "I don't know yet" and continues reading. The First Reader reads new text for 5 minutes. Then, the Second Reader reads new text for 5 minutes.

MINI-LESSONS

After students complete training, they will need additional support to become excellent at retelling, making main idea statements, and predicting. As a result, the Grades 2–6 PALS manual includes a set of short mini-lessons to improve students' skills in completing the PALS activities. For example, students often select too many characters or topics when they choose "the most important who or what" for paragraphs. One of the brief mini-lessons addresses this problem and can improve students' ability to do this much better. There are also three mini-lessons to help students use PALS with nonfiction texts.

High School PALS Reading

High School PALS contains the same activities as Grades 2–6 PALS, with the same purposes (see Table 5.6). There are two notable differences. First, the High School

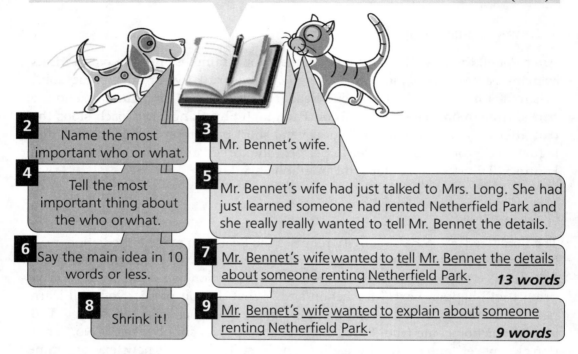

1 "My dear Mr. Bennet," said his lady to him one day, "have you heard that Netherfield Park is let at last?" Mr. Bennet replied that he had not.

"But it is," returned she; "for Mrs. Long has just been here, and she told me all about it." Mr. Bennet made no answer.

"Do you not want to know who has taken it?" cried his wife impatiently.

"*You* want to tell me, and I have no objection to hearing it."

This was invitation enough.

Austen (1813)

2 Name the most important who or what.

3 Mr. Bennet's wife.

4 Tell the most important thing about the who or what.

5 Mr. Bennet's wife had just talked to Mrs. Long. She had just learned someone had rented Netherfield Park and she really really wanted to tell Mr. Bennet the details.

6 Say the main idea in 10 words or less.

7 Mr. Bennet's wife wanted to tell Mr. Bennet the details about someone renting Netherfield Park. **13 words**

8 Shrink it!

9 Mr. Bennet's wife wanted to explain about someone renting Netherfield Park. **9 words**

FIGURE 5.10. The steps in Paragraph Shrinking, for a text sample from *Pride and Prejudice* (Austen, 2001; original work published in 1813). The Reader reads a paragraph [1], and the Coach tells the Reader where to stop. In this case, the Coach had the Reader read several paragraphs because the dialogue made each paragraph very short. Then, the Coach used the first Paragraph Shrinking prompt [2] to have the Reader identify the subject of the paragraph [3]. The Coach gives the second prompt [4] to have the Reader talk through his ideas about the important details in the paragraph [5]. The Coach gives the third prompt [6] to have the Reader synthesize the information in the paragraph. The response to the third prompt is called a *main idea statement*. The Coach counts the words in the Reader's main idea statement to assure it contains fewer than 10 words. Notably, the subject (the who or what from the first step) counts only as one word, as the underline [7] indicates. In this case, the Reader's main idea statement exceeds 10 words, so the Coach issues the "Shrink it" correction [8]. The Reader tries again to make a main idea statement with fewer than 10 words [9]. When they finish, the Coach marks 3 points on the point sheet, one for each step.

PALS Coach prompts the Reader more often. Second, the High School PALS motivation system is individualized and the adolescents earn PALS "dollars" instead of points.

There are two sets of prompts for Partner Reading and for Paragraph Shrinking. In Partner Reading, the Coach prompts the Reader when he or she makes a word identification error. The Coach will say, "Look at the parts of the word" or "Say the word very slowly." If neither of these strategies works, the Coach provides the answer. In Paragraph Shrinking, the Coach uses different strategies for different purposes, as Table 5.9 shows.

For the motivation system, students receive PALS dollars for academic behaviors, including being present for PALS, being focused, cooperating, catching mistakes, and using helping strategies. The teacher awards all of the dollars on each student's Record of Earnings Card, using his or her judgment about how many to award. Students learn to record their daily earnings in a Checkbook Register. Each month, the teacher gives each student a PALS Catalogue, and students purchase items from the PALS Store by writing a check. Figure 5.11 provides details.

IMPLEMENTING PALS READING

In this section, we provide suggestions for implementing PALS. We first address some tasks teachers must do before beginning PALS, namely, scheduling PALS, organizing for PALS, choosing texts, and pairing students. We then address the initial implementation, including the initial training and fidelity of implementation. Finally, we discuss the ongoing use of PALS, focusing on teacher monitoring, dealing with pair problems, and maintaining students' motivation during PALS. Finally, we discuss "off-label" uses of the PALS programs.

TABLE 5.9. Paragraph Shrinking Errors and Helping Strategies for High School PALS

Error	Coach response
Reader says too many who's or what's.	"Remember to choose the most important who or what."
Reader's main idea statement is incorrect (first time).	"That's not quite right. Try again."
Reader's main idea is incorrect (second time), or the reader expresses difficulty.	Asks Wh Questions (Who? What? When? Where? Why? How?) to help the Reader come up with a main idea statement.
Reader's main idea statement is more than 10 words.	"Shrink it."

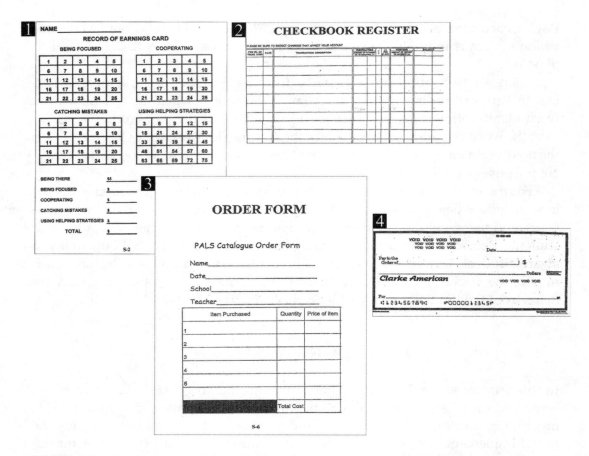

FIGURE 5.11. How students earn PALS dollars. First, the teacher awards PALS dollars during PALS for the activities listed on the Record of Earnings Card [1], and students total their earnings each day. Then, they enter their earnings in the checkbook register [2]. Once a month, the teacher provides students with the PALS Catalogue and the students order prizes from the Catalogue using the Order Form [3]. Each student writes the teacher a check for the cost of the items ordered [4], and the student deducts the amount from the checkbook register. From L. S. Fuchs et al. (n.d.). Reprinted with permission from the authors.

It is important to note that this section contains many helpful details, but some aspects of implementation are best taught through professional development (PD) provided by a PALS presenter. It is not strictly necessary to obtain PD, and virtually all of our best tips are contained in the following sections. However, some small but important details may not become clear to you without additional in-person support. In one K-PALS study, the best effects for K-PALS were obtained by combining initial PD with a set of follow-up booster sessions in which a PALS presenter met with teachers and provided ongoing implementation support (Stein et al., 2008). So, we hope the following tips are helpful to you, but we also recommend in-person PD. Information about professional development is located on the PALS website.

Before PALS Begins

Scheduling PALS

One important immediate decision concerns the schedule for PALS implementation. Two questions must be answered: (1) How many days per week should teachers conduct PALS? and (2) When should PALS implementation begin?

In terms of the weekly schedule, we recommend 3 full days of PALS per week, each lasting the recommended amount of time for that particular level (see Table 5.10). The PALS studies were conducted using a 3-day schedule, so we recommend this schedule. In some schools, it is not possible to conduct PALS in this way. In some cases, teachers and administrators will decide together that PALS lessons will be divided into two parts and conducted over 2 days. For example, in First Grade PALS, teachers will conduct Hearing Sounds and Sounding Out, Saying Sounds, Sounding Out, and Sight Words on 1 day. On the following day, they will do Story Reading, the Speed Game, and Partner Reading. We are reluctant to recommend this approach, as it slows students' reading skills development.

One approach to PALS implementation is to alternate PALS Reading and PALS Math across days. This allows for a consistent PALS time and offers students some variation, and it can improve students' long-term enjoyment of both versions of the program. Whether students get more PALS Reading or PALS Math depends on the needs of the students in the school, that is, whether there is a greater need for improvement in reading or mathematics.

TABLE 5.10. Implementation Questions and Answers

Question	Kinder-garten	First Grade	Grades 2–6	High school
How many training lessons are there?	5[a]	7	12	6
How many lessons are there in total?	72	71	—[b]	—[b]
How many minutes are pre-Partner Reading lessons?	20–25[c]	25–30	—[d]	—[d]
How many minutes are complete lessons?	25–30[c]	40–45	35–45	35–45
How many days a week should PALS be done?	3–4	3–4	3–4	3–4
How many weeks does training take?	2	2	2½–4[e]	6[f]
Can lessons be repeated?	Yes	Yes	No[g]	No[h]
Are there nonfiction reading procedures?	No	No	Yes[i]	Yes[j]

[a]There is also an Introduction week, with four 5–minute lessons, conducted before the training lessons.
[b]There is no limit on the number of lessons.
[c]The length of the activities is at the teacher's discretion.
[d]Lessons always include Partner Reading.
[e]Teachers often do training over 12 consecutive days, even when they follow the 3-day-per-week schedule.
[f]Training lessons 1 to 5 take 6 weeks. Lesson 6 on nonfiction is introduced after that and can take 2 weeks to teach.
[g]Students' skills are improved through mini-lessons rather than repeating training lessons, although training lessons can be repeated if necessary.
[h]Training lessons can be repeated if necessary.
[i]A series of mini-lessons.
[j]Lesson 6 teaches nonfiction reading procedures.

In terms of deciding when to start PALS during the year, it is best to wait at least 1 month from the beginning of school, regardless of the level. This gives students the opportunity to acclimate to their teacher's routines and procedures. It allows teachers to create a classroom culture conducive to conducting PALS. If teachers begin implementation too soon, the students may be unprepared to work together. This will reduce their ability to do PALS well and may lead to students disliking PALS, which will make it more difficult to maintain throughout the year.

PALS lessons can be conducted for most of the year. The Kindergarten and First Grade programs have daily lesson sheets that include 72 and 70 lessons, respectively, which means they could be completed in about 24 weeks, short of 36 weeks in a typical year. However, these levels of PALS will last most of the year because teachers often find they need to repeat lessons at least once so students reach high levels of accuracy. In line with the recommendation of Archer and Hughes (2011), it is appropriate to repeat a lesson if students' overall accuracy falls below 80%. The Grades 2–6 and High School programs can be taught all year long after training, as long as there are books for students to read.

Pairing Students

It is very important that students are paired thoughtfully because the students are each other's teachers. As already stated, the basic principle is that students are paired so that one student in each pair is higher in reading skill than the other, but the gap between their skill levels is not extreme. There are two ways teachers can pair students.

RANKING STUDENTS

To make the pairs, the first step is always to rank order students by reading skill level. Importantly, the rank ordering can be approximate, as teachers adjust pairs depending on students' compatibility. There are three ways to rank students: (1) use existing test scores for students, (2) administer and use progress monitoring data, or (3) use teacher judgment.

Using Existing Test Scores. If test scores are used, the measure should match the focus of the particular PALS program. For Kindergarten, we recommend letter–sound fluency at the beginning of the year. Letter–sound fluency scores are the number of letters' sounds (e.g., *c* = /k/) a student can read in a minute. Toward the end of the year, sight word fluency or decoding fluency would be appropriate. Sight word fluency is the number of sight words a student can read in a minute, and decoding fluency is how many nonwords (e.g., *vip*) a student can read in a minute. For First Grade PALS, we recommend letter–sound fluency, sight word fluency, or decoding fluency at the beginning of the year. Toward the end of First Grade, passage fluency could be used. Passage fluency is the number of words a student can read in a minute in a text. For Grades 2–6 PALS, we recommend using either passage reading fluency or reading comprehension scores to determine students' rank order. A variety of other measures could be used at any of these grades, including tests created by a teacher, school, or district. The only critical requirement is that the measure address the same skills as PALS.

Administering and Using Progress Monitoring Data. If no good information is available to guide decisions about pairing, it may be appropriate to administer a progress monitoring (PM) assessment to place the students. Letter–sound fluency, sight word fluency, decoding fluency, and passage fluency are all forms of PM that could be used. An important benefit of using PM is that the assessments take very little time to administer to each student, although they must be administered individually. An entire class can be assessed in less than an hour. For Grades 2–6 PALS, another form of PM is the CBM Maze (Fuchs & Fuchs, 1992), a measure in which approximately every seventh word is replaced by a choice of three words. The Maze is designed to measure fluency and reading comprehension. It is useful because it can be group administered, and thus an entire class can be assessed within 10 minutes.

Teacher Judgment. We often recommend that teachers rely on their own judgment to determine the rank ordering. As we described above, the pairs will be adjusted for students' compatibility, so it is not necessary for the rank order to be perfect. If the highest reader in a class was shown to be the second-highest reader on a reading comprehension test, it would make little difference in the selection of a partner for PALS. This method is also very efficient. We suggest teachers look at their class lists and write rankings for each student. It is quick and simple and sufficiently accurate for making pairs.

MAKING THE PAIRS

There are two methods for making pairs. The first method is the *high-low* method, which involves matching the highest and lowest readers, the second highest and second lowest, and so on. Powell and Fuchs (Chapter 6, this volume) provide detailed instructions on the *high-low method* in their section titled "Pairing Scheme" (pp. 218–219). The second is the *high-average/average-low* method. Figure 5.12 illustrates this approach. For this method, the teacher begins with the list of ranked students. She then divides the class in half, writing the names of the top half of the class in one column in rank order and the names of the bottom half of the class in rank order in a column next to the first. In a class of 16 students, therefore, student 1 and student 9 are partners. Then, the teacher adjusts the pairings based on students' compatibility. If the teacher knows that student 1 and student 9 will argue, she does not pair them. Two critical things to remember are these: (1) one student should be higher in reading skill than the other, and (2) the students in every pair should be likely to get along.

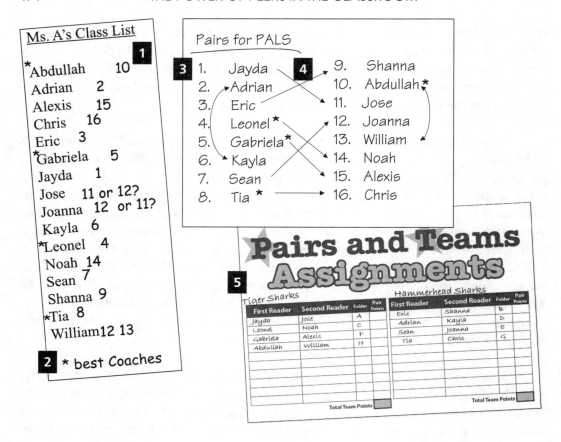

FIGURE 5.12. How teachers make pairs. For fictional Ms. A's small class, she takes an alphabetized class list (left side) and writes the rank order of the students based on her judgment [1]. She has a few questions and makes a couple of adjustments, but she spends a limited amount of time on ranking the students as she will make multiple compatibility adjustments. She also places asterisks next to the names of students who will likely be good Coaches [2]. Next, she rewrites the class list in the rank order [3], writing the top half of the class on the left and the bottom half on the right. At this point, she does not change the rank order. She also puts the asterisks next to the names of the good Coaches. Next, she draws arrows between students on the left and right sides, making adjustments for the sake of compatibility [4]. For example, Jayda and Shanna do not get along well, so Ms. A will not put them together. She knows that Jayda and Jose will work well together, and she believes that the gap between their abilities is not too large. She also tries to put good Coaches with her most needy students. Ms. A knows, for example, that Tia will be very patient with Chris. She chooses Tia for Chris instead of Leonel—who is perhaps a slightly better Coach—because she thinks the gap between Leonel, her fourth highest reader, and Chris, who is a year below grade level, is too large. Finally, she writes the pairs' names on the Pairs and Teams Assignments chart [5], being careful to put pairs with strong readers and weak readers on both teams. She also allows the teams to choose team names from a list of ocean creatures from the class's science unit. Pairs and Teams Assignments from D. Fuchs et al. (2008). Reprinted with permission from the authors.

The pairs work together for 4 to 6 weeks, and then students work with a new partner. It is important to change pairs regularly to keep PALS fresh. This helps assure students continue to enjoy PALS across the entire year. In Grades 2–6 PALS, this means the pair may not have finished a book. One student can finish reading the book during independent reading time or for homework and then turn it over to the other student.

DEALING WITH ODD NUMBERS OR ABSENTEES

If a class has an odd number of students or an absent student leaves another without a partner, a triad must be created. A triad is a group of three students, in which the students each coach the other students for an entire activity.

If the class has an odd number of students, an ongoing triad must be created. Students in triads get less practice than other students, so it is important that students with disabilities and struggling readers are not placed in triads. In addition, students act as both First and Second Reader in the same lesson, so triads cannot be based on reading skill level. Three average- or high-achieving students should be placed in the triad, and all three should be cooperative. One student is designated "the rover." When a student is absent, the rover works with the absent student's partner, and there is no longer a triad.

Absentees create the need for a temporary triad. In these cases, the teacher chooses a pair for the absentee's partner that is reading a text of similar difficulty to the original pairs and in which the three students are likely to get along. If two students are absent, their partners simply pair up for the day and there is no need for a triad.

In the triad, each student is assigned to be the Coach for one activity. The other students act as the First and Second Reader for that activity. For the next activity, a different student is the Coach and the other two read. For example, in Grades 2–6 PALS, Student A would be the Coach for Partner Reading. Student B would read first. Student C would read second. Both Student B and Student C would retell. For Paragraph Shrinking, Student B would become the Coach. Student C reads first, and Student A reads second. For Prediction Relay, Student C would become the Coach. Student A reads first, and Student B reads second. For Grades 2–6 PALS, the Triad Reading Schedule (Figure 5.13) can be used to help students remember what to do. It assures that the jobs rotate over the entire week, such that each student coaches an activity only once. This rotation prevents students from continually missing the same activity.

Choosing Texts for Each Pair

Students should read texts at the instructional level of the lower-performing reader and the independent reading level of the higher performing reader. Pairs often vary in ability, so each pair may read a different text. In K-PALS and First Grade

Triad Reading Schedule

1st Reader: _____

2nd Reader: _____

3rd Reader: _____

The student who is not reading or coaching will always mark points.

Day 1: _____

	Reads First	Reads Second	Coach
Partner Reading and Retell	1st Reader:	2nd Reader:	3rd Reader:
Paragraph Shrinking	3rd Reader:	1st Reader:	2nd Reader:
Prediction Relay	2nd Reader:	3rd Reader:	1st Reader:

Day 2: _____

	Reads First	Reads Second	Coach
Partner Reading and Retell	2nd Reader:	3rd Reader:	1st Reader:
Paragraph Shrinking	1st Reader:	2nd Reader:	3rd Reader:
Prediction Relay	3rd Reader:	1st Reader:	2nd Reader:

Day 3: _____

	Reads First	Reads Second	Coach
Partner Reading and Retell	3rd Reader:	1st Reader:	2nd Reader:
Paragraph Shrinking	2nd Reader:	3rd Reader:	1st Reader:
Prediction Relay	1st Reader:	2nd Reader:	3rd Reader:

Teacher Reference · 267

FIGURE 5.13. Triad Reading Schedule from Grades 2–6 PALS. Teachers fill in the entire chart with the names of the three students in the triad. The teacher gives this chart to the triad to help them remember what job they should do each day. From D. Fuchs et al. (2008). Reprinted with permission from the authors.

PALS, students generally read decodable books, books with controlled vocabulary that permit students to practice reading skills. The pair reads each book multiple times before they are given a new book. Notably, Kindergarten and First Grade teachers do not have to choose texts before PALS begins, as their students begin Partner Reading 10 weeks into the program.

In Grades 2–6 PALS and High School PALS, however, teachers must select texts right away. These levels of PALS lend themselves to reading chapter books, as these longer texts reduce the number of texts that must be located. Picture books and nonfiction books tend to be short, and pairs will sometimes complete them even before finishing a single lesson.

The Common Core State Standards (National Governors Association Center for Best Practices & Council of Chief State School Officers, 2010) emphasize the importance of reading nonfiction, so using nonfiction texts is important. Grades 2–6 PALS and High School PALS accommodate this easily, but we often recommend that teachers have a backup book for pairs to read if they finish the assigned nonfiction text. One alternative to having backup books is for teachers to provide leveled book boxes containing a variety of nonfiction texts and instruct pairs that they may select one book from the box. As will be obvious to most teachers, students can take a long time choosing a book, so we recommend having a "30-second rule" or some other procedure for making sure the text selection happens quickly.

Teachers sometimes like to assign a reading to their entire class, such as a selection from a science or social studies text or a chapter book that the teacher feels all students should read. For example, one school district in which we did research required students to read "essential literature" (e.g., *Charlotte's Web*, White & DiCamillo [1952], and *Mufaro's Beautiful Daughters*, Steptoe [1987], in fourth grade), and teachers sometimes assigned these texts to students for PALS. One caution about this approach relates to the levels of the pairs: If the pair is not ready to read grade-level text, it is not a good idea to require them to read this text during PALS. The students will become frustrated, start to dislike PALS, and comprehend little. When teachers do assign all students the same text, we recommend that they monitor the pairs carefully to make sure all can read the text with adequate accuracy, fluency, and comprehension.

Organizing for PALS

Once the schedule is set, students are paired, and books are chosen (in Grades 2–6 and High School), teachers must prepare materials (see Table 5.4). For all levels of PALS, each pair will need a pocket folder to hold their materials and a point sheet. K-PALS and First Grade PALS require daily lesson sheets. Teachers often copy all of the lessons at the beginning of the year and create packets of six to eight lessons for students to keep in their folders. To avoid making copies every year, some teachers create binders containing every Student Decoding Lesson. Each lesson sheet is placed in a heavy sheet protector, and all of the sheets are placed in a binder. Students mark happy faces with a wax pencil or a dry-erase marker. At the end of each lesson, the pair just erases their marks. Using binders prevents the need to copy additional lessons when repeating a lesson. In Grades 2–6 PALS and High School PALS, the materials in the folder should be durable, as they will be used the entire year. We recommend that teachers copy the Question Card and Correction Card onto colored cardstock (thick paper) and laminate them. We also suggest a different color be used for each item, so the teacher can refer to it by color as well as by name. Teachers will also, of course, need a timer. We recommend a countdown timer (e.g., a kitchen timer), rather than a stop watch (which counts only up), so that teachers do not have to pay attention to the time while monitoring. We also suggest that teachers get a timer that counts minutes and seconds, not hours and minutes. Or timer applications for smartphones and tablets can be used instead.

Teachers also need to determine where each pair will work and how students will get to their PALS spots. It is necessary to decide ahead of time where each pair will work. Students in each pair should sit next to each other, at two adjacent desks or at a table. The lesson sheet or book should be between the students, with the other materials (e.g., point sheet) within reach of the Coach. Sometimes teachers allow pairs to sit on the floor. This works well for K-PALS and First Grade PALS. For Grades 2–6 PALS and High School PALS, it can be more difficult, with the need for both students to easily see the book, and we do not recommend this to teachers just starting out with PALS. A sample desk setup for Grades 2–6 PALS is shown in Figure 5.14.

Teachers also need to decide how students will get their PALS materials and get to their PALS location. One simple way to avoid movement is to rearrange students' seats for all activities, such that their PALS partner is their partner all day. If the teacher does this, one student (e.g., the First Reader in each pair) gets the PALS folder from the folder box. If teachers would prefer to group students differently, there are moving rules in each program where moving procedures are explained. Teachers designate one student in each pair a Mover and the other a Stayer. The Mover gets the PALS folder and goes to the desk next to the Stayer.

First Reader's Desk   Second Reader's Desk

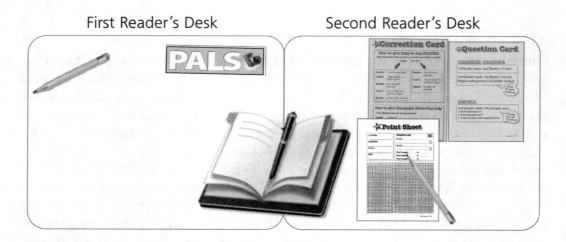

FIGURE 5.14. A sample desk setup for Grades 2–6 PALS. Notice that the book is in the middle, between the students. The arrow on the book represents a sticky note flag to remind the Second Reader where to start during Partner Reading. The Second Reader, who coaches first, has the point sheet right next to the book to make it easy to mark points, and the Question Card and Correction Card are within reach. Images of PALS materials from D. Fuchs et al. (2008). Reprinted with permission from the authors.

Initial Implementation

Training Lessons

After teachers prepare their materials, they begin teaching students to do PALS. For every level, there is a set of training lessons designed to help students learn the PALS procedures. The number of training lessons varies by level (see Table 5.10). Each manual includes a script for the teacher to follow. It is not necessary to read the script verbatim. The script is provided for convenience and efficiency. We recommend that teachers try using the scripts, as they are often more efficient when following the script than when adlibbing and usually find them less awkward than they first imagined. If teachers do use the scripts, we encourage them to match the scripts to their speaking and teaching style. Only the specific prompts the Coach uses must be said verbatim. These prompts must be taught exactly as written and used consistently so that the Coaches become accustomed to saying them as designed.

In Grades 2–6 PALS and High School PALS, the students use texts assigned by the teacher to practice the activities during training. These texts should be easier than the texts the pairs are capable of reading. By using easier texts during training, students can focus more on learning how to do the PALS activities than on deciphering the text. Another suggestion for initial training is to complete it as quickly as possible. Often, teachers will conduct the training lessons daily—as opposed to 3 or 4 days a week—in order to finish training in less time and begin full implementation. This is particularly appropriate for Grades 2–6 and High School PALS, where the students tend to be especially eager to begin practicing PALS on their own and are generally capable of learning the procedures quickly. As we have already emphasized, students' retellings, main idea statements, and predictions will be quite weak during training and immediately afterward. We recommend that teachers focus initially on students' accuracy in following the procedures and begin to emphasize quality after procedural accuracy is high.

Fidelity of Implementation

As we hope is clear now, we have tried to design PALS to make it easy for teachers to use and with attention to details that can smooth implementation. Each version of the program has gone through several iterations, as Douglas Fuchs and Lynn S. Fuchs—and, later, the rest of the authors—worked with teachers to refine the procedures. As a result, we believe that the strategies taught here are efficient, and research shows them to be effective.

We therefore recommend that teachers implement PALS with fidelity. Implementing PALS with fidelity means teaching pairs the exact procedures for each of the activities and insisting that they use them. It means using the points system to reinforce academic behaviors. It also means doing PALS as often as recommended or more often. We do not recommend breaking up lessons, as we discussed above in terms of scheduling.

However, implementing PALS with fidelity does not require perfect adherence to every minute detail. In a recent study, we actually permitted teachers to make a range of changes to Grades 2–6 PALS, and our data suggest that giving teachers some flexibility outside of the core elements of the program may have led to better reading improvement than standard PALS (Fuchs et al., 2012; McMaster et al., 2014). For example, some teachers added a written Paragraph Shrinking activity, in addition to the oral one used here. Other teachers added questioning activities or activities to practice vocabulary. What was consistent for these activities was the use of "PALS-like" approaches, particularly a structured interaction between peers with particular language the pair would use, and the use of a reinforcement system.

In our work with schools, we have observed other changes that do not affect fidelity. For example, in First Grade PALS, some teachers use a different system for Hearing Sounds, not following our "starting with the thumb" procedure. Instead, they tap each of their fingers against the thumb, following the procedure in their reading series. In K-PALS, teachers sometimes ignore the graphics we provide for each letter-sound (e.g., an apple for *A*) and refer to the clue pictures they have previously taught. So, provided that teachers do the activities following the prescribed procedures and use the point system, other minor changes are acceptable. We recommend that teachers monitor their own fidelity of implementation. Upon request, we can make copies of our fidelity checklists available. A sample checklist is given in Figure 5.15.

Ongoing Implementation

Teacher Monitoring

One of the great advantages of PALS is that teachers have time to *monitor* each student's performance without worrying at all whether the other students are finishing activities and need something else to do. Every student will be working. Teachers can provide feedback to students about their sound production, decoding, fluency, retelling, summarizing, or predicting, refining each student's skills in whatever is needed. We do not, therefore, recommend teachers use this as an opportunity to work with a separate group of students or complete other non-PALS tasks. In every version of PALS, an ongoing script is provided to guide the teacher through each lesson after training. Figure 5.16 shows the script, called the PALS Teacher Command Card, from Grades 2–6 PALS.

Teachers can reinforce specific behaviors as they monitor students. We recommend that teachers begin each activity by telling the students, "Today, I am looking to see . . ." and giving the class a target behavior. Teachers can walk around the room and provide performance-based feedback relative to the target behavior. Teachers can also give pairs bonus points, marking the point sheet with a colorful marker, glittery gel pen, stamper marker, or small sticker to make it obvious that the pair received points from the teacher. After each activity, we also recommend

Reading PALS Implementation Checklist Fidelity Time 2

Teacher: _____ School: _____ Observer: _____

Timeslot and Date: _____ # of Students present: _____ Appr. Session #: _____

For each item, please mark a checkmark in the appropriate column. A "+" is awarded if the behavior is observed about 80% of the time. For items that refer to the entire class, please award a "+" only if 80% (e.g., in a class of 20 students, 8 out of 10 pairs) has exhibited the behavior.

For some items, "NA" may be marked to indicate that the item did not occur (e.g., review, correction.)

Time Started: _____ Time Ended: _____ Total Time for PALS: _____

GENERAL — Teacher Implementation

+	—	NA	Organization and Set-Up
1			Teacher announces, "It's time for PALS" or there is some other obvious transition that indicates that the PALS session has begun.
2			Teacher distributes PALS materials, students pick up materials from the teacher, if necessary (books, question cards and new score cards), or students already have materials . This must take less than 2 minutes from the time of the first command in order to receive a "+". Time of first command: Time completed:
3			Students move, if necessary, within 2 minutes of the first command to move to their PALS places. Students must complete the move in less than 2 minutes from the time of the first command in order to receive a "+". Time of first command: Time completed:
4			Students have been assigned PALS seats, either at desks or on the floor.
5			Students are arranged so that students can easily follow along as their partner reads and teachers can easily navigate from pair to pair.
6			If today is the last PALS session of the week, the teacher tallies up team points.
7			Teacher tells students to put away PALS materials at the end of the lesson, or students are observed putting away the PALS materials. Time of first command: Time completed:

+	—	NA	Monitoring and Motivation
1			Teacher awards bonus PALS Points or provides specific positive reinforcement to at least 1 pair behaving appropriately **during set-up time.** Teacher issues corrective feedback and does not award bonus points to pairs behaving inappropriately. "NA" if teacher does not award bonus points.
2			Teacher awards bonus PALS Points or provides specific positive reinforcement to at least 1 pair behaving appropriately **at the end of the lesson.** Teacher issues corrective feedback and does not award bonus points to pairs behaving inappropriately. "NA" if teacher does not award bonus points.

Reading Assignments:

Comments:

FIGURE 5.15. Part of the fidelity checklist for Grades 2–6 PALS.

that the teacher provide specific praise to pairs regarding the target behavior, using social reinforcement in addition to the points-based reinforcement. Sometimes teachers will link the specific behavior to a classwide reward. We created Super Points, which are issued when teachers observe all students engaged in the desired behavior. After the class earns 10 Super Points, the students receive a reward (e.g., 10 minutes free reading time).

Teachers also sometimes have pairs model for the entire class between activities, choosing a pair that exhibits a target behavior. The chosen students appreciate being chosen. In addition, the model shows the class what the teacher expects of them. These models are most effective when the teacher draws the class's attention to the target behavior shown by the model pair and follows up during the actual

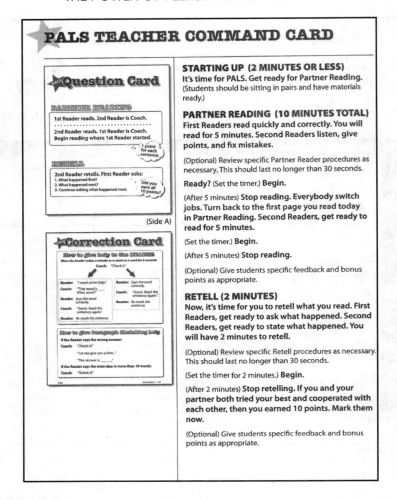

FIGURE 5.16. PALS Teacher Command Card (front). Teachers can read the instructions directly from this script to run PALS. Eventually, the Command Card becomes unnecessary, but it can be used by substitute teachers, parent volunteers, or other adults new to PALS. Thus, PALS can be implemented even when the teacher is absent. From D. Fuchs et al. (2008). Reprinted with permission from the authors.

lesson by providing points and additional social reinforcement to pairs that exhibit the behavior.

Addressing Pair Problems

Inevitably, your initial intuitions about which students to pair will be incorrect sometimes. So, pair problems are quite likely. There are several ways to handle such problems. The first approach is for teachers to talk with pairs that have experienced disagreements in recent lessons immediately before the PALS lesson begins. Teachers can provide the pair with a target behavior that requires cooperation and that will be praised during the lesson. Then, the teacher monitors the pair and praises students whenever they engage in the target behavior. We have observed that praising students often can cause pair problems to go away without further intervention.

If problems persist, it is important that the teacher does not change the student's partner based on a single complaint. As many teachers are painfully aware, letting one student do something means all the students want to do it. We have seen entire classes suddenly find their partners unsatisfactory! So, teachers generally insist that problematic pairs be told to work together. If the problems persist after a week, teachers may change the pairs.

If a particular student seems to have difficulty working with a partner, the student may—rarely—lose the privilege of working with a partner. In these cases, the student will do PALS on his or her own, doing all of the things the Reader does without Coach support. This means, of course, that the student receives no feedback, and the student's partner must be re-paired. However, some students better appreciate the value and enjoyment of working with a peer after a short period of time working alone. We emphasize that this strategy should be used rarely, and we recommend avoiding it for students already diagnosed with attention deficit/ hyperactivity disorder, emotional or behavior disorders, or other related disabilities because these students tend to experience difficulties working with others and should have opportunities to improve their social skills. These students also should receive extensive teacher support, possibly including explicit teacher instruction and modeling, to develop their ability to work with a partner.

Maintaining Student Motivation during PALS

Students and teachers are almost always initially very excited about PALS and enjoy it very much. Over time, the luster can wear off and students like it less. Usually, about halfway through the school year, students' motivation during PALS begins to flag. There are several ways to avoid this, or reverse it if it occurs. First, we remind teachers we work with that students' attitudes about PALS are largely shaped by teacher's attitudes about PALS. That is, we often observe that classrooms where students are less motivated are led by teachers who exhibit signs of fatigue as well. So, we emphasize the importance of teachers staying positive and motivated. Second, we recommend that teachers change pairs. We insist that pairs change every 4 to 6 weeks because it keeps PALS feeling fresh. We often find that teachers are busy and do not feel they have the time to make new pairs. So, the same pairs will stay together for more than 6 weeks, and the students tire of each other. Third, we recommend strategies to motivate the whole class. Emphasizing the team competition (except in Kindergarten) is one way to do this. Sometimes, teachers will issue a class challenge to beat the previous week's point total as well. Another method is to use Super Points or some other way of rewarding the entire class. We generally find that some combination of the above ideas for maintaining PALS gets students motivated again.

Off-Label Uses of PALS

Given PALS' research base and its limited cost, we are often asked whether it is appropriate to use PALS out of level. Here are some examples: Many schools use First Grade PALS as a remediation program for struggling older readers, students in second, third, or fourth grades who have serious decoding problems. Teachers create small groups and serve as the Coach while the students in the group act as the Readers. K-PALS is sometimes used with struggling first graders in a similar way. Teachers also sometimes use Grades 2–6 PALS with students in sixth through eighth grade, and occasionally teachers use Grades 2–6 PALS with high school students instead of the High School PALS.

We call these "off-label" uses to emphasize the idea that they are used for a different purpose than the purpose for which they were tested, in the way that medications are sometimes used. We have two comments about these off-label uses of PALS Reading.

First, these make good sense from a practical point of view. PALS requires minimal daily preparation, as all of the lessons are contained within the teacher guide. Given how busy teachers are during the day, they often appreciate having a program that provides systematic instruction with little planning. The procedures are also relatively easy to learn and can be implemented—after training and practice—by a paraprofessional, a parent volunteer, or another thoughtful adult who has not received extensive training in reading content and pedagogy.

The second point is that using the PALS programs out of level is something teachers should undertake with caution. We cannot explicitly endorse out-of-level uses, as we have not tested the programs in these ways and want to speak only within the limits of the data we have collected. We noted these uses here because we often hear about these practices when we work with schools and because these approaches make sense to us too. However, we have not tested the programs this way. We recommend that teachers monitor students' progress carefully and regularly when they use PALS out of level. We recommend that teachers make changes if students' outcomes do not appear to improve quickly. This is one reason that remediation should be accompanied by regular PM (see Kearns, Lemons, Fuchs, & Fuchs, 2014, and Lemons, Kearns, & Davidson, 2014, for information about implementing interventions).

CONCLUSION

PALS Reading is an evidence-based program that provides students extensive reading practice. It has been tested by comparing the performance of students participating in PALS Reading to the performance of their peers who do not get PALS, and for kindergarten, first grade, second through sixth grade, and high school, students in PALS have performed better than their peers not in the program. The program has been changed and refined as the developers worked with teachers to assure that PALS implementation is practical given the real-world conditions teachers face. Each version is the product of this iterative design process. It is our hope that the descriptions provided here contain sufficient detail to allow practitioners to understand what PALS involves, why it might be effective, and how it might feel to implement.

In closing, I (Devin M. Kearns) would like to endorse PALS as someone who learned about PALS after leaving the classroom. I was fortunate to work with my co-authors on a large evaluation of the Grades 2–6 program, and, during that project, I helped many teachers implement PALS. I was envious of these teachers, who got to see their students experience success with PALS' clear, simple procedures and the opportunity to read many texts. I still wish I had been able to teach Grades 2–6 PALS to my third graders in Los Angeles and to give them the same opportunities PALS students have. The best I can do now is to encourage other teachers to try the program. So, if you're a classroom teacher reading this chapter, let me encourage you: Get your hands on a manual and give PALS Reading a go. I think you'll like it.

REFERENCES

Archer, A. L., & Hughes, C. A. (2011). *Explicit instruction: Effective and efficient teaching.* New York: Guilford Press.

Austen, J. (2001). *Pride and prejudice.* Peterborough, Ontario, Canada: Broadview Press.

Baker, J. M., & Zigmond, N. (1990). Are regular education classes equipped to accommodate students with learning disabilities? *Exceptional Children, 56,* 515–526.

Burns, M. K. (2007). Reading at the instructional level with children identified as learning disabled: Potential implications for response-to-intervention. *School Psychology Quarterly, 22*(3), 297–313.

Clay, M. (1985). *Early detection of reading difficulties.* Portsmouth, NH: Heinemann.

Cohen, J. (1988). *Statistical power analysis for the behavioral sciences.* New York: Routledge.

Dion, E., Fuchs, D., & Fuchs, L. S. (2005). Differential effects of Peer-Assisted Learning Strategies on students' social preference and friendship making. *Behavioral Disorders, 30,* 421–429.

Dolch, E. W. (1936). A basic sight vocabulary. *Elementary School Journal, 36,* 456–460.

Elbro, C., de Jong, P. F., Houter, D., & Nielsen, A. M. (2012). From spelling pronunciation to lexical access: A second step in word decoding? *Scientific Studies of Reading, 16,* 341–359.

Fuchs, D., Fuchs, L. S., & Burish, P. (2000). Peer-Assisted Learning Strategies: An evidence-based practice to promote reading achievement. *Learning Disabilities Research and Practice, 15,* 85–91.

Fuchs, D., Fuchs, L. S., Mathes, P. G., & Martinez, E. A. (2002a). Preliminary evidence on the social standing of students with learning disabilities in PALS and No–PALS classrooms. *Learning Disabilities Research and Practice, 17,* 205–215.

Fuchs, D., Fuchs, L. S., Mathes, P., & Simmons, D. (1997). Peer-Assisted Learning Strategies: Making classrooms more responsive to diversity. *American Educational Research Journal, 34,* 174–206.

Fuchs, D., Fuchs, L. S., Simmons, D. C., & Mathes, P. G. (2008). *Peer-Assisted Learning Strategies: Reading methods for Grades 2–6.* Nashville, TN: Vanderbilt University.

Fuchs, D., Fuchs, L. S., Svenson, E., Yen, L., Thompson, A., McMaster, K., et al. (2011). *Peer-Assisted Learning Strategies: First-Grade Reading PALS.* Nashville, TN: Vanderbilt University.

Fuchs, D., Fuchs, L. S., Thompson, A., Al Otaiba, S., Yen, L., McMaster, K., et al. (n.d.). *Peer-Assisted Learning Strategies: Kindergarten reading teacher manual*. Nashville, TN: Authors.

Fuchs, D., Fuchs, L. S., Thompson, A., Al Otaiba, S., Yen, L., Yang, N. J., et al. (2001b). Is reading important in reading-readiness programs?: A randomized field trial with teachers as program implementers. *Journal of Educational Psychology, 93*, 251–267.

Fuchs, D., Fuchs, L. S., Thompson, A., Al Otaiba, S., Yen, L., Yang, N. J., et al. (2002b). Exploring the importance of reading programs for kindergartners with disabilities in mainstream classrooms. *Exceptional Children, 68*, 295–311.

Fuchs, D., Fuchs, L. S., Yen, L., McMaster, K., Svenson, E., Yang, N., et al. (2001a). Developing first-grade reading fluency through peer mediation. *TEACHING Exceptional Children, 34*(2), 90–93.

Fuchs, D., McMaster, K., Sáenz, L., Fuchs, L. S., Kearns, D. M., Lemons, C., et al. (2012, September). *An IES-funded effectiveness study of a top-down and bottom-up approach to bring to scale an evidence-based reading program*. Paper presented at the annual conference of the Society for Research on Educational Effectiveness, Washington, DC.

Fuchs, L. S., & Fuchs, D. (1992). Identifying a measure for monitoring student reading progress. *School Psychology Review, 21*(1), 45–58.

Fuchs, L. S., & Fuchs, D. (2003). Curriculum-based measurement: A best practice guide. *NASP Communique, 32*(2), 1–4.

Fuchs, L. S., Fuchs, D., & Kazdan, S. (1999). Effects of peer-assisted learning strategies on high school students with serious reading problems. *Remedial and Special Education, 20*, 309–319.

Fuchs, L. S., Fuchs, D., Kazdan, S., Mathes, P., Prentice, K., & Sáenz, L. (n.d.). *Peer-Assisted Learning Strategies (PALS) for high school students*. Nashville, TN: Vanderbilt University.

Hollands, F. M., Pan, Y., Shand, R., Cheng, H., Levin, H. M., Belfield, C. R., et al. (2013). *Improving early literacy: Cost-effectiveness analysis of effective reading programs*. New York: Center for Benefit-Cost Studies of Education, Teachers College, Columbia University.

Kearns, D. M., Lemons, C. J., Fuchs, D., & Fuchs, L. S. (2014). Essentials of a tiered intervention system to support unique learners: Recommendations from research and practice. In J. Mascolo, D. Flanagan, & V. Alfonso (Eds.), *Essentials of planning, selecting, and tailoring interventions for the unique learner* (pp. 56–91). Hoboken, NJ: Wiley.

Lemons, C. J., Kearns, D. M., & Davidson, K. A. (2014). Data-based individualization in reading. *TEACHING Exceptional Children, 46*(4), 20–29.

Lipsey, M. W., Puzio, K., Yun, C., Hebert, M. A., Steinka-Fry, K., Cole, M. W., et al. (2012). *Translating the statistical representation of the effects of education interventions into more readily interpretable forms*. Retrieved November 15, 2013, from National Center for Special Education Research website, *http://ies.ed.gov/ncser/pubs/20133000*.

McMaster, K. L., Jung, P. G., Brandes, D., Pinto, V., Fuchs, D., Kearns, D, et al. (2014). Customizing a research-based reading practice. *The Reading Teacher, 68*(3), 173–183.

National Governors Association Center for Best Practices & Council of Chief State School Officers. (2010). *Common Core State Standards for English language arts and literacy in history/social studies, science, and technical subjects*. Washington, DC: Author.

National Institute of Child Health and Human Development. (2000). *Report of the National Reading Panel: Teaching children to read: An evidence-based assessment of the scientific research literature on reading and its implications for reading instruction* (NIH Publication No. 00-4754). Washington, DC: U.S. Government Printing Office.

O'Connor, R. E., White, A., & Swanson, H. L. (2007). Repeated reading versus continuous reading: Influences on reading fluency and comprehension. *Exceptional Children, 74*, 31–46.

Rafdal, B. H., McMaster, K. L., McConnell, S. R., Fuchs, D., & Fuchs, L. S. (2011). The effectiveness of Kindergarten Peer-Assisted Learning Strategies for students with disabilities. *Exceptional Children, 77*, 299–316.

Sáenz, L. M., Fuchs, L. S., & Fuchs, D. (2005). Peer-assisted learning strategies for English language learners with learning disabilities. *Exceptional Children, 71,* 231–247.

Scarborough, H. (2001). Connecting early language and literacy to later reading (dis)abilities: Evidence, theory, and practice. In S. Neuman & D. Dickinson (Eds.), *Handbook of early literacy research: Vol. 1* (pp. 97–110). New York: Guilford Press.

Sindelar, P. T., Monda, L. E., & O'Shea, L. J. (1990). Effects of repeated readings on instructional- and mastery-level readers. *Journal of Educational Research, 83,* 220–226.

Snow, C. E., Burns, M. S., & Griffin, P. (Eds.). (1998). *Preventing reading difficulties in young children.* Washington, DC: National Academy Press.

Stein, M. L., Berends, M., Fuchs, D., McMaster, K., Sáenz, L., Yen, L., et al. (2008). Scaling up an early reading program: Relationships among teacher support, fidelity of implementation, and student performance across different sites and years. *Educational Evaluation and Policy Analysis, 30,* 368–388.

Steptoe, J. (1987). *Mufaro's beautiful daughters.* New York: HarperCollins.

White, E. B., & DiCamillo, K. (1952). *Charlotte's web.* New York: HarperCollins.

CHAPTER 6

Peer-Assisted Learning Strategies in Mathematics

SARAH R. POWELL and LYNN S. FUCHS

As highlighted in this book and elsewhere, peer tutoring is a beneficial strategy for teaching students across elementary, middle, and high school (Bowman-Perrott et al., 2013; Codding, Chan-Iannetta, George, Ferreira, & Volpe, 2011). In this chapter, we focus on peer tutoring in mathematics with the Peer-Assisted Learning Strategies (PALS) program (Fuchs et al., 1997). PALS was based in part on a set of core principles established with the classwide peer-tutoring model (CWPT; Delquadri, Greenwood, Whorton, Carta, & Hall, 1986). With PALS Math, higher-performing students are paired with lower-performing students. One student in the pair starts as a Coach and helps the Player work step by step through math problems. The Coach and Player switch roles throughout the lesson. In this chapter, we discuss the research supporting PALS Math and how to implement PALS Math in kindergarten, grade 1, and grades 2–6. We also discuss how to effectively pair students for PALS Math, how to differentiate PALS Math lessons, and how to conduct PALS Math with high levels of fidelity.

With peer-tutoring programs, students are paired together to practice academic skills. Peer tutoring improves academic outcomes, and with the interaction between peers, social outcomes typically improve as well (Robinson, Schofield, & Steers-Wentzell, 2005). When students act as peer tutors, their mathematics understanding improves, and when students are on the receiving end of peer tutoring, they receive one-on-one individual attention with appropriate feedback (Carmody & Wood, 2009). Importantly, as schools use models of inclusion, peer tutoring is a strategy that can be utilized in general education settings (Harper & Maheady, 2007; Kroeger & Kouche, 2006), as it has proven effective in improving mathematics outcomes for students with and without disabilities (Fuchs et al., 1997; Fuchs, Fuchs, & Karns, 2001).

Peer tutoring, in general, has been recognized as an evidence-based practice by the What Works Clearinghouse (*ies.ed.gov/ncee/wwc*), and, specifically, PALS Math has been recognized by the Best Evidence Encyclopedia (*www.bestevidence.org*) as an evidence-based practice. An evidence-based practice has been determined, through high-quality research, to be effective for most students most of the time. It is important to note that peer tutoring is effective when students are trained and supervised by teachers (Maheady & Gard, 2010). Additionally, peer tutoring requires structure for the pairs. With peer tutoring, teachers do not have student peers work in an unstructured way on random pages in a mathematics textbook. With an evidence-based peer-tutoring program like PALS, students are assigned specific roles within the pair and provided with training in how to work productively on mathematics activities, and the students are assigned specific mathematics skills on which they require assistance.

OVERVIEW OF PALS MATH

To extend the CWPT framework beyond working on calculation problems and drill and practice, Fuchs et al. (1996, 1997) developed PALS Math, expanding the curriculum to address most strands of the mathematics curriculum in kindergarten through sixth grade and to provide structured instruction that included, but was not limited to, practice. See Table 6.1 for an overview of skills by grade level.

PALS Math Research

In kindergarten, Fuchs, Fuchs, Karns, Yazdian, and Powell (2001) randomly assigned 20 teachers to teach PALS Math or act as a business-as-usual control. After teacher implementation of PALS Math for 15 weeks, students who participated in the PALS Math lessons demonstrated significant mathematics growth over students who did not receive PALS. The overall effect size (ES) favoring PALS students was 0.24, but lower-performing students and those with disabilities demonstrated larger gains, with ESs ranging from 0.41 to 0.46. In a similar way, at Grade 1, Fuchs, Fuchs, Yazdian, and Powell (2002) randomly assigned 20 teachers to PALS Math or business-as-usual conditions. After 16 weeks of PALS, students who participated in PALS outperformed business-as-usual students on mathematics outcomes taught during PALS (ES = 0.31). At Grades 2 through 4, Fuchs et al. (1997) randomly assigned 40 teachers to conduct PALS Math or participate in a business-as-usual condition. After 18 weeks of PALS, students participating in PALS outperformed business-as-usual students with ESs ranging from 0.42 to 0.73.

TABLE 6.1. Overview of PALS Math by Grade Level

Grade level	Duration	Days per week	Minutes per session	Topics	
K	16 weeks (with an additional 14 weeks of challenge game boards)	2	20	Number recognition Comparing numbers Addition and subtraction	
1	18 weeks (with an additional 11 weeks of challenge game boards)	3	20	Number concepts Comparing numbers Addition and subtraction concepts Place value Addition and subtraction Missing addends	
2	34 weeks (of possible lessons)	2	30	*Computation:* Adding basic facts Adding without regrouping Adding with regrouping Subtracting basic facts Subtracting without regrouping Subtracting with regrouping	*Applications:* Applied computation Charts and graphs Counting Fractions Measurement Money Number concepts Names of numbers Word problems
3	42 weeks (of possible lessons)	2	30	*Computation:* Adding Subtracting with regrouping Multiplying basic facts Multiplying Dividing basic facts	*Applications:* Applied computation Charts and graphs Counting Decimals Fractions Measurement Money Number concepts Names of numbers Word problems
4	44 weeks (of possible lessons)	2	30	*Computation:* Adding Subtracting Multiplying basic facts Multiplying Dividing basic facts Dividing Adding and subtracting fractions	*Applications:* Area and perimeter Charts and graphs Decimals Fractions Grid reading Measurement Number concepts Names of numbers Word problems

(continued)

TABLE 6.1. *(continued)*

Grade level	Duration	Days per week	Minutes per session	Topics	
5	38 weeks (of possible lessons)	2	30	*Computation:* Adding Subtracting Multiplying Dividing Reducing/renaming fractions Adding and subtracting fractions Adding and subtracting decimals	*Applications:* Applied computation Charts and graphs Geometry Decimals Fractions and factors Measurement Money Numeration Word problems
6	40 weeks (of possible lessons)	2	30	*Computation:* Adding Subtracting Multiplying Dividing Adding and subtracting fractions Multiplying and dividing fractions Adding and subtracting decimals Multiplying decimals Dividing decimals	*Applications:* Applied computation Charts and graphs Geometry Measurement Numeration Percentages Proportions Ratios and probability Variables Word problems

Collectively, this research base indicates that PALS Math improves the mathematics outcomes of students in the elementary grades. In the rest of this chapter, we describe Kindergarten PALS Math, Grade 1 PALS Math, and Grades 2–6 PALS Math. We conclude with a description of strategies to pair students effectively for peer tutoring, to differentiate instruction, and to measure fidelity of the PALS Math programs.

PALS MATH PROGRAMS

Currently, PALS Math is available for kindergarten through sixth grade. The kindergarten program and first-grade programs are fairly similar. We describe them in separate sections, however, because each program has its own manual. We describe PALS Math for students in Grades 2 through 6 in a combined section because a single teacher manual (with corresponding grade-level materials manuals) guides implementation at these grades. Each PALS Math manual is relatively low in cost ($40 to $65) and can be purchased by visiting the PALS website (*kc. vanderbilt.edu/pals*).

Kindergarten PALS Math

Teachers use a manual to guide implementation of Kindergarten PALS (K-PALS) Math (Fuchs, Fuchs, Yazdian, Powell, & Karns, 2011b). The manual comprises basic information about implementation of K-PALS, teacher guides, student game board templates, templates for extra materials, and templates for challenge game boards. Teachers use the templates to make materials for each pair.

Basics

K-PALS is conducted two times a week for 16 weeks. Each week is a "lesson." Every lesson has 2 "days," lasting approximately 20 minutes each. The lessons are broken into three primary skill categories: number recognition (six lessons), comparing numbers (four lessons), and addition and subtraction (six lessons). See Table 6.2 for a list of skills by lesson.

During every day, two activities occur. First, in classwide format, the teacher introduces or reviews a skill, which is represented on the K-PALS "game board." This teaching segment, which takes 5 to 10 minutes, reviews important mathematical concepts or terminology and helps students understand how the pair uses the game board to structure the pair's practice on that lesson's skill. This prepares the Coach and Player to work together in productive fashion on the game board. After this brief, classwide lesson, the students break into pairs to work together on

TABLE 6.2. K-PALS Lessons

Lesson	Category	Skill
1	Number Concepts	Training; Recognition of numerals (0–10)
2		Recognition of numerals (0–10)
3		Recognition of numerals (0–19)
4		Pictorial representation of numbers (0–9)
5		Pictorial representation of numbers (0–19)
6		Writing numerals (0–9)
7	Comparing Numbers	Which is greater? (pictorial representations)
8		Which is less? (pictorial representations)
9		More and less (numbers)
10		More and less (number line)
11	Addition and Subtraction	Addition concepts (pictorial representations)
12		Subtraction concepts (pictorial representations)
13		Addition and subtraction (pictorial representations)
14		Addition (manipulatives)
15		Subtraction (manipulatives)
16		Addition and subtraction (manipulatives)

a shared game board. The higher-performing student in the pair starts as Coach. The Coach asks questions of the Player to work through each game board problem. If the Player makes a mistake, the Coach helps out by providing appropriate feedback. Pairs work together in this way for 10 to 15 minutes.

Lessons

Each lesson includes 2 days: Day 1 and Day 2. During Lesson 1, teachers introduce students to the K-PALS Rules (see Figure 6.1) and show students how to act as Coach and Player. To provide extra practice for learning how to act as Coach and Player, Lesson 1 actually contains 3 days. Starting with Lesson 2, students work on the lesson's skill for 2 days each week. Teachers use the game boards that accompany each lesson. Teachers also have the option of using "challenge game boards" that extend the number set of a lesson. For example, with Lesson 2, students work on identifying numbers 0–20. The challenge game boards for Lesson 2 feature numbers 0–99. Teachers may opt to use the challenge game boards following the original Lesson 2 (i.e., identifying numbers 0–20) or some teachers use the challenge game boards after completing the entire set of 16 K-PALS lessons (see Table 6.2) as a way of reviewing while extending student learning.

PALS RULES

1. Talk only to your partner, and talk only about math.

2. Use a soft PALS voice.

3. Be nice and helpful.

FIGURE 6.1. K-PALS rules. From Fuchs, Fuchs, Yazdian, Powell, and Karns (2011b). Reprinted with permission from the authors.

Game Boards

Each day, every pair shares one game board. So in a classroom of 20 students with 10 pairs, the teacher needs 10 game boards. See Figure 6.2 for a sample game board from a lesson on comparing numbers. On the left, in individual boxes, are the Coach's prompts. The Coach asks each prompt for every problem. The Player's problems are on the right side of the game board. On this game board, each problem for the Player is in a box with pictures and a dashed line running vertically down the middle of the box. The Player works each problem as the Coach asks the prompts. When the Player and Coach reach the smiley face and flag on the game board, two actions occur. First, the Player colors a smiley face on the pair's Smiley Sheet (see Figure 6.3). Second, the flag signals the students to switch roles: The Coach becomes the Player, and the Player becomes the Coach.

Because K-PALS takes place two times a week in kindergarten, the Smiley Sheet has smiley faces separated into Day 1 and Day 2 sections. When the Player reaches a smiley face on the game board, the Player marks one smiley face on the Smiley Sheet. To not waste time, it is helpful to teach Players to mark a smiley face using a slash or X because some Players take a long time trying to color in the smiley face. The Player marks a smiley to reward him- or herself for positive

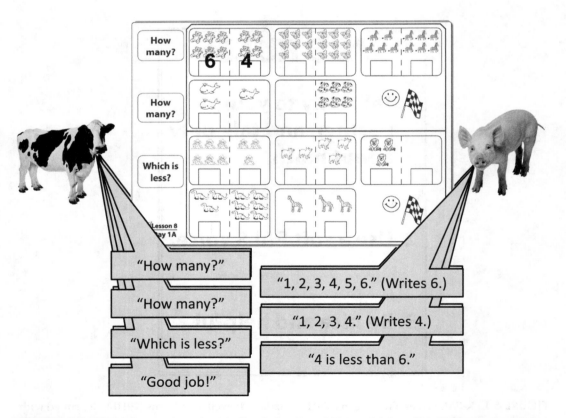

FIGURE 6.2. K-PALS game board with Coach (cow) and Player (pig) actions. From Fuchs, Fuchs, Yazdian, Powell, and Karns (2011b). Reprinted with permission from the authors.

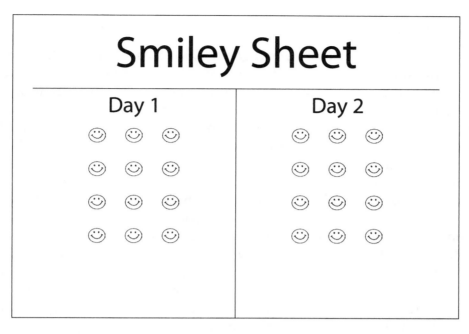

FIGURE 6.3. K-PALS Smiley Sheet. From Fuchs, Fuchs, Yazdian, Powell, and Karns (2011b). Reprinted with permission from the authors.

mathematics work. The pair can also earn smiley faces from the classroom teacher. As pairs work together, the teacher walks around, listens to pairs, and provides necessary feedback. If the teacher observes the pair following the PALS Rules and demonstrating positive pair behavior, the teacher may award a smiley face on the Smiley Sheet. For example, a teacher may award a smiley face for a pair "using soft voices" or for a Coach explaining addition to the Player in a "nice, helpful way." Having the teacher award extra smiley faces helps with classroom management during a PALS session. At the end of the lesson, the number of marked smiley faces is an indicator to the teacher and pair about the pair's success with the lesson. Note that the marked smiley faces are not tied to any tangible reward system.

Some game boards and lessons require the use of additional materials. The cost of materials is minimal, however, and many teachers have the necessary items in their classroom. Therefore, purchasing new materials is at minimal cost or unnecessary. Teachers use two-pocket folders to organize the game boards and Smiley Sheet for a lesson. Each pair shares one folder. Typically, teachers stuff the folders with the game boards for a specific lesson (e.g., Lesson 7 Day 1 and Lesson 7 Day 2) and the Smiley Sheet. For Lesson 7, a Bean Sheet Mat, which is copied from the manual onto cardstock, accompanies the lesson. The pair also needs approximately 20 beans (in a plastic bag) to work through problems. The Bean Sheet and bag of beans can also be placed in the two-pocket folder. Other materials include spinners, number lines, and work mats. All templates for work mats (including the Bean Sheet Mat) are included in the manual.

The Teacher's Role

Every lesson is accompanied by a teacher guide, which is scripted to show teachers how to introduce the lesson. See Figure 6.4 for a sample teacher guide from Lesson 3. Teachers should not read the guide verbatim. Instead, teachers become familiar with the guide before teaching and then deliver the lesson in their own words. Teachers are encouraged to tie in PALS lessons to their mathematics curriculum, but they should not alter the PALS lessons in major ways. The teacher's role at the beginning of each lesson is to demonstrate how the Coach provides the lesson's prompts, how the Player responds to the prompts, and how the Coach helps the Player when the Player makes a mistake. During the teacher lesson, the teacher should have the Day 1 game board from the lesson displayed. Many teachers make the game board larger, often through display on a projector, so all students can see and interact with the game board. Many teachers ask students to gather around a "carpet area" so students can see the game board, come up, and practice with the teacher, and learn how to write on the game board. Typically, the teacher guide is much longer on Day 1 than Day 2 of each lesson. On Day 2, the teacher briefly reviews the game board to allow for more pair work.

Once the students break into pairs, the teacher monitors pairs by walking around the classroom, listening to student pairs, engaging pairs in discussion, and awarding extra smiley faces when pairs follow the PALS Rules and demonstrate positive pair behavior. At the end of 10 to 15 minutes, teachers ask students to put all materials back in the two-pocket folder, and a student pair collects folders.

All lessons follow a similar format. This makes it easy for teachers and students to learn the PALS strategies and implement the lessons.

Grade 1 PALS Math

Similar to K-PALS, teachers use a manual to guide implementation of Grade 1 PALS Math (Fuchs, Fuchs, Yazdian, Powell, & Karns, 2011a). The manual contains all information, teacher guides, student game board templates, templates for extra materials, and templates for challenge game boards that a teacher needs to implement Grade 1 PALS. Teachers use templates to make materials for each pair. For example, in a classroom of 22 students, the teacher makes 11 sets of materials for 11 pairs.

Basics

Grade 1 PALS is conducted three times a week for 18 weeks. Similar to K-PALS, each week is a "lesson." Every lesson has 3 "days," lasting approximately 20 minutes each. The lessons are broken into six categories: number concepts (3 lessons), comparing numbers (3 lessons), addition and subtraction concepts (4 lessons), place value (2 lessons), addition and subtraction (5 lessons), and missing addends

You already know that when you come to the number 10, you "flash" all of your fingers. Now, here's a new thing. When you come to numbers higher than 10, you "flash" 10, like this (hold up all 10 fingers). Then you count up the rest, one at a time.

So, to show 11 on my fingers, I flash 10 fingers and say "10." (Flash 10 fingers to students and then close fingers.) Then, I count up the rest, one finger at a time: "11." (Extend fingers out one at a time while counting up.)

To show 12, I first flash 10 fingers and say "10." (Flash 10 fingers to students.) Then I count up the rest: "11, 12." (Demonstrate to students.)

Let's look at the next problem. I'll be the Coach, and you'll all be the Players (Point to 15.) "What number?"

STUDENTS: 15.

"Show how many."

STUDENTS: Flash 10 fingers and say, "10." Then count up using fingers, "11, 12, 13, 14, 15."

For two-digit numbers, a helpful clue is to look at the first number. The first number shows how many tens to flash. For 15, we know to flash 1 ten because the first number is 1. The second number tells how many ones to count. For 15, we know to count up 5 ones because the second number is 5.

Good job. Who will be my Player to help me show 18?

> Pick a student to be the Player and demonstrate the procedure.
> Continue to practice with the students as Players.
> Make mistakes in both numeral names and number of fingers.
> Help students with correction procedures as needed.
> Stop when you are sure they understand the procedure.

Before we break into partners, let's review the Coach's words.

> Echo read the Coach's words with the entire class until they are comfortable with the wording.

38 - Lesson 3

FIGURE 6.4. K-PALS Teacher Guide. From Fuchs, Fuchs, Yazdian, Powell, and Karns (2011b). Reprinted with permission from the authors.

(1 lesson). See Table 6.3 for a list of skills by lesson. An additional 11 lessons are available with the challenge game boards.

Two activities occur every day. First, the teacher introduces or reviews a game board with the class for 5 to 10 minutes. The teacher demonstrates the role of the Coach and Player so the students know how to act as Coach and Player when working with their partner. The teacher may also review important mathematical concepts or terminology. Second, student pairs work together on a shared game board. The higher-performing student in the pair starts as Coach. The Coach asks questions of the Player to work though each game board problem. If the Player makes a mistake, the Coach helps by providing appropriate feedback. Pairs work together for 10 to 15 minutes.

Lessons

Each lesson includes three days: Day 1, Day 2, and Day 3. During Lesson 1, teachers introduce students to the PALS Math Rules. These rules are the same rules used in K-PALS (see Figure 6.1). Also during Lesson 1, the teacher shows students how to be the Coach and how to respond as the Player. After students receive training

TABLE 6.3. Grade 1 PALS Lessons

Lesson	Category	Skill
1	Number Concepts	Training; Recognition of numerals (0–10)
2		Recognition of numerals (0–50)
3		Drawing representations of numbers (0–50)
4	Comparing Numbers	More and less (0–20)
5		More and less (0–20)
6		Greater, equal, and less (0–20)
7	Addition and Subtraction Concepts	Addition (0–10; manipulatives)
8		Subtraction (0–10; manipulatives)
9		Addition and subtraction (0–10; manipulatives)
10		Addition and subtraction (0–10; pictorial representations)
11	Place Value	Tens and ones (0–20; manipulatives)
12		Tens and ones (0–50; pictorial representations)
13	Single-Digit Addition and Subtraction	Addition (0–12)
14		Subtraction (0–12)
15	Double-Digit Addition and Subtraction	Addition (0–99)
16		Subtraction (0–99)
17		Addition and subtraction (0–99)
18	Missing Addends	Solving for unknowns (0–12)

on the Grade 1 PALS strategies, all lessons run similarly. On Day 1 of a lesson, the teacher introduces or reviews the lesson's skill. Students participate in brief pair practice. Days 2 and 3 of each lesson include a briefer teacher introduction to provide the students with more time to work in pairs.

Game Boards

A game board guides pair work for all 3 days of each lesson. The pair shares the game board. See Figure 6.5 for a sample game board from a lesson on place value. On the left, in individual boxes, are the Coach's prompts. The Coach asks each of these prompts for every Player problem. The Player's problems are on the right side of the game board. On this game board, each problem for the Player is a separate number, and the Player works each problem as the Coach asks the prompts.

As with K-PALS, when the Player and Coach reach the smiley face and flag on the game board, two actions occur. First, the Player colors a smiley face on the pair's Smiley Sheet. (See Figure 6.3 for an example of the Kindergarten Smiley

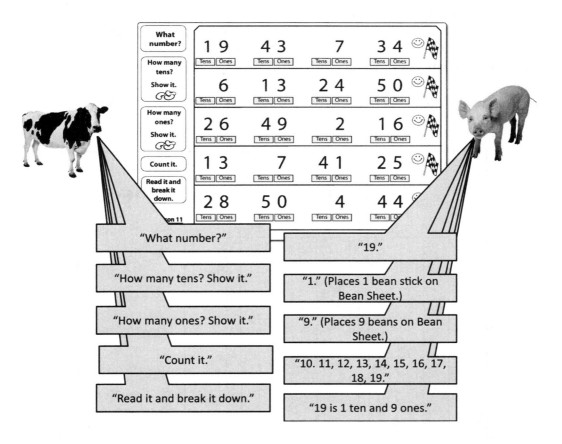

FIGURE 6.5. Grade 1 PALS game board with Coach (cow) and Player (pig) actions. From Fuchs, Fuchs, Yazdian, Powell, and Karns (2011a). Reprinted with permission from the authors.

Sheet—the Grade 1 Smiley Sheet has space for 3 days of smiley faces.) The Player marks a smiley face to reward the Player for doing good math work. Pairs also earn smiley faces from the teacher for following PALS Rules and demonstrating positive pair behavior. Having the teacher award extra smiley faces helps with classroom management. At the end of the lesson, the number of marked smiley faces is an indicator to the teacher and pair about the pair's success with the lesson. The marked smiley faces are not tied to any tangible reward system. The flag on the game board signals for the students to switch roles: the Coach becomes the Player, and the Player becomes the Coach.

Several lessons require the use of additional materials, which is similar to K-PALS. In fact, some of the additional materials are the same, so it is possible for kindergarten and first-grade teachers to share materials (e.g., beans, number lines, spinners). The cost of materials is minimal, however, and many teachers have items in their classroom that can be used, so purchasing new materials should be minimal or unnecessary. Teachers should use two-pocket folders to organize the game boards and Smiley Sheet for a lesson. Each pair shares one folder. Typically, teachers stuff the folders with the game boards for a specific lesson (e.g., Lesson 12 Day 1, Lesson 12 Day 2, and Lesson 12 Day 3) and the Smiley Sheet. For several lessons, teachers copy templates from the manual onto cardstock (see Figure 6.6 for a sample Bean Place Value Work Mat template). Pairs use loose beans and beans sticks (with 10 beans glued into each stick) to represent ones and tens. Additional materials include spinners, number lines, and work mats. All templates for work mats (including Bean Place Value Work Mats) are included in the manual.

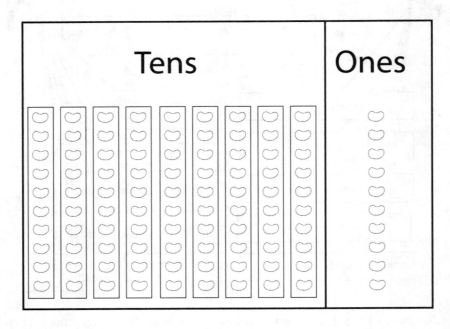

FIGURE 6.6. Bean Place Value Work Mat. From Fuchs, Fuchs, Yazdian, Powell, and Karns (2011a). Reprinted with permission from the authors.

The Teacher's Role

Teachers use a guide, provided in the Grade 1 PALS manual, to learn how to introduce each lesson. The sample K-PALS teacher guide in Figure 6.4 is very similar to the Grade 1 PALS guides. As with K-PALS, teachers should become familiar with the guide before delivering the lesson, and then deliver the lesson using their own language (i.e., teachers should not read the guide verbatim). Whenever Grade 1 PALS lessons are similar in content to the teacher's first-grade math curriculum, teachers should make explicit connections for students between PALS lessons and the classroom math curriculum. Teachers should not, however, change the PALS Math lessons in major ways.

For each lesson, during Day 1 teachers introduce or review the lesson's skill. The teacher displays the lesson's Day 1 game board in a format that is readily viewed by all students in the classroom (e.g., projector, Smart Board). The teacher acts as Coach (with the class acting as Players) and then reverses roles, so the teacher acts as Player (with the class acting as Coaches). This ensures that students understand the Coach and Player roles before they break into pairs. The teacher also provides students with strategies for helping partners when Players make mistakes. A standard correction statement is taught: The Coach always says, "Stop. You missed that one." Then the Coach explains what the mistake is and helps the Player correct it. Teachers emphasize to students that the Coach does not tell the Player the correct answer. Instead, the Coach provides hints to help the Player find the correct answer. Error correction is difficult for students at first, because they think that giving the correct answer is most helpful. With teacher practice, demonstration, and reminders, however, students learn to use the error correction procedure well. The teacher guide is longer on Day 1 than on Day 2 or 3 of each lesson. As with K-PALS, this approach provides children with more practice on the subsequent day(s).

In fact, in Grade 1 PALS, the Day 2 guide is limited to a brief announcement (see Figure 6.7). The teacher uses the announcement guide to conduct a short lesson at the beginning of Day 2, at which time the teacher can also review any difficulties that he or she observed during Day 1 pair practice. For example, if the teacher observed many students struggling with the Coach's prompts, he or she could spend more time reviewing the prompts on Day 2. Many times it is helpful to review possible Player errors and discuss how the Coach could help correct such errors. On Day 3, based on the teacher's observations of Day 2, the teacher opts to conduct a brief review or allow the students to break directly into pairs.

During paired work, the teacher constantly monitors the pairs by walking around the classroom. Teachers can select pairs to sit with for several minutes of instructional support and feedback as necessary. Teachers award extra smiley faces on the Smiley Sheet when they observe students demonstrating positive pair behavior, following the PALS Rules, and providing good explanations or help. After most pairs have completed their game board or at the end of 10 to 15 minutes, the teacher directs students to place all materials back in the two-pocket folder, and

ANNOUNCEMENT
for Day 2

Today, you'll be doing the same activity at last time. But, you'll have larger numbers on your game board.

Demonstrate how to show numbers higher than 19 (e.g., 20, 25, 30, 36, 40, 41, 50 and 53) by drawing bundles of 10 and drawing marks for ones.

Example: 36

Coach: "What number?"
Player: "36."
Coach: "Draw how many."
Player: Draws 3 bundles of 10 in the tens box. Draws 6 lines in the ones box.
Coach: "Write the number."
Player: Writes 3 in the tens box and 6 in the ones box.
Coach: "Read it and break it down."
Player: "36 is 3 tens and 6 ones."

FIGURE 6.7. Grade 1 PALS announcement. From Fuchs, Fuchs, Yazdian, Powell, and Karns (2011a). Reprinted with permission from the authors.

students move on to the next classroom activity. Teachers should ensure that each student in the pair acts as both Coach and Player during each lesson. To ensure equitable time in both roles, many teachers use a timer. Once the students break into pairs, the teacher may see that he or she has 12 minutes for students to work in pairs. The teacher then sets the timer for 6 minutes, and when the timer beeps, the teacher says, "If you have not already done so, switch roles. Players, mark a smiley on the Smiley Sheet." Then the Coach becomes the Player and the Player becomes the Coach.

Grades 2–6 PALS Math

PALS Math for students in Grades 2 through 6 is quite different from K-PALS or Grade 1 PALS. We will refer to this program as Grades 2–6 PALS. For Grades 2–6 PALS, teachers use two manuals in second, third, fourth, fifth, or sixth grade to guide implementation of PALS Math. For Grades 2–6, there is one "Teacher Manual" that contains all information teachers need to implement Grades 2–6 PALS (Fuchs, Fuchs, Karns, & Phillips, 2009a). At each grade, there is also a "Student Manual" (Grade 2, Fuchs et al., 2009b; Grade 3, Fuchs et al., 2009c; Grade 4, Fuchs et al., 2009d; Grade 5, Fuchs et al., 2009e; & Grade 6, Fuchs et al., 2009f). Each teacher needs one Student Manual at the grade level he or she teaches. The Student Manual at a particular grade level includes all the templates needed to copy lesson materials for each pair at that grade level.

Basics

Grades 2–6 PALS occurs two times per week, for 30 minutes each "day." Teachers use a "lesson," which focuses on one skill, for a 2-week period. Thus, a specific lesson has a total of 4 days across 2 weeks. In contrast to K-PALS and Grade 1 PALS, teachers do not conduct a teacher-directed lesson each day. Instead, the teacher arranges the students into pairs, and the teaching occurs at the pair level.

Each Grades 2–6 PALS day includes two activities: coaching and practice. During coaching, students work in pairs. The higher-performing math student in the pair starts as the Coach, and the other student acts as the Player. The Coach coaches the Player through the first half of a Coaching Sheet. The Coach provides feedback as necessary. Then, the Coach and Player switch roles and complete the rest of the Coaching Sheet. The teacher monitors all student pairs, provides appropriate feedback, and awards extra points on the pair's Point Sheet. Coaching typically lasts 15 to 20 minutes. During practice, each student in the pair works individually on a Practice Sheet for 5 minutes. At the end of 5 minutes, the students switch Practice Sheets and check one another's work for correct answers. Each student earns 1 point for each correct answer, and the students mark their points on the pair's Point Sheet. The pair with the highest score at the end of the day helps collect PALS materials. Practice lasts approximately 10 minutes.

Lessons

Each lesson includes 4 days of material: Day 1, Day 2, Day 3, and Day 4. Days 1 and 2 of a lesson occur during 1 week, and Days 3 and 4 of the same lesson take place the following week. To introduce students to the PALS Math activities of coaching and practice, the teacher conducts 4 training days (over a 2-week period). The teaching load during training is heavy, but it ensures that students will be able to participate successfully in PALS for the rest of the school year. After training, teachers do not conduct teacher-directed lessons each day. Instead, they allow the teaching to occur between the Coach and the Player.

Teachers use two types of lessons with students: computation and applications. Computation lessons involve addition, subtraction, multiplication, or division of whole or rational numbers. Applications lessons involve math skills such as gathering information from charts and graphs, counting money, calculating perimeter, or solving word problems. The applications problems are similar to real-world math problems that often appear on standardized math assessments. At each grade level, the lessons are divided into computation and applications categories. Teachers should conduct PALS Math training using computation lessons, and after students are comfortable with the coaching and practice activities of PALS, the teacher can use either computation or applications lessons.

Teachers can choose lessons one of two ways: (1) the lessons can be concurrent with what the teacher is teaching (e.g., a fourth-grade teacher teaching decimals may opt to use one of the applications lessons focused on decimals in fourth grade), or (2) the lessons can act as a review for a skill that the teacher has already taught (e.g., the same fourth-grade teacher may use an applications lesson on fractions—which was taught in a previous unit—while the class is working on decimals). Using PALS lessons as a review allows teachers to spend more classroom instruction time focused on developing math knowledge and less time reviewing.

As teachers and students become familiar with Grades 2–6 PALS, teachers can also individualize the lessons to fit the needs of pairs. Some teachers will choose a lesson and have all pairs in the classroom work on the same lesson. Other teachers, however, differentiate the lessons based on the math needs of the pair. For example, a teacher may have several pairs ready for an applications lesson focused on calculating area and perimeter. Perhaps six pairs work on this lesson. The teacher may have four other pairs not ready for work on area and perimeter, and these pairs need to review their multiplication skills. The teacher may select a computation lesson focused on multiplication for these four pairs. In this way, PALS lessons can be used to remediate or extend math learning.

Coaching Materials

For the coaching portion of each lesson, pairs need the following materials: Coach's Question Sheet, Coaching Sheet, and Coaching Answer Sheet. The Coach uses the Coach's Question Sheet to guide the Player through the Coaching Sheet. See Figure 6.8 for a sample Coach's Question Sheet. The Coach asks the questions in the box for each new math problem. The Coach asks the numbered questions to work through each problem. The arrow indicates that the Coach needs to keep asking the questions until the problem is solved.

The Player uses the Coaching Sheet to do all math work related to answering the Coach's questions. See Figure 6.9 for a sample Coaching Sheet that accompanies the Coach's Question Sheet in Figure 6.8. The computation Coaching Sheets are always divided into four rows. The Coach and Player do something different on each row. On row 1, the Coach asks questions from the Coach's Question Sheet to the Player. On row 2, the Player "self-talks" as the Coach provides feedback. With self-talk, the Player uses the Coach's questions as a guide and talks aloud about every step to the problem. For example, for the problem 35 + 96, the student might say, "I see a plus sign, so I need to add. I start in the ones column: 5 plus 6 is 11. I have to regroup, so I write a 1 under the equal line and regroup a 1 to the tens column. Now, I add 1 plus 3 plus 9. That's 13. I write a 3 under the equal line and regroup a 1 to the hundreds column. Now, I just need to write a 1 in the hundreds column. My answer is 131." At the end of row 2, the Coach and Player switch roles. It is helpful for the students to exchange materials. That is, the second Coach takes the Coach's Question Sheet, and the second Player takes the Coaching Sheet. On row 3, the second Coach asks questions from the Coach's Question Sheet to the Player. On row 4, the second Player self-talks while the Coach provides feedback.

On all four rows, as the Player writes each digit, the Coach checks the Player's work. The Coach draws a circle around each correct digit. If a digit is incorrect, the

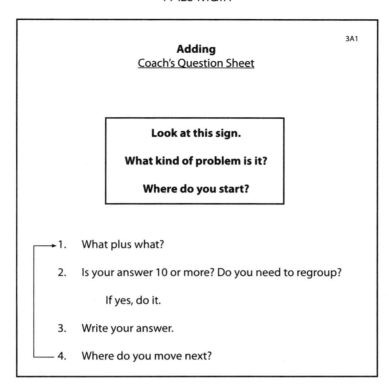

FIGURE 6.8. Coach's Question Sheet from Grade 3 computation: Adding. From Fuchs, Fuchs, Karns, and Phillips (2009c). Reprinted with permission from the authors.

Coach helps the Player correct the mistake. After the Player corrects the mistake, the Coach draws a triangle around the corrected digit. Once the Player finishes an entire problem, the Coach checks the Player's answer against a Coaching Answer Sheet. If the entire answer is correct with no triangles, the Coach draws a circle around the entire problem. (See Figure 6.10 for an example of circled and triangled digits.) The Coach checks the Player's work as the Player writes each digit. So, the Coach circles or triangles after the student writes the ones place answer. Then, the Coach asks the prompts for the tens place. After the Player writes the tens place answer, the Coach circles or triangles. The Coach should learn to check digits as the Player writes each digit to ensure that a mistake made earlier in a problem does not cause mistakes later in a problem.

The Coach circles or triangles each digit for several reasons. First, it helps the Coach catch Player mistakes quickly. Many times in math, a mistake in one answer column may contribute to subsequent errors. Second, circling and triangling helps the Coach focus on the Coach's questions and the Player's work. Some Coaches could rattle off questions without paying attention to the Player's answer, and the circling and triangling helps hold the Coach's interest. Third, circling and triangling digits help the teacher know where mistakes occur. Teachers can look at Coaching Sheets and determine whether the triangles are an accidental mistake or the result of a larger problem related to not understanding math concepts

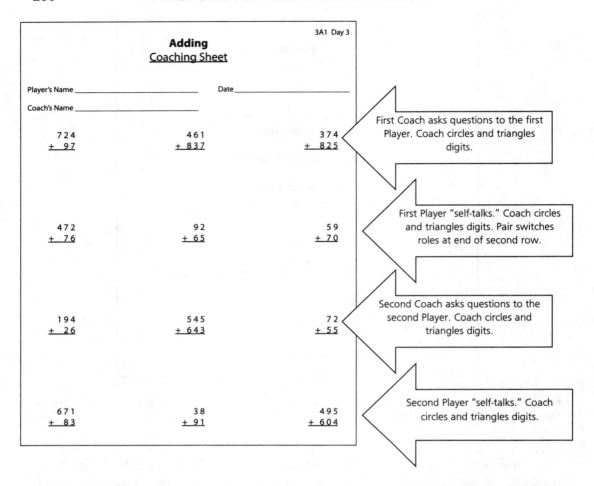

FIGURE 6.9. Coaching Sheet from Grade 3 computation: Adding. From Fuchs, Fuchs, Karns, and Phillips (2009c). Reprinted with permission from the authors.

(e.g., regrouping, finding common denominators). The Coach draws a large circle around a problem (with no incorrectly answered digits) for two reasons. First, the large circle gives the Player a mark of affirmation. Second, large circles (or the absence of large circles) can be an indicator to teachers as to which pairs may need some teacher attention or feedback during the lesson. It is fairly easy to glance around the classroom at Coaching Sheets, and if a teacher does not see many big circles, the teacher can head directly over to the pair to observe or provide assistance.

The Coaching Answer Sheet (see Figure 6.11) provides answers for the Coach to check the Player's work. It is helpful for the teacher however, to encourage the Coach to do the math work in his or her head as the Player works. This gives the Coach extra math practice. After the Player has finished the entire problem, the Coach can peek at the Coaching Answer Sheet to make sure all digits are correct. If the Player has no triangles drawn around a digit, the Coach draws a large circle around the entire problem.

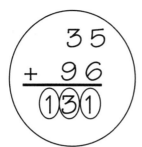

The Player answered each digit correctly (on the first try), so the Coach circles each digit in the answer. Because the Player answered each digit correctly without any correction, the Coach also draws a large circle around the entire problem.

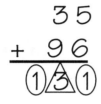

The Player answered the digit in the ones place correctly, so the Coach circles it. In the tens place, however, the Player initially wrote a 2. The Coach provided feedback to the Player by asking the Player to "add again." The Player corrected the digit, and the Coach draws a triangle around the 3. The Player answered the digit in the hundreds place correctly, so the Coach circles it. Because the Player had at least one triangled digit, the Coach does not draw a large circle around the entire problem.

FIGURE 6.10. Example of circled and triangled digits.

Practice Materials

For the practice portion of a PALS lesson, each student in the pair needs his or her own Practice Sheet, and the pair shares a Practice Answer Sheet. The Practice Sheet (see Figure 6.12) comprises 25 computation problems in 25 boxes. The computation problems are cumulative, meaning that a range of operations appears on each Practice Sheet. For example, on a Practice Sheet from a lesson on addition, students work on both addition and subtraction problems to ensure that students pay attention to the operator symbols (e.g., + and –). Each partner in a pair works independently on the Practice Sheet for 5 minutes. Teachers should set a timer to make sure all students work for the same amount of time for every lesson. If students finish a Practice Sheet early, which is not a regular occurrence, the student can sit quietly.

At the end of 5 minutes, partners switch Practice Sheets. The last Coach gets the Practice Answer Sheet out and places it between the two students. See Figure 6.13 for an example Practice Answer Sheet. Instead of scoring each digit, students score the Practice Sheet for correct answers. For example, if the answer is 63 and the student wrote "63," the scorer draws a circle around the entire problem. If the answer is 63 and the student wrote "53," the scorer does not draw anything. After scoring all the answered problems, the scorer counts the number of circles (i.e., correctly answered problems) and writes this number at the top of the Practice Sheet and circles it. The students in each pair then exchange Practice Sheets, so each student has his or her own Practice Sheet. The number circled at the top of the sheet is the student's score. The student marks this score on the Point Sheet. In Figure 6.12, the student Steffen scored Miranda's work. Miranda answered eight problems

(text continues on p. 211)

Adding

Coaching Answer Sheet

Name _____   Date _____

Scored by _____

```
   11
  724            461            374
 + 97          + 837          + 825
  821           1298           1199


    1
  472             92             59
 + 76           + 65           + 70
  548            157            129


   11
  194            545             72
 + 26          + 643           + 55
  220           1188            127


    1
  671             38            495
 + 83           + 91          + 604
  754            129           1099
```

FIGURE 6.11. Coaching Answer Sheet from Grade 3 computation: Adding. From Fuchs, Fuchs, Karns, and Phillips (2009c). Reprinted with permission from the authors.

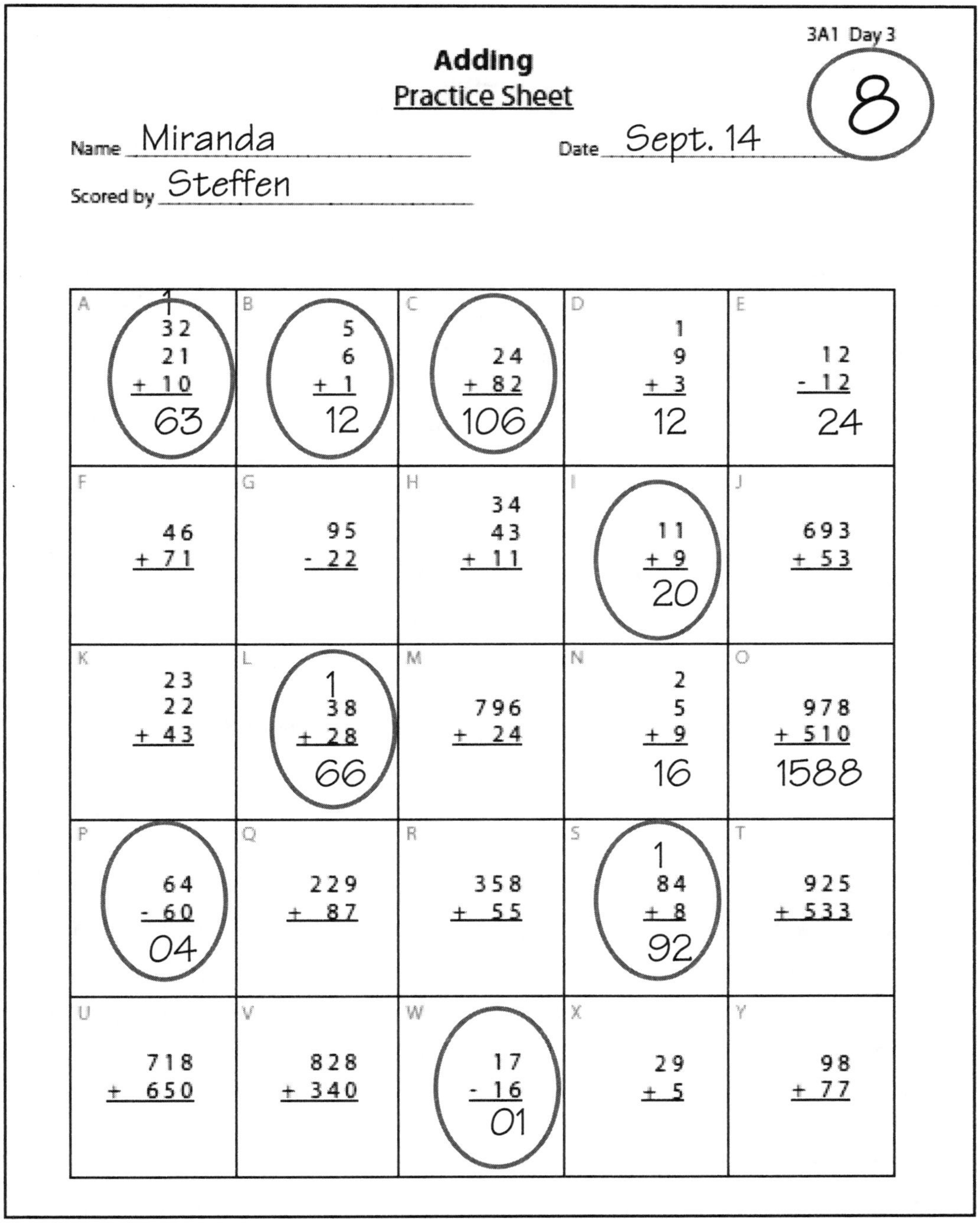

3A1 Day 3

Adding

Practice Sheet

8

Name Miranda

Date Sept. 14

Scored by Steffen

A 1 / 32 / 21 / + 10 / 63	B 5 / 6 / + 1 / 12	C 24 / + 82 / 106	D 1 / 9 / + 3 / 12	E 12 / - 12 / 24
F 46 / + 71	G 95 / - 22	H 34 / 43 / + 11	I 11 / + 9 / 20	J 693 / + 53
K 23 / 22 / + 43	L 1 / 38 / + 28 / 66	M 796 / + 24	N 2 / 5 / + 9 / 16	O 978 / + 510 / 1588
P 64 / - 60 / 04	Q 229 / + 87	R 358 / + 55	S 1 / 84 / + 8 / 92	T 925 / + 533
U 718 / + 650	V 828 / + 340	W 17 / - 16 / 01	X 29 / + 5	Y 98 / + 77

FIGURE 6.12. Scored Practice Sheet from Grade 3 computation: Adding. From Fuchs, Fuchs, Karns, and Phillips (2009c). Reprinted with permission from the authors.

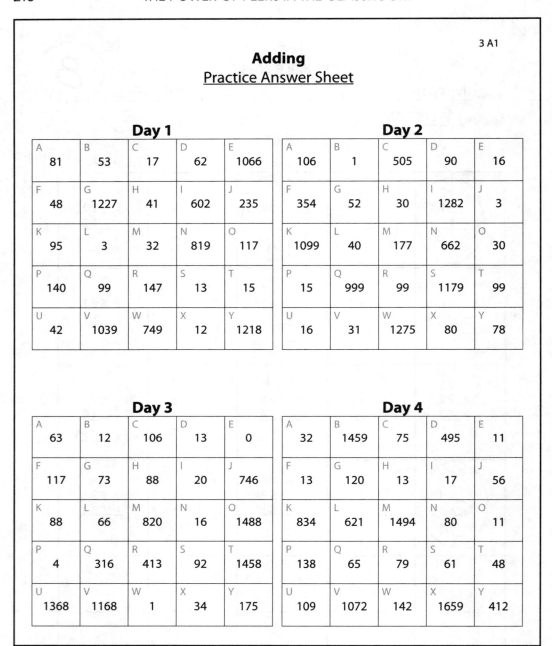

FIGURE 6.13. Practice Answer Sheet from Grade 3 computation: Adding. From Fuchs, Fuchs, Karns, and Phillips (2009c). Reprinted with permission from the authors.

correctly, so Steffen wrote an 8 at the top of Miranda's Practice Sheet. Miranda marks 8 points on the Point Sheet.

Other Pair Materials

The Coach and Player share a Point Sheet (see Figure 6.14) for the PALS lesson. During coaching, the teacher walks around and awards points to pairs demonstrating positive PALS behaviors such as using a soft voice, helping a Player correct a mistake, and using a helping strategy. The pair does not mark points on the Point Sheet during coaching. During practice, each student earns 1 point for each correctly answered problem on his or her Practice Sheet. Both students mark their points on the Point Sheet. The pair with the highest number of points at the end of the PALS lessons gets to collect the materials.

To help organize the coaching and practice materials, teachers should prepare two two-pocket folders for each pair. One folder is labeled "Coach" on the outside of the folder; the other is labeled "Player" on the outside. On the inside of both folders, "Coaching" is written on the left-hand pocket. All coaching materials for either the Coach or Player will be placed in this pocket. "Practice" is written on

POINT SHEET

Day 1

1	2	3	4	5	6	7	8	9	10
11	12	13	14	15	16	17	18	19	20
21	22	23	24	25	26	27	28	29	30
31	32	33	34	35	36	37	38	39	40
41	42	43	44	45	46	47	48	49	50
51	52	53	54	55	56	57	58	59	60
61	62	63	64	65	66	67	68	69	70
71	72	73	74	75	76	77	78	79	80

Day 2

1	2	3	4	5	6	7	8	9	10
11	12	13	14	15	16	17	18	19	20
21	22	23	24	25	26	27	28	29	30
31	32	33	34	35	36	37	38	39	40
41	42	43	44	45	46	47	48	49	50
51	52	53	54	55	56	57	58	59	60
61	62	63	64	65	66	67	68	69	70
71	72	73	74	75	76	77	78	79	80

Day 3

1	2	3	4	5	6	7	8	9	10
11	12	13	14	15	16	17	18	19	20
21	22	23	24	25	26	27	28	29	30
31	32	33	34	35	36	37	38	39	40
41	42	43	44	45	46	47	48	49	50
51	52	53	54	55	56	57	58	59	60
61	62	63	64	65	66	67	68	69	70
71	72	73	74	75	76	77	78	79	80

Day 4

1	2	3	4	5	6	7	8	9	10
11	12	13	14	15	16	17	18	19	20
21	22	23	24	25	26	27	28	29	30
31	32	33	34	35	36	37	38	39	40
41	42	43	44	45	46	47	48	49	50
51	52	53	54	55	56	57	58	59	60
61	62	63	64	65	66	67	68	69	70
71	72	73	74	75	76	77	78	79	80

FIGURE 6.14. Grades 2–6 PALS Point Sheet. From Fuchs, Fuchs, Karns, and Phillips (2009a). Reprinted with permission from the authors.

the right-hand pocket. All practice materials for either the Coach or Player will be placed in this pocket. It is easy to place the materials in the folders because the order of materials from the manual corresponds with placing them in the Coach's folder and then the Player's folder.

The Teacher's Role

Teachers show students the basic tenets of coaching and practice with four training lessons implemented at the beginning of the PALS program. The training guides and necessary teacher materials are included in the Grades 2–6 Teacher Manual. Teachers should not read the training guides verbatim. They should become familiar with the training materials and deliver the lesson using their own style. Day 1 of training includes introducing students to the Coach's Question Sheet and Coaching Sheet. Students also learn about circling and triangling correct and incorrect digits. Day 2 of training includes practicing coaching, where the Coach asks questions to the Player. On Day 3, students learn about self-talk. On Day 4, students learn to work on the Practice Sheet and check partner answers. By the end of the 4 days of training, students should be familiar enough with PALS to be able to complete a full lesson with both coaching and practice activities. During all days of training and for the first few weeks of PALS, teachers should use computation lessons for all students.

There is not a separate guide for each lesson after training. Instead, the teacher uses a Command Card to guide the students through the coaching and practice activities of a lesson. See Figure 6.15 for the first page of the Command Card. When students work in pairs, the teacher monitors them by walking around the classroom, listening to student pairs, engaging pairs in discussion, and awarding extra points when students demonstrate positive pair behaviors. During practice, the teacher should also continue to monitor students to ensure they are working independently on their own Practice Sheet.

To ensure that all PALS days run 30 minutes, it is helpful for the teacher to use a timer. Coaching in which the first Coach asks questions and the first Player self-talks should last approximately 7 to 10 minutes. When the timer beeps, the teacher encourages students to switch roles if they have not already done so. Coaching in which the second Coach asks questions and the second Player self-talks lasts another 7–10 minutes. When the timer beeps, the teacher asks students to put coaching materials away in the folders, and each student gets out a Practice Sheet. The teacher times the students for 5 minutes as they work on their Practice Sheet. When the timer beeps, the teacher asks the students to get out the Practice Answer Sheet. Students grade one another's Practice Sheets and mark points on the Point Sheet for the last 5 minutes of the PALS day.

After students are familiar with coaching, teachers provide a brief training session on helping and explaining. This session typically occurs after 2 successful weeks of PALS lessons. During helping and explaining training, the Players learn

PALS Command Card

1. **It's time for Coaching.**

2. **The list of Coaching pairs is posted on the board. Are any partners absent?**

3. **Second Coaches, stand and get the folders.**

4. **Second Coaches, sit with your partner.**

5. **Second Coaches, take the Player folder.**

6. **First Coaches, take the Coach folder.**

7. **Second Coaches, take out the Coaching Sheet. Write your name, your partner's name, and the date at the top.**

8. **First Coaches, take out the Point Sheet and put it on your desk so I can mark points. Also, make sure you have the Coaching Answer Sheet.**

9. (Wait until students have names and dates written. Review correction procedures and Coach's Question Sheet, if necessary.) **First Coaches, you are the Coach on rows one and two. Second Coaches, you are the Player on rows one and two. Remember, after the first row of problems, the Coach will stop asking the Player questions. The Player will self-talk through row two.**

   After the first two rows of problems, when you get to row three, STOP. It will be time to change materials and jobs. (If you want all pairs to switch Coaches at the same time, instruct them to wait at the end of row two. Then, halfway through the allotted Coaching time, instruct students to switch jobs.) **Second Coaches, it will be your turn to Coach. At that time, get the Coach's Question Sheet and the Coaching Answer Sheet from your partner. First Coaches, you will be the Player, and you'll get the Coaching Sheet from your partner.**

   Begin. (Monitor for correct PALS procedures and for understanding of assigned skills. Provide help as needed and award extra points on the Point Sheet when warranted.)

10. (When most students are finished or after 15–20 minutes:) **Stop.** (Award bonus points and point out good PALS behaviors you observed.)

11. **Second Coaches, make sure your name, your partner's name, and the date are on the Coaching Sheet.**

12. **Second Coaches, get the Player folder. Place the Coaching Sheet in the back of the *Coaching* pocket.**

FIGURE 6.15. Grades 2–6 PALS Command Card (first page). From Fuchs, Fuchs, Karns, and Phillips (2009a). Reprinted with permission from the authors.

how to ask for help from the Coach, and the Coach learns how to provide helpful explanations and feedback. Several weeks after the helping and explaining training, teachers train students on math strategies. These math strategies may be used by the Coach when the Player makes a mistake. See Figure 6.16 for a poster outlining the math strategies.

After at least 8 successful weeks of PALS, teachers have the option to start using some of the applications lessons (see Figure 6.17). Teachers need to conduct a brief training on the differences between computation and applications lessons. On the Coaching Sheet, stop signs signal for the Coach to stop asking questions to the Player. The Player starts self-talk after the stop sign. The flag signals for the Coach and Player to switch roles.

On applications Practice Sheets (see Figure 6.18), students always work on the lesson's skill at the top of the sheet and work on a computation review at the bottom. Sometimes the point values change by problem, but the Practice Sheet score is always a maximum of 25 across both computation and application Practice Sheets.

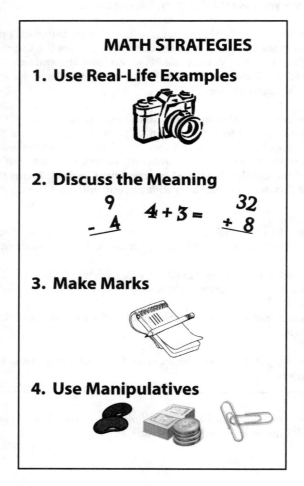

FIGURE 6.16. Grades 2–6 PALS Math strategies poster. From Fuchs, Fuchs, Karns, and Phillips (2009a). Reprinted with permission from the authors.

Counting
Coaching Sheet

T 2AP 1

Player's Name _____   Date _____

Coach's Name _____

Fill in the blanks.

28, 30, 32, ___, ___	36, 38, 40, ___, ___	50, 60, 70, ___, ___
12, 14, 16, ___, ___	55, 56, 57, ___, ___	44, 45, 46, ___, ___
75, 80, 85, ___, ___	90, 92, 94, ___, ___	10, 20, 30, ___, ___
81, 82, 83, ___, ___	72, 74, 76, ___, ___	78, 80, 82, ___, ___
64, 66, 68, ___, ___	6, 8, 10, ___, ___	35, 40, 45, ___, ___
85, 86, 87, ___, ___	20, 30, 40, ___, ___	95, 96, 97, ___, ___
30, 40, 50, ___, ___	27, 28, 29, ___, ___	65, 70, 75, ___, ___
45, 50, 55, ___, ___	78, 80, 82, ___, ___	20, 30, 40, ___, ___
55, 60, 65, ___, ___	66, 68, 70, ___, ___	90, 92, 94, ___, ___
93, 94, 95, ___, ___	87, 88, 89, ___, ___	15, 20, 25, ___, ___
22, 24, 26, ___, ___	50, 60, 70, ___, ___	37, 38, 39, ___, ___
17, 18, 19, ___, ___	18, 20, 22, ___, ___	46, 48, 50, ___, ___

FIGURE 6.17. Grades 2–6 applications Coaching Sheet. From Fuchs, Fuchs, Karns, and Phillips (2009a). Reprinted with permission from the authors.

T 34AP 4

Charts and Graphs
Practice Sheet

Name _____   Date _____

Scored by _____

Ducks in Parks in Nashville

Centennial Park	🦆 🦆 🦆 🦆
Cedar Hills Park	🦆 🦆
Shelby Park	🦆 🦆 🦆 🦆 🦆 🦆

Key: Each  🦆 means 10 ducks.

Fill in the blanks. (Each blank counts 2 points)

How many ducks are there at Shelby Park?
A. _____

How many ducks are there at the three parks altogether? **B.** _____

How many fewer ducks are there at Cedar Hills Park than at Shelby Park? **C.** _____

How many more ducks are there at Centennial Park than at Cedar Hills Park?
D. _____

How many ducks are there at Centennial Park?
E. _____

How many ducks at Shelby Park and Centennial Park altogether?
F. _____

Solve. (1 point each)

G. 654 - 34	**H.** 25 + 18	**I.** 43 - 16	**J.** 657 + 432	**K.** 52 + 15
L. 81 - 23	**M.** 417 - 61	**N.** 84 - 56	**O.** 700 + 604	**P.** 234 - 43
	Q. 74 - 15	**R.** 47 - 28	**S.** 125 + 45	

FIGURE 6.18. Grades 2–6 applications Practice Sheet. From Fuchs, Fuchs, Karns, and Phillips (2009a). Reprinted with permission from the authors.

See Figure 6.19 for a sample Coach and Player dialogue from an applications lesson on telling time. Notice the Coach circles and triangles digits on the applications Coaching Sheet in the same manner as on a computation Coaching Sheet.

PAIRING STUDENTS

Creating effective pairs is integral to the success of PALS Math. To pair students, teachers rank order their students based on math performance and then use a pairing scheme to organize the students into partners. The ultimate goal of pairing is to pair higher-performing students with lower-performing students. Please note that teachers always arrange pairs; students never choose their own PALS partners.

Rank Ordering

To create a rank order of students, teachers make a numbered list starting with 1. The strongest math student in the class is listed at the top of the list (i.e., 1). The second-best math student receives the rank of 2 and so on. The weakest math stu-

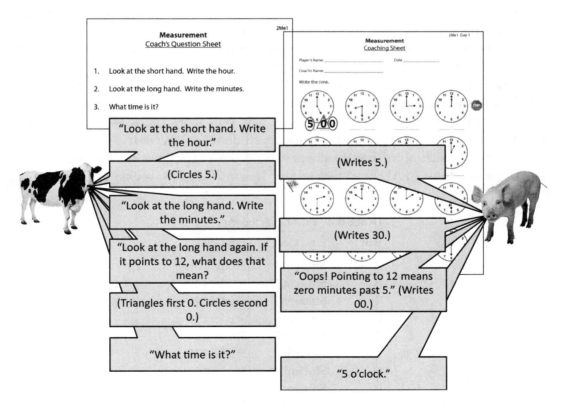

FIGURE 6.19. Grade 2 applications Coaching Sheet with Coach (cow) and Player (pig) actions. From Fuchs, Fuchs, Karns, and Phillips (2009b). Reprinted with permission from the authors.

dent in the class is listed at the bottom. For example, in a classroom with 22 students, the lowest-performing math student is ranked 22.

The rank order does not have to be perfect. Teachers often ask which assessment should be given to students to help determine rank order. We avoid recommending specific math assessments. Instead, we suggest teachers use any math assessment information that is routinely available. Teachers should not stress over developing the rank order. If higher-performing math students are toward the top of the rank order and lower-performing math students toward the bottom, then the rank order will work well.

Pairing Scheme

To explain this pairing scheme, we will use an example from a classroom of 18 students. See Table 6.4 for the scheme. The highest-performing math student is 1; the lowest-performing math student is 18. To provide the lowest-performing students in the class with tutors who can help explain math concepts and procedures, students 1, 2, and 3 are paired with the three-lowest performing students: 18, 17, and 16. Write the names of Students 1, 2, and 3 in the First Coach column. Then, pair Student 18 with Student 1, Student 17 with Student 2, and Student 16 with Student 3. To pair the students in the rest of the class, write the names of Students 4 through 9 in the First Coach Column. Then, starting with Student 10, write the names of the students in descending order in the First Player column.

Teachers should evaluate the pairs before announcing partners to the class. It is possible the pairing scheme pairs together two students with conflicting personalities or creates a pair where the higher-performing student would not be a good Coach for the given lower-performing student. At Grades 2–6, the teacher also needs to consider which lessons the pair will work on. It is important for teachers to evaluate the pairs and reassign students as necessary. Once students start working with a partner, teachers should maintain pairs for 4–6 lessons in K-PALS and Grade 1 PALS and two to four lessons (i.e., 4–8 weeks) in Grades 2–6.

TABLE 6.4. Pairing Scheme

Pair	First Coach	First Player
A	Student 1	Student 18
B	Student 2	Student 17
C	Student 3	Student 16
D	Student 4	Student 10
E	Student 5	Student 11
F	Student 6	Student 12
G	Student 7	Student 13
H	Student 8	Student 14
I	Student 9	Student 15

When pairs are kept together for several weeks, students learn how to work well with their partners, and getting students into work positions for pair practice is quick and easy.

Odd Numbers of Students

All classrooms have odd numbers of students on some days because an odd number of students are enrolled in the classroom (even in such classrooms, the number of students is sometimes even because a student is absent) or because a student is absent from a classroom that has an even number of students. For either situation, the teacher needs to create a PALS triad. There are two options for creating a triad: (1) if two students are firm on the lesson's skill and one student is weak on the lesson's skill, then the stronger students should be assigned as "first Coaches" and the weaker student as the "first Player" (when two students act as the Coach, they take turns, problem by problem, fulfilling the role of Coach); (2) if only one student is firm on the lesson's skill and the two remaining students are weak on the skill, designate the stronger student as "first Coach" and the two remaining students as "first Players." The Players take turns, problem by problem, fulfilling the role of Player as the Coach read the Coach's prompts.

If teachers have to create a more permanent triad (i.e., the teacher has an odd number of students in his or her classroom, such that a triad is unnecessary only with student absences), it is important for the teacher not to place the lowest-performing math students in the triad. The lowest-performing two or three students in any classroom should receive one-on-one peer attention during PALS (i.e., these students should not be permanently assigned to a triad, where the student might only answer every other problem).

Management of Pairs

To help PALS run smoothly, classroom management is important. We have learned several strategies that help with the implementation of PALS Math. First, once a teacher determines pairs, he or she should assign pairs to work positions within the classroom. We find it easiest to arrange students sitting side by side at desks or tables. See Figure 6.20 for an example from Grades 2–6 PALS. The Coach has the Coach folder (with the Player folder tucked inside it) and the Coach's Question Sheet out for Coaching. The Player has the Point Sheet, Coaching Sheet, and a pencil. When it is time for the pairs to switch roles (i.e., the Coach becomes the Player and the Player becomes the Coach), the students can (1) exchange materials or (2) exchange seats.

If the teacher assigns pairs to work positions, students waste less time deciding where to work and spend more time focused on learning math with their partner. Some teachers in kindergarten or first grade may allow partners to sit next to one another on the floor. While convenient for some teachers, this arrangement

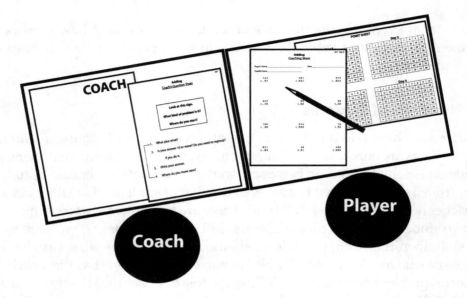

FIGURE 6.20. Sample pair arrangement. From Fuchs, Fuchs, Karns, and Phillips (2009c). Reprinted with permission from the authors.

makes it challenging for the teacher to circulate around the classroom effectively and observe all pairs (i.e., it requires teachers to constantly be crouching down and standing up).

Second, teachers should assign roles to the Coach and Player for moving into work positions. Often, teachers can ask Players to pick up the PALS folders containing all necessary lesson materials and Coaches to pick up a pencil. Once the students have their materials, they can meet at their assigned work position and start working as a pair. Only one pencil is necessary for each pair, and eliminating extra pencils or other writing materials as distractions encourages pairs to focus on PALS. In a similar way, teachers should assign roles for returning PALS materials at the end of a day of pair work.

Third, pairs respond positively to extra smiley faces (Kindergarten and Grade 1) and extra points (Grades 2–6). To maintain positive pair relationships, it is important that all students understand how to behave when working with a partner. In all the PALS Math programs, teachers introduce rules for pair behavior during training, but teachers may want to revisit behavior guidelines throughout the implementation of PALS. At all grade levels, as a teacher circulates among pairs and sees pairs working together effectively, the teacher should award an extra smiley or set of points and let the pair know why extra smileys or points are awarded (e.g., "I like how you are using soft PALS voices," "That was a nice way to tell the Player he is doing a good job," or "I'm giving you two points for that detailed self-talk"). Pairs respond positively to the possibility of getting extra smiley faces or points from the teacher, and this helps create an environment where many pairs can work in the same classroom in an effective manner.

IMPLEMENTATION OF PALS MATH

Teachers should schedule PALS Math as part of their regular school schedule. For example, a fourth-grade teacher may schedule PALS to take place on Tuesday and Fridays from 1:45 to 2:15 p.m. Teachers should conduct PALS Math consistently so students become familiar with the PALS strategies and practice mathematics with PALS regularly.

Differentiation

To best meet the needs of all students, some teachers choose to differentiate PALS Math lessons based on student performance. In Kindergarten and Grade 1 PALS, teachers can reuse lessons to provide more practice if students struggled with the lesson initially. Teachers can also opt to use the challenge game boards to extend the learning of students who were successful with lessons initially.

In Grades 2–6 PALS, teachers choose lessons to (1) match what the teacher is currently teaching or (2) act as a review for a skill the teacher has taught previously. For example, one third-grade teacher who is currently teaching a unit on fractions may choose to use the PALS fractions lesson for third grade with all dyads. Another third-grade teacher currently teaching a unit on fractions may select a PALS lesson on multiplication facts, which was taught previously in the school year, for review.

Grades 2–6 PALS can also be differentiated within the classroom. That is, all students do not work on the same lesson. If teachers choose to use PALS in this way, the lesson should be a skill the lower-performing student in a pair needs to practice. For example, a fifth-grade teacher may have many of her student pairs working on a PALS lesson focused on word problems. This same teacher, however, may assign two pairs to work on a PALS lesson focused on division computation because the students in these pairs need extra practice on division. Some teachers have even greater variety among the skills students are working on within the classroom to optimize PALS as a differentiation strategy. There is no reason different pairs need to work on the same skill. As both Coaching and Practice function in the same manner across lessons, it is completely feasible to have different pairs working on different lesson skills in the same classroom. Additionally, teachers may pull materials from other grade levels if students need remediation or extension. For example, a fifth-grade teacher may pull third-grade lessons for several pairs. Do note that the pulling from lessons across grade levels only works for the Grades 2–6 PALS materials.

Fidelity

To ensure proper implementation of PALS Math, we developed fidelity checklists to accompany the lessons. There are Kindergarten and Grade 1 checklists and one for Grades 2–6. Each checklist contains key components of a PALS lesson that teachers

Pair observed _____ & _____

Value	
1	Students begin activities when asked.
1	Coaches use correct commands on side of game board to participate in their role.
1	Coaches use proper correction procedure when applicable.

Correction Procedure: "Stop, you missed that one. Can you figure it out?" (waits 4 seconds). Coach helps Player find the answer through demonstration, he/she does not tell answer unless Player continually struggles.

Value	
1	Players point and respond appropriately in their role.
1	Students reverse roles appropriately when signaled on their game boards.
1	Students cooperate with helpful explanations (do not get point if argumentative).
1	Students work quietly.
1	Students stay on task.
1	Students appropriately award themselves "smiley faces."

Comments:

FIGURE 6.21. Excerpt from Kindergarten and Grade 1 fidelity checklist.

and students must do to demonstrate that PALS is being implemented as designed. See Figure 6.21 for a sample checklist from Grade 1 PALS. On the checklists, if a behavior is observed, the teacher/pair earns 1 point. If a behavior is not observed, no point is awarded. The sum of observed points is divided by the total possible points to calculate fidelity. A fidelity percentage of 96% means the teacher and pairs are addressing 96% of the important components of a PALS lesson. Teachers should aim for fidelity above 90%.

CONCLUSION

From our work with teachers in school districts across the United States and Canada, teachers remark that PALS Math is relatively easy to implement in the classroom. Teachers like that they are using an evidence-based program, and they comment that their students benefit from PALS Math both academically and socially. Students enjoy working with pairs and acting as a teacher, and the students often explain concepts better to other students than teachers can. The research on PALS Math demonstrates that students make positive gains on mathematics outcomes after participating in peer tutoring, and we are confident that teachers and students benefit from using the PALS Math programs.

REFERENCES

Bowman-Perrott, L., Davis, H., Vannest, K., Williams, L., Greenwood, C., & Parker, R. (2013). Academic benefits of peer tutoring: A meta-analytic review of single-case research. *School Psychology Review, 42*, 39–55.

Carmody, G., & Wood, L. (2009). Peer tutoring in mathematics for university students. *Mathematics and Computer Education, 43*, 18–28.

Codding, R. S., Chan-Iannetta, L., George, S., Ferreira, K., & Volpe, R. (2011). Early number skills: Examining the effects of classwide interventions on kindergarten performance. *School Psychology Quarterly, 26*, 85–96.

Delquadri, J., Greenwood, C. R., Whorton, D., Carta, J. J., & Hall, R. V. (1986). Classwide peer tutoring. *Exceptional Children, 52*, 535–542.

Fuchs, L. S., Fuchs, D., Hamlett, C. L., Phillips, N. B., Karns, K., & Dutka, S. (1997). Enhancing students' helping behavior during peer-mediated instruction with conceptual mathematical explanations. *Elementary School Journal, 97*, 223–249.

Fuchs, L. S., Fuchs, D., & Karns, K. (2001). Enhancing kindergartners' mathematical development: Effects of Peer-Assisted Learning Strategies. *Elementary School Journal, 101*, 495–510.

Fuchs, L. S., Fuchs, D., Karns, K., Hamlett, C. L., Dutka, S., & Katzaroff, M. (1996). The relation between student ability and the quality and effectiveness of explanations. *American Educational Research Journal, 33*, 631–664.

Fuchs, L. S., Fuchs, D., Karns, K., & Phillips, N. (2009a). *Peer Assisted Learning Strategies: Teacher manual*. Nashville, TN: Authors.

Fuchs, L. S., Fuchs, D., Karns, K., & Phillips, N. (2009b). *Peer Assisted Learning Strategies: Second grade*. Nashville, TN: Authors.

Fuchs, L. S., Fuchs, D., Karns, K., & Phillips, N. (2009c). *Peer Assisted Learning Strategies: Third grade*. Nashville, TN: Authors.

Fuchs, L. S., Fuchs, D., Karns, K., & Phillips, N. (2009d). *Peer Assisted Learning Strategies: Fourth grade*. Nashville, TN: Authors.

Fuchs, L. S., Fuchs, D., Karns, K., & Phillips, N. (2009e). *Peer Assisted Learning Strategies: Fifth grade*. Nashville, TN: Authors.

Fuchs, L. S., Fuchs, D., Karns, K., & Phillips, N. (2009f). *Peer Assisted Learning Strategies: Sixth grade*. Nashville, TN: Authors.

Fuchs, L. S., Fuchs, D., Karns, K., Yazdian, L., & Powell, S. (2001). Creating a strong foundation for mathematics learning with kindergarten Peer-Assisted Learning Strategies. *TEACHING Exceptional Children, 33*(3), 84–87.

Fuchs, L. S., Fuchs, D., Yazdian, L., & Powell, S. R. (2002). Enhancing first-grade children's mathematical development with Peer-Assisted Learning Strategies. *School Psychology Review, 31*, 569–583.

Fuchs, L. S., Fuchs, D., Yazdian, L., Powell, S., & Karns, K. (2011a). *Peer Assisted Learning Strategies: First Grade Math PALS*. Nashville, TN: Authors.

Fuchs, L. S., Fuchs, D., Yazdian, L., Powell, S., & Karns, K. (2011b). *Peer Assisted Learning Strategies: Kindergarten Math PALS*. Nashville, TN: Authors.

Harper, G. F., & Maheady, L. (2007). Peer-mediated teaching and students with learning disabilities. *Intervention in School and Clinic, 43*, 101–107.

Kroeger, K. D., & Kouche, B. (2006). Using Peer-Assisted Learning Strategies to increase response to intervention in inclusive math settings. *TEACHING Exceptional Children, 38*(5), 6–13.

Maheady, L., & Gard, J. (2010). Classwide peer tutoring: Practice, theory, research, and personal narrative. *Intervention in School and Clinic, 46*, 71–78.

Robinson, D. R., Schofield, J. W., & Steers-Wentzell, K. L. (2005). Peer and cross-age tutoring in math: Outcomes and their design implications. *Educational Psychology Review, 17*, 327–361.

CHAPTER 7

Maximizing the Benefits of Working Cooperatively with Peers

KIMBER L. WILKERSON and JENNA L. LEQUIA

Walking down the halls of a typical American school, it is not unusual to see students working together: huddled over an art project; conferring with each other on drafts of a writing assignment; sitting shoulder to shoulder in front of a computer screen bantering about which option to choose next. Given the student–teacher ratio in typical, traditional schools, a general education teacher would be hard-pressed to keep everyone on task without relying on some form of peer-mediated instruction throughout the day. Explicitly and consciously arranging students into small groups with their peers for instruction is commonly referred to as cooperative learning, and the practice is prevalent across grade levels and content areas.

In this chapter we provide a brief overview of the evidence base that supports the use of cooperative learning across grade levels, highlighting benefits for students with disabilities who are included in those cooperative learning groups with peers. We also provide sample cooperative learning lesson elements and an illustrative lesson plan to hopefully prompt ideas and provide inspiration for ways that cooperative learning could be put to good use in your own classrooms and schools. When grouping peers together there are inevitable pitfalls: students chatting about their weekend plans instead of analyzing a poem; classmates growing short-tempered with the one student in their group who is chronically off task; friends deciding that the "smart" student should complete the bulk of certain tasks so that they all get a good grade, undermining the teacher's best intentions. These kinds of pitfalls can be avoided by fine-tuning lesson plans. In this chapter we also provide suggestions for ways to tweak lesson plans in order to capitalize on group interaction in the most instructionally productive ways.

224

Because it is also common for general educators to be joined in the classroom by other educational professionals, or even adult volunteers, we also suggest strategies for incorporating paraprofessionals and other educational professionals into the implementation of small-group work. It is our belief and hope that attention to all these details will allow teachers to get the most out of the common classroom practice of having students work together.

WHAT IS "SMALL-GROUP INSTRUCTION"?

Small-group instruction is an instructional arrangement wherein students within a class are divided into groups for the purpose of learning (Lou et al., 1996). Cooperative learning is a specific small-group instructional arrangement. In a lesson that relies on cooperative learning, the teacher typically arranges students into groups of three to five students, with students intentionally grouped by the teacher. Important considerations for group composition are provided in a separate section later in the chapter.

Small-group instruction—including cooperative learning specifically—contrasts with whole-class instruction, wherein a whole class of students works toward the same instructional objective. Utilizing small-group instruction enables teachers to increase instructional time and increase opportunities for students to respond to and practice new academic skills with their peers, which has been linked to higher outcomes for students—including those with disabilities. Conversely, excessive reliance on whole-class instruction and individual seatwork sets the stage for off-task behavior by students who need more hands-on instructional guidance to be successful.

Another benefit of small-group instruction is that it increases a teacher's ability to individualize instruction, a necessary but challenging prospect for teachers in general education settings. With students working in small groups, teachers can choose to give instructions or explanations to the whole class or just to specific groups of students as needed. Using small-group arrangements during instructional time also gives teachers an opportunity to vary assignments (within or across groups) or to individualize instruction within the larger group by spending time with selected groups. Using small groups is one way for general education teachers to differentiate instruction. (See Regan, Evmenova, Mastropieri, & Scruggs, Chapter 2, this volume, for more information on differentiated instruction.)

BENEFITS OF WORKING COOPERATIVELY WITH PEERS

Overwhelmingly, the literature has demonstrated that working cooperatively with peers in small groups has a variety of benefits for students of all grade levels, as well as teachers of all major content areas (McMaster & Fuchs, 2002). The components of small-group instruction increase the feasibility (Ling, Hawkins, & Weber, 2011), efficiency (Ledford & Wolery, 2013), and quality (Jones & Henriksen, 2013) of instruction, while also allowing for teachers to meet the needs of learners of diverse ability levels (Johnson & Johnson, 1999; Zentall, Craig, & Kuester, 2011). For students, working cooperatively with peers has been shown to enhance academic achievement in all content areas (Gillies 2003, 2006; Gillies & Ashman, 2000; Kamps et al., 2008), self-efficacy as a learner (Gillies, 2003), and social skills (Kuester & Zentall, 2012; Ledford & Wolery, 2013). In the remainder of this section we outline specific strategies and provide a summary of benefits to both teachers and students that have been associated with these strategies.

Benefits for Teachers

Perhaps one of the most important benefits that the use of small-group arrangements affords teachers is the ability to accommodate diverse learning needs (Johnson & Johnson, 1999; Zentall et al., 2011), ultimately increasing the efficiency of instruction (Ledford & Wolery, 2013) and promoting the inclusion of students with disabilities—even those students with moderate to severe intellectual disabilities (Piercy, Wilton, & Townsend, 2002)—in the general education classroom (Gillies & Ashman, 2000; Stevens & Slavin, 1995). See Strain and Bovey (Chapter 9, this volume) for more information on peer-mediated interventions for students with severe disabilities.

Consider the use of cooperative learning groups with elementary students who have attention-deficit/hyperactivity disorder (ADHD), a population that has been shown to encounter social failure (Zentall et al., 2011). Teachers who have a student with ADHD in their classroom may want to address that student's social skills needs as part of everyday instruction. The use of cooperative learning groups allows teachers to target both social and academic goals for all members of a group while they collaborate to achieve a common goal. For example, one requirement of a cooperative learning group can be the display of a specified number of predefined social skills (e.g., listening to peers, discussing the assignment with group mates, taking turns sharing ideas), while simultaneously demonstrating understanding of the academic content. Integrating instruction and practice of social skills into academic group work allows a teacher to address the social and behavioral needs of a student with ADHD in authentic and inclusive education tasks.

In addition to improving the efficiency of instruction, research has shown that having students work cooperatively with their peers enhances the quality of instruction provided by teachers (Jones & Henriksen, 2013). Upon evaluating teacher and student behaviors during cooperative and small-group learning in a variety of subject areas in eighth-grade classrooms, it was found that the use of cooperative learning groups increased the amount of feedback provided to students in the form of speculative and/or challenging questions (Gillies, 2006). Working cooperatively with peers also fosters the active involvement of all students in each step of the learning process (Gillies & Ashman, 2000; Johnson & Johnson, 1999). Further, such arrangements allow for explicit instruction on behavioral or social expectations through prompts directed to the entire class or one group. Small-group instructional arrangements, especially those with interdependent contingencies, allow teachers to bring attention to appropriate social behaviors rather than resorting to reactive disciplinary actions or comments (Gillies, 2006; Ling et al., 2011).

The incorporation of various interdependent contingencies to small-group instructional arrangements provides additional benefit to teachers. Due to the interdependent nature of these reward contingencies, it is possible to implement them in ways that require fairly low effort on the part of teachers, thus increasing the feasibility of implementation (Ling et al., 2011). Finally, the use of small-group instructional arrangements decreases dependency on teachers to provide all learning opportunities. When having students work cooperatively with their peers, teachers are able to capitalize on other students modeling behaviors or skills that are being targeted during a small-group instructional session (Ledford & Wolery, 2013). This arrangement increases the number of learning opportunities that students with disabilities are exposed to through observing their peers.

Benefits for Students

Small-group instructional strategies have also been shown to be beneficial to students in the areas of motivation, self-efficacy as a learner, academic achievement, social development and social acceptance. Positive outcomes in the aforementioned areas have been demonstrated across grade-levels and core content areas (McMaster & Fuchs, 2002). When students work cooperatively with their peers, there are positive effects on learners of diverse ability levels: students without disabilities (Hawkins, Musti-Rao, Hughes, Berry, & McGuire, 2009; Gillies, 2006; Song & Grabowski, 2006), students at risk for a disability (Kamps et al., 2008; Kuester & Zentall, 2012; Ling et al., 2011), and students with disabilities (Gillies & Ashman, 2000; Ledford & Wolery, 2013).

Academic Achievement

When selecting teaching methods and approaches, perhaps one of the most important things to consider is the effect of a strategy on student academic outcomes. Often times, new methods or strategies are pursued in an attempt to improve student learning. The literature on the use of small-group instruction has demonstrated positive gains in various content areas for students of all grade levels (McMaster & Fuchs, 2002). Even targeting social skills has been suggested to contribute to the academic achievement of students with disabilities working cooperatively with their peers (Gillies & Ashman, 2000). In an evaluation of cooperative learning groups that incorporate individual accountability as well as group goals, Stevens and Slavin (1995) attribute academic achievement gains to the explanations of concepts and skills provided when students work in groups with their peers. The researchers noted a direct relationship wherein the more elaborate the explanations provided in the group, the better the group members' performance on achievement tests. (See Scornavacco et al., Chapter 4, this volume, for more information on promoting peer discourse.)

Motivation

An essential element of teaching students with and without disabilities is motivation. One way that teachers can address or increase student motivation is having students work in groups with their peers (Kuester & Zentall, 2012; Song & Grabowski, 2006). Whether a teacher is looking to increase intrinsic motivation for the process of learning or plans to explicitly address motivation by incorporating an interdependent reward contingency, such strategies offer ample opportunities to increase student motivation. The literature suggests that cooperative learning arrangements result in higher productivity on tasks than independent arrangements, as students who regularly work cooperatively with peers grow accustomed to sharing perspectives, ideas, and knowledge about the topics being covered (Johnson & Johnson, 1999).

Self-Efficacy

An additional benefit of having students work cooperatively with their peers, which is related to level of motivation, is an increased sense of self-efficacy as a learner. Bandura (1977) identifies four factors that contribute to self-efficacy: mastery experiences, social modeling, social persuasion, and psychological responses. Many of these are essential elements of small-group instructional arrangements. When students work in cooperative arrangements with their peers, their perceived ability as a learner has been shown to improve (Jones & Henriksen, 2013; Stevens & Slavin, 1995). Gillies (2003) examined the use of cooperative groups for students in eighth grade and found that placing students in structured groups with a specific shared problem-solving task was associated with students having strong perceptions that the work they were doing together in groups was of high quality. As a student, understanding how to obtain assistance for a problem that you are unsure how to solve is just as important as knowing the answer—both of these, process and outcome, are emphasized in cooperative learning groups.

Social Development

As previously mentioned, placing students in small-group arrangements with peers to work on tasks provides ample opportunities to explicitly target, teach, and model appropriate social skills. At the elementary level, cooperative learning groups have been associated with improvement in sharing and listening to diverse perspectives (Stockall, 2011). It has been noted that explicit instruction on social skills may be necessary to modify the social behaviors of students with disabilities (Zentall et al., 2011); arranging students in groups with their peers provides opportunities for these students to practice targeted social skills and observe typically developing peers engaging in targeted and other appropriate social skills (Ledford & Wolery, 2013). Additionally, incorporating small-group instructional arrangements increases the collaborative skills of all students (Gillies, 2003), which has the proximal benefit of improving the classroom climate, and the distal benefit of reinforcing skills that are essential to success in work settings.

Social Acceptance

The use of small-group arrangements not only provides increased academic performance, it also promotes the social inclusion of students with disabilities (Gillies & Ashman, 2000; Stevens & Slavin, 1995). Including students with disabilities in general education classrooms requires planning and preparation. In order to foster quality inclusive environments, it is necessary that students with disabilities have the opportunity to work cooperatively with typically developing peers to achieve a common goal (Alquraini & Gut, 2012). While such arrangements have the potential for these students to learn appropriate social skills from observing their peers (Ledford & Wolery, 2013), the arrangement also affects the peers. The increased exposure and interaction with students with disabilities helps typically developing peers understand that these students have things in common with them, ultimately increasing typically developing peers' social acceptance of students with disabilities (Kuester & Zentall, 2012; Stevens & Slavin, 1995). The use of cooperative learning groups has also been shown to increase the number of friends students have overall (Stevens & Slavin, 1995).

LESSON QUALITIES THAT MAXIMIZE BENEFITS FOR STUDENTS

In order to best capitalize on the strength of small-group instruction, teachers should be mindful of four important lesson plan elements:

1. Group composition
2. Nature of the group task
3. Individual accountability
4. Relative ability of group members

These four elements can have a significant impact on increases in task-related interactions and increases in academic achievement. Each of these four elements is further described and illustrated in the following sections. Figure 7.1 provides a graphic depiction of a summary of the step-by-step decision process and instructional elements that educators should consider when designing cooperative learning lessons.

Step 1: Group Composition

Form groups consciously
- Heterogeneous groups (i.e., mixed ability groups)
  Math or Science tasks
- Homogenous groups (i.e., similar ability groups)
  Reading tasks

Step 2: Nature of Group Task

Arrange for positive interdependence
- Identify group goal
- Specify roles
- Incorporate group contingency

Step 3: Individual Accountability

Incorporate plan for assessing individual students
- Quizzes
- Summary sheet
- Roles in group project (e.g., expertise in area)

Step 4: Relative Ability of Group Members

Create equal opportunities for success
- Improve on individual past performance
- Allow for multiple forms of contribution

Step 5: Roles of Educational Professionals

Identify roles for various educational professionals
- Assist with progress monitoring of groups
- Facilitate discussion within groups
- Monitor and reward appropriate behavior

FIGURE 7.1. Step-by-step outline of how to arrange cooperative learning groups.

Group Composition

The decision to place students in heterogeneous versus homogeneous ability groups with peers depends on the nature of the learning task (Noddings, 1989). With regard to subject area of instruction, a meta-analysis of within-class grouping found that overall effect sizes for homogeneous and heterogeneous ability instructional groups in mathematics and science were not significantly different; in reading, however, placing students in homogeneous ability groups with peers was superior (Lou et al., 1996). This finding may be due to the fact that tasks in math and science are typically more hierarchical; thus, group discussion and assistance from peers of varying abilities may be more likely to benefit student progress (Lou et al., 1996).

Lou et al.'s (1996) meta-analysis also determined that the effects of homogeneous versus heterogeneous groups were not stable across student ability. Students whose academic skills were low learned significantly more when placed in heterogeneous groups with peers, regardless of subject matter. This outcome is most likely because students who are farthest from mastery of a particular content have the most to gain from peer interaction around learning tasks. When placed in homogeneous groups, with other students who are equally far from mastery, struggling students then lack access to models of more capable thinkers as well as peers who can stretch their learning. When placed in heterogeneous groups, students whose grasp of the content is initially more tenuous can think through the academic tasks at hand with peers whose understanding is more advanced than their own. Lev Vygotsky named this learner space the "zone of proximal development," referring to the distance between a learner's current, actual developmental level and his or her potential level of development (1978, p. 86). Working with peers whose development (i.e., understanding of the current academic task), is slightly advanced allows a student to edge his own mastery of the task forward. Teachers who structure learning tasks to take advantage of the heterogeneity in their classrooms are capitalizing on this phenomenon. See Figure 7.2 for a depiction of different options for group composition for cooperative learning groups.

The benefit of participating in learning tasks with peers of differing abilities applies to social learning as well. For students who exhibit challenging behavior, the social benefits of learning alongside peers who are more socially adept are well established. This research underscores that the social and academic growth of students with disabilities is maximized by their participation in heterogeneous ability groups during small-group instruction, particularly in math and science.

Nature of the Group Task

Designing a cooperative learning lesson starts with learning objectives that are cooperative in nature or require interdependence to complete successfully. Simply placing students in groups and asking them to complete an assignment that could just as easily have been completed alone will not reap the positive social and aca-

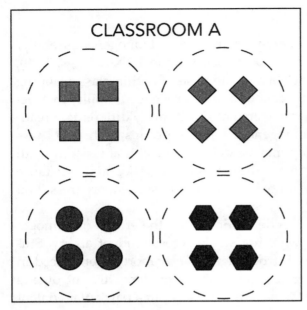

Homogeneous Groups

Classroom A is arranged in homogeneous learning groups. When using homogeneous peer groups, students are placed in groups by ability level (e.g., all high-achieving students work together). Grouping peers homogeneously by ability is beneficial when working on *reading* tasks, where a specific level of mastery is necessary.

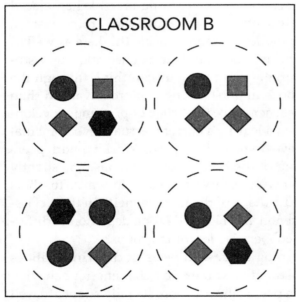

Heterogeneous Groups

Classroom B is arranged in heterogeneous learning groups. In heterogeneous peer groups, students are placed with peers who have differing ability levels (e.g., mixed ability groupings). Using mixed ability groups is beneficial when the task is in the area of *math or science* where most tasks are hierarchical in nature and students who are lower achieving can learn from their peers who have mastered the targeted concept or skill.

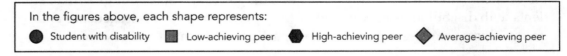

FIGURE 7.2. Variations in composition of cooperative learning groups.

demic benefits that small-group work has to offer. Learning objectives that encourage or, ideally, require students to work together are an important foundational element of successful cooperative learning lessons.

Although it may seem obvious, one important part of designing a cooperative lesson to keep in mind is that the task must include a true group goal, otherwise known as *positive interdependence*. Positive interdependence exists when individual students perceive that their accomplishments contribute positively to the accomplishments of others. When students in small groups are recognized for the accomplishments of their group as a whole, positive interdependence is in place and the learning is considered cooperative. When students are physically placed into small groups with peers for instruction but no structure is in place for positive interdependence, the learning is considered competitive or individualistic in nature. Students working toward a collaborative or group goal have been found to develop concepts that are richer and more precise than students who work independently under competitive or individualistic goal structures (Kol'tsova, 1978).

Ensuring that students work toward a group goal is best facilitated by assigning group tasks. A group task is one that requires some type of input from all the peers in the group in order for the group to be successful (Cohen, 1994). A task that could easily be completed by the individual group members without each other's input or assistance is not likely to facilitate interaction for all group members. This is particularly true for students who struggle to master new content or who struggle socially; these are the students who may be perceived by their peers as having little to offer the group. To circumvent this problem, Cohen and Cohen (1991) suggest utilizing a classroom management system that encourages students to be responsible for each other's success, issuing specific roles during group work to help ensure that groups function in a prespecified manner and utilizing ill-structured tasks (i.e., ones that do not have a single correct answer) for group collaboration. Figure 7.3 presents sample cooperative learning group tasks in the form of lesson objectives that incorporate positive interdependence. Figure 7.4 includes sample group tasks that lack elements that encourage positive interdependence, along with suggestions on how to improve those tasks to optimize their effectiveness for promoting social competence and collaboration among peers.

Positive interdependence in small-group work can be created through goal interdependence, as described previously, but can also be promoted through contingencies and reward structures, referred to as *reward interdependence*. This is an effective technique that teachers can use to create a cooperative learning group task for which all peers in the group receive a reward when the group collectively has met some standard. In behavioral literature, this concept is referred to as an interdependent group contingency. When an interdependent group contingency is set up, peers will encourage each other to ensure that the group is successful. Instigating an interdependent group contingency has the added effect of ensuring

Cooperative Learning Lesson Objectives	Evidence of Positive Interdependence
Academic: When working in small groups and playing the question game, students will correctly answer a minimum of three comprehension questions. *Social*: When working in small groups, students will take turns when choosing and answering question cards.	Students are responsible for asking questions of the other members in their small groups. This activity cannot be completed successfully unless each student actively participates by asking and answering questions aloud.
Academic: While working in pairs, students will ask "who," "what," and "where" questions related to the book they are reading. Also, while working in pairs, each student will answer his or her partner's questions using details from the book they are reading. *Social*: Students will interact positively in relation to their shared reading tasks, which include shared questioning and answering responsibilities.	Students decide with their partners how many pages each will read before switching roles. The students also decide how many pages they will read before stopping to generate questions. Each student is responsible for asking one question at each stopping point. The activity cannot be completed unless both partners are actively listening and responding.
Academic: Students will work together to create and act out a short play. All members of the group will articulate different points of view via the different characters in the play. *Social*: Students will use their group roles to work together cooperatively and use conflict resolution skills when creating a script for their play.	Each student has a role that he or she must fulfill in order for the group to act out their play.
Academic: Students will accurately measure the length of three different jumps by using strips of paper. Students will accurately use strips of paper to measure how many units are in their longest and shortest jumps. *Social*: Students and their partners will work cooperatively by helping each other mark their jumps with tape on the ground and rolling out long strips of paper.	Partners need to share supplies and help each other roll out the paper to measure the length of each partner's jump. The students cannot do this by themselves because there are not enough materials and the task is physically difficult to accomplish without at least one helper.

FIGURE 7.3. Sample cooperative learning tasks that encourage positive interdependence. Sample lesson objectives provided by Grace Doval and Jaime Ropski.

Group task that lacks positive interdependence	Potential problem	Suggestions for increasing positive interdependence
In small groups, students will create a cartoon that demonstrates their understanding of analogies.	One student may complete the task for the whole group.	• Give each student in the group a role in the cartoon creation. Examples include illustrator, copy editor, and timekeeper. • Require groups to create a brainstorm list on chart paper that contains at least two ideas from each group member before they begin drafting the cartoon.
Students study a map together to prepare for a U.S. history test.	Students will not necessarily be invested in their partners' level of preparation for the test and may not utilize the study session productively.	• Give students a script to follow to quiz their partners on the important map features. Have students "sign off" on their partners' study sheet(s) when they have gone over the map questions at least two times. Give credit on the test for students who signed off on their partners' study sheets.

FIGURE 7.4. Solutions to potential problems with group tasks.

that all group members actively participate and thus have the chance to benefit academically. See Figure 7.5 for examples of interdependent group contingencies that would be appropriate in a variety of subjects and across grade levels.

According to Slavin (1995), creating an interdependent group contingency is the best way to avoid small-group work in which one or more members "slack off" or where low-status or low-ability students are discouraged by the other members of the group from participating. By making increased achievement the group goal for *all* members and by rewarding groups that accomplish their goal (i.e., reward

Appropriate grade level	Subject area	Sample interdependent group contingency
Elementary	Any	Students will self-assess their contribution to the group work using a checklist. *If all group members complete the checklist, the whole group gets a sticker.*
	Science	In small groups, students complete a K-W-L chart ("K" = Know, "W" = Want to know, "L" = Learned). Groups are instructed that each member of the group must add an item to the "K" and "W" columns and have those items checked by a teacher before they can retrieve the materials for the science activity. When checking the K-W-L charts, the teacher can place a star next to at least one "W" ("Want to know") item for each member of the group. (Note: the teacher may have to facilitate the addition of more "W" entries to ensure that the items will be addressed by the upcoming activity.) At the end of the activity, *groups will receive a reward if each member can complete the "L" section of the chart* with an entry that corresponds to the starred "W" items.
Middle school	English	After having been instructed to brainstorm a list of analogies on chart paper, with each member being expected to contribute, *groups will be graded on the degree to which all group members' ideas are reflected* in the final brainstorm list.
	Science	Students are each given 10 previously unknown vocabulary words to study. (Note: word lists can be individualized by the teacher, or even selected from a pool of words by the students themselves.) Students are put into small groups and instructed to help each other learn the new words. *Each group whose members all score at least 8 out of 10 on the vocabulary quiz gets to choose a song* to play during Friday lab cleanup.
High school	Math	After completing a small-group study activity reviewing a practice test, *all members of the group get 3 extra points on the test if every member of the group increases his or her score* from the score achieved on the previous attempt at the practice test.
	History	Groups of three students will be assigned to research a specific political movement and write a three-paragraph summary. As part the assignment, each student will have a first draft edited by one group mate and the teacher. The second group mate will review the final draft to make sure that all suggestions on the first draft (from the peer and the teacher) have been incorporated into the final draft. *Final grades for the project will be based on* the quality of the final draft, the extent to which feedback was incorporated, and *the extent to which peers made sure that their group mates incorporated feedback.*

FIGURE 7.5. Sample interdependent group contingencies and group reward structure. *Italicized* text denotes the rewarded interdependence in each example.

interdependence), all members of a group will be more likely to interact, maximizing academic growth for all. Various researchers have supported this notion, reporting that the greatest effects of cooperative learning come when groups are rewarded for the increased achievement of all the members of their groups (Davidson, 1985; Ellis & Fouts, 1993; Manning & Lucking, 1991; Slavin, 1983). The sample group contingencies in Figure 7.5 could be adapted for use in a wide variety of inclusive classrooms to promote cooperative behavior when working in groups with peers.

Another consideration for teachers when designing a group task is to think about ways that the task could be individualized for specific students. The importance and merit of this facet of small-group instruction is underscored by researchers' findings that the effectiveness of small-group work as an instructional strategy is magnified when teachers are able to individualize instructional materials across groups (Lou et al., 1996). This individualization can take the form of assigning roles that are crafted to allow students with a range of strengths and abilities to be pushed to learn and grow, or it can take the form of individualizing specific tasks expected of students under the umbrella of an encompassing group goal. The sample lesson in Figure 7.6 provides examples of ways that tasks can be individualized, through the use of accommodations and role differentiation, without losing access to the benefits of cooperative group learning. See Section V of the sample lesson plan for specific examples of accommodations made for learners with disabilities. The lesson plan in Figure 7.6 also includes the other lesson plan elements that are recommended for effective cooperative learning instruction.

Overall, positive interdependence that is established by utilizing group rewards in conjunction with group goals maximizes the positive effects of small-group instruction on academic growth for all students. Tudge (1992) contends that adding these factors to group work introduces the element of motivation that is lacking in most work in the Vygotskian and Piagetian traditions. It may not matter, for example, how much overlap exists in students' zones of proximal development if they simply refuse to speak to each other. Adding the elements of explicit group goals and group rewards provides the motivation for the valuable interaction to take place. Attention to these additional elements acknowledges that contextual factors also influence learning when peers come together around academic tasks.

This acknowledgment that students may need motivation to participate fully and effectively in group work may be especially relevant for students with emotional and behavioral disorders or other students with disabilities who have social skill needs delineated in their individualized education programs (IEPs). These students are prime candidates for missing the benefits of task-related peer interaction if they are left in small groups with little structure and where their participation in the group task may not be a welcome prospect to peers. Additionally, it is well established that students with emotional and behavioral disorders, particularly, frequently respond well to behavioral interventions.

(text continues on p. 240)

Cooperative Learning Lesson Plan

Curriculum Area: Math   Time Frame: 9:00–10:00

Name of lesson: Jump Measuring   Grade level: 2

I. Enduring understandings:
- Students will accurately measure the length of three different jumps by using strips of paper.
- Students will accurately use strips of blue paper to measure how many units are in their longest and shortest jumps.
- Students will work cooperatively with their partner(s) by helping each other mark their jumps with tape on the ground and rolling out the long strips of paper to measure their jumps.

Essential questions:
- How can I accurately measure how far I can jump using blue strips of paper as the units?
- How many yellow strips of paper are in a blue strip of paper?
- How can I work with a partner to help me accurately track and measure my jump?

II. Common Core State Standards addressed in this lesson:
CCSS.MATH.CONTENT.2.MD.A.1

Measure the length of an object by selecting and using appropriate tools such as rulers, yardsticks, meter sticks, and measuring tapes.

CCSS.MATH.CONTENT.2.MD.A.4

Measure to determine how much longer one object is than another, expressing the length difference in terms of a standard length unit.

CCSS.MATH.CONTENT.2.MD.A.2

Measure the length of an object twice, using length units of different lengths for the two measurements; describe how the two measurements relate to the size of the unit chosen.

III. Evidence of understanding/learning (student assessment procedures):
Students will fill out a worksheet and answer the questions. I will use this to check for understanding, and the adults in the classroom will also supervise when the students jump to make sure that they are following directions and measuring correctly and accurately (using the skills and rules that are discussed at the beginning of the lesson).

In the first part of the worksheet, the students have to figure out which jump is the longest and shortest. The students know and understand the difference between "long" and "short" so they should be able to answer these questions on their own. The additional questions on the worksheet will be used to check for understanding. The adults in the classroom will observe the students as they are using the blue and yellow strips of paper to measure the length of their jumps. The blue strips of paper are twice the size of the yellow strips, and the students will have to understand this in order to use both of the strips of paper to measure. Using observations, I will look to see which students understand this concept, and which students need more help with it. Based on their worksheets and the strips of paper that they will attach to them, I will be able to see how accurate their answers are when comparing the length of their jumps to the blue and yellow strips of paper.

(continued)

FIGURE 7.6. Sample cooperative learning lesson plan.

IV. Lesson objectives and outcomes:
   A. Academic: Students will accurately measure (using the rules of measuring) the length of three different jumps by using strips of paper.

   Students will accurately use strips of blue paper to measure how many units are in their longest and shortest jumps.

   B. Social: Students will work cooperatively with their partner(s) by helping each other mark their jumps on the ground with tape and rolling out the long strips of paper.

V. Lesson objectives for students with unique learning characteristics:
   Cailey:
   - Cailey often does not participate in class activities, so my main goal is for her to participate. In addition, I have the same social and academic goals and expectations for her as I do for the rest of the class. Socially, I would like to stress the importance of Cailey working with her partner instead of working alone and refusing to work with others, as she has done in the past.
   - If Cailey leaves the classroom or does not want to participate, I will invite her into the activity multiple times, and if she does not decide to participate then she will not participate. I also will try to work with her to see if that gets her to become more interested in working on this activity.

   Carlisle:
   - Carlisle also has the same social and academic goals as the rest of the class, but I would like to stress the social goal for him as well. He often does not work well with other students in the class, and I would really like to see him help out his partners. He worked with the same partners in one of the last measuring activities and did a great job, so I would like to see the same for this lesson. If he is being contrary with his peers during this activity, I will have him take a break and finish what he missed during snack/recess.

   Leslie:
   - For Leslie, I would like to stress the measurement vocabulary and the size of the blue and yellow strips. I think that she will have a hard time understanding that the blue strip is twice the size of the yellow strip, as well as the other measurement rules, so I will make sure to stress this with her. I will also talk with her specifically about one measuring rule—do not leave space between the strips of paper—so that she will keep this rule in mind, and I will call on her to share it at the end of the lesson.

VI. Materials: jumping worksheet, tape, rolling paper, blue and yellow strips, rules for measuring strips of paper, scissors, paper clips

VII. Key or new vocabulary and concepts:
   - Measurement
   - Units
   - Frog, rabbit, human jump

(continued)

FIGURE 7.6. (continued)

VIII. Teaching procedure and techniques:

  a. **Introduction or anchor activity (30 seconds)**

   Students will meet at the carpet.

   "Raise your hand if you think that you can jump really far" (watch as students raise their hands). "Great! Today we are going to measure how far you can jump!"

  b. **Instructional sequence**

Instructions and demonstration (15 minutes):

- "You are going to work with a partner to mark and measure three different jumps: a frog jump, a rabbit jump, and a kid jump. For the frog jump, you will start from a squatting position, starting and ending with both your hands and feet on the floor" (choose student to demonstrate). "For the rabbit jump, you will jump from an almost standing position with your knees bent, feet together, and hands staying in front" (choose student to demonstrate). "For the kid jump, you will do the same thing as the rabbit jump, but you can use your arms to pump forward" (choose student to demonstrate).
  - ○ "When you do each of your three jumps, you will begin at the piece of tape that is marked on the floor. Your toes should be behind that piece of tape (demonstrate). After you jump you MUST land with both of your feet next to each other. If your feet are not next to each other, then your partner will mark the foot that is furthest back. When you land with both of your feet together, you will stand where you landed while your partner puts a piece of tape behind your HEELS to mark where you landed."
  - ○ "Make sure that you are working with your partner for this part. You will not be able to do it on your own. Then, you will take a strip of paper. Have your partner hold it at the starting line and roll it out to where your partner taped your landing spot on the floor. Cut the piece of paper where your landing spot was. Then, write your name and the jump you did on the piece of paper. Repeat this for each of the jumps for you and your partner."
- "Once you complete all three jumps, you will decide which jump was the longest and which was the shortest. You are going to measure those two jumps using these blue strips of paper. Mrs. A told me that you did a great job using these strips of paper last week, so I am expecting you to do the same today."
  - ○ "Are these strips of paper the same size?"
  - ○ "No, the blue piece is twice the size of the yellow piece."
  - ○ Demonstrate measuring a line on the chalkboard with the yellow and blue strips.
    - ▪ "Should I start at the edge or go over the edge with my strip?"
    - ▪ "What do I do if I do not have enough strips to reach the whole line?"
      - □ "Use your finger or chalk to mark where you were."
      - □ "Use yellow or blue pieces."
    - ▪ "Can I leave spaces between each strip?"
    - ▪ "What if my paper goes over/under my ending line?"
    - ▪ "Can I overlap the strips?"
    - ▪ "Can I move the strips in a crooked line?"

Dismiss students to stations

  c. **Activity (35 minutes)**

   Walk around to assist, observe, and answer student questions.

   When students are finished, they can record their jumps on the chart in the front of the room. If there is not time, they can record it next time.

   - Chart: longest jump, shortest jump, blue strips, yellow strips (figure this out—yellow is half of the blue).

(continued)

FIGURE 7.6. *(continued)*

d. **Closure (10 minutes)**
Have students write the length of their longest jump and shortest jump on the board.
- Look at results and discuss.
"I saw a lot of you measuring your jumps in different ways. What are some of the rules we need to remember when we are measuring our jumps?"
Discussion and reflection on working with partners.
- "How did your partner help you with this activity?"
- "Could you have completed this activity without your partner?"
"Next time, we are going to figure out how to find the difference between our longest and shortest jumps."

Transition to next activity
I will have the students give me their worksheet and pieces of paper from their jumps (paper clip them together), and then dismiss the students to either get on their jackets for recess or wash their hands for lunch.

IX. **Extension and enrichment:**
If students finish measuring their jump using the blue and yellow strips early, I will have them practice measuring using popsicle sticks and their own feet. They may also solve the difference between their longest and shortest jump if they finish all of this.

X. **Application/maintenance/generalization of skills and concepts:**
Students will continue using measurement throughout their schooling experience and in everyday life. Upcoming lessons will reinforce these skills and we will build on them now, as teachers will in future grade levels.

XI. **Additional cooperative learning elements:**

Group Processing: The discussion at the conclusion of the lesson will give me feedback from the students and get them to think about how well they worked in partners and how their partners helped them in this activity.

Social Skills: When students are working in partners, they need to interact by sharing supplies and communicating while measuring the length of their jumps.

Face-to-Face Interactions: Partners need to assist one another in marking where each partner jumped to, as well as helping roll out the paper and cutting to measure the length of their jump. The students will not be able to do the assignment by themselves because there are too many materials and the paper will roll up if one person is not holding the other end.

FIGURE 7.6. *(continued)*

Individual Accountability

While the importance of having all group members invested in their peers' success has been established, it is also important to incorporate a mechanism for individual accountability. A lesson that includes individual accountability ensures that growth or success for each student in each group is given attention. Individual accountability is in place when the teacher overseeing the lesson can ascertain on an individual basis whether or not students have met the learning objectives. Examples of ways that individual accountability can be ensured include:

- Individual quizzes
- Individual summary sheets submitted along with group summary sheets
- Group lessons that require individual students to acquire expertise on a topic and share information on that topic with their peers in order to complete the group project

In all these examples, a teacher could easily check an individual student's learning and hold each student accountable for mastering learning objectives. See Figure 7.7 for classroom examples of ways that teachers can incorporate individual accountability into cooperative learning lessons. These examples correspond to sample lesson plans referenced in earlier sections of this chapter.

When incorporating individual accountability, it is important to do so in a way that does not undermine the positive interdependence that was established by the creation of a group goal. Consider one of the examples from Figure 7.7. If a high school teacher were to individually assess students on their understanding of an assigned text that was explored and studied by students collaboratively in cooperative groups, this approach would certainly have the intended effect of holding each student accountable for the learning objectives. However, if the only assessment were the individual students' performance on a test, the students would have little incentive to be invested in their group mates' acquisition of the content. However, if the teacher also assigned a grade to the groups based on their completion of a self-assessment form using group processing or required students to turn in

Appropriate grade level	Example of individual accountability
Any	By fulfilling activities associated with assigned group roles, all students are required to be active participants in their groups.
K–1	Every student will have to write at least one new adjective on his or her group's poster. Everyone will have a different color marker, so this will make it clear to the teacher and students in the group that each student has contributed.
3–5	During a shared reading activity, each student is responsible for generating his or her own question at each stopping point. Each student is also responsible for answering his or her partner's questions at each stopping point.
6–8	Students complete all tasks associated with their roles in the group and contribute at least one idea for the group's culminating play. During the lesson, students write ideas for the play on separate pieces of paper. The final product must include at least one idea from each group member.
9–12	Each student in the group is responsible for knowing the assigned text well enough to answer the comprehension questions individually.

FIGURE 7.7. Examples of ways to include individual accountability in cooperative learning lessons. Lesson elements provided by Emma Becher, Grace Doval, Tiffany Mason, and Jaime Ropski.

a study sheet completed collectively by all group members prior to the individual tests being administered, the teacher would be ensuring that the groups still had reason to be invested in high-quality interaction with their peers.

Relative Ability of Group Members

As underscored earlier in the chapter, the relative abilities of the members of a group—both in academic as well as social domains—have a significant impact on the success of cooperative learning groups as a mode of instruction. Assuming an increase in the social acceptance of students with disabilities is a goal, the cooperative learning group tasks that teachers create must involve quality interactions. One important way to promote quality interaction is to ensure that all group members believe they have an equal opportunity for success. If tasks are structured in such a way that certain members of the group can succeed more easily than others, the stage for divisiveness may be set. Placing students in heterogeneous-ability cooperative learning groups will not necessarily lead to an increase in positive interactions unless some structure is built into the activity to create an "even playing field." Creating group tasks in which all students believe they can contribute to the good of the group helps promote acceptance and leads to more positive interactions and, it is hoped, to increased achievement.

Some manifestations of cooperative learning have these characteristics. For example, researchers at Johns Hopkins University have developed cooperative learning techniques that allow students to contribute to their group's goal by improving their own past performance. In these methods, group rewards are given to groups based on the extent to which individual members meet or exceed their own earlier levels of achievement. These methods prevent peers from viewing low-achieving students as burdensome and promote acceptance of students for whom mastery of academic content is more challenging, including some students with disabilities (Madden & Slavin, 1983; Slavin, 1984).

Because students with emotional and behavioral disorders and learning disabilities also struggle academically, methods that provide equal opportunities for success for all students—such as having students work cooperatively with peers— should be maximized in order to increase positive peer interactions. Increases in peer interactions around academic tasks should then lead to better understanding of the academic content around which the interactions take place.

To create cooperative learning activities that provide students with disabilities with equal opportunities for success, teachers sometimes have to be highly creative. When using a cooperative learning method such as Slavin's (1995) Student Teams Achievement Divisions, groups are rewarded for their joint performance on quizzes, but students add to their group's performance depending on how much they improve from their previous quiz score. This modification allows students to compete with themselves rather than feeling like they must meet the same criteria as all of the peers in their group to be deemed successful.

Other forms of cooperative learning produce equal opportunities for success by allowing for alternative forms of assessment or by using group projects that allow for multiple forms of contribution (e.g., one person creates illustrations, one reads a defining passage aloud, one summarizes) as assessment activities. In these ways, students are allowed to contribute according to their strengths while everyone is still held responsible for learning and demonstrating that learning.

SUGGESTED SOLUTIONS FOR COMMON PROBLEMS IN COOPERATIVE LEARNING ARRANGEMENTS

While use of cooperative learning groups is associated with many benefits for students and teachers alike, some implementations of cooperative learning groups can lead to problems in the classroom. These problems can usually be successfully averted or corrected for the future by attending to a few important details. The scenarios below provide depictions of common problems that teachers encounter when using small-group instruction and tips for addressing those problems.

Scenario 1. Problems with Small-Group Composition: How Much Heterogeneity Is Too Much?

Ms. Joyce teaches sophomore English. During a poetry unit, she decides to arrange her students into small groups for a cooperative peer editing activity. Ms. Joyce consciously creates heterogeneous ability groups in hopes that this will benefit her most academically challenged students by allowing them more individual attention and practice at editing. However, when the students are instructed to meet with their groups for the first time, Ms. Joyce notices almost immediately that Group 1 is going to have problems.

Group 1 comprises Ruth, a quiet student who is the strongest writer in the class; Ali, a friendly, capable student who does not exhibit any behavior difficulties; and Darryl, a student with a learning disability with a pattern of noncompliance when it comes to teacher requests. Ms. Joyce had hoped that Darryl would feel at ease with Ruth and Ali and that he would exhibit less disruptive behavior in a small group of three students. She also hoped Darryl would benefit from Ruth's expertise in writing. What she noticed, however, is that as soon as Ruth began giving a verbal overview of her written response, which was the first step of the small-group peer editing assignment, Darryl became increasingly boisterous. Although he was being complimentary to Ruth, it seemed clear to Ms. Joyce that Darryl was self-conscious about his own written response. Ten minutes into the group activity, Darryl was making loud jokes and refusing to participate seriously.

Ms. Joyce had set up an interdependent contingency, wherein part of the students' overall grade on the paper would be based on the success of their group's peer editing exercise. Unfortunately, what Ms. Joyce saw unfolding was that Darryl had little to gain, since he assumed he would eventually get a poor grade on the assignment no matter whom he worked with. Since Ruth was a shy student, she was not well equipped to redirect Darryl's raucous jokes. Also, since Ruth's grade was the highest in the class, she had little motivation to ensure Darryl's success. (There was little chance that Ruth would get anything other than an A in the course overall.) Ali was more invested in the peer editing process—and the activity in general—than either Ruth or Darryl. However, Ali—like the rest of the students in the class—was also aware of Ruth's status as the strongest student and seemed more set on deferring to Ruth than on actually working to get Darryl back on task. At the moment when Ms. Joyce realized that Group 1 was on an unproductive path, Ms. Joyce decided to address the situation by pulling Darryl out of the group to work with her individually, directing Ruth and Ali to finish the assignment as a pair, thus undermining the success of the cooperative activity and reinforcing the idea that Darryl could not be successful in a group.

In this scenario, Ms. Joyce and her students experienced the negative effect of too much heterogeneity. In order to prosper from interaction with peers, it is important for students to work with others who are within their zones of proximal development. Given the wide range of abilities that are typically found in general education classrooms, the gap between the strongest student in a particular academic domain and the student with the greatest needs is often too great for those students to work productively in a small group together. In this example, Darryl might have benefited more from a small group consisting of Ali and one other student who also struggled, but whose performance in the class was somewhere between Ali and Darryl. With that group composition, Darryl would not have felt as self-conscious about his writing and may have had better, more productive role models. Another benefit would have been that Ali would have been placed in the role of de facto group expert, which might have been good for her self-concept as well. If Ms. Joyce were worried about having two struggling students in the same group, she could have made a point to sit down with the group for part of their work time, so as not to overburden Ali in the role of teacher.

The take-home message: Manage the bands of heterogeneity so that the gap between the strongest student and the most challenged student in a group is not too great.

Scenario 2. When a Group Goal Is Too Much Pressure for Students Who Struggle

Mr. Sumi decides to place his fifth-grade students in cooperative learning groups as part of a unit on the Harlem Renaissance. He decides to use a "jigsaw" strategy. As a first step, Mr. Sumi organizes all the students in his class into "expert" groups, where each expert group of five students is charged with doing research on a particular aspect of the Harlem Renaissance. After three class sessions, during which the groups of experts spend time researching their group's topic collectively, new "jigsaw" groups, consisting of one student from each expert group, are formed. Mr.

Sumi decides to motivate the expert groups by saying that each expert group will be evaluated by how well the other students in the later jigsaw groups learn the content from each expert.

Nate is a student with a behavioral disorder who is prone to anxiety and mistrust in social situations. He has been assigned to the expert group that will be researching music and dance. Mr. Sumi chose this group specifically for Nate because of Nate's interest in music; he correctly predicted that the content would be of high interest to Nate. Unfortunately, what he did not predict was that Nate would become so stressed by the prospect of being responsible for teaching the music and dance content to the later jigsaw group that he actually stayed home from school for all 3 days that the jigsaw groups were meeting. At the end of the unit, Mr. Sumi felt deflated because he believed he had created a situation that led to Nate's status in the larger class—and with his "expert" group mates specifically—being compromised.

A suggestion for Mr. Sumi for the future would be to look for ways to provide scaffolding to students like Nate. In this example, Mr. Sumi could have arranged for Nate to have extra support at another time during the day to review the music and dance content, or Mr. Sumi could have arranged for a paraprofessional to spend time with the music and dance expert group with the explicit objective of providing academic and emotional support to Nate without singling him out. Also, because Mr. Sumi spent so much time and thought designing the complex assignment, pulling together resources for the groups to use, and carefully choosing the students who would be working together, he did not spend as much time thinking about the critical skills that are required for students to teach each other content. In this example, if Mr. Sumi had devoted a class session at the beginning of the unit to explaining what the students could expect in the two different groups and teaching the students *how* to teach their peers when they were put together in jigsaw groups, Nate might have been less stressed by the activity. Just as it is important to preteach the social skills needed to work cooperatively, it is important to teach the interaction skills necessary to complete collaborative assignments. A class session or two at the beginning of a unit can pay off in much higher-quality work later in the unit—as well as throughout other units later in the semester.

The take-home message: Students with disabilities may need support prior to and during cooperative learning activities in order to be successful.

Scenario 3. Oil and Water: What If Some Students Just Don't Get Along?

It is important to remember that cooperative learning is a tool to help students make gains in content knowledge and improve their social skills. If all goes well, these two areas of improvement will, in turn, fuel each other. This is not the same as having a goal of facilitating specific students getting along with other specific students. If a teacher is aware that two students do not get along, it is fine to put those students in different groups. In fact, it is probably preferable to put them in separate groups so that time and energy can be spent on the learning task—not on managing interpersonal dynamics.

As in Scenario 1, students should be placed in groups that will help them learn and practice new skills. If students do not get along, it may be too much to expect them to find common ground around a cooperative learning task. Just as with Scenario 1, this kind of disparity between specific group members can result in group dysfunction and hurt the other students in the group. This is not to suggest that students only work with friends, but that teachers take care to form groups that have a high likelihood of success.

The take-home message: Take interpersonal relationships into account when forming groups.

INCORPORATING OTHER EDUCATIONAL PROFESSIONALS

The use of cooperative group arrangements is highlighted in much of the literature on the inclusion of students with disabilities—even significant disabilities—in general education classrooms (Alquraini & Gut, 2012; Stevens & Slavin, 1995). Including students with disabilities in the classroom with typically developing peers was initiated by federal legislation and is increasingly pursued in schools across the nation. There are various service delivery models that support inclusive education; many of these models require collaboration across professionals and additional personnel (e.g., co-teaching and instructional assistants; Idol, 2006). Additionally, students with disabilities often receive services from related professionals, such as speech–language pathologists (SLPs), occupational therapists (OTs), and physical therapists (PTs). Increasingly, many of these related services are being offered in natural settings—or general education classrooms—instead of in segregated therapy rooms. With a variety of professionals being present in the classroom setting, there is potential to find ways to incorporate them into classroom activities, such as small-group instructional arrangements.

While small-group instructional arrangements emphasize the interactions between peers to overcome a common problem or complete a task, educational professionals still play an essential role in ensuring the effective use of such strategies. Educational professionals need to facilitate learning and interactions in small-group instructional arrangements, modeling ways to acknowledge individual peer contributions; providing positive feedback on progress; offering prompts using speculative, challenging questions; and monitoring student progress on targeted skills (Gillies, 2006; Stockall, 2011). There is potential for a variety of professionals from various backgrounds to be present in the classroom while small-group instruction is occurring, creating an opportunity for sharing the responsibility of providing this feedback to the small groups in the classroom. While supporting a specific student with a disability in a small group, paraprofessionals or other related service professionals can, and should, remain cognizant of the progress the group is making and keep them on track (see Jitendra et al., 2013). This requires collaboration and ultimately a community of practice where strategies and other professional wisdom from the general educator (or special educator) are imparted to other professionals who are willing to share this responsibility (Alquraini & Gut, 2012; Mortier, Hunt, Leroy, Van de Putte, & Van Hove, 2010). This will not only increase the frequency with which small groups receive feedback, but also the quality of inclusion that students with disabilities encounter when they are included with their general education peers.

As previously mentioned, social skills are directly incorporated and targeted in cooperative learning groups. Considering that improving social skills may be one of the goals that SLPs have for students with disabilities on their caseload, what better way is there to teach and practice these skills than in the general education classroom in an authentic setting where social skills are being refined by all students? The SLP can also provide support for other students who may be struggling with syntax or some other communication-based difficulty. For students with significant disabilities, the OT can help foster active participation within the group by teaching and/or creating opportunities for the student to use an augmentative and alternative communication device. Incorporating these adults into whole-class activities will create a high-quality inclusive educational setting.

Jitendra and colleagues (2013) evaluated the use of two different types of small-group peer-tutoring arrangements facilitated by paraprofessionals to address the difficulties some students were having with math (see Powell & Fuchs, Chapter 6, this volume, for more information on peer-mediated strategies for mathematics). The two approaches to tutoring that were considered were schema-based instruction (SBI) and standards-based curriculum (SBC), or practice as usual. SBI focuses on gaining understanding of the structure of problems, increasing the likelihood that a solution can be reached when encountering similar problems in the future; emphasis is placed on "think-alouds" to monitor and reflect on the process. Results indicated that students in both groups improved: students with low performance on the pretest gained more on the posttest when in the SBC group, while students with high performance on the pretest gained more on the posttest when in the SBI group. The study also showed that paraprofessionals were able to successfully facilitate the tutoring session, on average demonstrating high levels of fidelity.

Stevens and Slavin (1995) demonstrated the positive effects of the use of cooperative group arrangements on a systems level (i.e., cooperative schools). The authors note that the key element of change for the successful implementation of a cooperative school was the collaboration of educational professionals, which can include all of those previously mentioned. Encouraging the use of open dialogue in the planning and preparation of lessons can make it easy to incorporate others into the planned activities. While schoolwide change may not be feasible in all settings, we should consider the components that may be: open dialogue in lesson planning, involvement of all professionals who are in the classroom, and shared responsibility of facilitating group learning and interaction. It may be necessary to touch base as a team periodically to ensure that all members understand their roles. This need for continuous communication can be addressed using traditional means or by incorporating technology (e.g., texts, e-mail) to keep all of the team members current on upcoming lessons.

CONCLUSION

In this chapter, we presented strategies for implementing one popular and effective form of peer-mediated instruction: cooperative learning groups. As discussed, it is important to remember that while teachers frequently utilize small-group learning techniques, there is a continuum of benefits associated with various forms of small-group work, with research demonstrating that some group strategies are more effective than others. When designing instruction that relies on group learning, teachers should consider the ways in which the individual needs of students can be met through peer mediation; creating learning tasks that rely on group goals and on the learning of all students to accomplish those goals will be most productive. In order to maximize benefits of small-group instruction, teachers should consider ways that other classroom resources (e.g., related service providers and paraprofessionals) might be relied upon in planned ways to increase the impact of instruction for all students. While use of cooperative learning groups has been prevalent in schools for decades, the new challenges of including all students in the general education classroom space, along with the new demands of meeting increasingly higher academic standards, ensure that use of small-group instruction will continue to evolve and be refined.

REFERENCES

Alquraini, T., & Gut, D. (2012). Critical components of successful inclusion of students with severe disabilities: Literature review. *International Journal of Special Education, 27,* 42–59.

Bandura, A. (1977). Self-efficacy: Toward a unifying theory of behavioral change. *Psychological Review, 84,* 191–215.

Cohen, B. P., & Cohen, E. G. (1991). From groupwork among children to R&D teams: Interdependence, interaction and productivity. *Advances in Group Processes, 8,* 205–226.

Cohen, E. G. (1994). *Restructuring the classroom: Conditions for productive small groups* (ERIC Document Reproduction Service No. ED 347 639). Washington, DC: Office of Educational Research and Improvement.

Davidson, N. (1985). Small-group learning and teaching in mathematics: A selective review of the research. In R. E. Slavin, S. Saran, S. Kagan, R. Hertz-Lazarowitz, C. Webb, & R. Schmuck (Eds.), *Learning to cooperate, cooperating to learn* (pp. 211–230). New York: Plenum Press.

Ellis, A. K., & Fouts, J. T. (1993). *Research on educational innovations.* Princeton Junction, NJ: Eye on Education.

Gillies, R. M. (2003). The behaviors, interactions, and perceptions of junior high school students during small-group learning. *Journal of Educational Psychology, 95,* 137–147.

Gillies, R. M. (2006). Teachers' and students' verbal behaviors during cooperative and small-group learning. *British Journal of Educational Psychology, 76,* 271–287.

Gillies, R. M., & Ashman, A. F. (2000). The effects of cooperative learning on students with learning difficulties in the lower elementary school. *Journal of Special Education, 34,* 19–27.

Hawkins, R. O., Musti-Rao, S., Hughes, C., Berry, L., & McGuire, S. (2009). Applying a randomized interdependent group contingency component to classwide peer tutoring for multiplication fact fluency. *Journal of Behavioral Education, 18,* 300–318.

Idol, L. (2006). Toward inclusion of special education students in general education. *Remedial and Special Education, 27,* 77–94.

Jitendra, A. K., Rodriguez, M., Kanive, R., Huang, J., Church, C., Corroy, K. A., et al. (2013). Impact of small-group tutoring interventions on the mathematical problem solving and achievement of third-grade students with mathematics difficulties. *Learning Disability Quarterly, 36,* 21–35.

Johnson, D. W., & Johnson, R. T. (1999). Making cooperative learning work. *Theory into Practice, 38,* 67–73.

Jones, C. D., & Henriksen, B. M. (2013). Skills-focused small group literacy instruction in the first grade: An inquiry and insights. *Journal of Reading Education, 38,* 25–30.

Kamps, D., Abbott, M., Greenwood, C., Wills, C., Veerkamp, M., & Kaufman, J. (2008). Effects of small-group reading instruction and curriculum differences for students most at risk in kindergarten: Two-year results for secondary- and tertiary-level interventions. *Journal of Learning Disabilities, 41,* 101–114.

Kol'tsova, V. A. (1978). Experimental study of cognitive activity in communication (with specific reference to concept formation). *Soviet Psychology, 17*(1), 23–38.

Kuester, D. A., & Zentall, S. S. (2012). Social interaction rules in cooperative learning groups for students at risk for ADHD. *Journal of Experimental Education, 80,* 69–95.

Ledford, J. R., & Wolery, M. (2013). Peer modeling of academic and social behaviors during small-group direct instruction. *Exceptional Children, 79,* 439–458.

Ling, S., Hawkins, R. O., & Weber, D. (2011). Effects of a classwide interdependent group contingency designed to improve behavior of an at-risk student. *Journal of Behavioral Education, 20,* 103–116.

Lou, Y., Abrami, P. C., Spence, J. C., Poulsen, C., Chambers, B., & d'Apollonia, S. (1996). Within-class grouping: A meta-analysis. *Review of Educational Research, 66,* 423–458.

Madden, N. A., & Slavin, R. E. (1983). Effects of cooperative learning on the social acceptance of mainstreamed academically handicapped students. *Journal of Special Education, 17,* 171–182.

Manning, M. L., & Lucking, R. (1991). The what, why, and how of cooperative learning. *Social Studies, 82,* 120–124.

McMaster, K. N., & Fuchs, D. (2002). Effects of cooperative learning on the academic achievement of students with learning disabilities: An update of Tateyama-Sniezek's review. *Learning Disabilities, Research, and Practice, 17,* 107–117.

Mortier, K., Hunt, P., Leroy, M., Van de Putte, I., & Van Hove, G. (2010). Communities of practice in inclusive education. *Educational Studies, 36,* 345–355.

Noddings, N. (1989). Theoretical and practical concerns about small groups in mathematics. *Elementary School Journal, 89,* 607–623.

Piercy, M., Wilton, K., & Townsend, M. (2002). Promoting the social acceptance of young children with moderate-severe intellectual disabilities using cooperative-learning techniques. *American Journal on Mental Retardation, 107,* 352–360.

Slavin, R. E. (1983). When does cooperative learning increase student achievement? *Psychological Bulletin, 94,* 429–445.

Slavin, R. E. (1984). Team assisted individualization: Cooperative learning and individualized instruction in the mainstreamed classroom. *Remedial and Special Education, 5*(6), 33–42.

Slavin, R. E. (1995). *Cooperative learning: Theory, research, and practice* (2nd ed.). Needham Heights, MA: Allyn & Bacon.

Song, H., & Grabowski, B. L. (2006). Stimulating intrinsic motivation for problem solving using goal-oriented contexts and peer composition. *Educational Technology Research and Development, 54,* 445–466.

Stevens, R. J., & Slavin, R. E. (1995). The cooperative elementary school: Effects on students' achievement, attitudes, and social relations. *American Educational Research Journal, 32,* 321–351.

Stockall, N. (2011). Cooperative groups: Engaging elementary students with pragmatic language impairments. *TEACHING Exceptional Children, 44,* 18–25.

Tudge, J. (1992). Vygotsky, the zone of proximal development, and peer collaboration: Implications for classroom practice. In L. C. Moll (Ed.), *Vygotsky and education: Instructional implications and applications of sociohistorical psychology* (pp. 155–172). New York: Cambridge University Press.

Vygotsky, L. S. (1978). *Mind in society: The development of higher psychological processes.* Cambridge, MA: Harvard University Press.

Zentall, S. S., Craig, B. A., & Kuester, D. A. (2011). Social behavior in cooperative groups: Students at risk for ADHD and their peers. *Journal of Educational Research, 104,* 28–41.

CHAPTER 8

Peer-Supported Instruction
for English Learners

CATHERINE RICHARDS-TUTOR, TERESE ACEVES, and COLLEEN REUTEBUCH

Much of the research to date related to peer-supported instruction has focused on classroom implementation with native language speakers. However, schools and classrooms in the United States continue to reflect an increasingly diverse student population, including students who may understand, speak, read, and write in English with varying levels of proficiency. Students may come to school having had little to no formal schooling in their native language, experience in basic conversational English, or instruction in understanding and using academic English. These students may or may not have family members proficient in English to provide further exposure and assistance at home. In the classroom, these differences in experience and exposure to English become clear to teachers when they see some of their students struggle with understanding, speaking, and reading in English and expressing their thoughts, needs, and ideas through their writing in a second language.

It is clear that the increasing diversity in U.S. classrooms and the incredible need to support the language development and academic achievement of English learners requires teachers to consider effective instructional methods for this population. Teachers need knowledge of and experience with those instructional practices that support diverse students' culture, language, progress, and overall achievement. One instructional method that has potential for increasing achievement of English learners is peer-supported instruction. Often peer-supported instruction can be overwhelming for teachers with diverse classrooms. They wonder how to implement peer or small-group activities with students who may or may not have mastered the language of instruction. How can they provide joint opportunities for native English speakers and English learners at various stages of English language acquisition? What methods should they use to optimize peer-based activities with students who are learning to read in English for the first time and learning grade-level academic content in a language they are only just beginning to acquire? Much of the research to date related to peer-supported instruction has focused on class-room implementation with native language speakers. However, current research on peer-supported instruction provides a solid foundation for teachers of English learners to build upon in their classrooms. In this chapter we will (1) describe the general increase in student diversity nationwide, (2) describe the benefits of peer support for English learners, (3) present research-based instructional models that include peer support and are found to be appropriate for English learners, and (4) provide classroom examples of peer support specifically designed for this popula-tion.

INCREASE IN STUDENT DIVERSITY

According to the 2011 U.S. Census, 60 million people speak a language other than English at home (U.S. Census Bureau, 2011). Within this group, approximately 25 million people reported being a limited English speaker, an 81% increase from 1990. Nine percent of this population included children and youth between the ages of 5 and 15. In our public school system, between 2010 and 2011, there were an estimated 4.7 million students designated as English learners (U.S. Department of Education, 2013). During this time, increases in English learners were noted in all but 12 states, with the largest increases occurring in Kansas, South Carolina, Hawaii, and Nevada; many of these states typically are not associated with large numbers of these students.

As the number of English learners continues to increase, so does the critical need to support the language and learning of this diverse population. Yet, teachers continue to feel exceedingly unprepared to support the needs of English learn-ers in the classroom, contributing to their persistent underperformance of English learners in comparison to their native English-speaking peers. As evidenced in the National Assessment of Educational Progress, a national measure of student achievement, from 2002 to 2011, a consistent gap persists in the average reading performance of English learners and non-English learners in the fourth and eighth grades (see Figures 8.1 and 8.2).

In addition to the problem of ongoing underachievement, English learn-ers are overidentified in remedial and special education programs (Artiles & Klingner, 2006; Klingner et al., 2005). The reasons why many English learners continue to struggle academically or to be inappropriately referred to or placed in remedial and special education are complicated to say the least. Lack of early intervention, inappropriate referral for special education evaluation, and misun-derstanding regarding disability, culture, and first and second language devel-opment all contribute to this issue. To address this critical problem, teaching

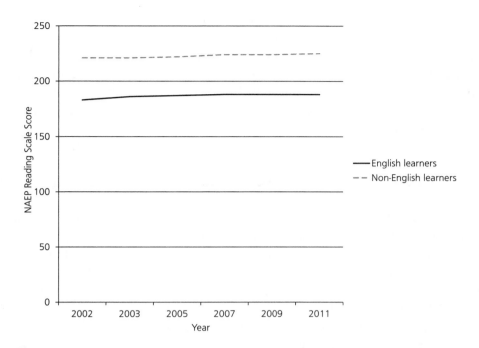

FIGURE 8.1. Average NAEP fourth-grade reading scores (NAEP Reading Scale score range = 0–500). U.S. Department of Education, National Center for Education Statistics, National Assessment of Educational Progress, selected years, 2002–2011 Reading Assessments, NAEP Data Explorer. See *Digest of Education Statistics 2012*, Table 142.

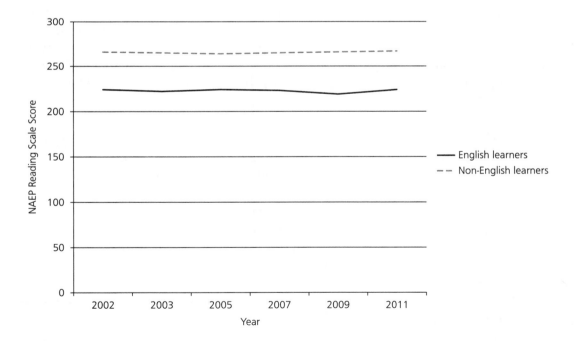

FIGURE 8.2. Average NAEP eighth-grade reading scores (NAEP Reading Scale score range = 0–500). U.S. Department of Education, National Center for Education Statistics, National Assessment of Educational Progress, selected years, 2002–2011 Reading Assessments, NAEP Data Explorer. See *Digest of Education Statistics 2012*, Table 142.

practices that are supportive of students' language and culture should be used (Klingner et al., 2005). Peer-supported instruction is a teaching practice that is supportive of students' language and culture and has the potential to both increase student achievement and reduce inappropriate referrals for special education evaluation.

BENEFITS OF PEER SUPPORT FOR ENGLISH LEARNERS

In contrast to whole-class instruction, partner and small-group cooperative activities allow students to better understand content while actively practicing speaking with peers and adults using academic language connected to their learning. Students are grouped or partnered with peers with varying levels of English proficiency, allowing them to learn content while having the opportunity to practice their English language skills in a safe environment. Teachers report that peer support provides a safe environment for struggling learners to thrive, perform, participate, and produce (O'Connor & Jenkins, 2013). Positive increases in academic achievement (Gersten et al., 2007; Scruggs, Mastropieri, & Marchak, 2012) as well as positive social and behavioral outcomes have been noted (Ginsburg-Block, Rohrbeck, & Fantuzzo, 2006).

Teachers can design peer-supported instruction to scaffold the language and literacy development of their English learners. When designed appropriately, peer support can provide teachers with a foundation of essential instructional practices known to encourage students' learning, language use, and development (Cloud, Genesee, & Hamayan, 2009; Gersten et al., 2007; Goldenberg, 2010; Goldenberg & Coleman, 2010; Haager, Klingner, & Aceves, 2009; O'Connor & Jenkins, 2013). Specifically, using peer support with English learners:

1. Allows for students to negotiate meaning while adjusting their language and literacy use according to the demands of the interaction.
2. Motivates students to be actively engaged in learning in a safe environment.
3. Provides appropriate models of language and literacy use.
4. Connects reading, writing, speaking, and listening skills.
5. Increases opportunities for application and practice of critical skills.
6. Allows for sharing and comparing of prior knowledge, understanding, and cultural and life experiences.
7. Encourages native language use when appropriate to support understanding and engagement.
8. Increases expectations for students to take active ownership of their own learning.
9. Provides informal assessment of literacy use, including academic literacy.
10. Supports individual differences, viewing these differences as resources for learning and growth.

When activities are appropriately planned and designed, pairing students or using cooperative groups provides students with additional practice in reading, writing, and oral conversation in English (Goldenberg, 2010). Peer support can benefit all students and replace independent activities teachers often use to provide practice or extended learning, such as completing worksheets or other independent seatwork (Gersten et al., 2007). Teachers can design these opportunities for students to receive extended learning and feedback from appropriate peer models.

The National Literacy Panel (NLP; August & Shanahan, 2006) and the Center for Research on Education, Diversity and Excellence (CREDE; Genesee, Lindholm-Leary, Saunders, & Christian, 2006) conducted two separate and extensive reviews of empirical research related to educating English learners. The authors of both reviews encouraged implementation of peer-supported activities with English learners as a useful strategy to promote student engagement and opportunities for students to interact with one another in motivating and structured activities. Specifically, the NLP found cooperative learning and Instructional Conversations (IC) to hold promise when used with them. Teachers using IC encourage students to dialogue about academic content during interactive, meaningful activities while making connections to their language, culture, background knowledge, and experiences with support from the teacher (Saunders & Goldenberg, 1999; Tharp, 1997; Tharp & Gallimore, 1991). Cooperative learning (Johnson & Johnson, 1987, 1989, 1999), involves organizing students with varying ability levels into small groups or teams in which each student has a designated responsibility to complete a specific task or activity.

DESIGNING PEER-SUPPORTED ACTIVITIES

In order to optimize outcomes for English learners it is important that teachers understand how to design peer-supported instruction beyond the lesson plan and activities to be completed. This includes assuring students are placed in appropriate classrooms, grouping students for content learning, pairing students appropriately, and preparing students for peer-supported instructional activities.

Placing Students in Appropriate Classroom Environments

Research generally suggests that English learners show more academic growth if placed in classrooms where they have opportunities to interact with students with varying levels of English proficiency. In other words, English learners should be assigned to classrooms with native English speakers and with other English learners of varying levels of proficiency in English. Within these heterogeneous classrooms instructional groupings can be assigned according to ability in content areas such as reading or math (Goldenberg & Coleman, 2010). However, for instruction specifically in English language development, these students should be grouped according to their appropriate level of English proficiency.

Grouping Students for Content Learning

When designing small-group or paired instruction to support content-area learning for English learners in heterogeneous classrooms, teachers should design these activities to achieve the maximum benefit to further students' language and learning outcomes. Depending on the purpose or goal of the activity, teachers may allow students to select their own group or partners based on preference or personal interest in a topic area or activity. Making allowances for a self-selected partner or small-group opportunities supports independence. However, there are times when small groups or partners should be carefully planned by the teacher in order to provide students with more strategic support when the focus is reinforcing academic content already taught by the teacher. During these activities, teachers can group or partner English learners with native English-speaking and/or bilingual peers who can provide the native language and/or English assistance to complete the activities. The focus during these interactions is to give these students access to the content and the opportunity to actively participate. In order to create these opportunities, teachers should ask themselves several questions:

1. Should some of the materials and/or assistance be provided in the native language?
2. How will English learners demonstrate their understanding?
3. Will they share in their native language or in English with their peers?
4. Will this be done verbally, using pictures, or through their writing?
5. Does the group or partner need to be bilingual so English learners can express their thoughts and ideas in their primary language?

Pairing Students Appropriately

Teachers must use information about their students, including their background, home and life experiences, culture, and language, to better inform their instruction and lesson planning. Students come to school with a variety of experiences with language and literacy in English and/or their native language. Native English speakers should be paired with English learners who have sufficient skills in English to communicate effectively with their partner (Goldenberg, 2010). When designing student pairings and group assignments, teachers should consider the goal of the activity (e.g., topic/content learning vs. tutoring), students' understanding and ability in the subject of the activity, the proficiency of English learners in understanding and using English, and overall compatibility. For example, in order to pair students for tutoring in basic reading skills, teachers would rank these students in the class according to their levels of reading and language proficiency. Separately, teachers similarly would rank the native English speakers in the class. Students with the highest rankings in each group would be paired, students with the next-highest rankings in the two groups would also be paired, and this would continue until all students were partnered (Echevarria & Short, 2011). Figure 8.3

English Learners			Native Speakers		
Students	*Language*	*Reading*	*Students*		*Reading*
1	Maria	Early Advanced	Basic	1	Robert	Proficient
2	Juan	Intermediate	Basic	2	Cindy	Proficient
3	Sergio	Intermediate	Basic	3	Carolina	Proficient
4	Laura	Early Intermediate	Below Basic	4	Paul	Basic
5	Chen	Early Intermediate	Below Basic	5	Sarah	Basic
6	Jin	Early Intermediate	Below Basic	6	Jenny	Basic
7	Seema	Beginning	Far Below Basic	7	Daniel	Basic
8	Avani	Beginning	Far Below Basic	8	Mathew	Below Basic

FIGURE 8.3. Sample class rankings for pairing English learners and native speakers.

provides an example of a classroom profile with corresponding scores for pairing purposes. In this classroom, pairings would include Maria with Robert, Juan with Cindy, Sergio with Carolina, and so on. Although in our example we use state testing designations to pair students, other assessments, such as curriculum-based measures (e.g., reading fluency), could be used. In a specific peer-assisted reading intervention, Peer-Assisted Learning Strategies (PALS), this method of pairing students is referred to as the *high-average/average-low* method (see Kearns, Fuchs, Fuchs, McMaster, & Sáenz, Chapter 5, this volume, for a description). Other alternative pairings for matching tutor and tutee partners are described by Powell and Fuchs (Chapter 6, this volume) for the purpose of using peer support during math tutoring sessions.

Regardless of the method for pairing students, teachers should consider students' social/behavioral compatibility, such as the ability of the English-speaking partner to serve as a supportive peer, and whether primary language support is appropriate and available, as well as the English learner's ability to communicate in English. For those students just beginning to learn basic skills in English, it would be appropriate to select an English partner who can be flexible, supportive, and patient. In this example, if the goal of the pairing is to work with a partner to extend an English learner's understanding in a topic area (e.g., the solar system, a novel, or a thematic unit), the teacher may choose an English-speaking partner who is bilingual and able to provide native language support as needed. The class ranking and matching methods described here are just a guide for pairing students. Ultimately, the teacher must use his or her judgment and consider these additional criteria when finalizing matched pairs or groupings.

Preparing Students to Work Collaboratively

As described in the previous section, it is very important to determine appropriate partners and groups, taking into consideration individual student differences (e.g., reading ability and social competence; O'Connor & Jenkins, 1996). However, teachers also need to prepare students to work cooperatively with one another and explicitly teach them to how to help their partner or group when necessary. When students are not prepared to work together or taught how to help each other, problems can occur (O'Connor & Jenkins, 2013). Difficulties can occur in pairs or cooperative groups if ELs do not have the language and communication skills necessary to solve problems and negotiate meaning. Students may have problems sharing responsibilities equally and completing their tasks. Merely grouping English learners with native speakers does not guarantee that the activity will be meaningful and productive (Genesee, Lindholm-Leary, Saunders, & Christian, 2006). Students may rush through an activity just to get it done. Lengthy and complex tasks that extend beyond the initial instruction provided by the teacher may challenge the ability of English learners to successfully contribute to the group or partner work. Similarly, native English-speaking peers may feel the need to complete the tasks themselves rather than take the time necessary to work with their less fluent or skilled partners.

Given these potential roadblocks to successful peer-supported learning opportunities, teachers should monitor these groups and prepare students in advance with the skills necessary to participate, problem-solve, and support one another. Teachers should carefully design the collaborative work or tasks students are expected to complete. These tasks should require skills previewed and practiced extensively first with the teacher. Moreover, teachers may need to provide strategies for how students can interact with one another during paired or small-group activities. The teacher may need to spend time modeling these interactions and provide clear instructions in order to scaffold these interactions.

> Teachers need to make sure students focus on extended and productive interactions (rather than quick task completion), which might require that both English learners and English speakers learn strategies for successful verbal interactions. Teachers should teach and model interaction strategies such as directing requests to specific individuals; providing clear, complete, and comprehensive answers; and demonstrating helpful attitudes among all participants. (Goldenberg & Coleman, 2010, p. 75)

All of these elements, supported by research, are necessary requirements when involving English learners in peer-supported activities. These requirements are summarized in Box 8.1.

A CLASSROOM SCENARIO: ENVISIONING PEER SUPPORTS IN THE CLASSROOM

The following scenario highlights how educators can contribute to the success of English learners through the implementation of peer supports.

BOX 8.1. REQUIREMENTS FOR SMALL-GROUP AND PEER ACTIVITIES INVOLVING ENGLISH LEARNERS

1. Design pairings and small groups with English learners and native speakers with comparable skills in the subject area.

2. Assign English learners in pairings and small groups if they have sufficient communication skills in English to interact successfully with their partner; students may need to be provided with sentence starters or specific vocabulary.

3. Monitor student participation during paired or small-group activities to ensure understanding, appropriate interaction, and on-task behavior.

4. Prepare students to problem-solve when disagreements occur or if they are confused.

5. Train students to support one another in a positive and productive manner.

6. Create activities or tasks that support previously taught and modeled content.

7. Teach students strategies for working with one another effectively and positively.

8. Model strategies for problem solving and engaging in positive interactions.

9. Provide clear and sufficient directions for task completion.

10. Supply templates, resources, and examples to scaffold activities and discussions.

Imagine a typical classroom setting made up of diverse learners with a range of cultural and experiential backgrounds. Several of the students may come from homes in which a language other than English is spoken, while others may speak little or no English at all. In addition, some learners will have academic, behavioral, or other issues that impede learning. Still others will require supplementary or accelerated instruction in order to benefit and remain engaged. Ms. Romero, the classroom teacher, focuses her instruction on meeting the wide range of students' needs within her classroom. Under her guidance, she enlists peers to support each other during academic tasks. Her efforts culminate in improved student outcomes in language learning and access to content knowledge, as well as a greater capacity to engage in appropriate and productive interactions. Students in Ms. Romero's class report that participating and contributing in class makes them feel like they matter and belong.

What makes the difference for struggling learners, including struggling English learners, in Ms. Romero's class is that student dyads or small groups are encouraged to talk, read, and write about the content as an alternative to Ms. Romero only lecturing about the topic. Peers assist each other in reading, thinking, and talking about concepts. Students discuss and debate literary and historical figures as well as trending news, and how the topics they study relate to their own lives and to their background knowledge. They solve complex problems and work in cooperative groups to find solutions and/or review them with their classmates.

Although "Ms. Romero" is a pseudonym, the description of her instruction is real. The peer-mediated approach she uses to support English learners and the positive results noted are also an accurate representation. Higher-level tasks, like reading for meaning or the application of knowledge and skills, will require purposely constructing peer supports for optimal results. As stated in the previous section, pairing and/or grouping students intentionally is a key step in implementing peer-supported instruction. Ms. Romero has been provided professional development in a variety of research-based peer-supported instructional models for English learners, which are described in detail in the next section.

IMPLEMENTING RESEARCH-BASED PEER-SUPPORTED INSTRUCTION FOR ENGLISH LEARNERS

Over the past decade or so the research base for using peer support for English learners has grown. In the What Works Clearinghouse practice guide focusing on literacy instruction and English language development instruction for English learners, Gersten et al. (2007) found strong evidence to support teachers' inclusion of weekly peer-supported instruction. This instruction should include pairing and grouping students at various academic ability levels as well as different English proficiency levels and should be provided in structured academic contexts. In this portion of the chapter we describe five specific instructional models that use peer support and have been found in at least one study that used quasi-experimental or experimental design to have a positive impact on these students. For each instructional model, we briefly describe the key elements of the instruction, describe the research base, highlight the specific instructional strategies that are particularly important for English learners, and provide a sample activity, supplementary materials, and/or lesson plan to get you started with integrating peer supports into your instructional practice.

Peer-Assisted Learning Strategies

PALS is a peer-tutoring program (see Chapters 5 and 6, this volume, for a more detailed description) that originally was developed to promote reading fluency and comprehension (Fuchs, Fuchs, Mathes, & Simmons, 1997); however, the model has been extended to math. It can be applied in elementary and secondary classrooms using existing instructional materials. Before beginning PALS, all students are placed into a tutoring dyad. These pairs are changed regularly and over a period of time as students work on a variety of skills. Next, students receive instruction on using specific prompts, corrections, and feedback. All partners serve as tutor and tutee during each session. An important feature of this instructional strategy is structured, frequent communication between tutors and tutees. Last, PALS students are trained to implement four structured activities including partner reading with retell, paragraph shrinking, and prediction relay (see Figure 8.4).

Partner Reading with Retell. Each student alternatively reads aloud for 5 minutes from the same connected text (i.e., words that are linked in sentences, phrases, and paragraphs vs. words in a list). For 2 minutes following after the text has been read, both readers alternate retelling the main ideas that happened in the story. The more proficient reader goes first. Text selection should match the less proficient student's reading level. Students use corrective procedures to help the student reading.

Error corrections include: "Stop, you missed that word. Can you figure it out?" If the reader does not figure out the word within 4 seconds, then the tutor states, "That word is _____. What word?" The reader says the word and continues reading.

Paragraph Shrinking. Develops comprehension through summarizing and identification of the main idea. Students using questioning techniques: "Name the who or what" and "Name the most important thing about the who or what."

Prediction Relay. Requires students to make predictions and confirm or disconfirm them. The steps include the following:
- Predict: What do you expect will happen?
- Read: The next half page.
- Check: Did the prediction come true?
- Shrink: Name who or what the page was about. Tell the most important things discussed.

FIGURE 8.4. PALS structured activities.

PALS utilizes a number of structured instructional activities that provide English learners with needed oral language and reading practice that fosters their overall reading development. PALS includes explicit teaching, routines, repetition, modeling and practice, and frequent opportunities to respond, all of which have been noted as essential for these students (Gersten & Baker, 2000; Gersten & Geva, 2003; Vaughn et al., 2006). Additionally, opportunities to improve comprehension are strengthened through the program's activities involving predicting and summarizing.

PALS Research and Effectiveness

Three studies of PALS have been conducted with English learners (Calhoon, Al Otaiba, Cihak, King, & Avalos, 2007; McMaster, Kung, Han, & Cao, 2008; Sáenz, Fuchs, & Fuchs, 2005). These studies have been conducted with students in kindergarten (McMaster et al., 2008), first grade (Calhoon et al., 2007), and third through sixth grade (Sáenz et al., 2005). In K-PALS (McMaster et al., 2008) English learners participate in two main instructional activities: Sound Play and Sounds and Words. Sound Play includes rhyming and first sounds. Sounds and Words consists of identifying the sounds of letters, reading sight words, reading decodable words, and reading sentences. First Grade PALS (Calhoon et al., 2007) consists of two activities: Sounds and Words (very similar to K-PALS) and Story Sharing. Story Sharing consists of reading trade books, making predictions, and story retelling. In the PALS study focused on third- through sixth-grade English learners (Sáenz et al., 2005), instruction included partner reading with story retelling, paragraph shrinking in which students needed to state the main idea in 10 words or less, and prediction relay, in which students made a prediction, read half the page, checked the prediction, and then used paragraph shrinking. PALS is typically implemented for about 3–4 days per week for approximately 18–22 weeks.

In each of the studies the impact of PALS was positive for English learners. Kindergarten English learners who received K-PALS performed significantly better on measures of phonemic awareness—with moderate effect sizes (ES) for both segmentation (ES = 0.69) and blending (ES = 0.65) and letter-sound recognition, with a moderate effect size (ES = 0.58)—than the English learners who did not receive K-PALS, and similarly to non-English learners who received K-PALS (McMaster et al., 2008). (See Box 8.2 for a brief description of effect sizes.) In the first grade PALS study students were in two-way dual immersion programs (Calhoon et al., 2007). Students who received PALS performed significantly better on measures of phoneme segmentation fluency (ES = 0.53), nonsense word fluency (ES = 0.50), and oral reading fluency (ES = 0.51). However, there were slightly different results for students who were proficient in English and English learners. PALS had more of an effect on English-proficient students' phoneme segmentation fluency and oral reading fluency and more of an effect on English learners' letter naming fluency and nonsense word fluency (Calhoon et al., 2007). For English learners in third through sixth grade who received PALS (Sáenz et al., 2005), large effects were found for reading comprehension (ES = 1.02) but not for reading fluency.

Research to Practice: What Educators Need to Know

Overall, the English learners who received K-PALS/PALS instruction showed improvements in reading achievement when compared to English learners who received typical instruction in reading. Findings from studies implementing K-PALS in kindergarten and PALS in first grade were found to have positive effects on foundational reading skills. Teachers who work in these early grades can use K-PALS/PALS to develop the important building blocks necessary for decoding and fluent reading (i.e., blending sounds together, isolating sounds, and recognizing letters and their corresponding sounds). As students move into upper elementary and on to the middle grades (4–8), "reading to learn" becomes the focus over "learning to read." Teachers who work with English learners in the upper elemen-

---

BOX 8.2. DESCRIPTION OF EFFECT SIZES

An effect size is essentially the magnitude of the differences between groups, in most cases the "intervention" or "treatment" group and the "control" or "comparison group." It gives us an estimate of the impact of an instructional model or intervention. The larger the effect size, the bigger the impact. Typically we report effect sizes to be small if they are about 0.20 or lower, moderate if they are about 0.50, and large if they are about 0.80 or higher (Cohen, 1988).

tary grades can help students improve their reading comprehension using PALS. However, teachers should keep in mind that some students will still need work on developing fluency at these grade levels, and PALS may not provide enough support. Teacher manuals, lesson plans, and student reproducible worksheets are available for purchase. Additional information can be found on the PALS website (*http://kc.vanderbilt.edu/pals*).

Collaborative Strategic Reading

Collaborative strategic reading (CSR) is a cooperative learning instructional model (see Chapter 4, this volume). Students of varying reading levels and language levels work in small groups and apply four specific strategies to access content-area reading material (Klingner & Vaughn, 1999). The instructional model was created specifically to assist students with disabilities, English learners, and other struggling learners in general education classrooms (Klingner, Vaughn, Arguelles, Hughes, & Leftwich, 2004). The goals of CSR are to improve reading comprehension and increase conceptual learning in ways that maximize students' involvement (Klingner & Vaughn, 1999). Structured peer discussion and collaborative activities are included throughout the before-during-after reading process, so together students use reading strategies to monitor their own comprehension, review and synthesize information, ask and answer questions, and take steps to improve their understanding (see CSR strategies in Figure 8.5). An important aspect of CSR is that students work in groups of four, with each member assigned a specific role and responsibility (see Figure 8.6 for group roles) as they put the CSR strategies into practice as part of a reading assignment (see sample lesson, Figure 8.7). The assignment of roles during CSR guarantees that each member has something specific to do and accomplish. Each member of the group is expected to complete a learning log while peers assist each other in completing different parts of the log and checking its accuracy and quality. (See the CSR sample learning log, Figure 8.8.) Typically, CSR is used two times per week for about 16–20 weeks.

CSR is effective for English learners because it allows for structured opportunities that facilitate meaningful discussion about academic content and understanding of text within student-led cooperative groups. Further, in CSR, these

---

Preview: Activate background knowledge and generate predictions.

Click and Clunk: Monitor understanding and use strategies to assist with unknown words/concepts.

Get the Gist: Determine the main idea of a passage.

Wrap-Up: Think about what was learned and make connections.

FIGURE 8.5. CSR strategies.

Leader: Guides the group through all the steps of CSR. Tasks include monitoring time, keeping everyone working together and on task.

Clunk Expert: Makes sure group members document clunks (i.e., words or concepts that are unclear) on their learning logs. Helps students use strategies to figure out unknown words or ideas by rereading and using content clues, analyzing word parts (i.e., roots and affixes), or connecting with cognates.

Gist Expert: Guides the individual members' development and sharing of a gist statement and determines if the gist contains the most important ideas (main idea and supporting details in 10 words or less).

Question Expert: Guides the students in their development of questions that address important ideas from the text and checks that all members write questions and answers.

FIGURE 8.6. CSR roles.

students are encouraged to use their first language to clarify meaning and make connections between their native language and English vocabulary (e.g., using cognates—words in different languages that share a similar root word—to determine word meaning, as in *bicycle* and *bicicleta*).

CSR Research and Effectiveness

CSR has been implemented with English learners in upper elementary classrooms in three research studies (Hitchcock, Dimino, Kurki, Wilkins, & Gersten, 2011; Klingner et al., 2004; Klingner, Vaughn, & Schumm, 1998). In the Klingner et al. (1998) study, English learners and non-English learners in fourth grade in the treatment group were taught CSR strategies during social studies; students in the control group were not taught the CSR strategies. The results of the study showed that both English learners and non-English learners who received CSR made moderate but significant gains in reading comprehension (ES = 0.43). In the Klingner et al. (2004) study the focus was on teacher implementation. The authors found a direct relationship between teacher implementation and student results; larger effect sizes were found for students with teachers who implemented CSR more often and with higher fidelity. They found that overall students made small but significant gains in reading comprehension (ES = 0.19), and that effect sizes were moderate for low-achieving students (ES = 0.51) and students with learning disabilities (LD) (ES = 0.38). On the other hand, Hitchcock et al. (2011) found that in a large-scale study of CSR, there were not significant differences between students in the treatment group and those in the control group. However, this study had wide variation in implementation of CSR; the authors found that only 21% of the teachers were observed using all of the core teaching strategies and that students were observed using all student strategies in only 35% of the classrooms, indicating that it is important for teachers using the strategy to use it as it was designed in order to impact student reading comprehension.

CSR Sample Lesson Plan	Supplemental Reading: Science	Grade 3
Time Allotment: 30 minutes	**Text:** Level 5.0	**Title**: *Sharks*

Rationale: Develop skills for enhancing comprehension of informational text by using strategies before, during, and after reading.

Standards:
- Know and use various text features to locate key facts or information in a text.
- Ask and answer questions about key details in a text.
- Identify the main topic and retell key details of a text.
- Ask and answer questions to help determine or clarify the meaning of words and phrases in a text.
- In life science, students recognize the interdependence of organisms in the natural world.

Student Materials:	**Teacher Materials:**
• Learning log • Assigned text	• Assigned text • Learning log for modeling • Photo of shark(s) for previewing • Timer

BEFORE READING (2–3 min.): Direct students to today's text, *Sharks*, and to:

Read–Title, subtitles, and key words.

Brainstorm–What do I already know?

Predict–What might I learn?

Optional–Highlight photo of sharks (use photo from books or on the Internet)

Explain that some believe sharks are terrifying and dangerous creatures, but in today's lesson students will discover that sharks have more to fear from humans.

Remind students that an important aim of CSR is for the students to work together to use CSR as they read and learn about . . . *Sharks*.

DURING READING (10–12 min.): Tell students they are going to read the passage (or part of the passage, depending on difficulty level) with their group members and work through CSR strategies by completing the learning log and fulfilling their assigned group role.

AFTER READING (10–12 min.): *Tell students that they will collaborate to:*
1. Generate questions and discuss the questions and answers with their group members.
2. Review what they just learned after reading and write a short summary that includes the main idea and key supporting details.

Teacher Closure (2–5 min.): After the review is completed, highlight what was accomplished during the session and facilitate any connections students can potentially take between the day's reading, other readings, and the real world (2–5 minutes).
- **Restate the purpose of the day's reading.** *In today's reading we learned many species of sharks are found around the world, most of which are harmless.*
- **Remind students of what they were able to accomplish during the session.**

Using CSR today, you worked together to read about sharks, their long existence that precedes dinosaurs, and that there are over 400 species of sharks in oceans and rivers.

Provide brief feedback about student performance and behavior during the lesson.

FIGURE 8.7. CSR sample lesson. Adapted with permission from the Meadows Center for Preventing Educational Risk (2013).

Learning Log

Topic _____

Before Reading

Activity: Brainstorm—What do I already know?

I know that _____ and _____.

Activity: Predict—What might I learn?

I think I might learn that _____ or I think I might learn about _____.

During Reading

Activity: Identify **clunks**—*words or concepts that I don't understand—and fix clunks to make sense.*

Text section	These do not make sense	The definitions or meanings
1		
Gist Statement	Who or what section 1 was about in 10 words or less:	
2		
Gist Statement	Who or what section 2 was about in 10 words or less:	
3		
Gist Statement	Who or what section 3 was about in 10 words or less:	

(continued)

FIGURE 8.8. CSR sample learning log. Adapted with permission from the Meadows Center for Preventing Educational Risk (2013).

After Reading

Activity: Question Generation—write questions and their answers.

Questions	Answers

Activity: Review—Write about the most important ideas in the text.

_____

_____

_____

_____

_____

_____

_____

_____

_____

_____

_____

FIGURE 8.8. *(continued)*

Research to Practice: What Educators Need to Know

Overall, both English and non-English learners who used CSR outperformed the comparison group, which received typical instruction, on measures of reading comprehension. Students who were low achievers or identified with an LD made the largest gains using CSR. Classroom teachers considering implementing CSR should note that in these studies students with teachers who followed the CSR model closely had the largest gains. Positive effects of CSR were dependent on quality and frequency of implementation. Teachers implementing CSR need to promote the use of the reading comprehension strategies before, during, and after reading as well as facilitate high-quality discourse in order for English learners to make sense of the text. When teachers do this, English learners benefit from instruction and make gains in reading comprehension. One huge advantage of CSR is that it can be used with a variety of text types that teachers already use. Sample lessons and videos can be found at *http://www.csrcolorado.org*. Additional information and sample materials are available at the IRIS Center (*http://iris.peabody.vanderbilt.edu/module/csr/#content*).

Instructional Conversations

IC is a teaching method that uses dialogue between the teacher and students and between students and students. There are five critical features of IC:

(a) It is interesting and engaging,

(b) It is about an idea or a concept that has meaning and relevance for students,

(c) It has a focus that, while it may shift as the discussion evolves, remains discernible throughout,

(d) There is a high level of participation, without undue domination by any one individual, particularly the teacher,

(e) Students engage in extended discussions—conversations—with the teacher and among themselves. (Goldenberg, 1991, p. 3)

Discussion-based lessons are geared toward creating rich opportunities for students' conceptual and linguistic development. IC fosters communication between small groups of students and the teacher or between peers with the clear instructional goal of promoting contemplation and comprehension. IC goes beyond traditional classroom practices in an effort to develop learners' thinking skills, including the ability to form, express, and exchange ideas. Teachers should select prompts to stimulate discussion, which includes such phrases as:

- "Tell me about why you agree or disagree."
- "Explain why you think that."
- "Can you give me an example?"
- "So, are you saying . . . ?"
- "Say more about . . ."

Ideally, the action of teachers and students engaged in dialogue leads to a more profound questioning and sharing of ideas and knowledge. It is through skillful questioning that learners are led not to correct answers, but rather to construct meaning. IC is dependent upon the teacher's subject matter mastery and knowledge of the students in his or her classroom, as well as both the teacher and peers skills to assist students' deep understanding of content. There are several proven techniques to assist student performance during IC and therefore promote deeper understanding of content. These are included in Figure 8.9.

The following steps serve as a basic guide when planning for an IC around a story or a book:

1. Select a text that will be of interest to students.
2. Read the text to gain a deeper grasp of it and how it relates to students.
3. Select a theme as a starting point to focus the discussion. Ponder what will be meaningful and interesting to students and help them make connections or extend their current knowledge.
4. Identify and provide or review key vocabulary and background knowledge that students will need in order to make sense of what they will be reading. Students sometimes need to be provided with relevant background knowledge or an opportunity to gain deeper understanding of concepts or ideas.
5. Decide on a starting point for the discussion to provide an initial focus. This might be a key concept or word (e.g., *freedom*, *mitosis*) or a key question that will help focus students' and the teacher's attention.
6. Think about possible ways the discussion might progress, how the initial focus might eventually lead to an exploration of the theme, and, ultimately, how the theme will tie into the story students are reading. For instance, consider the following questions: How might students respond to the initial focal point selected? What will you do if they do not respond? Do you have a story, illustration, or anecdote you can share that will help the discussion begin? How will you determine what portions of text to read before stop-

---

- **Modeling**—demonstrating the thought process or possible dialogue that may stem from a key word or concept.
- **Offering Explicit Feedback**—providing information about another's performance so that corrections can be made.
- **Contingency Managing**—applying consequences depending on whether or not the desired behaviors are demonstrated.
- **Directing**—specifying responses, clarifying information, and promoting decision making.
- **Questioning**—inquiry that invites or calls for a reply or justification.
- **Explaining**—making an idea, situation, or problem clear by describing it in more detail or revealing relevant facts or ideas.
- **Task Structuring**—organizing and sequencing a task into components.

FIGURE 8.9. Techniques for assisting with performance when using IC.

ping for discussion? What meanings and interpretations might students bring to this theme or text?

7. Consider some suitable follow-up activities, particularly ones that will help gauge what students have learned from the IC.

ICs are effective for ELs because they promote reading comprehension by allowing participants to appreciate and build on each other's experiences, knowledge, and understanding as it relates to text. In IC, English language development occurs through rich discussion among groups or partners. Language can be further developed by extending oral language practice with writing prompts or questions related to the text or topic of focus. This approach allows students to develop and practice their language skills, specifically academic language. In addition, ICs allow for modeling by English-proficient peers and the teacher and opportunities for practicing academic language through meaningful authentic discussion, all in a safe environment (lowering students' affective filter). Teachers use this model to tap into students' background knowledge, culture, and experiences using strategically placed and developed question prompts in order to encourage the engagement, interest, and participation of all students in the conversation. Typically, IC instruction is conducted multiple times a week for about 45 minutes (Saunders & Goldenberg, 1999).

IC Research and Effectiveness

Research on IC has focused on English learners transitioning from receiving the majority of their instruction in Spanish to receiving instruction in English (Saunders & Goldenberg, 1999). The goal of the instruction is to improve the reading achievement of students as well as improve English proficiency. Since English learners are often in classes with students who are fluent in English, the research examining IC has included both groups of students. Two studies have examined the impact of IC on the reading achievement and English proficiency of English learners in the upper elementary grades (Saunders, 1999; Saunders & Goldenberg, 1999). Both of these studies have been reviewed by the What Works Clearinghouse, which found that IC has a positive impact on the reading comprehension of English learners (USDOE, 2006).

In the Saunders (1999) study, the author examined the long-term impact of IC on students transitioning into English instruction in fourth and fifth grade. Students were initially randomized in second grade based on first-grade assessments. Following the transition to English, which typically occurred during fourth or fifth grade, students in IC and the comparison classes were matched and analyzed. The average effect size across the reading comprehension measures was large (ES = 0.79; USDOE, 2006); however significant effects were not found on the measures of language proficiency (USDOE, 2006). Similarly, in the Saunders and Goldenberg (1999) study, students in fourth and fifth grade who were transitioning into English instruction participated. Effect sizes were large for reading comprehension measures (ES = 0.81; USDOE, 2006).

Research to Practice: What Educators Need to Know

Teachers considering implementing IC should plan to do so within their broader language arts instruction. Teachers should expect that implementing IC will take time, given that researchers in the Saunders (1999) study (grades K–5) research team members worked closely with classroom teachers to provide intervention. Teachers should also note that when combined with literature logs, ICs have the potential to increase the reading comprehension of English learners and possibly their English proficiency as students read, write, and share responses about what was read. Additionally, literature logs, or writing entries, require students to independently write about personal experiences that were relevant to a character in the text or to provide detailed accounts of story events. Completed logs were discussed with the teacher and compared with those of other students in small groups. The full report and summary from the What Works Clearinghouse can be found at *http://ies.ed.gov/ncee/wwc/interventionreport.aspx?sid=236.*

Sheltered Instruction Observation Protocol Model

The Sheltered Instruction Observation Protocol (SIOP) model is a multicomponent instructional framework that was specifically developed to support English learners in developing English proficiency as well as mastering academic content (Echevarria, Vogt, & Short, 2012). The SIOP model helps teachers plan and deliver lessons that allow English learners to acquire academic knowledge as they develop English language proficiency. In this model, language and content objectives are systematically woven into the grade-level subject curriculum that teachers present to students through adapted instruction in English. SIOP is composed of 30 instructional features grouped into eight components meant to increase student engagement and outcomes in content-area instruction (see Figure 8.10). One of the eight components of SIOP is "Interaction," which includes "frequent interactions and discussion between teacher/student and among students, which encourage elaborated responses about lesson concepts" and "grouping configurations that support the language and content objectives of the lesson" (Echevarria et al., 2012, p. 295). Teachers using the SIOP model provide opportunities for interactions through the pairing or collaborative grouping of students for such activities as:

- *Think–pair–share*—a discussion strategy that requires learners to think about a question or prompt, then partner up with another to talk about what came to mind, and then finally to share with the larger group.
- *Role play or simulation*—performing or imitating someone else and their actions, attributes, and feelings.

- *Games*—purposeful play or sport to promote acquisition and practice of content knowledge along with language development.
- *Experiments*—procedures for discovering, verifying, refuting, or establishing the validity of a hypothesis or to demonstrate a known fact.
- *Text reading*—a process of activating one's thinking about the meaning of words and concepts, along with author's purpose and text pattern, in order to have a clear understanding of the text's main idea.

Preparation. Each SIOP lesson has language and content objectives that are linked to the curriculum and standards and taught systematically. Content concepts suit the grade and developmental level of the students. Lessons include meaningful activities that integrate concepts with language practice and supplemental materials to support the academic text.

Building Background. Teachers make connections between new concepts and past learning and between concepts and students' personal experiences. These connections help students organize new information as part of their cognitive processing. Further, teachers must explicitly teach and emphasize the key academic vocabulary of the concepts and provide opportunities for English learners to use this vocabulary in meaningful ways.

Comprehensible Input. Teachers modulate their rate of speech, word choice, and sentence structure complexity according to the proficiency level of English learners. They make content comprehensible through content ESL techniques. Teachers also explain academic tasks clearly, both orally and in writing, providing models and examples wherever possible.

Strategies. Teachers and students need to use strategies in SIOP lessons. Teachers must scaffold instruction, beginning at a level that encourages student success and providing support to move the students to a higher level of understanding and accomplishment. Teachers highlight study skills and learning strategies for students and create tasks and ask higher-order questions that require students to use the strategies and talk about them.

Interaction. High-quality classes provide frequent opportunities for interaction and discussion between teacher and students, and among students. It is through discussion with classmates and with the teacher that English learners practice important skills like elaborating, negotiating meaning, clarifying and confirming information, persuading, disagreeing, and evaluating.

Practice and Application. Effective SIOP lessons include activities that encourage students to practice and apply the content they are learning, and practice and apply the language skills they are learning too. These activities are most beneficial when they include visual, hands-on, and other kinesthetic tasks.

Lesson Delivery. Successful delivery of a SIOP lesson means that the content and language objectives were met, the pacing was appropriate, and the students had a high level of engagement throughout the class period. All students must have opportunities to practice their language skills within the context of the academic tasks.

Review and Assessment. English learners need to review key vocabulary and concepts, and teachers need to assess how well students retain the information—through frequent feedback to students and informal assessments throughout the lesson. Teachers should offer multiple pathways for students to demonstrate their understanding of the content.

FIGURE 8.10. Eight components of the SIOP model.

Figure 8.11 shows how the eight SIOP components are woven into a lesson plan. SIOP developers note that students will need explicit guidance to make the transition to academic tasks and that adjustments to instruction will be necessary for students' different learning styles. Instructional adjustments or enhances prescribed by the SIOP developers include use of:

- Visuals.
- Graphic organizers.
- Oral, written, physical, or pictorial communication.
- Students as resources for information about the topic.
- Hands-on and performance-based activities.
- Critical thinking and study skill development.
- Cooperative learning activities.
- Student interaction and peer tutoring among classmates.
- Process-oriented instruction with modeling.

Teachers typically implement SIOP lessons every day so that it becomes a routinized instructional practice. Additionally, each of the other instructional models described in this section could be implemented as part of a SIOP lesson and fit nicely within the framework.

In the last several decades, multiple studies have been conducted to examine the impact of the SIOP model on the achievement of English learners. Most recently the SIOP model was studied as part of the CREATE (Center for Research on the Educational Achievement and Teaching of English Language Learners) program, which was funded by the Institute of Education Sciences. CREATE specifically targeted instruction for English learners in the middle grades (4–8). SIOP was examined as an individual instructional model as well as the framework for the other instructional interventions.

SIOP Model Research and Effectiveness

One CREATE study examined the impact of SIOP on seventh-grade students in life science classes (Echevarria, Richards-Tutor, Canges, & Francis, 2011). Students in the SIOP classes made larger gains when compared to students in the control group—gains that approached significance. In another study examining these same classrooms (Echevarria, Richards-Tutor, Pham, & Ratleff, 2011), researchers found that there was a strong relationship between teacher implementation of the SIOP model, the fidelity of implementation, and student outcomes. Additional research examining SIOP in grades 6–12 found that students in English as a second language (ESL) classes who received SIOP instruction performed significantly better on both writing (ES = 0.31) and oral language (ES = 0.29) assessments with moderate effect sizes (Short, Fidelman, & Louguit, 2012). In an earlier study of SIOP (Echevarria, Short, & Powers, 2006), researchers found that English learners in grades 6–8 who received SIOP instruction performed better than students in the

SIOP LESSON PLAN

SUBJECT: Life Science

UNIT FOCUS: Investigating Genetics and Heredity

Lesson # 6   **Length of lesson 1 day**

STANDARD(S): In sexually reproducing organisms, each parent contributes half the genes acquired (at random) by the offspring (Next Generation Science Standard LS3.B)

LESSON TOPIC: Punnett Squares

OBJECTIVES:

Content: Students will . . .
- Use a Punnett square to predict the possible outcomes of genetic crosses.
- Demonstrate how to calculate probability.
- Review the difference between a homozygous and heterozygous genotype.

Language: Students will . . .
- Define key terms related to genetics and heredity and give examples in a written and visual format.
- Take notes on a graphic organizer to categorize new information.
- Write summary sentences.

KEY VOCABULARY: probability, Punnett square, *review homozygous, heterozygous*

MATERIALS: quarters, puppy Punnett square, three-column chart, butcher or poster paper, markers or colored pencils

MOTIVATION:

Read the content and language objectives of this lesson to the students.

Building Background (10 minutes)
- Put the students in groups of three to four and give each group a quarter. Ask the group to predict how many times they think the coin will land "heads up" and how many times it will land "heads down" if they toss the quarter 20 times. Tell them to reach a consensus for their prediction and record it on a piece of paper.
- Ask some groups to justify their prediction and ask some groups to write their prediction on the board.
- Tell the groups to test their prediction by tossing the coin 20 times and recording the outcome of each toss on the paper. Each member of the group should have a role (e.g., coin tosser, counter, presenter, and data recorder).
- Ask each group to look at their data and compare their prediction with their results. How accurate were their predictions? Ask some of the groups to share.
- Ask the presenter of each group to give you their group's data for the total number of tosses, the number of heads, and the number of tails and tally it on the board or overhead transparency for the class.
- Ask the students to compare the class's data with their group's data and think about any differences they see between their group's data and the class's data. After students do a Think–Square–Share, ask some students in each group to tell you what their group discussed.

(continued)

FIGURE 8.11. SIOP lesson plan example. Used with permission from the Center for Applied Linguistics and California State University, Long Beach. Copyright 2012.

- Discuss the students' analysis of this task and bring out the idea that there were only two ways for the coin to land and both ways were equally likely to occur. In other words, there is a one in two or 50% chance that the coin will land "heads up," and a one in two or 50% chance that the coin will land "heads down" (this also may be a time to review how to convert ratios to percentages). Tell the students that this coin toss task just demonstrated the concept of probability. Explain that Mendel was the first scientist to recognize that the principles of probability can be used to predict the results of genetic crosses.
- Students make a vocabulary card for probability.

PRESENTATION (20 minutes):
- Ask the students to refer to p. 90 in their text and explain that a Punnett square is a chart that can show the probability of allele combinations from a genetic cross.
- Students make a vocabulary card for "Punnett square."
- Read the "Punnett Squares and Phenotypes and Genotypes" section in the text and take notes using a three-column chart. Do as a class or in pairs, depending on level of students.
  - Geneticists use Punnett squares to show all the possible outcomes of a genetic cross and to determine the probability of a specific outcome occurring.
  - The alleles that one parent can pass on to the children is written across the top of the square and the alleles from the other parent are written down the left side. The boxes in the square are the possible combination of alleles that the offspring can inherit from its parents.
  - People use Punnett squares to calculate the probability that an offspring will inherit certain allele combinations.
  - People also use them to predict what allele combinations an organism will inherit from its parents.
  - Genotypes can be either homozygous or heterozygous
- Ask the students to help you complete a Punnett square for a litter of puppies. Put the puppy Punnett square transparency up for the students to see and ask them to help you complete it. Explain that this Punnett square shows a cross between two purebred dogs, one with black fur and one with white (use photos if possible).
  - Point out that the allele controlling fur color will be represented with FF for black fur and ff for white fur (you may also want to have the students review why there are two alleles for each purebred).
  - Review that black fur is represented with an F and white fur is represented with an f.
  - Complete the Punnett square with the students.
  - Students copy the Punnett square into their notes.
- In a Think–Pair–Share ask the students to look at the Punnett square and answer the following questions: What is the probability that the offspring of these two animals will have black fur? What is the probability that the offspring of these two animals will have white fur?
- Discuss answers as a class.

PRACTICE/APPLICATION (15 minutes):
- Put students in groups of three or four and give each group a piece of poster paper, markers or colored pencils, and a set of genetic crosses involving hybrid animals (e.g., one brown hamster [Bb] and one white hamster [bb]).
- Tell the students to create a Punnett square that represents the different allele combinations of the offspring of these genetic crosses. The Punnett square needs to include the correct phenotype symbols and a visual representation of each offspring possibility (refer students to p. 91 in the text for an example).
- Assign roles to each group member (e.g., presenter, illustrator, timekeeper, and coach) and teacher circulates and checks for accuracy.
- Each group presents its posters to the class.

(continued)

FIGURE 8.11. *(continued)*

REVIEW/ASSESSMENT (5 minutes):

Write two to three summary sentences about Punnett squares and probability on the Exit Sheet.

EXTENSION:

In the same groups, students will Send-A-Problem to another group.
- Students write a question based on their Punnett square poster (e.g., What is the probability that a hamster with Bb alleles and a hamster with bb alleles will have an offspring with white fur?). Model the format of the question type first.
- After the students write their question they send it to another group to solve.
- Ask a representative from each group to read the question and their answer. As a class, correct and confirm the responses.

FIGURE 8.11. *(continued)*

comparison group on a writing performance assessment. The effect size was large (ES = 0.83) for the overall writing scores, and students in the SIOP groups specifically performed better on the writing elements of language production, organization, and mechanics.

Research to Practice: What Educators Need to Know

The SIOP studies described indicate the potential for success of students not yet proficient in English when educators integrate language development into content-specific lessons. In all studies the level of SIOP implementation varied by teachers. Higher-quality implementation of SIOP was associated with more positive outcomes for students. Results indicate that with professional development and ongoing support content-area teachers implementing SIOP were able to vary their instruction to better target English learners' needs. In some of the studies, SIOP professional development was limited and implementation was observed over only a short amount of time, yet results were still promising. More time for teachers to learn and use the SIOP model may help them produce positive long-term outcomes for English learners. In addition, teachers who have English learners and native English speakers in their classes can expect that SIOP will not hinder the achievement of native English speakers, as the research studies found that using the model resulted in no disadvantage for these students. Sample lessons can be found on the CREATE website (*www.cal.org/create/resources/lesson-plans.html*), and more information about professional development for using the SIOP model can be found at *http://siop.pearson.com*.

Project SCALE

Project SCALE (Supporting Comprehension and Academic Language through Explicit Instruction in Social Studies for English Learners) is a multicomponent intervention developed and investigated as part of the CREATE center program (*www.cal.org/create*). This intervention is meant to enhance content knowledge through improved reading comprehension and vocabulary development. Project SCALE includes an instructional routine designed to promote content knowledge and enhance the literacy and language learning of students in middle school social studies classes. Peer support is integrated into many of the SCALE activities. SCALE's lesson structure is based on best practices for English learners that include making connections with students' background knowledge, active reading and content-acquisition strategies, and explicit instruction in specific content, as well as with academic language. The intervention, which consisted of nine 1-week units, was implemented for 50 minutes 5 days a week. There are seven key components to this intervention:

1. *Preview of lesson content.* The preview stage of the lesson involves activating students' background knowledge to provide opportunities for students to intentionally *connect new and prior learning.* At the beginning of each lesson, the introduction section gives teacher prompts for motivating and engaging students through reviewing key concepts from one or more prior lessons and making explicit links to the current lesson. For example, the teacher prompt might begin with "As we have discussed previously," or "Yesterday we learned that . . ." to focus students' attention on specific concepts, vocabulary words, or historical events from past lessons. Then the teacher is guided to link this with the key concepts to be taught in the current lesson, using such prompts as "Today we will see . . ." or "As we read, keep in mind . . ."

2. *Explicit preteaching of content-specific vocabulary and academic vocabulary with extended follow-up.* Following the introduction/activation component, the teacher provides *explicit instruction of selected content-specific and academic vocabulary.* Words are preselected from the reading materials that represent key concepts within the particular content to be covered. The vocabulary words are selected from state content standards and research-based academic vocabulary word lists. In subsequent lessons, teachers are directed to deepen and extend students' understanding of the vocabulary words through oral and written use of the words and systematic review.

3. *Strategic use of video.* For most of the lessons, short video clips (e.g., 2 to 7 minutes) are given to develop students' *background knowledge* of key ideas and themes from the lesson and to provide an alternative format of presentation of content. The purpose is to foster student engagement with the ideas and concepts initially without the added stress (for struggling readers) of reading difficult text. Lessons prompt teachers to introduce the video using one or two guiding questions to direct students' thinking and attention throughout the viewing. After students view the clip, the teacher should facilitate a short discussion centered on the questions.

4. *Active text reading.* The next step is engaging students in using *active reading strategies* to read the lesson text. The teacher chooses a text selection from the

curriculum focused on the lesson topic. Teachers are guided to select the passage carefully to ensure that the selection focuses specifically on the key ideas and provides opportunities for students to apply vocabulary knowledge. Before reading, the teacher provides focus questions to direct attention to the most important ideas. The students will be expected to answer the questions following the reading. Previewing the questions prior to reading is another element of *active reading strategies*. Teachers have flexibility to choose either a teacher read-aloud or partner reading format. The teacher read-aloud option provides a teacher model of active reading strategies, intentionally stopping to clarify vocabulary and check for understanding. In the partner reading format, the partners take turns reading, with one partner always in the role of following along and providing corrective feedback as was described with PALS (see Figure 8.4) (e.g., "You missed a word. That word is _____. Go back and read it again."). After reading the passage, the students work in pairs to answer the focus questions, then come back as a whole group for a teacher-led discussion.

5. *Use of writing with graphic organizers.* Following the text reading, the students further engage in analyzing the lesson content and practice using the vocabulary words through a writing activity using a graphic organizer. The activity is designed to lead students to synthesize and organize the key ideas from the lesson. Teachers provide brief instruction on how to complete the activity, and then students work collaboratively with their partners to identify and summarize the most important information. Students are encouraged to use the new vocabulary words in their written responses. The teacher rotates through the classroom to give feedback and guidance. A final whole-class discussion reviews the key ideas and vocabulary, making connections to prior learning.

6. *Strategic paired grouping.* Students work in pairs throughout the lesson to engage in text reading, oral discussion, and writing. In planning the lessons, teachers strategically organize the partner groups based on reading ability and English language proficiency status. Students worked with partners for approximately 15–20 minutes per lesson.

7. *SIOP lesson framework.* The SIOP Model framework (see SCALE sample lesson, Figure 8.12) was adopted, and SIOP components were woven into lesson design.

Project SCALE Research and Effectiveness

Project SCALE was also evaluated through the CREATE center (Vaughn et al., 2009). This project examined a social studies intervention for seventh-grade English learners and its impact on both vocabulary and reading comprehension. The instructional model was examined in two studies (Vaughn et al., 2009). In study 1, English learners showed growth on both reading comprehension and vocabulary measures. Effect sizes were large for comprehension ($g = 1.12$) and moderate for vocabulary ($g = 0.53$). In study 2, similar results and effect sizes were found.

(text continues on p. 284)

Slavery Divides the Country

Big Idea: Human Rights & Survival/Resistance

Lesson 1

Standards	7.4A Identify and discuss events and conflicts in the state of Texas
	7.21B Analyze information by sequencing and identifying cause-and-effect relationships
	7.5A Explain reasons for the involvement of Texas in the Civil War
Lesson Topic	Slavery in Texas

Objectives	Key Vocabulary
CONTENT—Students will:	• misery
• Learn about the injustice of slavery as an institution.	• plantation
LANGUAGE—Students will:	• plow
• Use key vocabulary in reading, writing, listening, and speaking throughout the lesson.	• unceasing
• Watch and listen to the video, write responses in their notebooks, and contribute in whole-class discussion.	
• Listen to and/or read the lesson passage, and write question responses in their notebooks.	
• (In the review/assessment activity) Discuss the beliefs of slave owners that allowed slavery to continue and write about how and why the balance of power between slaves and slave owners favored the slave owners.	

Materials	Preparation
• Student notebooks	• Post the objectives
• Overhead projector and transparency markers	• Links to background
• Video: "Jupiter and Thomas Jefferson"	• Discussion about beliefs of slave owners that allowed slavery to continue
• Outside Passage: "Slavery in the South" (in teacher's binder)	
• Transparency: Questions	
• Transparency: Balance of Power between Slaves and Slave Owners	

(continued)

FIGURE 8.12. Sample SCALE lesson with Vocabulary/Concept Cards. Used with permission from the Meadows Center for Preventing Risk.

Motivation (Engagement/Linkages)   3 min.

- Provide overview/background information on today's lesson.
  - *In the 1850s, farms were important in the South, including Texas. Many of the farmers grew cotton to sell, as there was a demand for cotton in the North and in Europe. Most Texas cotton was grown on plantations, or large farms.*
- Solicit students for knowledge of *plantation*.
  - *Slavery became a cheap source of labor for planters who had plantations. Slaves made up a large portion of the population in East Texas. Slaves held no power, and their white owners considered slaves to be property. This week we will examine the institution of slavery. We'll see how inhumanely one human can treat another and how slaves resisted.*

Presentation   30 min.

Vocabulary   (10 min.)

- Introduce today's vocabulary and discuss "turn and talk" questions among pairs and/or whole group. Students write vocabulary terms and synonyms in their notebooks.

Teacher-led Reading: "Slavery in the South" (in teacher's binder)   (10 min.)

- State the big idea of the reading.
- Preview the reading by asking questions to help activate background knowledge and guide students' thinking about what they will learn.
- Read the questions (on transparency) that students will focus on during the reading.
  - *Describe the kinds of work done by slaves in the cities.*
  - *Describe the kinds of work done by slaves on plantations.*
- Model thinking aloud as you read in order to make sense of text.
- As you read, demonstrate how to generate different types of questions, while allowing them to respond to these questions.

Video: "Jupiter and Thomas Jefferson"   (10 min.)

- Introduce the video.
  - *From the reading, we got an idea of the kinds of work slaves were forced to do. Of course, slaves were not happy with the way they were treated, and many tried to resist, or fight back.*
  - *Now let's watch a short video about the life of a particular slave, Jupiter. As you watch, listen for descriptions of the conditions under which slaves were forced to work, the ways they tried to resist, and the inhuman punishments they were given for resisting. Focus on the following questions: In what ways did the slaves try to resist? What were the consequences if they resisted? In what ways were the slaves' human rights violated?*
- Students watch the video clip.
- Students write their responses in their logs. They may discuss the answers in their pairs.
- Teacher summarizes the video, highlighting the questions above by using a few responses from the students.

(continued)

FIGURE 8.12. *(continued)*

Practice
5 min.

- After the reading, in pairs, have students discuss and write responses to the above question/s in their notebooks.
- Once students are done, begin discussion of the questions while helping students to center on the big idea/s in the selection.

Review/Assessment
10 min.

- Introduce the activity.
  - *Let's examine the institution of slavery. What were the beliefs of slave owners that allowed slavery to continue?*
- Prompt for answers such as "white supremacy" and "cheap labor."
  - *Today we looked at the lives of slaves, the work they were forced to do, and the harsh punishments they were given if they resisted. Tomorrow, we'll see that despite these hardships, slaves continued to resist.*
- Explain to students that they will work on a balance of power graphic organizer in which they will write about the ways in which slaves and slave owners had power and/or were powerless.
- Students write their responses in their graphic organizer.
- Students contribute their answers in a whole-class discussion.

(continued)

FIGURE 8.12. *(continued)*

misery
(miseria)

Suffering and unhappiness

Trowbridge Estate; www.flickr.com/photos/jaggers/7006194783
Attribution 2.0 Generic (CC BY 2.0)

Synonym: distress

The slaves faced great **misery** under their slave masters.

Misery can cause people to do things they would not normally do.

Turn and Talk

- What are some things that cause you misery?

plantation
(plantación)

A large farm or estate where cotton, tobacco, coffee, sugar cane, or other cash crops are grown

Frank and Frances Carpenter Collection www.loc.gov/pictures/item/93511081

Synonyms: large farm, farm estate

On large **plantations**, slaves had specific jobs.

Plantations are usually found in tropical areas.

Turn and Talk

- Why is it necessary to have many workers on a plantation?

(continued)

FIGURE 8.12. *(continued)*

plow
(prar)

To turn over soil using a heavy farm tool
that has a broad blade

Klearchos Kapoutsis www.flickr.com/photos/klearchos/5285358580
Attribution 2.0 Generic (CC BY 2.0)

Synonym: tilling land

Male slaves usually did the heaviest work, which involved **plowing** the fields.

Horses, donkeys, and tractors are usually used for **plowing** the field before planting.

Turn and Talk

- In your opinion, what would be the disadvantage of not plowing the field before planting?

unceasing
(incesante)

Continuous, endless

Carl Wycoff
Attribution 2.0 Generic (CC BY 2.0)

Synonyms: nonstop, persistent

A slave experienced years of **unceasing** labor.

The seemingly **unceasing** efforts by the teacher to get calculators for the entire class finally resulted in success.

Turn and Talk

- Share an activity that you would like to do unceasingly. What is it about the activity that makes you want to spend so many hours on it?

FIGURE 8.12. *(continued)*

Research to Practice: What Educators Need to Know

The SCALE intervention reported here was conducted in high-poverty schools. While students in the SCALE condition made improvements in content-specific comprehension and vocabulary, many students were noted as being well below grade level in achievement. Although they did improve, improvements were not substantial enough to help them meet or exceed grade-level standards.

English learners who participated in the SCALE intervention benefited from the instruction they received. They outperformed a comparison group who did not receive the intervention on both vocabulary and comprehension measures. English learners who participated in the intervention gained new vocabulary words at the same rate as students who were proficient in English. Although the SCALE intervention was developed to address the instructional and language needs of English learners, the students who were proficient in English also benefited. Teachers can feel confident that implementing the SCALE intervention will have positive effects on both the English learners and English-proficient students in their classrooms. Sample lessons are available for download at *www.meadowscenter.org/library/resource/english-learners-in-content-area-classes-social-studies.*

CONCLUSION

The unique learning needs of English learners necessitates that effective second-language instruction be embedded into content-area classes. This, in turn, requires educators to be provided with a sound knowledge base and the capacity to deliver instruction that supports language development, literacy, and content learning. Peer-supported instruction has the potential to powerfully impact the achievement of this group of students, as this type of instruction impacts both academic achievement and language development. Teachers using peer-supported instruction need to carefully consider how to pair and group students and explicitly teach students to work in groups cooperatively. Although the research on peer-supported instruction for English learners is limited, particularly when compared to the literature in this area with native English-speaking students, there are several peer-supported instructional practices that have the potential to increase the achievement of English learners. PALS, CSR, IC, the SIOP Model, and Project SCALE are instructional practices that use peer-supported instruction, and research has found that these practices increase the academic achievement and in some cases the language development of English learners. The peer-supported instructional activities and techniques, lessons, and suggestions presented in this chapter are meant to complement teacher-directed instructional approaches and content. Peer support is an approach that we believe educators can readily translate into relevant routines, structures, and learning opportunities that boost the language and academic achievement of both English learners and their native English-speaking peers.

REFERENCES

Artiles, A. J., & Klingner, J. K. (Eds.). (2006). Forging a knowledge base on English language learners with special needs: Theoretical, population, and technical issues. *Teachers College Record, 108,* 2187–2194.

August, D., & Shanahan, T. (2006). *Developing literacy in second-language learners: Report of the National Literacy Panel on Language-Minority Children and Youth.* Mahwah, NJ: Erlbaum.

Calhoon, M. B., Al Otaiba, S., Cihak, D., King, A., & Avalos, A. (2007). Effects of a peer-mediated program on reading skill acquisition for two-way bilingual first-grade classrooms. *Learning Disability Quarterly, 30*(3), 169–184.

Cloud, N., Genesee, F., & Hamayan, E. (2009). *Literacy instruction for English language learners*: Portsmouth, NH: Heinemann.

Cohen, J. (1988). *Statistical power analysis for the behavioral sciences* (2nd ed.). Hillside, NJ: Erlbaum.

Echevarria, J., Richards-Tutor, C., Canges, R., & Francis, D. (2011). Using the SIOP model to promote the acquisition of language and science concepts with English learners. *Bilingual Research Journal, 34*(3), 334–351.

Echevarria, J., Richards-Tutor, C., Pham, V., & Ratleff, P. (2011). Did they get it?: The role of fidelity in improving teaching for English learners. *Journal of Adolescent and Adult Literacy, 4,* 425–434.

Echevarría, J., & Short, D. (2011). The SIOP® Model: A professional development framework for comprehensive schoolwide intervention. Washington, DC: Center for Research on the Educational Achievement and Teaching of English Language Learners. Retrieved from *www.cal.org/create/publications/briefs/pdfs/professional-development-framework.pdf.*

Echevarria, J., Short, D., & Powers, K. (2006). School reform and standards-based education: A model for English-language learners. *Journal of Educational Research, 99*(4), 195–211.

Echevarria, J., Vogt, M., & Short, D. (2012). *Making content comprehensible for English learners* (4th ed.). Boston: Pearson.

Fuchs, D., Fuchs, L. S., Mathes, P. G., & Simmons, D. C. (1997). Peer-assisted learning strategies: Making classrooms more responsive to diversity. *American Educational Research Journal, 34,* 174–206.

Genesee, F., Lindholm-Leary, K., Saunders, W., & Christian, D. (2006). *Educating English language learners: A synthesis of research evidence.* New York: Cambridge University Press.

Gersten, R., & Baker, S. (2000). What we know about effective instructional practices for English-language learners. *Exceptional Children, 66,* 454–470.

Gersten, R., Baker, S. K., Shanahan, T., Linan-Thompson, S., Collins, P., & Scarcella, R. (2007). *Effective literacy and English language instruction for English learners in the elementary grades.* Washington, DC: National Center for Education Evaluation and Regional Assistance, Institute of Education Sciences, U.S. Department of Education. Retrieved from *http://ies.ed.gov/ncee/wwc/pdf/practice_guides/20074011.pdf.*

Gersten, R., & Geva, E. (2003, April). Teaching reading to early language learners. *Educational Leadership, 60,* 44–49.

Ginsburg-Block, M. D., Rohrbeck, C. A., & Fantuzzo, J. W. (2006). A meta-analytic review of social, self-concept, and behavioral outcomes of peer-assisted learning. *Journal of Educational Psychology, 98*(4), 732–749.

Goldenberg, C. (1991). *Instructional conversations and their classroom application* (Educational Practice Report 2). Santa Cruz, CA: National Center for Research on Cultural Diversity and Second Language Learning.

Goldenberg, C. (2010). Improving achievement for English learners: Conclusions from recent reviews and emerging research. In G. Li & P. A. Edwards (Eds.), *Best practices in ELL instruction* (pp. 15–43). New York: Guilford Press.

Goldenberg, C., & Coleman, R. (2010). *Promoting academic achievement among English learners: A guide to the research.* Thousand Oaks, CA: Corwin.

Haager, D., Klingner, J. K., & Aceves, T. C. (2009). *How to teach English language learners: Effective strategies from outstanding educators, grades K–6.* San Francisco: Jossey-Bass.

Hitchcock, J., Dimino, J., Kurki, A., Wilkins, C., & Gersten, R. (2011). *The impact of collaborative strategic reading on the reading comprehension of grade 5 students in linguistically diverse schools: Final Report* (NCEE 2011–4001). Washington, DC: National Center for Education Evaluation and Regional Assistance, Institute of Educational Sciences, U.S. Department of Education.

Johnson, D. W., & Johnson, R. T. (1987). *Learning together and alone* (2nd ed.). Englewood Cliffs, NJ: Prentice-Hall.

Johnson, D. W., & Johnson, R. (1989). *Cooperation and competition: Theory and research.* Edina, MN: Interaction Book Company.

Johnson, D. W., & Johnson, R. (1999). Learning together and alone: Cooperative, competitive, and individualistic learning (5th ed.). Boston: Allyn & Bacon.

Klingner, J. K., Artiles, A. J., Kozleski, E., Harry, B., Zion, S., Tate, W., et al. (2005). Addressing the disproportionate representation of culturally and linguistically diverse students in special education through culturally responsive educational systems. *Education Policy Analysis Archives, 13*(38), 1–39.

Klingner, J. K., & Vaughn, S. (1999). Promoting reading comprehension, content learning, and English acquisition through Collaborative Strategic Reading (CSR). *Reading Teacher, 52*(7), 738–747.

Klingner, J. K., Vaughn, S., Arguelles, M. E., Hughes, M. T., & Leftwich, S. A. (2004). Collaborative strategic reading: "Real-world" lessons from classroom teachers. *Remedial and Special Education, 25*(5), 291–302.

Klingner, J. K., Vaughn, S., & Schumm, J. S. (1998). Collaborative strategic reading during social studies in heterogeneous fourth-grade classrooms. *Elementary School Journal, 99*(1), 3–22.

McMaster, K. L., Kung, S.-H., Han, I., & Cao, M. (2008). Peer-assisted learning strategies: A "tier 1" approach to promoting English learners' response to intervention. *Exceptional Children, 74*(2), 194–214.

O'Connor, R. E., & Jenkins, J. R. (1996). Cooperative learning as an inclusion strategy: A closer look. *Exceptionality, 6*(1), 29–51.

O'Connor, R. E., & Jenkins, J. R. (2013). Cooperative learning for students with learning disabilities: Advice and caution derived from the evidence. In H. L. Swanson, K. R. Harris, & S. Graham (Eds.), *Handbook of learning disabilities* (2nd ed., pp. 507–525). New York: Guilford Press.

Sáenz, L. M., Fuchs, L. S., & Fuchs, D. (2005). Peer-assisted learning strategies for English language learners with learning disabilities. *Exceptional Children, 71*(3), 231–247.

Saunders, W. M. (1999). Improving literacy achievement for English learners in transitional bilingual programs. *Educational Research and Evaluation, 5*(4), 345–381.

Saunders, W. M., & Goldenberg, C. (1999). Effects of instructional conversations and literature logs on limited- and fluent-English-proficient students' story comprehension and thematic understanding. *Elementary School Journal, 99*(4), 277–301.

Scruggs, T. E., Mastropieri, M. A., & Marchak, L. (2012). Peer-mediated instruction in inclusive secondary social studies learning: Direct and indirect learning effects. *Learning Disabilities Research and Practice, 27,* 12–20.

Short, D. J., Fidelman, C. G., & Louguit, M. (2012). Developing academic language in English language learners through sheltered instruction. *TESOL Quarterly, 46*(2), 334–361.

Tharp, R. G. (1997). *From at-risk to excellence: Research, theory, and principles for practice* (Research Report 1). Santa Cruz, CA: Center for Research on Education, Diversity and Excellence.

Tharp, R. G., & Gallimore, R. (1991). *The instructional conversation: Teaching and learning in social activity* (Research Report 2). Santa Cruz, CA: National Center for Research on Cultural Diversity and Second Language Learning, University of California, Santa Cruz.

U.S. Census Bureau. (2011). Language spoken at home by ability to speak English for the population 5 years and over (Table B016001). *2011 American Community Survey.* Retrieved from *http://factfinder2.census.gov.*

U.S. Department of Education, National Center for Education Statistics. (2013). English language learners (NCES 2013-037). Retrieved from *https://nces.ed.gov/programs/coe/indicator_cgf.asp.*

U.S. Department of Education, Institute of Education Sciences, National Center for Education Evaluation and Regional Assistance, What Works Clearinghouse (2006). Intervention report: Instructional conversations and literature logs. Retrieved from *http://ies.ed.gov/ncee/wwc/pdf/intervention_reports/WWC_ICLL_102606.pdf.*

Vaughn, S., Linan-Thompson, S., Mathes, P. G., Cirino, P. T., Carlson, C. D., Pollard-Durodola, S. D., et al. (2006). Effectiveness of Spanish intervention for first-grade English language learners at risk for reading difficulties. *Journal of Learning Disabilities, 39,* 56–73.

Vaughn, S., Martinez, L. R., Linan-Thompson, S., Reutebuch, C. K., Carlson, C. D., & Francis, D. J. (2009). Enhancing social studies vocabulary and comprehension for seventh-grade English language learners: Findings from two experimental studies. *Journal of Research on Educational Effectiveness, 2*(4), 297–324.

CHAPTER 9

The Power of Preschool Peers to Influence Social Outcomes for Children with Special Needs

PHILLIP S. STRAIN and EDWARD H. BOVEY II

In this chapter, we describe the step-by-step procedures for implementing peer-mediated intervention for social skills at the preschool level. We begin by reviewing some of the needs experienced by young children with significant social delays. Next, we review three decades of precedent research aimed at improving the social skills and relationships of preschool-age children with autism spectrum disorder (ASD) and other significant developmental concerns. This research has focused on the utilization of typically developing peers as agents of intervention, culminating in a comprehensive treatment model, the Learning Experiences an Alternative Program for Preschoolers and Parents (LEAP) Preschool, which embodies much of the learning from this research. Next, we provide the reader with a detailed description of the procedural aspects of peer-mediated intervention. Finally, we consider some lessons learned about the conditions that enhance the impact of peer-mediated intervention in the social domain.

YOUNG CHILDREN WITH SOCIAL DELAYS

Perhaps the most conspicuous group of children who experience significant social delays are children with ASD. Indeed, social delays are a defining characteristic of this population as ASD is, in part, defined by persistent deficits in social communication and social interaction, including deficits in social reciprocity, nonverbal communication, and developing and maintaining relationships (American Psychiatric Association, 2013). While there is great variability within this clinical group, it is not uncommon for preschoolers with ASD to actively avoid social contact, seldom if ever, initiate social interactions, and more often than not fail to respond to the social initiations of others. While most of the research on peer-mediated strategies has focused on this population, the strategies have been replicated widely. Many other groups of children experience significant social delays, including children with mental retardation, children with emotional and behavioral disorders, multiply disabled children, and children at risk due to poverty. Indeed, the peer-mediated strategies discussed in this chapter have been replicated across each of these groups (see Kohler & Strain, 1990).

Besides peer-mediated intervention strategies, most of the other intervention research has focused on adults teaching discrete social skills in one-to-one, adult–child arrangements (see Goldstein, Lackey, & Schneider, 2014, for review) or evaluated a social skills curriculum delivered by adults in the context of a preschool setting (see Joseph & Strain, 2003, for review). It is clear that both alternatives yield benefits, but with limitations. The one-to-one tutorial approach has failed to yield behavioral changes beyond the confines of the original instructional settings (Turner-Brown, Perry, Dichter, Bodfish, & Penn, 2008). The curricular approaches have shown better generalized outcomes, but results have not been particularly strong for children with developmental disorders (Barton et al., 2013).

STUDIES THAT SET THE STAGE FOR PEER-MEDIATED INTERVENTION

With the benefit of hindsight, it is clear that the significant social behavior benefits for participants in our research program have been dependent on questioning basic assumptions and practices regarding: (1) the assessment of social behavior, (2) what should be the foci for change, and (3) who are the best intervention agents.

Assessment of Social Behavior

Regarding the social behavior of young children with ASD and other developmental concerns, years ago early intervention work focused exclusively on changing discrete, singular behaviors of individuals. Social behaviors were measured in a fashion identical to reciting math facts or staying on task during pre-academic instruction. In fact, there was nothing particularly social about early behavioral measures of intervention outcomes. Beginning in 1974, Strain and colleagues (Strain & Timm, 1974) began to use an observational coding system that would capture the dyadic or reciprocal nature of social behavior, thereby preserving essential information regarding who does what with whom and with what behavioral effects. With such a coding system it was shown in a series of studies that adult-mediated prompting and social reinforcement directed to an individual or toward that individual's peer group equally affected the social behavior of all parties (Strain, Shores, & Kerr, 1976; Strain & Timm, 1974). This finding helped solve the troubling educational challenge of delivering social reinforcement in a fashion that would not result in class peers feeling either singled out or unfairly ignored.

Over the years, the essentials of this observational system remained intact, with additions focusing on a more finely grained portrayal of specific social behaviors (e.g., sharing, asking someone to play, and demonstrating affection). Interestingly enough, this coding system has been used with study participants across an 80-year age span and with participants identified as having learning disabilities, ASD, behavioral disorders, and multiple disabilities. More important, the coding system has generated information on a wide variety of intervention issues. For example, the code has shown that where generalization across settings does occur, it is attributable to high levels of peer responsiveness in these settings. Likewise, when generalization does not occur, it is the consequence of minimal peer responsiveness in these settings (Hecimovic, Fox, Shores, & Strain, 1985; Strain, 1983). The code has also revealed that day-to-day variability in children's social behavior during active intervention is also a direct consequence of peer responsiveness (Kohler, Strain, & Shearer, 1992).

At a more macro level of analysis, the code has been of significant value as well. For example, inclusive early childhood settings alone have been found to have a facilitative impact on the social interactions of preschoolers with ASD. On the other hand, autism-only settings appear to be developmentally toxic when social behavior is considered (Strain, McGee, & Kohler, 2001). Moreover, the code has been used to determine the degree and quality of social integration in inclusive preschool settings (Kohler & Strain, 1996). While there is no direct evidence to link the development of our social interaction coding system to improved quality-of-life outcomes for individuals, an inferential case can be made. For example, prior efforts to explain the lack of generalization associated with social skill interventions focused on either faulty instructional tactics or learner characteristics. It would not be too harsh to describe this prevailing logic as classical victim blaming. That is, if generalization did not occur, then the learners' "defective" mental processes were likely to blame. In sharp contrast, the coding system has placed the spotlight for the lack or presence of generalization on the responsiveness of peers in the generalization setting itself. Moreover, the use of this coding system in inclusive as well as developmentally segregated settings for young children with ASD has questioned, in no uncertain terms, the prevailing mode of service delivery. Access to more inclusive settings for young children with ASD can represent access to the most effective intervention strategies for addressing the core social deficit of ASD (Strain et al., 2001; Strain, Schwartz, & Barton, 2012).

What Are the Key Social Behaviors to Target?

When we began our peer-mediated intervention studies, the prevailing strategy for determining which social skills to increase rested on a simple deficit model. If children did not greet others, then greeting was taught, and so on. While this approach may be reasonable for children with limited skill deficits, it is inefficient for youngsters with more pervasive needs. Simply put, the universe of potential social skills to teach is endless. We felt there had to be a better strategy—a strategy that would permit some logical, empirically defensible prioritization of skills to teach.

A series of naturalistic observation studies (e.g., Strain, 1983; Tremblay, Strain, Hendrickson, & Shores, 1981) was launched in an attempt to specify behaviors and patterns of behavior that distinguish the interactions of young children with friends, whether or not those children have disabilities. At the level of discrete behaviors, four essential skills emerged: (1) sharing toys and materials, (2) organizing play by making suggestions as to what to do (e.g., "Let's play trucks"), (3) assisting others (e.g., showing where a puzzle piece goes, helping a friend climb up a jungle gym), and (4) showing affection when a peer is hurt (e.g., saying "that's OK" and giving a hug). Interestingly, the information that emerged from this empirical analysis revealed that, in addition to discrete skills, *patterns* of behavior were equally important for the development of friendships. Specifically, for preschool children to have friends, it is important for them to engage in social exchanges of a minimum length. For preschoolers, length is not simply a matter of time but rather a matter of the number of turns in an interaction episode. On average, preschool children with friends have interactions that consist of at least four social turns. Children without friends often engage in the same discrete behavior (e.g., sharing, assistance), but their exchanges are fleeting (Tremblay et al., 1981) and appear to hold little developmental significance. Thus, one of the major scientific contributions from this line of research is this "empirical definition" of the often elusive concept of social responsiveness. By preserving sequences of behavior across time the code was able to reveal critical aspects of peer social behavior beyond discrete skills.

Determining the Best Intervention Agents

Initial attempts at social behavior intervention in the field as a whole involved the exclusive use of teacher-manipulated antecedent and consequent events. By far, the most immediate changes in child behaviors were produced by combining various antecedents (e.g., teachers' verbal and physical prompting) with contingent social attention from adults (Strain et al., 1976; Strain & Timm, 1974).

Although we were successful in making rather profound improvements in the social responsiveness of young children, it was clear that they immediately returned to their isolate behavior patterns when intervention was terminated. In part, we suspected that the lack of maintenance was an artifact of the research designs that we employed. Specifically, when rich, relatively continuous reinforcement schedules are begun, suddenly withdrawn, and reinstated, requirements for demonstrating experimental control usually are met. Unfortunately, when such powerful control of behavior is obtained, children may quickly discriminate that a particular time or setting is an occasion to be social, and all other occasions are periods for isolation.

In an attempt to reduce the effects of sudden condition shifts on children's behavior, we employed response-dependent prompt fading and adult social reinforcement schedule thinning with three preschool boys with ASD (Timm, Strain, & Eller, 1979). After a period of 40 days under response-dependent conditions, two of the three boys' positive interactions were being maintained by one prompting and one reinforcement event per 5 minutes.

It was at this rather optimistic point in the development of teacher-mediated intervention that the data became much less impressive. Going back to original observation protocols from earlier teacher-mediated intervention studies, we asked the question (using conditional probability analyses), "What are the immediate temporal consequences of reinforcement delivery?" Simply put, we found that the immediate consequence of reinforcement delivery by adults was the termination of child–child interaction. For example, if two children were sharing blocks and the adult said, "Good, you're sharing so nicely," the immediate impact was a cessation in sharing followed by both children physically orienting toward the adult. Although the overall, day-to-day effect of intervention was positive, reinforcement delivery unintentionally limited the duration of social exchanges (Shores, Hester, & Strain, 1976). Given these intervention limitations and logistical complexities, we began a systematic study of the potential use of peers as more natural instructional agents.

An analysis of the peer social intervention literature suggests a few distinct criteria for selection of the peer trainer:

1. The child must attend preschool regularly, to ensure uninterrupted intervention.
2. The child must display positive social initiations during free-play periods.
3. The child must follow adult directions reliably.

Unlike many job descriptions, this one does not include minimum age (peer trainer ages have ranged from 2 years to 80 years), previous experience (only one had prior training), or a certain type of education (several of the peer trainers were themselves enrolled in classes for children with behavioral disorders).

In one study, data collected during five pre-baseline free-play sessions supported the choice of the peer trainer (Strain, Kerr, & Ragland, 1979). This child exhibited the greatest vocabulary and played for longer periods of time than others in his class. In other investigations, teachers simply nominated the peers as trainers. Despite such an informal selection procedure, none of the peer trainers (a total of 55 in our studies) required replacement, and all proved successful at their task.

Teaching a child to alter the isolate behavior of others seems like a major undertaking. Yet, our studies have relied on a rather simple role-playing and rehearsal format that takes place before any actual intervention sessions. The child is given an explanation of the task, such as "try hard to get others to play with you." "Training to expect rejections" is accomplished through a role-play strategy in which the adult ignores every other initiation by the peer trainer, explains this behavior, and finally encourages the peer trainer: "Keep trying, even when children don't play at first" (Strain, Shores, & Timm, 1977, p. 291).

These training steps were repeated, usually in four 20-minute daily sessions, until the peer trainer could reliably make social bids to the occasionally reluctant adult. In one study involving a peer trainer with mental retardation (Young & Kerr, 1979), the initial training required more time and structure. A verbal request to play was taught first. Then, the peer was taught to make this request while handing the adult a toy. These practice sessions continued until the peer trainer initiated appropriately on 80% of the role plays.

In all studies, the peer trainer rehearsed in the actual play setting and used toys that were selected, based on careful reinforcer preference assessment, for the isolate children. The adult frequently praised the peer trainer's efforts during this practice. Praise has been supplemented during some of the studies by tangible rewards.

LAYING THE GROUNDWORK FOR PEER-MEDIATED INSTRUCTION

As with most structured interventions to promote children's social interactions there are various steps that practitioners can take to maximize the impact of peer-mediated social skills training. These steps, as enumerated below, involve purposeful planning around the overall classroom environment, general social promotion strategies, and the use of play activities that enhance social interactions.

Assessing the Classroom Environment

The classroom environment plays a critical role in the number of opportunities for social interactions among children. There are five basic steps staff should follow to ensure that social interactions are occurring in the classroom.

1. Teachers must plan for how they will encourage social interactions during curriculum planning meetings.
2. Teachers need to make time to teach social skills (either during structured group times or in small groups).
3. Staff need to arrange the environment to promote social interactions by choosing materials with high social value and limiting selected materials so children have to share.
4. Adults need to regularly prompt for interactions between children.
5. Staff should have a plan in place to reinforce child-to-child interactions to ensure their continued occurrence.

	Yes	Sometimes	No
1. Are there typically developing children available for daily interaction?			
2. Are all class activities structured to promote social interactions?			
3. Are typically developing children offered specific and consistent instruction to foster interaction with peers?			
4. Are interactions mostly child directed, not teacher directed, during free play?			
5. Are social skills goals included in children's IEPs?			
6. Do teachers provide children with positive feedback when they are playing nicely together?			
7. Does the teacher help by supporting and suggesting play ideas?			

FIGURE 9.1. Social interaction procedural checklist.

Figure 9.1 is designed to help adults assess the children's environment. The more questions for which you can answer "yes," the more opportunities there are for social interactions in your classroom.

STRATEGIES FOR PROMOTING SOCIAL INTERACTIONS

The following are general ideas and strategies teachers can use to increase social interactions in the classroom.

Set Up/Arrange Materials

Set up or arrange materials for an activity in advance that are novel or unique to the area. Unusual materials are a good way to facilitate a reaction. Other materials that are not typical for the activity or arranged in advance may be spontaneously brought into the area once the interest and nature of the child's play becomes more evident. Materials that are planned in advance of the activity may not always fit the child's interest during the activity. The following are examples.

1. The teacher places a box of large cardboard blocks in the gross motor area

for the children to stack at the bottom of the slide. Children enjoy sliding down the slide and knocking over the blocks.

2. The teacher places letter cards on the side of a climber in the gross motor area. Alex (the focal child) directs the teacher to crawl her toy dinosaur up the cards by naming the letter on the next card he wants the dinosaur to crawl on.

3. The teacher encourages Alex and two other children to bring cars over to the slide for races. She directs the children to hold the cars up at the top and wait for Alex to say, "Ready, set, go!"

Join the Activity

Join the activity to enrich the quality of the child's play and/or participation. Assume an activity-related role in play with the child. This involves more than actively commenting on what the child is or may be doing during the activity. The following are examples.

1. After reading a book about cowboys, the teacher assumes the role of a bad guy, steals some food from the table where Mike is playing (sociodramatic area), then encourages Mike to be the sheriff and capture her.

2. The teacher takes on the role of a small creature she is manipulating. The creature she is holding keeps trying to get the lid off a container that holds more creatures that Alex wants. She seeks directions from Alex during the play and encourages him to chant, "Pull, pull" as the creature attempts to lift the lid.

3. The teacher actively participates in a game of basketball with Alex and his peers. She occasionally steals the ball and runs with it, she holds the ball beyond the children's reach, and redirects the ball back to Alex's hands as needed.

Require Expansion

Require expansion in response to a child's initiation by asking follow-up questions or by intentionally delaying a response to the child in an effort to make the child repeat or elaborate on his verbalization. The following are examples.

1. Once Alex has made a basic request for a toy, the teacher withholds the toy and asks a series of questions to gain more information and extend the interaction. "You want the car. What color is it?" "Is it a big or little car?" "Where are you going to take it?"

2. The teacher acts like she does not hear Mike's request to stack the blocks; she holds the block, turning it over and over while looking across the room. Mike repeats the request with more specific details about where and how

to stack it. The teacher responds to these repeated overtures by complying with the child's requests.

Encourage Activity-Related Talk

Encourage activity-related talk by modeling or inviting participation in songs/nursery rhymes, chanting, reading, counting, or appropriate reciting. The following are examples.

1. The teacher slowly sings "Three Little Monkeys" and plays the part of the alligator, while the children work to keep the monkeys away from her.
2. The teacher models, and then encourages Mike to say, "Ready, set, go" as other children get ready to slide into the blocks at the bottom of the climber.
3. The teacher invites Mike to say "1, 2, 3, go" as the other children prepare to race their cars down the slide.
4. The teacher models lines from a Winnie the Pooh book that Mike knows well to encourage him to interact with peers.
5. The teacher directs Alex to count blocks as they are being stacked at the bottom of the slide.

Invite the Child to Direct Teacher Behaviors

While playing with the child, situations occur in which she or he can direct the play scenario. The teacher can then ask the child questions related to her role in their play together. Caution should be taken to have such questions flow naturally during play. The child should not be inundated with questions related to the teacher's role in the activity. The questions are most natural when both teacher and child are working together to solve a problem during play. The following are examples.

1. The teacher intentionally gets some creatures "stuck" in a place out of Alex's reach. The teacher asks, "Alex, they are stuck! What should I do?" He responds by telling the teacher to pull hard or lift him up so he can try. He takes on a very active role in directing the teacher's behaviors so he can get his creatures.
2. The teacher could intentionally stack the blocks incorrectly, violating Alex's expectations. He would immediately react, and she could ask him to explain how to correctly stack them.

Encourage Focal Child–Peer Interactions

Encourage focal child–peer interactions by inviting children to attend to each other and play together. The teacher wants the children to join in an activity together, without prompting for verbal or nonverbal interaction. The following are examples.

1. The teacher sets up an activity where Mike pretends to be Tigger. The teacher then asks two peers if they would like to be Winnie the Pooh and Piglet.
2. The teacher notices a peer building a road in the block area and tells the child to look at Alex and ask if he would like to help.

Invite Children to Exchange Materials

Sharing is an important social behavior, but one that often needs to be directly taught and prompted for. Teachers can facilitate sharing and exchanging materials in a variety of ways. The following are examples.

1. The teacher asks Mike to hand a peer a block to help build a tower.
2. A group of children race cars down the slide. After the race, the teacher tells Alex to give his friends their cars so they can race again.
3. Several children are having a tea party. The teacher tells Alex to hand cups and cookies to each peer.

Invite Children to Talk or Engage in Nonverbal Interactions

Invite children to talk to each other or engage in nonverbal interactions by prompting either the focal child or the peer(s). The following are examples.

1. After they win the basketball game, the teacher suggests that the team members give each other a high five.
2. The teacher encourages children to include Mike in their plans and be sure to ask him for his ideas.
3. The teacher asks Mike to pick which peer would be next to knock over the stack of blocks and then prompts Mike to say, "Ready, set, go!" at the right time.

PLAY ACTIVITIES FOR PROMOTING SOCIAL INTERACTIONS

The toys, materials, and activities you make available in the classroom can help promote social interactions. While many early childhood teachers set up activities so each child has his or her own materials (cup of crayons, scissors, glue sticks, etc.), this approach can greatly inhibit peer-to-peer social interactions. If you limit the materials that are available and insist that materials be shared or provide toys that require two children to operate, there will be more opportunities for children to play together. By being thoughtful in how you set up activities, important skills such as sharing and taking turns will occur more naturally. Below we outline suggestions across a variety of typical early childhood classroom activities for using your materials thoughtfully to promote interaction between children in the classroom.

Art Activities

Examples of Materials

- Crayons
- Watercolor paint
- Stickers
- Paint dabbers

- Markers
- Tempura paint
- Glue bottles and sticks
- Scissors

- Fingerpaint
- Stamps
- Chalk and chalk boards
- Tape

Traditional Use of Art Materials

All children are given paper and their own art materials (crayons, markers, paints, scissors, etc.), allowing each child to work at his or her own pace and complete the project independently. Children stand on opposite sides of a painting easel working independently on their own pictures.

Using Materials to Promote Social Interactions

Using the same activities you can reorganize the materials to encourage sharing, working together, and cooperative play.

- Place crayons and/or markers in cups and have two to three children share a cup, asking each other for the cup when they need a different color.
- Limit the number of glue sticks or glue containers to encourage children to ask for turns.
- Have children work collaboratively on large pieces of paper at the art easel or stand two easels next to each other and have children paint side by side so they can view and comment on each other's work.

Dramatic Play

Examples of Materials

- Dress-up clothes
- Doctor's kit
- Camping equipment
- Shoes
- Kitchen (food, pots, pans)
- Stuffed animals (vet clinic)

- Community helpers (fireman, police, etc.)
- Grocery carts, cash register
- Babies
- Birthday party materials
- Barber shop/beauty salon
- Construction equipment

Traditional Use of Dramatic Play Materials

Most early childhood classrooms have a house/dramatic play area that is stocked with traditional house items (play food, pots and pans, dress-up clothes, baby dolls). These materials are usually available in the play area, and children can choose to play with them if they want to. However, over the course of the school year, these same materials lose their luster and become less interesting to the children because of their constant availability. Additionally, children's roles become stagnant and predictable (e.g., Mom, Dad, child).

Using Materials to Promote Social Interactions

Periodically changing the materials and theme of the dramatic play area promotes children's interest and engagement and helps support the development of pretend play skills. Changing the materials also lets children take on a variety of new roles, which encourages more advanced pretend play. Below are some examples of ways to promote additional social interactions.

- Identify themes for your dramatic play area, set up materials in advance, and preteach possible roles and play sequences with the class before free play.
- Introduce simple, single themes and give children time to develop the themes.
- Assist in setting up play scenarios by suggesting roles to the children and helping them learn the roles.
- Add novel and "real-life" materials to the play area.
- Pair children who need exposure to new sociodramatic activities with children who are familiar with the activity.

Sensory Activities

Examples of Materials

- Sand (wet or dry)
- Birdseed
- Macaroni/pasta
- Bowls, cups
- Scoops and rakes
- Animals, people, fish
- Water
- Rice
- Cornmeal
- Measuring cups
- Cars, trucks, boats
- Shells, stones
- Beans
- Dirt
- Scrap paper
- Funnels
- Spray bottles
- Scissors

Traditional Use of Sensory Materials

One "messy" table with one kind of material is in the classroom, generally with the long side of the rectangular table pushed against a wall. The material in the table usually remains the same for long periods, or, conversely, the table is rarely opened because of the potential mess it creates. Strict limits are placed on the number of children who can play at the table (one or two children), or sufficient materials are provided (cups, buckets, scoops, etc.) so children can all play independently at the table.

Using Materials to Promote Social Interactions

Here again, some quick modifications can greatly enhance the social value of these sensory play experiences.

- Move the "messy" table away from the wall or push the short side of the table against the wall so children can stand on the long sides facing each other and in closer proximity to each other.
- Frequently change the materials in the table to maintain novelty and attract children consistently to the activity.
- Limit materials in the table (one large bucket, one or two shovels) to encourage and promote sharing.
- Encourage children to bury/hide materials for their friends to find.
- Encourage children to share materials and take turns with preferred items.

Manipulative Activities

Examples of Materials

- Small blocks
- Bristle blocks
- Sorting bears
- Play-Doh

- Puzzles
- Lego/Duplo blocks
- Mr. Potato Head
- Theraputty

- Peg boards
- Lincoln Logs
- Magnet tiles

Traditional Use of Manipulative Materials

Each child is given or has a basket of manipulatives to play with. Children generally play independently with their materials. Limited interactions take place between children.

Using Materials to Promote Social Interactions

Set up the area with designated materials available and regularly rotate the manipulatives to encourage interest. Utilize materials that encourage children to play and work collaboratively.

- Put a student "in charge" of the materials. Other students must ask the materials captain to pass them some materials.
- Encourage children to work together on puzzles, building, etc.
- Have one child select the materials and another child direct the action (where to put the Mr. Potato part).

PEER-MEDIATED STRATEGIES:
THE SOCIAL SKILLS CURRICULUM

This social skills curriculum has been developed over the past 30 years and has been extensively researched in early childhood settings (Strain & Bovey, 2008). It continues to be utilized as a tool for parents and teachers in increasing levels of interaction between children. This is especially important for students in inclusive classroom settings since some children with disabilities exhibit decreased levels of social interaction (Strain, Kohler, Storey, & Danko, 1994). The current curriculum consists of five social skills that were chosen because evidence suggests that they result in more lengthy interactions between children and create the potential for the development of friendships (Kohler et al., 1992). The five skills are:

1. Getting your friend's attention
2. Sharing—giving something to a peer
3. Sharing—asking for something from a peer
4. Play organizers—giving a peer a direction around play
5. Compliments—giving a compliment to a peer

The following scripts are for teachers and parents to use when teaching the social skills curriculum. The purpose of these scripts is to establish the appropriate steps in the instruction process as well as to give adults potential things to say to their audience about each skill. Social skill instruction for each skill follows the same sequence: (1) describing the skill, (2) demonstrating the skill with an adult, 3) demonstrating the skill incorrectly, (4) having a child demonstrate with an adult, (5) having a child practice the skill with another child, and (6) reviewing the reinforcement strategy. Consistently following this sequence provides children with predictability within the routine and supports their skill acquisition. A great opportunity for teaching the skills is to utilize 2 or 3 minutes during your structured large-group time (e.g., circle time). For the greatest impact from your instruction you should do your social skills instruction as the last activity in your large group before going to center time (free play), when the children will be expected to use the targeted skill(s). Teach one skill a day until the steps involved in that skill are well understood by the children and children are demonstrating use of the skill throughout free play times. Always review all skills previously learned before moving on to new skills. In addition to the verbal instruction, we suggest the utilization of posters that accompany each skill to provide a visual reminder of the steps required to complete each skill. The posters can be used during instruction and then hung in toy/play areas of the classroom or home where children will have opportunities to interact.

We encourage teachers to be creative when teaching these skills. Children respond well to puppets acting out the various social skills. They also enjoy watching their teachers role-play these skills, especially when teachers demonstrate the wrong way to interact. When they exaggerate these interactions, it drives home the point, and children see how silly the wrong way can be. While it can take time for teachers to become comfortable with the presentation of these skills, consistent delivery of the content will enable them to develop their own style of presenting the skills. To facilitate this process we have included two sample scripts (see Appendices 9.1 and 9.2) for providing social skills instruction to large groups of students.

Creating the Posters for Social Skills Instruction

The following section contains pictures, adult tip sheets, and scripts with which to teach children social skills. Use the pictures for each skill to create the posters designed to prompt children to practice the skills. Add the adult tip sheets to the backs of the posters to provide yourself with the steps for training each skill (see Figure 9.2). Use the scripts as reminders of what to say when completing the training with the children.

The posters can serve two purposes when using the social skills package: (1) they can be displayed during training when you are giving descriptions of the skills, and (2) they can serve as reminders of the skills after the training, when the children are involved in a play activity. Feel free to call the children's attention to them during play, saying, "Remember to _____."

During training present the posters while you are describing the skill. Be sure to point out what the pictures represent (e.g., "Look, the bug in the picture got the other bug's attention and now he's sharing the soccer ball."). After training the posters should be placed where the children can easily see them while they are involved in a play activity. You can make several copies to put in all the play centers. Or you can move the posters to where the children are playing. By pointing to these posters and giving verbal reminders, you can prompt the children to use the skills that they have learned.

There are five posters, one representing each of the skills to be taught: (1) Getting your friend's attention; (2) Sharing—giving something to a peer; (3) Sharing—

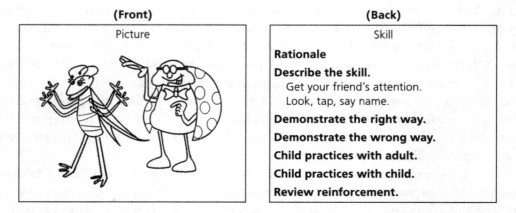

FIGURE 9.2. Sample for creating a social skills poster.

asking for something from a peer; (4) Play organizers; (5) Compliments. For each poster there is one picture and a corresponding tip sheet (see Figures 9.3 and 9.4 on the next page). The scripts familiarize teachers with the steps within each skill, and they provide suggestions on what exactly to say when presenting them.

The following are suggestions for making these posters:

1. Use bright colors to color in the pictures.
2. Poster board may be used as backing for the posters to strengthen them and enable them to last for years to come.
3. If possible, laminate the pictures onto the poster board.
4. Place the cheat sheet on the back of the poster.

Prompting and Reinforcing Social Interactions

It is important for teachers to learn how to prompt students to interact in ways that keep the children's play natural, fun, and continuing. Remember the following points when prompting and reinforcing children:

- *Place children in positions where they can interact.* If you have four children, place two children together so they can play with each other. If you only have three, try to give two children turns to be together.

- *Be sure children look at each other and use names.* Many times a child will be talking to another child, but that child will not know because he is not in view or did not hear his name. You can say, "Who are you talking to? Say his name." "Are you looking at your friend? He can't hear you."

- *Remind children to try again if they do not get a response.* Many times a child will not respond to another child's initiations. Tell the child to try again a few more times by saying something again or tapping a child on the shoulder for attention. If a child still does not respond, you may want to help a little if possible and always be sure to reinforce the child for trying.

- *Remind children to "play with your friends."* This simple reminder may be all that is needed at times to promote interactions.

- *Tell children exactly what to say in simple sentences.* Many times children need help in coming up with an interaction statement. You may have to specifically tell them what to say to their friend:

    o Say, "Give it to me, Sally."
    o Say, "Put it here, John."
    o Say, "Come over here, Joey."

- Arrange materials so they are more social. Sometimes you can create lengthy interactions by using the techniques listed and arranging materials in a specific way. For example, if children are doing puzzles, you can place two children near each other and tell them to help each other put a puzzle together. Give all the

FIGURE 9.3. Social skills poster: Getting Attention (front).

Skill 1
Getting Attention

- Rationale.

- Describe the skill.
  - ➤ Look at your friend.
  - ➤ Tap your friend's shoulder.
  - ➤ Say your friend's name.

- Demonstrate.
  - ➤ The right way.
  - ➤ The wrong way.

- Practice.
  - ➤ Child with adult.
  - ➤ Child with child.

- Review reinforcement.

FIGURE 9.4. Social skills poster: Getting Attention (back).

pieces to one child and tell him or her to hand them one at a time to the other child to put in. To John you might say:

  o "Give a piece to Joe."
  o "Say, 'Here John.'"
  o "Put it right in his hand."
  o "Did he do it?"
  o "Give him five."

• Reinforce interactions. If you see children interacting, wait until the interaction is over. Then make reinforcing statements such as:

  o "You are such a good friend helping Cindy like that."
  o "I like the way you are all playing together."
  o "What good friends you are."
  o "Did you make that together?"

When children hear such statements they will interact more easily.

Finally, it is important to remember that social interactions do not and should not be occurring all the time. Thus, we need to be mindful of the prompting that adults provide to children around social interactions. The following are important reminders to teachers and parents to fully support and encourage peer social interactions.

1. Don't make children interact all the time. If you see a natural peer social opportunity, then prompt for it. Try for approximately five interactions to occur per activity—not the entire time.
2. Children sometimes give more physical help to another child than is necessary. Remind them to ask or talk to their friends first.
3. Don't interrupt a peer-to-peer interaction. If you want to reinforce children for interacting or playing together, wait until the interaction has ended.
4. Stand back when you can and let children play. If you are in the direct area of the children all of the time, they tend to interact with you rather than with each other.

LESSONS LEARNED ABOUT PEER-MEDIATED INTERVENTIONS

The peer-mediated social skill intervention is designed to occur within the context of preschool/PreK classrooms. The preschool context can be thought of as a mediator of effects, with key dimensions of preschool environments having an influence on the success of the peer-mediated social skills intervention. Over the course of conducting the intervention across a wide variety of settings, three dimensions seem crucial: the ratio of typically developing children to those with social needs, the organization of adults within the classroom, and the utilization of materials and toys to maintain children's interest. Next we describe each of these factors.

The Ratio of Typically Developing Children to Children with Social Needs Is Critical

When LEAP began, the classroom composition was six typically developing children and six children with autism. Classrooms ran efficiently, outcomes were quite satisfying, and all seemed fine with this arbitrary 50:50 ratio. We observed that when classrooms are populated with equal or fewer numbers of typically developing children, (1) peers needed more and more reinforcement to maintain contact with classmates and (2) on many occasions during choice time children with skill deficits would be in close proximity to each other, often resulting in what appeared to be a "contagion effect" around problem behavior. That is, when one child started to engage in problem behaviors, others would follow.

A ratio of two or three typically developing children to every child with social needs and a maximum of 15 children are recommended. Observed benefits include: (1) natural groupings of children almost always provide typical peer models for children with social needs, (2) typical peers almost always have other typical peers with whom to interact, (3) multiple peers take turns interacting with classmates, providing essential generalization opportunities and eliminating burnout of typical peers, and (4) teachers are much more capable of individualizing social skill instruction, collecting daily data, and making instructional decisions based upon their data.

Adult Organization and Clear Roles and Responsibilities Affect Children's Learning

One hallmark of an efficient and effective preschool classroom is adults' ongoing, active engagement with children in the classroom. Every minute adults spend organizing materials, planning an activity, or discussing how to conduct an activity with other adults during classroom time results in lost opportunities for naturalistic social skill instruction. To maximize children's engagement, necessary for the implementation of naturalistic teaching, two key adult strategies are needed. First, staff must utilize a zone-based approach to classroom management, dividing the classroom into different, concurrent areas or activities throughout most of the day. McGee, Morrier, and Daly (1999) define a zone as "more than just the physical area of the center, but also the goal, activity, environmental arrangement, and teaching routine." Instead of adults being assigned a certain group of children for whom they are responsible, they are responsible for providing instruction to the children who choose to participate in activities in an assigned classroom zone. This offers two key advantages over a traditional child-focused or person-to-person approach. One, a zone-based approach allows for more fluid transitions within the classroom, decreasing idle wait time and reducing the associated inappropriate social behaviors that often accompany waiting. Second, because children are receiving instruction from a variety of adults and peers across different areas and activities, generalization of social behaviors is addressed directly.

To effectively manage a zone-based approach in the classroom, adults need to have a clear understanding of their roles and their responsibility for monitoring the various zones and then develop an adult schedule for the day to ensure all zones and activities are prepared and monitored (see Figure 9.5). As part of this schedule, time is allocated for adults to set up materials for activities prior to the children arriving at the center or activity. When children arrive, a teacher is waiting with the materials available for meeting students' needs so that they can immediately engage in the activity. Staff rotate responsibilities for teaching lessons, which enables them to gain experience and expertise in all teaching areas.

Toys and Materials Must Be Carefully Selected

Children learn by doing and through active participation with materials. Why then do many teachers insist on large-group (circle) times where the decidedly nonsocial expected behavioral response is simply to sit, listen, and watch the teacher (Hoyson, Jamieson, & Strain, 1984; Sainato, Lyon, & Strain, 1987; Winett & Winkler, 1972)? Large-group times need to be as active and social as other times of the day

Activity	Responsibilities
Table Time	Greeting/Sign in: Lisa Table 1: Ginny Table 2: Kelly
Circle	Teach: Ginny Monitor: Lisa Set up centers: Kelly
Centers	Monitor Zone 1: Ginny Monitor Zone 2: Lisa Monitor Zone 3: Kelly
Story Circle	Teach: Kelly Monitor: Ginny Set up snack: Lisa
Snack	Table 1: Lisa Table 2: Ginny Monitor/books: Kelly
Outside	Swings: Kelly Slide: Lisa Monitor: Ginny
Closing Circle	Teach: Lisa Monitor: Kelly Backpacks: Ginny

FIGURE 9.5. Adult responsibility schedule.

through the use of materials, song props, motor movement, and finger plays. For example, all of the traditional preschool songs used during circle time are chosen because they either utilize props that can be passed out and collected by a child or they have specific motor actions (with props or finger plays) that go with the song. This allows children to participate at a variety of different levels (e.g., socially or by watching, motor participation, verbal participation, and combining motor and verbal participation).

Similarly, big books, the use of puppets, felt boards, and/or having the children act out a story with props and materials during story time are more exciting and engaging ways to conduct this routine, both for typically developing children and children with social needs. Similar to the large-group time example, story time often consists of a teacher sitting in front of the children reading a story with the behavioral expectation that the children simply sit and listen. Providing children with additional visual stimuli, props, and/or opportunities for social or motor participation changes the behavioral expectation and allows for more active forms of child participation.

Two of the most common reasons for low levels of engagement in classrooms are that the children are bored with the toys and activities (centers) in the classroom and that they lack the skills necessary to initiate and sustain their play (Lawry, Danko, & Strain, 2000). This is true of all children. The implementation of a toy rotation (systematically varying the toys available in a play area) has been shown to increase engagement levels by over 10% in less than 1 month (McGee, Daly, Izeman, Mann, & Risley, 1991), and rotating different centers in the classroom on a weekly basis can provide an additional boost. It is, however, important to note that if children lack the skills to sustain their play in a center, additional time with those materials may be required to teach the necessary skill set so that children can maintain their independent behavior. Thus, it becomes a balance between giving children enough time with specific materials to learn how to use them and maintain their engagement and making sure that materials and centers are rotated on a frequent enough basis to maintain novelty and interest.

RESEARCH FINDINGS

In implementing peer-mediated interventions over the last 40 years, practitioners have often expressed concerns about possible negative impacts on typical peers. Interestingly, the impact on typical peers provides some of the most compelling evidence in support of this intervention approach. Two studies are of particular relevance in this regard. In the first study, peers participating in peer-mediated intervention for a 2-year period as part of the LEAP preschool model were compared on standardized measures of cognitive, language, social development, and problem behavior to comparable children enrolled in preschool settings with no special needs children and with no use of peer-mediated intervention. No differences were observed between groups except in problem behavior, in which children in LEAP who received instruction in peer-mediated strategies engaged in significantly fewer episodes of tantrums, opposition to adult requests, and aggression toward peers (Strain & Hoyson, 2000).

In the second study, 40 typical 4- and 5-year-old children were randomly selected from among LEAP enrollees and compared on a measure of peer social acceptance with 40 children of similar ages who were nominated by their teachers as the "social stars" of their class (Strain & Hoyson, 2000). The social stars had no exposure to peer-mediated intervention or children with special needs. After 1 year of enrollment, profound differences were noted between groups. When exposed to a video of a child labeled as "not like you" who was unsuccessful at putting a puzzle together, the "social stars" suggested that these children "should be punished" and that "children like that are no good." Conversely, children who had a history as peer mediators suggested overwhelmingly that "they could help the child with the puzzle" (Strain & Hoyson, 2000).

This simple study suggests that participation as an intervention agent can alter the entire social ecology for children with special needs. It also highlights the fact that social behavior change is not like any other developmental domain. Here, one needs a partner to succeed, and the dispositions and skills that a partner brings have a profound impact on children's opportunities for development.

In addition to the social outcomes identified above, for participants in peer-mediated intervention a number of broader short- and long-term outcomes have been achieved, including:

1. Typically developing peers as young as 36 months can be taught to utilize facilitative social and communicative initiations with their peers with ASD (Goldstein & Wickstrom, 1986; Strain & Danko, 1995; Strain & Bovey, 2008).
2. Peers' use of facilitative strategies results in higher rates of communicative interaction for preschoolers with ASD (Goldstein & Wickstrom, 1986; Strain, 1987; Kohler & Strain, 1999).
3. The peer facilitative strategies produce "day one" effects, suggesting that the delayed social and communicative abilities of many young children with autism may be attributable, in part, to the socially nonresponsive, developmentally segregated settings in which they are most often educated (Strain & Odom, 1986; Kohler & Strain, 1992).
4. For many children who receive peer-mediated intervention, their eventual level of social participation falls within the typical range for their age cohorts (Strain, 1987).
5. The potency of peer-mediated intervention extends across settings (Strain, 1987; Strain & Hoyson, 2000) and time periods (Strain, Goldstein, & Kohler, 1996).

These results, largely from single-case experimental designs, have been replicated in a recent, large-scale randomized trial (Strain & Bovey, 2011), and ongoing research is evaluating the maintenance of intervention effects into the sixth grade. Taken together, the body of research on peer-mediated intervention indicates that the practice is feasible in typical preschool settings, that benefits accrue to all parties involved, and that the effects are both substantial and sustainable.

REFERENCES

American Psychiatric Association. (2013). *Diagnostic and statistical manual of mental disorders* (5th ed.). Arlington, VA: Author.

Barton, E. E., Steed, E. A., Strain, P. S., Dunlap, G., Powell, D., & Payne, C. J. (2013). An analysis of classroom-based and parent-focused social-emotional programs for young children. *Infants and Young Children, 27*, 3–29.

Goldstein, H., Lackey, K. C., & Schneider, N. J. B. (2014). A new framework for systematic reviews: Application to social skills interventions for preschoolers with autism. *Exceptional Children, 80*(3), 262–286.

Goldstein, H., & Wickstrom, S. (1986). Peer intervention effects on communicative interaction among handicapped and nonhandicapped preschoolers. *Journal of Applied Behavior Analysis, 19*, 209–214.

Hecimovic, A., Fox, J. J., Shores, R. E., & Strain, P. S. (1985). The effects of integrated and segregated settings on the generalization of newly acquired social behaviors of socially withdrawn preschoolers. *Behavioral Assessment, 7*, 367–388.

Hoyson, M., Jamieson, B., & Strain, P. S. (1984). Individualized group instruction of normally developing and autistic-like children: The LEAP curriculum model. *Journal of the Division for Early Childhood, 8*, 157–172.

Joseph, G. E., & Strain, P. S. (2003). Comprehensive evidence-based social-emotional curricula for young children: An analysis of efficacious adoption potential. *Topics in Early Childhood Special Education, 23*, 65–76.

Kohler, F. W., & Strain, P. S. (1990). Peer-assisted interventions: Early promises, notable achievements, and future directions. *Clinical Psychology Review, 10*, 441–452.

Kohler, F. W., & Strain, P. S. (1992). Applied behavior analysis and the movement to restructure schools: Compatibility and opportunities for collaboration. *Journal of Behavioral Education, 2*, 367–390.

Kohler, F. W., & Strain, P. S. (1996). The social interactions between preschoolers with disabilities and their peers: Methods for assessment, intervention, and analysis. In N. Singh (Ed.), *Practical approaches to the treatment of severe behavior disorders* (pp. 83–97). Pacific Grove, CA: Sycamore.

Kohler, F. W., & Strain, P. S. (1999). Maximizing peer-mediated resources within integrated preschool classrooms. *Topics in Early Childhood Special Education, 19*, 92–102.

Kohler, F. W., Strain, P. S., & Shearer, D. D. (1992). The overtures of preschool social skill intervention agents: Differential rates, forms, and functions. *Behavior Modification, 16*, 525–542.

Lawry, J., Danko, C., & Strain, P. S. (2000). Examining the role of the classroom environment in the prevention of problem behaviors. *Young Exceptional Children, 3*, 11–18.

McGee, G. G., Daly, T., Izeman, S. G., Mann, L. H., & Risley, T. R. (1991). Use of classroom materials to promote preschool engagement. *TEACHING Exceptional Children, 23*(4), 43–47.

McGee, G. G., Morrier, M. M., & Daly, T. (1999). An incidental teaching approach to early intervention for toddlers with autism. *Journal of the Association for Persons with Severe Handicaps, 24*(3), 133–146.

Sainato, D. M., Lyon, S. L., & Strain, P. S. (1987). Facilitating group instruction for handicapped preschool children. *Journal of the Division for Early Childhood, 12,* 23–30.

Shores, R. E., Hester, P., & Strain, P. S. (1976). The effects of amount and type of teacher–child interaction on child–child interaction. *Psychology in the Schools, 13,* 171–175.

Strain, P. S. (1983). Generalization of autistic children's social behavior change: Effects of developmentally integrated and segregated settings. *Analysis and Intervention in Developmental Disabilities, 3,* 23–34.

Strain, P. S. (1987). Comprehensive evaluation of young autistic children. *Topics in Early Childhood Special Education, 7,* 97–110.

Strain, P. S., & Bovey, E. (2008). LEAP preschool. In J. Handleman & S. Harris (Eds.), *Preschool education programs for children with autism* (pp. 249–281). Austin, TX: PRO-ED.

Strain, P. S., & Bovey, E. H. (2011). Randomized, controlled trial of the LEAP model of early intervention for young children with autism spectrum disorders. *Topics in Early Childhood Special Education, 31*(3), 133–154.

Strain, P. S., & Danko, C. D. (1995). Caregivers' encouragement of positive interaction between preschoolers with autism and their siblings. *Journal of Emotional and Behavioral Disorders, 3,* 2–12.

Strain, P. S., Goldstein, H., & Kohler, F. W. (1996). LEAP: Peer-mediated intervention for young children with autism. In E. Hibbs & P. Jensen (Eds.), *Psychosocial treatments for child and adolescent disorders.* Washington, DC: American Psychiatric Association.

Strain, P. S., & Hoyson, M. (2000). On the need for longitudinal, intensive social skill intervention: LEAP follow-up outcomes for children with autism as a case-in-point. *Topics in Early Childhood Special Education, 20,* 116–122.

Strain, P. S., Kerr, M. M., & Ragland, E. U. (1979). Effects of peer-mediated social initiations and prompting/reinforcement procedures on the social behavior of autistic children. *Journal of Autism and Developmental Disorders, 9,* 41–54.

Strain, P. S., Kohler, F. W., Storey, K., & Danko, C. (1994). Teaching preschoolers with autism to self-monitor their social interactions: An analysis of results in home and school settings. *Journal of Emotional and Behavioral Disorders, 2,* 78–88.

Strain, P. S., McGee, G., & Kohler, F. W. (2001). Inclusion of children with autism in early intervention: An examination of rationale, myths, and procedures. In M. J. Guralnick (Ed.), *Early childhood inclusion: Focus on change* (pp. 337–363). Baltimore, MD: Brookes.

Strain, P. S., & Odom, S. L. (1986). Peer social initiations: An effective intervention for social skill deficits of exceptional children. *Exceptional Children, 52,* 543–551.

Strain, P. S., Schwartz, I., & Barton, E. (2012). Providing intervention for young children with autism spectrum disorders: What we still need to accomplish. *Journal of Early Intervention, 33,* 321–332.

Strain, P. S., Shores, R. E., & Kerr, M. M. (1976). An experimental analysis of "spill-over" effects on social interaction among behaviorally handicapped preschool children. *Journal of Applied Behavior Analysis, 9,* 31–40.

Strain, P. S., Shores, R. E., & Timm, M. A. (1977). Effects of peer initiations on the social behavior of withdrawn preschoolers. *Journal of Applied Behavior Analysis, 10,* 289–298.

Strain, P. S., & Timm, M. A. (1974). An experimental analysis of social interaction between a behaviorally disordered preschool child and her classroom peers. *Journal of Applied Behavior Analysis, 7,* 583–590.

Timm, M. A., Strain, P. S., & Eller, P. H. (1979). Effects of systematic, response-dependent fading and thinning procedures on the maintenance of child-child interaction. *Journal of Applied Behavior Analysis, 12,* 308.

Tremblay, A., Strain, P. S., Hendrickson, J. M., & Shores, R. E. (1981). Social interactions of normally developing preschool children: Using normative data for subject and target behavior selection. *Behavior Modification, 5,* 237–253.

Turner-Brown, L., Perry, T. D., Dichter, G. S., Bodfish, J. W., & Penn, D. L. (2008). Brief report: Feasibility of social cognition and interaction training for adults with high functioning autism. *Journal of Autism and Developmental Disorders, 38*(9), 1777–1784.

Winett, R. A., & Winkler, R. C. (1972). Current behavior modification in the classroom: Be still, be quiet, be docile. *Journal of Applied Behavior Analysis, 5*(4), 499–504.

Young, C. C., & Kerr, M. M. (1979). The effects of a retarded child's social initiations on the behavior of several retarded school-age peers. *Education and Training of Mentally Retarded, 14,* 185–190.

APPENDIX 9.1. Sample Script: Getting Your Friend's Attention

Preparation

Decide how you are going to teach the social skills (puppets, role playing, etc.) and have the necessary materials ready.

General Introduction to the Peers

"Today we are going to learn about getting our friends to play with us. It is very important that children learn to play with each other. One way to get your friend to play with you is by getting his or her attention."

Step 1: Describe

"One way you can get your friend to play with you is by getting his or her attention. When you get your friend's attention, you:

"1. Look at your friend.
"2. Tap your friend on the shoulder.
"3. Say your friend's name.

"Here is a poster that shows a bug getting his friend's attention. He is looking at her, touching her shoulder, and saying her name."

Step 2: Demonstrate—Adult with Adult

"Let's practice getting a friend to look at you.
"Now watch me. I'm going to get _____'s attention. Tell me if I do it right."
Demonstrate.
"Did I get _____'s attention?
"That's right—I looked at my friend, said his [or her] name, and touched him [or her] gently on the arm."

Step 3: Demonstrate the Wrong Way

"Let's try again."
Demonstrate the wrong way. Tap the child or other teacher on the shoulder but do not say his or her name. (You can do other wrong ways here that may represent what you currently see in your class, like tapping too hard or saying the person's name over and over without giving that person a chance to respond.)

"Did I do it right?
"What did I do wrong?
"That's right. I should have looked at my friend, tapped him on the shoulder, and said his name."

Step 4: Child Practice with Adult

Invite a child up to the front of the group.

"Now I want you to practice getting your friend's attention. Let's pretend I'm your friend and you're going to get my attention.

"Remember to:

"1. Look at me.
"2. Say my name.
"3. Gently tap me on the shoulder if I'm not looking at you."

Use the reminder "Remember to get your friend's attention" each time you have the child take a turn. This will help the children remember what to do when they hear you say this during a play session.

"If you forget to get your friend's attention, I'll remind you by pointing to the poster."

Step 5: Practice with the Target Child

Invite a second child up to the front of the group.

"Now I want you to practice getting _____'s attention. Remember you're going to:

"1. Look at him [or her].
"2. Say his [or her] name.
"3. Tap him [or her] on the shoulder.

"If you get stuck, I'll remind you by pointing to the poster."

Allow the child to try and get his or her friend's attention. If the child demonstrates correctly but the target child doesn't respond, encourage the child to be persistent and try again. Then provide physical assistance to help the child respond if necessary.

Step 6: Describe Your Reinforcement Strategy

Give specific instructions as to why students are getting prizes (such as "You got your friend to look at you" for peers, or "You looked at your friends!" for target students).

"Now, if a teacher sees you getting your friend's attention while we play today, you will get a superstar. Later, you will turn in the superstar to get a prize. But remember, we have to see you get your friend's attention."

APPENDIX 9.2. Sample Script: Sharing—Giving to a Peer

Preparation

Decide how you are going to teach the social skills (puppets, role playing, etc.) and have the necessary materials ready.

General Introduction to the Peers

"Today you are going to learn how to be a good friend. Sometimes your friends in class do not know how to play with other children. You are going to learn how to help them play."

Step 1: Describe

"One way you can get your friend to play with you is to share a toy with him or her.
　"When you share you need to:

　"1. Get your friend's attention (look, tap, say your friend's name).
　"2. Hold out a toy.
　"3. Say, 'Here.'
　"4. Wait for your friend to take the toy (or put it directly in his or her hand).

　"Here is a poster that shows a bug sharing with his friend."

Step 2: Demonstrate—Adult with Adult

"Let's practice sharing with a friend.
　"Now watch me. I'm going to share with _____. Tell me if I do it right."
　Demonstrate.
　"Did I share with _____?
　"What did I do?
　"That's right. I got _____'s attention by looking at him, tapping him on the shoulder, and saying his name. I held out the toy and said, 'Here.' And I waited for him to take the toy."
　Repeat this procedure using different examples of sharing (e.g., share the trucks, shovels, blocks, dolls).
　Make sure each child has several opportunities to answer.

Step 3: Demonstrate the Wrong Way

"Let's try again."
　Demonstrate the wrong way.

　"Did I do it right?
　"What did I do wrong?
　"That's right. I should have looked at my friend, tapped him on the shoulder, said his name, held out a toy and said, 'Here.'"

Step 4: Child Practice with Adult

"Now I want *you* to practice sharing. Let's pretend I'm your friend and you're going to share something with me. Remember to:

"1. Get my attention (look, tap, say my name).
"2. Hold out a toy.
"3. Say, 'Here.'
"4. Wait for me to take the toy (or put it directly in my hand)."

Use the reminder "Remember to share with your friend" each time you have the children take a turn. This will help them remember what to do when they hear you say this during a play session.

"If you forget how to share I'll remind you by pointing to the poster."

Step 5: Practice with the Target Child

"Now we're going to have another friend come up and join us and I'm going to ask you to practice sharing with him or her. I'll help you remember to share by saying 'Remember to share with your friend.' Remember you are going to:

"1. Get _____'s attention.
"2. Hold out a toy.
"3. Say, 'Here.'
"4. Wait for your friend to take the toy (or put it directly in your friend's hand).

"If you get stuck, I'll remind you by pointing to the poster."

Allow the child to try and share with his or her friend. If the child demonstrates correctly but the target child doesn't respond, encourage the child to be persistent and try again. Make sure the child holds out the toy until the peer takes it or the child places it directly in the peer's hand. If the target child doesn't respond, you can provide physical assistance if necessary.

Step 6: Award Prizes to Students

Give specific praise as to why students are getting prizes (such as "You got your friend to look at you" for peers or "You looked at your friends!" for target students).

Index

Note: Page numbers in *italics* indicate figures, boxes, and tables.